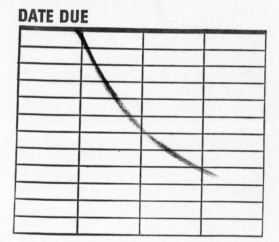

CALVINISM AND
THE AMYRAUT HERESY

MOSES AMYRALDVS EVANGELII MINISTER ET IN ACADEMIA SALMVRIENSI THEOLOGIÆ PROFESSOR 9.

CALVINISM AND
THE AMYRAUT HERESY

Protestant Scholasticism and Humanism

in Seventeenth-Century France

BRIAN G. ARMSTRONG

The University of Wisconsin Press

Madison, Milwaukee, and London

1969

PUBLISHED BY
THE UNIVERSITY OF WISCONSIN PRESS
BOX 1379, MADISON, WISCONSIN 53701

THE UNIVERSITY OF WISCONSIN PRESS, LTD.
27-29 WHITFIELD STREET, LONDON, W.1

PRINTED IN THE UNITED STATES OF AMERICA BY
HEFFERNAN PRESS, INC.
WORCESTER, MASSACHUSETTS

SBN 299-05490-X
LC 72-84949

FRONTISPIECE FROM A PORTRAIT HOUSED IN
THE LIBRARY OF THE SOCIETY OF FRENCH PROTESTANTISM IN PARIS.
COURTESY PASTEUR HENRI BOSC. PHOTOGRAPH BY MICHEL CABAUD.

To Carol,
Brett, and Curt

CONTENTS

ILLUSTRATIONS

PREFACE

A S IS QUITE OFTEN TRUE OF SPECIALIZED STUDIES, some of the contents of this book are of a rather technical nature. In order not to make this a test of the reader's ability to read foreign languages of another century, I have translated or presented in translation all materials incorporated in the body of the text. The original is frequently reproduced in the notes.

Within the text the terms *Reformed, Calvinist* and *Huguenot* have been used interchangeably. *Orthodoxy, orthodox Calvinism* and *scholasticism* have also been used more or less synonymously. In addition, *Heilsgeschichte* and *heilsgeschichtlich* are frequently used, though I am aware this is anachronistic. By these terms I mean simply the awareness that the concept and work of salvation has a history, that there has been a gradual unfolding of the process of redemption within history.

It will be noticed that rather copious footnotes have been supplied. This I have done because of the extreme rarity of many of the volumes with which I worked, particularly Amyraut's writings. It appears likely that many copies of these works were destroyed after Louis XIV's revocation of the Edict of Nantes, hence most are very rare. All of the passages reproduced in the footnotes are exact reproductions of the original except for the standardization of *u, v, i,* and *j.* There are frequent misspellings and improper accentuations in the originals. These have been reproduced without the addition of *sic* except in cases where the meaning might be missed were some attention not drawn to the mistake in the text. All translations are mine unless otherwise indicated.

Of course every study owes much to a host of scholars and friends. I cannot hope to acknowledge all I owe, but I wish to acknowledge some of the more outstanding debts of which I am aware. To the late Dr. Kenneth Gapp, librarian of Speer Memorial Library, Princeton Theological Seminary, Princeton, New Jersey, this study owes its present form, for his untiring cooperation and work resulted in the collection of works necessary to carry on my research. Indeed, the entire staff of Speer Library was at all times most helpful, and perhaps in particular Miss Isabelle Stouffer, assistant librarian. Also I should like to thank Dr. Lefferts A. Loetscher, who introduced me to the study of Amyraut some years ago and who has taken a lively interest in my work over the years. Again my thanks go to my good friend John Bray, who ransacked many European libraries on my behalf, ferreting out Amyraut volumes and supplying me with a xerox copy of an important work. And especial thanks go to Dr. Roger Nicole, who has supplied much bibliographic help, has generously granted the privilege of using, in his home, the extensive materials he has collected relating to Amyraut, has been quick to lend these materials at various times, and has read the entire manuscript, making valuable suggestions. While I fundamentally disagree with his interpretation of Amyraldian thought, I owe much to his warm-hearted assistance.

I should also like to give particular thanks to Dr. Norman V. Hope, Dr. Georges A. Barrois, and Dr. Edward A. Dowey, Jr. Dr. Barrois gave invaluable aid on some translations, and valuable hints in many other areas. Especially, though, I wish to express appreciation to Dr. Dowey, who spent many long hours reading the manuscript and discussing with me the various portions of the work; he never failed to provide inspiration and helpful advice. Dr. Joseph O. Baylen, head of the department of history at Georgia State College, has given valuable aid on many technical and practical matters.

Finally, I am deeply grateful to my wife, Carol, who, besides typing an impossible manuscript several times, proofreading it, and performing one hundred other menial tasks relating to the study, has given help and encouragement without reservation.

KEY TO ABBREVIATIONS

BECAUSE OF THE GENERAL LACK of familiarity with Amyraut's writings I have generally avoided abbreviations in the citations unless accompanied with an explanation. The Calvin material has been cited according to what seems to be the standard form: *CO*, 8:165 would mean volume 8 of the *Calvini opera* volumes in the *Corpus Reformatorum,* page or column 165. *OS,* IV.75.6–9 means volume 4, page 75, lines 6 through 9 of the five-volume *Opera selecta* collection edited by Barth and Niesel. In like manner the Luther citations have followed the standard form. *W.A.* XL.69.4–7 means volume 40, page 69, lines 4 through 7 of the Weimar edition of Luther's works.

Other abbreviations are as follows:

AHR	*American Historical Review*
ARG	*Archiv für Reformationsgeschichte*
BHR	*Bibliothèque d'Humanisme et Renaissance*
Bulletin	*Bulletin de la société de l'histoire du protestantisme français*
CH	*Church History*
DNB	*Dictionary of National Biography*
ERE	Hastings' *Encyclopedia of Religion and Ethics*
JHI	*Journal of the History of Ideas*
PRE	Herzog's *Real-Encyclopädie für protestantische Theologie und Kirche*
RTP	*Revue de théologie et philosophie*
ZKG	*Zeitschrift für Kirchengeschichte*

INTRODUCTION

THE INTELLECTUAL TRADITIONS of the sixteenth and seventeenth centuries are still but imperfectly known. In particular, to paraphrase Geoffrey Treasure, there are large gaps remaining between the very specialized monographs and the general histories of the period. Richard Popkin has recently given a most helpful, somewhat general picture of one aspect of the intellectual climate of this period in his *History of Scepticism from Erasmus to Descartes*.[1] The sceptical tradition he so carefully illustrates is limited, for the most part, to the Roman Catholic world, for the Catholics found in this new Pyrrhonism an effective weapon in the ideological warfare with the Protestants. A recent article by Julien-Eymard d'Angers has shown that, on the other hand, the sceptical position was by no means unanimously adopted by Catholic thinkers.[2] Rather there were, at least in the early years of the seventeenth century, many prominent Catholic intellectuals who may be called according to d'Angers "Christian humanists," and who were not at all in agreement with the tradition which professed distrust of the senses and the rational equipment of man. Of course these two disparate intellectual currents by no means exhaust the possibilities that were open to and followed by thinkers in the Roman Catholic communion.

Even with these studies and others, our knowledge of the

1. Assen, 1960.
2. "Problèmes et difficultés de l'humanisme chrétien (1600–1642)," *XVIIe Siècle*, nos. 62–63 (1964), 4–29.

seventeeth-century world is less complete than of any post-Middle Ages century. There are several scholarly works on selected great thinkers of this period, and there has been considerable interest in the latter years of this *Grand Siècle* since Paul Hazard's epochal *La Crise de la conscience européenne, 1680–1715*,[3] but few attempts have been made to deal synthetically with the early and middle years of the century. Even Louis XIV had to wait until very recently for an adequate biographer![4] Hazard has, correctly I believe, seen Pierre Bayle as a pivotal figure for the Enlightenment, but he too has had no adequate biographer until E. Labrousse's work of the past few years.[5]

This study of mine is by no means intended to provide a road map of the intellectual traditions which led to the Enlightenment. Indeed, my designs are very modest and very limited. I intend only to introduce some of the forces at work within one limited tradition, that today called Calvinism, and this restricted even further to one country, France. I believe it will show that the French Calvinists fall into two broadly defined intellectual traditions, one which relates most directly to impulses present in the medieval world and which I have called Protestant scholasticism, the second which relates most directly to impulses spawned by the Renaissance and which I have called French humanism.

If in general the thought of the sixteenth and seventeenth centuries is but imperfectly known, the situation is worse with regard to the thought of Calvinism. A study has finally been completed which claims to identify the main authors of the Westminster Confession, the basic confessional document of the largest branch of the Calvinist Churches.[6] No satisfactory treatise, however, deals with the history of the ideas which culminated in this document. Is there one main intellectual tradition embodied

3. 3 vols. (Paris, 1934).

4. J. B. Wolf, author of *Louis XIV* (New York, 1968).

5. Elisabeth Labrousse, *Pierre Bayle*, 2 vols. (La Haye, 1963–65). For Bayle's intellectual heritage see also Walter Rex III's *Essays on Pierre Bayle and Religious Controversy* (The Hague, 1965), and Donald Brush's *Montaigne and Bayle* (The Hague, 1966).

6. Jack B. Rogers' *Scripture in the Westminster Confession* (Grand Rapids, 1967).

in it, or several? Does it represent a middle-ground consensus of differing opinions or a near-unanimous report of commissioners essentially in agreement? Does it represent the thought of the great John Calvin or is it a substantial modification of his thought? These and a host of other questions are still unanswered with regard to the very statement of faith of most Calvinist Churches.[7]

In larger context, does the historical movement known as Calvinism represent a generally uniform intellectual tradition, and how faithfully does this movement represent the teachings of John Calvin? Perhaps the most overlooked problem in research having to do with the thought of Calvinism concerns the relationship of the thought of Calvin himself to that of his followers. It is axiomatic that thought does not remain static and that most great thinkers have been but imperfectly understood by their successors. Interestingly, these principles seem never to have been applied with rigor and care in order to determine the precise relationship of Calvin's thought to the expression of faith known as Calvinism. Since the Calvinist thinkers of the late sixteenth and seventeenth centuries rarely even take the trouble to refer to Calvin himself, the interest evolves into surprise. The question then arises whether these orthodox Calvinists can in fact be regarded as proper representatives of Calvin's thought, an assumption which until very recent times seems to have remained unquestioned by historians of Calvinism. I believe that Calvin's religious thought is still commonly judged in the light of what eventuated in Calvinism, and that a careful comparison of his writings with those of representative Calvinists of the seventeenth century reveals a radical change of emphasis. In fact, this change of emphasis is so pronounced that at many points the whole structure of Calvin's thought is seriously compromised.

In seeking to approach the above question, the researcher is greatly assisted by a controversy within French Calvinism in the seventeenth century. The controversy revolved around Moïse Amyraut, a theology professor at the most illustrious of the

---

7. The same statement would also be true if applied to the confessional document of the Dutch Reformed churches, *The Canons and Decrees of the Synod of Dort.*

French Reformed universities, the Academy of Saumur. Amyraut (Moses Amyraldus) was without contest the most influential Reformed theologian of the seventeenth century. During his tenure as professor of theology at the Academy of Saumur (1626–64) this academy had the largest enrollment of any of the Reformed divinity schools.[8] Largely through his influence, by mid-century the tide had turned so that the majority of French pastors and theologians were Amyraldians,[9] and some who were favorable to this theology were teaching in such staunchly orthodox centers as the Genevan Academy.[10] He took his stand foursquare against the teaching of the orthodoxy of international Calvinism. Occasionally overtly, but perhaps most dramatically by implication, he claimed that orthodox Calvinist theology was a corruption of Calvin's thought. In a most explicit manner he propounded a theological method and teaching which disputed orthodox Calvinist teaching and which he claimed was a return to Reformation thought, in particular to that of John Calvin. Amyraut displayed a thorough acquaintance with the mass of the Calvin corpus and a sophisticated sensitivity to the intricacy of Calvin's theological position. The insights he had into Calvin's thought are nothing short of remarkable when seen in the light of the fact that almost the whole of international Calvinism was far removed from Calvin's thought. Since Amyraut had to stand trial for heresy, the claim that he was true to Calvin is most interesting, for it would mean that less than one hundred years after Calvin's death the communion which generally bore his name considered his teaching heresy.

The approach of this study, then, has been to use Amyraut as a model, to explicate his teaching, and to relate it in the crucial

8. See the excellent discussion of the Saumur school in Bourchenin, *Etude sur les académies protestantes en France au XVIe et au XVIIe siècle* (Paris, 1882), pp. 137–46, 404–28, and pp. 469–70, where Bourchenin gives a very interesting and significant listing of the best-known students of the Saumur Academy.

9. This is admitted even by the rabidly anti-Amyraldian Scottish theologian George Smeaton in *The Doctrine of the Holy Spirit,* 2nd ed. (Edinburgh, 1889), p. 362.

10. Notably the son of the rigidly orthodox professor at Geneva Théodore Tronchin (1582–1657), Louis Tronchin (1629–1705), who openly defended the Salmurian theology and was even rector of the Genevan Academy, 1663-68.

points to that of Calvin. Moreover, I have sought to contrast this teaching with that of his orthodox Calvinist opponents. Most assuredly, it is only against the background of that orthodox Calvinism that much of Amyraut's work either makes sense or has lasting significance. In the process of this comparison of Amyraut with Calvin and then with Amyraut's orthodox contemporaries it became apparent that two very different intellectual traditions were operative. Both the methodology and content of the teaching of Calvin and Amyraut were found to contrast sharply with those of orthodox Calvinists of the seventeenth century. The latter showed themselves to be much more interested in metaphysics and systematization, and so were preserving elements of medieval scholasticism quite in contrast to the humanistically shaped thought of Calvin and Amyraut.

It is hoped, then, that this study will both provide an introduction to the intellectual trends within French Calvinism, to the teaching of Amyraut and the relation of his thought to that of Calvin, and furnish an insight into the removal of orthodox Calvinist thought from Calvin into a narrower, more defensive, more intolerant, and more impervious system. In addition, it is hoped that it may serve as a contribution to the woefully neglected topic of Calvin interpretation in the seventeenth century. There has not been an attempt to deal with every aspect of Amyraut's thought, but rather to observe its main features, with special attention to those teachings which were under the most sustained attack.

The limitation noted above leaves a host of topics which cry out for investigation. Amyraut had able and illustrious colleagues and backers who supported him and who even struck out in different directions, claiming as he did the support of Calvin, and representing the humanist genre. Among these men might be mentioned two who were his colleagues at Saumur, Louis Cappel and Josué de la Place, and two who were associated with the great Paris Reformed Church, Jean Daillé and David Blondel. None of these men has been the object of a scholarly study. Moreover, the whole question of the movement of Amyraldian teaching into a second generation needs careful study. It has been universally accepted that Claude Pajon, Amyraut's successor at Saumur, was representative of Amyraldian thought. My research leads me to believe that Alexander Schweizer, Otto Ritschl, and François Laplanche are mistaken, that a man like Louis Tronchin of Geneva was a more faithful representative of that thought. I hope that this study will inspire further research in this area.

CALVINISM AND
THE AMYRAUT HERESY

1

THE HISTORICAL
AND THEOLOGICAL BACKGROUND

SEVENTEENTH-CENTURY FRANCE was the France of the Edict of Nantes. This is a consideration which cannot be taken lightly, and especially in a study concerned with religious matters.[1] Though the liberties granted to the Protestants by the Edict were always in jeopardy and never fully enjoyed, and after the death of Mazarin in 1661 were short-lived,[2] though the freedom to worship for Protestants was rigidly restricted to specified localities, it is nevertheless true that the Edict made of the Reformed Church a legal institution and afforded the *religion prétendue réformée*[3] relative liberty. This state of relative liberty existed especially during the period of activity of Moïse Amyraut (ca. 1620–64) and in the place of his work (Saumur, originally one of the *places de sûreté,* and during the greatest part of Amyraut's life a village where Catholics and

1. In the words of Jacques Pannier in the first of his excellent studies on the Reformed church at Paris (actually Charenton), "on ne puisse jamais trop insister sur l'importance exceptionnelle de cet acte dans l'histoire de France et dans l'histoire de la civilisation universelle" (*L'Eglise réformée de Paris sous Henri IV* [Paris, 1911], p. 34).

2. For a well-documented, detailed study showing that the Catholic Church never surrendered its *une-loi, une-foi, un-roi* religio-political ideal, see Elie Benoist's massive *Histoire de l'édit de Nantes,* 5 vols. (Delft, 1693–95); also the opening chapters of John Viénot's *Histoire de la réforme française de l'édit de Nantes à sa révocation* (Paris, 1934).

3. The pejorative term (often simply R.P.R.) used by Roman Catholic churchmen to refer to Protestants.

Protestants were on unusually friendly terms).[4] It was the one positive result of the long, bitter Huguenot-Catholic wars of religion fought during the latter half of the sixteenth century.

PROTESTANT-CATHOLIC CONTROVERSY IN FRANCE DURING THE SEVENTEENTH CENTURY

While armed hostilities virtually ceased after the Siege of La Rochelle, that campaign of 1628 which finally annihilated the political arm of French Protestantism, they were followed by a period of religious controversy *par excellence*. The Protestant churchmen furiously sought to justify their existence as well as to show the novelty and irrationality of the Roman Catholic positions. The civil war of the seventeenth century was fought with the pen, a warfare which produced a barrage of pamphlets, with seemingly every capable churchman disputing at length on one, and often many, of the points at issue.

To penetrate this mass of literature is a difficult undertaking, but Alfred Rébelliau's old and learned discussion appears to present a reliable schema by which such an undertaking may be facilitated.[5] Rébelliau's basic argument is that during the first

4. The Oratorians had established a college at Nôtre Dame des Ardilliers in 1617 which Walter Rex judges was "perhaps even more brilliant than the Protestant Academy" and notes that such illustrious persons as Father Thomassin taught there, "as did Abel de Sainte-Marthe, Jean Morin, André Martin (Ambrosius Victor), Leporcq, and Bernard Lamy" (*Essays on Pierre Bayle* [The Hague, 1965], pp. 121–22). Rex goes on to point out that the professors at the Academy attended lectures at the Oratory and vice-versa, that Morin secured the printing privileges for Cappel's *Critica sacra*, that the teachers at the Oratory asked permission to attend the viewing of La Place after his death in 1655, etc. See also J. Prost, *La Philosophie à l'académie protestante de Saumur* (Paris, 1907), pp. 7off.

5. See his immensely erudite *Bossuet, historien du protestantisme* (Paris, 1892), *passim*, but esp. pp. 4–59. This study by Rébelliau remains one of the best introductions to seventeenth-century French church history. In fact, it is primarily Catholic historians who have contributed to the scholarship of this period. See, among others, the studies in the series published by the Catholic University at Louvain: Gustave Thils, *Les Notes de l'église dans l'apologétique catholique depuis la réforme* (Gembloux, 1937) and Remi Snoeks, *L'Argument de tradition dans la controverse eucharistique entre catholiques et réformés français au XVIIe siècle* (Louvain and Gembloux, 1951). Two recent studies from the Protestant perspective have, however, helped to balance the weight of scholarship. They are the abovementioned work of W. Rex and that of René Voeltzel, *Vraie et fausse Eglise selon les théologiens protestants français du XVIIe siècle* (Paris, 1956).

quarter of the seventeenth century the controversy had an encyclopedic character, with every possible issue debated. Moreover, he contends that the spirit of the protagonists was such that the controversy reached an impasse. On both sides there was an obstinate refusal to compromise on even the smallest particular in the entrenched positions of the respective communions. Insult and villification bred insult and villification.

By 1640, however, this atmosphere had noticeably changed. In the first place, the mood of the controversialists was "singularly more restrained and calmer."[6] Secondly, the encyclopedic character of the controversy was gone: "The debate is no longer spread out over one hundred subjects of unequal importance, but is centered upon a few essential points."[7] And finally, there was a new dimension introduced; a new historical consciousness began to emerge, producing some very learned discussions on the teaching of past centuries.

While furnishing a helpful characterization of the milieu in which Amyraut lived,[8] these considerations are even more significant for our purpose; for, in fact, each one of them is to some extent a contribution of the *école de Saumur* to the arena of controversy. And although Rébelliau gives no hint that this idea ever crossed his mind, since he discusses the Reformed position as one consistent testimony, I believe that his treatise alone would be sufficient to substantiate this claim.

It perhaps needs to be said that one may find here and there

6. *Bossuet, historien du protestantisme*, p. 14.

7. *Ibid.*, p. 23. Rébelliau maintains that two issues, successively, became the center of controversy in the middle and latter part of the century: from 1640–60, the Eucharist, and from 1660–85, the Church.

8. It would be a mistake to try to understand Amyraldian theology without a keen awareness of the importance of this historical background of controversy. The Protestants had become obsessed, in the course of controversy, with the argument that the Reformed Church was the true and catholic church. While this was not nearly so evident among Saumur theologians, they were unusually sensitive about maintaining rapport with the Roman Catholics and about producing a theological system which would be readily understood by Catholic churchmen. (Indeed, Pierre du Moulin accused the Amyraldians of being too friendly with members of the Roman Church.) Cosmopolitanism was a marked feature of Amyraldianism, perhaps of Amyraut in particular, and unquestionably influenced Saumur theology as the theologians of this school endeavored to be both cosmopolitan and Reformed in this age of controversy.

an orthodox theologian (and *ipso facto* an opponent of Amyraldianism) who would also speak to one of these points. My point, however, is that as a group the Amyraldians were the only ones within the Reformed Church who consistently contributed in these three areas. And it seems not too much to say that concerning the first point, namely, that a more conciliatory spirit appeared in the course of controversy, the Amyraldians were the exclusive contributors. Their cosmopolitanism went far toward producing a more congenial atmosphere in the realm of controversy. The great Charenton church reportedly ministered to many of the king's court and to some foreign ambassadors. It is natural that these ministers, Amyraldians all, were eager to maintain the best possible relations with the Roman churchmen. And we may regard Jean Daillé as speaking for his fellow ministers in this matter when he said:

> We do not hide our sentiments upon religion from those outside our faith, but we explain ourselves thereon to them in a way that is proper both to their edification and to our safety. We, then, dispose of all the goods capable of wounding those who hear us, so that there is nothing injurious or offensive, nothing which smacks of hate or contempt. . . . As to those truths (of which thank God there are many . . .) which are agreeable to our adversaries, these we uncover and expose with full liberty. For those which necessitate a rejection of their errors . . . , it is necessary that we express ourselves thereon with great discretion, showing them sweetly the reasons for our sentiments, so that they may see that it is not a light consideration, but by the constraint of a necessary reason that we separate ourselves from their belief.[9]

This remarkable passage is sufficient to document the respect and care with which the Amyraldians treated the points at issue with the Catholics. It certainly reveals a radically different spirit from the orthodox. Compare, for example, Pierre du Moulin's *Nouvelles Briques pour le bastiment de Babel, c'est a dire erreurs de l'eglise romaine nouvellement forgez, pour establir la grandeur de l'evesque de Rome,*[10] for which he penned no

---

9. From Daillé's 47th sermon in the collection *Sermons sur l'épître aux Colossiens* (Geneva, 1662) as quoted in Pannier, *L'Eglise réformée de Paris sous Louis XIII* (Paris, 1922), p. 514.

10. La Rochelle, 1604; Sedan, 1624; Geneva, 1637.

dedicatory epistle because it would be too dangerous to the one to whom it was addressed.

Another instance of the improved spirit toward those of the Roman communion is the very nature of the theology of both Amyraut and the professor who so profoundly influenced him, John Cameron. Cameron was known to have taught that Peter was the first bishop of Rome, and both he and Amyraut were attacked by du Moulin for being too lenient to Roman Catholics.[11]

Before leaving this matter it is necessary to point out that the entire credit for an improved atmosphere of controversy probably ought not to be given the Amyraldians since the Oratorians, and as Rébelliau suggests the Jansenists, had contributed to it from the Catholic side. Yet on the other hand, the two most active Catholic orders at this time, the Jesuits and Capuchins, seldom if ever revealed a "more conciliatory spirit." In any case, the contention is only that in the Reformed communion it was the Amyraldians who led the way in demonstrating a spirit of reasonableness.

Concerning the second of Rébelliau's theses, that there was a notable reduction of the topics debated, the influence of the Salmurians is much less striking. In the first place, Rébelliau's contention is generally to be accepted that "it is chiefly on the side of the Catholics that this diminution is noticeable."[12] Again, by the time it was most noticeable (1650 and after) Amyraldian theology had won the day in France, except for small pockets of resistance around La Rochelle and in the province of Bas-Languedoc. For this reason it is somewhat difficult to find an outstanding example. Nevertheless, if one compares Cameron or Amyraut with Daniel Chamier or du Moulin one can see in the Amyraldians a definite tendency toward reducing the debated

11. See du Moulin's *Réponse à Samuel Langle, où est contenue la doctrine de M. Amyrault* (n.p., n.d.), pp. 5ff., for his remarks on Amyraut. In his *de Mosis Amyraldi adversus Fridericum Spanhemium libro judicium* (Rotterdam, 1649), p. 213, he says of Cameron: "Petrum dicebat esse fundamentum Ecclesiae. Non ferebat, idque me praesente, hominem qui diceret in Ecclesia Romana homines servari non posse. Quam persuasionem cum Milleterius sub ejus disciplina imbibisset, facili transitu ad Pontificios defecit."

12. *Bossuet, historien du protestantisme*, p. 13.

points to central issues. There is nothing in either Cameron or
Amyraut which compares with the incredibly multifarious *Pan-
stratiae catholicae* of Chamier, in four thick folio volumes.[13] Nor
for that matter is there anything in either of these men which
compares with du Moulin's *Nouveauté du papisme*,[14] which fills
more than one thousand quarto pages. On the contrary, when
Cameron leveled his one broadside against the Roman Church
he dealt only with the doctrine of the Church and was thereby
enabled to strike a more telling blow. Amyraut, in turn, penned
but three treatises specifically designated for the Reformed-
Catholic controversy, and these dealt with justification, the
merit of works, and the Eucharist.[15]

As we turn to the third of Rébelliau's points, the introduction
of the *élément historique* into the Protestant-Catholic controversy, we come to perhaps the most dramatic and unique of all
the Salmurian contributions. Doubtless this owed its existence to
a *"humanistische Erbe"* which Hans Emil Weber has noted
lived on at Saumur, even when it had largely disappeared from
other Reformed academies such as the Genevan.[16] At any rate,
when one looks for a historical consciousness and for historical
research within the Reformed communion in France in the
seventeenth century he must for the most part turn to the
Amyraldians. So when Gustave Thils looks for Calvinist theologians who composed learned works in history he must speak
of men "such as du Plessis-Mornay, Aubertin, Blondel, Daillé,"[17]
all Salmurians.

13. Geneva, 1626; Frankfurt am Main, 1627. Even these were incomplete, for
Chamier was killed before he could complete the work!

14. Sedan, 1627. Many successive editions.

15. *De la justification* (Saumur, 1638); *Du merite des oeuvres* (Saumur, 1638);
and *De l'elevation de la foy et de l'abaissement de la raison en la creance des
mysteres de la religion* (Saumur, 1640, 1641; Charenton, 1644, 1645). The first two
were written in answer to a treatise by Théophile Brachet de la Milletière (1596–
1665) which propounded the reunion of the Reformed and Catholic communions
on the basis of the theological position espoused in that treatise. Though many
Reformed theologians wrote rejoinders to de la Milletière, to my knowledge only
Amyraut singled out justification as the main point of controversy.

16. *Reformation, Orthodoxie und Rationalismus* (Gütersloh, 1937), p. 135. C. Borgeaud in *Histoire de l'Université de Genève: L'Académie de Calvin* (Geneva, 1900)
says that when Isaac Casaubon left Geneva in 1596, the humanist orientation of
that academy also left for good (p. 216ff).

17. *Les Notes de l'église*, p. 67.

It was du Plessis-Mornay himself, the great Calvinist statesman and founder of the Saumur Academy, who produced one of the first scholarly forays into the Patristic period in order to prove the novelty of the Roman Catholic doctrine of the Eucharist. The work, entitled *De l'institution, usage et doctrine du saint sacrement de l'eucharistie en l'eglise ancienne*,[18] ranges over all the topics at issue with the Catholics and in that sense belongs to the encyclopedic genre of controversial pieces characteristic of the sixteenth century. However, the main theme remains that of the Eucharist, and du Plessis took great pains to show that the seventeenth-century Catholic teaching at that point, and especially the idea of sacrifice, was a late corruption of the Church's teaching, that in fact the idea of sacrifice and transubstantiation originated sometime in the Age of Charlemagne.

But perhaps even more significant for the historical dimension in the Protestant-Catholic controversy was the work of John Cameron. We shall have occasion to show, in the final section of this chapter on his theology, that one of the unusual features of his education was an emphasis upon the study of history. This orientation he brought with him as he entered the arena of controversy in France, and it was to alter substantially the nature of that controversy. In 1617 he published his *Traicté auquel sont examinez les prejugez de ceux de l'eglise romaine contre la re-ligion reformee.*[19] In this work he recovered with uncommon emphasis the Reformation principle of examination, and put it to work as a polemic device in his historically oriented attack on the Roman Church.[20]

18. La Rochelle, 1598. For a discussion of this work see Snoeks, *L'Argument de tradition dans la controverse eucharistique*, pp. 35–56. See also Pontien Polman, *L'Element historique dans la controverse religieuse du XVIe siècle* (Louvain and Gembloux, 1951), pp. 267ff.

19. La Rochelle, 1617. English trans. under the title *An Examination of those plausible Appearances which seeme most to commend the Romish Church, and to prejudice the Reformed* (Oxford, 1626). I have not had access to either of the above and have used the Latin translation in Cameron's *Opera* (Geneva, 1642), pp. 553–92. The ensuing discussion owes much to Rex's account in *Essays on Pierre Bayle*, pp. 9–20. Rex's work first drew my attention to the treatise of Cameron, and the reader is referred thereto for a more complete analysis of it.

20. By "principle of examination" is meant a critical investigation of an issue being discussed within the Church in order to determine (1) its origin and (2) whether or not the commonly held teaching conformed to the Scriptures. Cam-

With the principle of examination occupying the central place in this treatise, Cameron develops his argument with respect to the marks of the Church claimed by Roman Catholics. Rex notes that the work is "extra-ordinarily lively if compared to other Calvinist works of this period."[21] The argument is tightly knit and carefully developed so that it makes interesting reading even today—a statement one does not make about many seventeenth-century polemic pieces! Right from the outset the novelty and independence of Cameron's argument is evident. He begins with an appeal to common experience. This experience reveals that even the most sagacious men (*prae cateris eminent*) frequently err in judgment even though they yearn to embrace only truth; the *intellectus,* which irresistibly inclines to that which it perceives to be true, is blinded because of the corruption of the passions. This, Cameron says, we all recognize to be true in the affairs of civil life, but we should recognize that it is also true in religious matters, where the consequences are infinitely more serious. Consider, he says, the poor Indians who flock to idols, or the Turks who follow the folly of a false religion, or the Jews who have followed the traditions of the Fathers rather than the *gloriam Dei in facie Christi.*[22]

Having set forth examples to which the Catholics would readily subscribe, Cameron then turns his argument to serve the Protestant cause. He argues that since we know this propensity of human nature which so frequently and easily produces a corruption of one's judgment in religious matters, it is infinitely more necessary to subject the basis of religious doctrines to careful examination, in order to determine if truth in this realm is so clear and evident (*perspicua & evidens*) that one is completely satisfied by it.[23] Is it not possible, he asks, that the same bad turn taken by the Jews has also been taken by the Christian Church?

---

eron's use of this principle was not novel in itself—what was new was the rigor with which he applied it and the absolute prominence it received in every phase of his argumentation. He seems to have applied it more consistently than even the early Reformers, clearly reflecting, it would appear, a humanist heritage.

21. Rex, *Essays on Pierre Bayle,* p. 12.
22. Cameron, *Opera,* p. 554, 1. Ch. 2, *ad fin.*
23. *Ibid.,* p. 555, 2. Ch. 5, *ad init.*

He then proceeds to an examination of the *notae ecclesiae* which had become a prominent part of the Roman Catholic polemic against the Reformed. He selects "antiquity" as the *nota ecclesiae* around which to build his argument, for he believes it is *praejudicium illud omnium gravissimum*.[24] Thils, who says this particular mark had its origin in the canon of Vincent of Lerins, defines it as the unique mark of the Catholic Church, for this church alone "is one with the Fathers and the ancient doctors."[25] Now Cameron at this point surprises the reader accustomed to the Protestant polemics of the period, for he concurs with the claim that the true church would have antiquity on her side. At this point, however, he introduces a new twist to the argument.

In a recent article W. von Leyden has shown that during the Renaissance the term "antiquity" was understood in various ways.[26] One approach, found in the work of Vives and Descartes, was that antiquity was only properly understood as a synonym for truth.[27] Nothing deserves the name of antiquity except that which is true. As Cameron develops his argument by proposing to examine whether or not the antiquity claimed by the Catholics is in fact coextensive with truth, he seems to reflect this understanding. But, of course, such an argument presupposes a certain belief of what truth is. Cameron maintains that truth is only infallibly found in the writings of the Apostles, in the Scriptures. So his argument returns to the Bible as the sole arbiter of all disputes. This is in the best tradition of the Reformation. What marks Cameron's novelty here is (1) his argument that religion is subject to corruption and therefore must always be judged in terms of its starting point and, (2) that he applies a Renaissance theory of history to substantiate this.

This radical reversion to Scripture carried with it another element which was also in the tradition of the Reformation but which did not receive such prominence or consistent application in other Reformed writings of Cameron's time; specifically, his

24. *Ibid.*, p. 567, 2. Ch. 15, *ad init.*
25. *Les Notes de l'église*, p. xii.
26. "Antiquity and Authority: A Paradox in the Renaissance Theory of History," *JHI* 19 (1958): 473–92.
27. *Ibid.*, p. 490.

distinction between Apostolic and post-Apostolic. Though this
distinction had been commonly made by the Reformers, the
general practice had been to quote the early Fathers as in some
measure authoritative, especially since it was also generally held
that the Church had not become corrupt until some time after
the third century. But Cameron, having argued that frequent
errors are made in the religious realm, and having redefined
antiquity, could no longer regard the Fathers of the first centuries as authoritative. Since antiquity and truth are coextensive,
what was important was not who said it, or when it was said, but
rather whether what was said was in accord with Scripture.

While a return to Scripture as true antiquity might appear,
at first glance, to have diminished the historical and augmented
the dogmatic element of the debate, because of the strong emphasis upon the principle of examination such was not the case.
In fact, there was another aspect of Cameron's argument which
was taken up by his disciple, Jean Daillé (1594–1670).[28] Daillé
asked, What about these oft-cited references from the Fathers?
Are they in fact speaking to the issues of our time? In his
Traicté de l'employ des saincts peres[29] he answered this question

28. Pierre Bayle reports that "Ceux de la religion disaient ordinairement en
France, que depuis Calvin ils n'avaient point eu de meilleure plume que M.
Daillé" (*Dictionnaire historique et critique s.v.* Daillé, Jean). Born January 6,
1594, in Chateleraut, Daillé was reared by an uncle of *generosité rare*, a trait
exhibited by Daillé throughout his life. He studied at Saumur ca. 1610 under the
celebrated Scottish philosopher, Marc Duncan. He entered the household of du
Plessis-Mornay in October, 1612, as tutor of du Plessis' two sons. In actual fact
Daillé was the benefactor in this arrangement, for the great Mornay took a singu-
lar interest in him and for seven years imparted to him the fruits of his study. At
the same time Daillé spent much time at the Academy, learning from the illustrious professors there, particularly from John Cameron. The years 1619–21 were
spent traveling with du Plessis' sons, during which time he formed a close friendship with Fra Paolo Sarpi. Upon returning to France he became pastor in Poitou;
then M. du Plessis having died "in his arms," he gathered together Mornay's
Memoires and *Correspondence* and oversaw their publication. In 1625 he was
called to be pastor of the church at Saumur, but left after a year and became
pastor at Charenton where he stayed until his death in 1670. His career at Charenton was particularly distinguished as pastor and man of letters. He was a close
friend of many of the most learned men of the time, including Balzac, Conrart,
Mersenne, and Sarrau. He was moderator of the last national synod (Loudun,
1659). And he was an energetic exponent of Amyraldianism. See the biography by
his son Adrien (Quevilly, 1670), from which the foregoing has been taken.

29. *Traicté de l'employ des saincts peres, pour le jugement des différends qui*

in the negative. This work, called by Bayle a *chef-d'oeuvre*,[30] shows that Daillé had a remarkable knowledge of the Patristic period. He subjects the writings of the first three centuries to a careful analysis, taking special note of the occasion for each writing, and concludes that the matters of which they speak "have very little rapport with the present-day controversies, of which they never speak, unless perhaps incidentally . . ."[31] Again such a position seems to deny the importance of history, but since the position taken demanded a masterful knowledge of the early Fathers, it served rather to increase research in the history of the Church. And in the Reformed communion the Amyraldians led the way. David Blondel, for instance, who exposed the fallacy of the argument that a woman was once Pope, was generally recognized as the premier church historian among the Reformed. And Rébelliau, not taking into consideration du Plessis-Mornay's treatise, contends that the first exhaustive study of the Fathers apropos the doctrine of the Eucharist was done by the Parisian pastor, Edme Aubertin (1595–1652).[32] And it is noteworthy that, as Rébelliau says, this *savant défi* was not taken up by the Catholics until mid-century.

The Nature of French Protestant Theology

It is not only important for our study of Amyraut and the warring trends within French Calvinism to understand something of the position of the Huguenots *vis-à-vis* Catholicism, but it is also requisite that we give some consideration to the theological setting of Amyraut's time and communion. It was, of course, to Calvinist theology that Amyraldianism contributed most specifically. Since Amyraldianism is properly a chapter in the history

---

sont aujourd'huy en la religion (Geneva, 1631). English translations, *The Right Use of the Fathers* (London, 1651; London, 1843). Latin translation, *De usu patrum* (Geneva, 1656).

30. *Dictionnaire, s.v.* Daillé, Jean.

31. *Traicté de l'employ des saincts peres,* French ed., p. 20.

32. *Bossuet, historien du protestantisme,* pp. 50–51. Rébelliau contends that Aubertin "introduisait brillamment dans la controverse protestante la méthode historique, par son ouvrage sur *l'Eucharistie de l'ancienne Eglise,*" and adds that "les catholiques furent longtemps à relever la savant défi."

of Calvinism, we must understand what "Calvinism" meant at this time in France.

French Calvinist thought is unique within the body of international Calvinism. There is no desire here to prolong or renew the once lively debate concerning the origin of French Protestantism, that is, whether the Reformation was "an importation into France"[33] or primarily an indigenous movement. Yet while recent scholarship tends to challenge the older historians who argued with many words and much feeling for the national origin thesis,[34] the results of this study have led me to the same conclusion in at least a modified form. For the most part they have borne out the analysis of Jacques Pannier that "the origins of French Protestantism, of its confession of faith, of its discipline

33. The phrase of Preserved Smith in *The Reformation in Europe* (1920; New York: Collier Paperbacks, 1962), p. 151. This position is generally espoused by Catholic historians, as well as by J. Viénot, R-J. Lovy, J. Cadier, W. G. Moore, and to a degree R. M. Kingdon.

34. See for example J. H. Merle D'Aubigné's old *History of the Great Reformation of the Sixteenth Century*, Eng. trans., 5 vols. (New York, 1843) 3: 341ff., which begins with the Waldenses and moves through the "Christian Humanists." Recent authors subscribing to this thesis are E. Doumergue, Brunetière, M. P. Reynaud (not a Protestant), O. Douen, F. Busson, Mignet, J. Pannier, L. Romier and, in general, E. Léonard. The question, to be sure, is complex, but I suspect that the differences are largely semantic, that the word *Reformation* is being employed with different meanings. However, I think it necessary to insist on the old position, even in the face of the recent trend towards speaking of these years as the "Age of Reformation," including in that term the Catholic Church as well as the Protestant (H. Grimm, Daniel-Rops, P. Janelle, H. Jedin, etc.). Of course if this characterization were adopted without reservation it would tend to weaken my argument; yet I contend that the emphasis upon justification by faith, and the Bible in the vernacular, is not common to reform movements other than the Protestant. (A possible exception is the movement among the *dejados* of Spain, involving especially Pedro Ruiz de Alcaraz [d. 1529?] and Juan de Valdés [ca. 1500–41]. See the Ph.D. diss. on Valdés by José Nieto, Princeton Theological Seminary, 1967, pt. 1, ch. 1.) I want to emphasize that I am contending for French *origins* of the Reformation; not that Lutheranism did not mightily reinforce, and even reshape to some degree, this nascent movement. At the bottom of my argument lies the consideration that there was in France not only the discontent with the old order common to almost all of Europe, but a positive theology, with many Protestant emphases, in the process of formulation. For a noteworthy attempt to reorient this whole debate, to deny the validity of the question of whether Lefèvre was Protestant or Catholic, see Lucien Febvre, *Au coeur religieux de XVIe siècle* (Paris, 1957), ch. 1.

are essentially French."[35] What can be stressed in particular is the development of the intellectual tradition of the French Protestant Church along lines which repeatedly point to an indomitably independent spirit. This I believe can be demonstrated to be true even with regard to Geneva, the training ground of most of the French ministers.

To appreciate fully the independent spirit of French Protestantism, its national origin and essentially humanistic orientation must be taken into consideration. The French Reformation was at bottom a product of Renaissance humanism, and French Protestantism generally maintained a religious outlook characterized by the spirit of humanism. There were within the French Protestant movement some notable exceptions to this prevailing spirit, to be sure, and any true picture of it will not always present perfect symmetry. In fact, almost from the very first one finds indications of the struggle between a prevalent humanism and the expression of a religious orientation more nearly akin to medieval scholasticism—a struggle which would become rather bitter in the following century. As we shall see, this scholastic tendency is evident in the confession of faith drafted by the French Protestant Church. Nevertheless, it can be said without serious qualification that by the early seventeenth century the humanist orientation was a distinguishing feature of French Calvinism. This study has failed to provide any definitive answers as to why the French Calvinists remained attached to the humanist spirit while the rest of continental Calvinism slowly reverted to a religious expression more closely resembling medieval scholastic thought than the thought of the early reformers. Yet such seems to be the case. French Calvinism simply never developed the scholastic tendency to the extent charac-

35. *Les Origines de la confession de foi et de la discipline des églises réformées de France* (Paris, 1936), pp. 25–26. The recent studies, R. Mehl, *Explication de la confession de foi de la Rochelle* (Paris, 1959) and H. Jahr, *Studien zur Uberlieferungsgeschichte der Confession de foi von 1559* (Neukirchen, 1964), do not contribute much to an historical understanding of the confession. Jahr's detailed listing of its various printings does, however, dramatically point up its importance, and may lead to a restudy of the relative importance of Reformation confessions, since the French confession was perhaps the most widely distributed of any.

teristic of later sixteenth-century Geneva, Leyden or Amsterdam.

A distinctly French humanistic impulse was in great measure responsible for the emergence and growth of the French Reformation. There is, of course, a certain international character to the ideas circulated at this time, but this does not mean that they have no national characteristics. Lucien Romier may well be correct when he argues that "there is no reform more national or local than the French Reformation . . ."[36] before the wars of religion. Doubtless it was its indigenous start that left French Protestantism free of compunction to pattern itself after any model. It is possible to argue, then, not only for the national origin of French Protestantism, but also that the important documents in the life of the Church—the French Bible and the Confession of Faith—were essentially products of the French Church itself. There can be very little contesting this position with regard to Olivétan's French Bible. On the other hand, there is considerable disagreement over the precise relation of the Confession of Faith to its origin and acceptance. I believe that the evidence points toward an independent course for the French Church even with respect to John Calvin, in spite of the fact that Calvin himself was a product of French humanist circles and remained faithful to the humanist orientation throughout his life.

My contention for the essentially national origin of French Protestantism, which does not seek to deny the tremendous influence of Lutheran writings in the years after 1518, is based primarily on the conviction that the *causa causans* of the Protestant Reformation was the teaching on justification by faith. The description of this doctrine as the *articulus stantis et cadentis ecclesiae* is an exact statement not only of Luther's position, but of Calvin's and Reformed Protestantism's as well.[37]

36. L. Romier, *Origines politiques des guerres de religion* (Perrin, 1914), 2:225.

37. Calvin's statement, which had appeared by 1539, that justification "praecipuum esse sustinendae religionis cardinem" (*Institutio*, III, xi.1; *OS*, IV.182.15–16) may be regarded as a comparable sentiment. The nuance peculiar to the French Protestant expression of the doctrine of justification by faith is further argument for a "national origin" thesis. That is, Lefèvre's very close conjunction of faith and works, which led Merle d'Aubigné to suspect that he perhaps did not "sufficiently mark the distinction between justification and sanctification" (*History*

Since justification by faith is the "article of the Reformation," French Protestant historians have every right to point with pride to the 1512 commentary on the Epistles of St. Paul by Jacques Lefèvre d'Étaples (Faber Stapulensis, d. 1536).[38] Herein Lefèvre boldly set forth what can only be described as a Protestant doctrine of justification. "It is God alone," he wrote, "who gives that righteousness which is by faith; it is God alone who solely by grace, justifies unto eternal life," and then went on to distinguish two kinds of righteousness (one which is of our own works, the invention of man and temporal, the other of grace, the work of God alone and eternal) in a manner much like Luther's celebrated active-righteousness, passive-righteousness distinction in the argument to his 1531 *Lectures on Galatians.*[39]

---

of the Great Reformation, 3:359), is a characteristic of French Reformed theology. Lucien Febvre has documented this in Farel and Roussel and makes the generalization that "d'une façon générale, le souci de ne pas exclure totalement les oeuvres a tousjours été marqué chez les Français, au moins de la premiere génération" (*Au coeur religieux du XVIe siècle,* p. 52). One can, I believe, extend this to comprehend the main exponents of French Protestantism. Certainly it is true of Calvin, who apparently felt the need of so stressing works that he discussed sanctification or regeneration before justification in book III of the *Institutio.* It is overwhelmingly true of Amyraut and most of the Amyraldians.

38. *Sancti Pauli epistolae XIV* (Paris, 1512; 2nd ed., 1515). The best analyses of Lefèvre's thought remain Augustin Renaudet's *Préréforme et humanisme à Paris* (Paris, 1916; 2nd ed., 1953) and *Humanisme et Renaissance* (Paris, 1958). Most proponents of the national origin thesis for French Protestantism lean heavily on Lefèvre. See Raoul Stéphan, *Histoire du protestantisme français* (Paris, 1961), p. 24ff. Stéphan speaks of Lefévre as "l'homme qui a vraiment préparé la Réforme en France et dont on ne saurait exagérer l'influence . . ."

39. ". . . solus enim deus est qui hanc justitiâ per fidem tradit: qui sola gratia ad vitam justificat aeternam. Justitia illa: legis dicitur. haec:fidei. illa:operum. haec. gratiae. illa:humana est. haec: divina. illius: homo. huius: deus author est. Illa: ad terrena & transitoria. haec: ad divina & aeterna justificat bona. illa: praeparat. haec consummat. ergo illa: via. haec finis. illa: umbratile vestigium atque signum. hec: lux & veritas" (*Sancti Pauli epistolae XIV. Comm. on Rom. 3,* p. 71, 2). Compare Luther's distinction in *W.A. XL* 42ff. The strong dualism running through the writings of Lefèvre is more evident in his style of argument than is the same tendency in Luther. Lefèvre's all-embracing interpretation of Romans is in terms of the opposition of law and gospel, and he is constantly making comparisons between the features and personalities of the Old and New Testament dispensations. In his discussion of the circumcision of the heart and the circumcision of the flesh he says: "Haec: in spiritu circuncisio. illa: in litera. haec: occulta. illa: manifesta. hec: veritas. illa: huius signum et umbra. haec: a deo fit.

Moreover, and consistent with the dualism which was illustrated in the preceding note, Lefèvre also spoke derogatorily of the merit of works, seeing all human effort as applicable only to earthly righteousness and not to spiritual or heavenly righteousness. Furthermore, there is a Protestant flavor to his explanation of redemption which, to some extent, anticipates Calvin's doctrine of election:

> Yea, those who are perishing desire to be saved but our will, our choice, our works are powerless in this matter. However the election of God is most efficacious and most powerful. Indeed, it alone is able to work in us and give us salvation. Therefore when we are converted it is not our conversion which makes us elect, but rather it is the will, grace, and election of God.[40]

And to these "Protestant" soteriological teachings we might also add his denial of the doctrine of transubstantiation and his insistence upon the sufficiency of the Scriptures in determining matters of salvation.[41]

Besides incorporating these Protestant-like doctrines in his works, Lefèvre also provided principles of exegesis which greatly abetted the Protestants, notably Luther, in their rejection of the four-fold exegesis of the Schoolmen and in their espousal of the doctrine *sola scriptura*. In the preface to his text and com-

---

illa: ab homine. per hanc: filii dei secundû spiritum cognoscimur. per illâ: secundum carnê filii Abrahae. illa enim: filiationis hominis est signû. haec: signû filiationis dei. illam habêtes: terrâ Chananeorû possederût. habentes vero hâc: haereditabunt regnû coelorû. Et hic et ille judaeus & haec et illa circuncisio adeo inter se differunt: ut spiritus atque caro coelû et terra lux et tenebrae novum et antiquum ut et ferme ex opposito per totû respôdeât. spiritualibus tamen viris et qui eloquia dei in luce evangelii vidêt: carnalia spiritualiû manifeste sunt symbola. Et nos Christum Jhesum." There is in this a *heilsgeschichtlich* tendency which includes an awareness of history not common in the 15th and 16th centuries.

40. "Immo et qui pereunt: salvari volunt. sed inefficax est ad hoc ipsum nostra voluntas nostra electio nostra opera: dei autem electio efficacissima et potentissima. Immo sola quae salutem nobis et facere et donare potest. Ergo cum convertinur: nostra conversio nos non facit electos sed dei voluntas gratia et electio" (*Sancti Pauli epistolae XIV. Comm. on Rom. 11*, p. 89, 2).

41. See J. T. McNeill, *The History and Character of Calvinism* (New York, 1954), p. 96; G. L. Mosse, *The Reformation*, Berkshire Studies in European History, 3rd ed. (New York, 1963), p. 20.

mentary on the Psalms, Lefèvre maintained the sole admissibility of the literal sense of biblical texts.[42] By literal he did not mean what we would understand by that term today; rather he meant a prophetic interpretation based on the literal text. This enabled him to set forth a strongly christological interpretation of the Psalms, an interpretation adopted by Luther.[43]

The above points having been made, I should make clear that I am not claiming that Lefèvre was a Protestant. On this matter there is but little doubt that Renaudet is correct in his judgment that the writing of Lefèvre is that "of a spiritual man, but not of a reformer."[44] His mysticism is much like that of the Pseudo-Dionysius, Raymond Lull, and Nicholas of Cusa, and is most certainly at odds with the theocentric religion of the Reformers, perhaps especially Luther. But our point is not that Lefèvre was a Protestant, but that he both produced an atmosphere of reform and inspired others to become thoroughly committed to Luther's movement.

Perhaps the most notable of Lefèvre's disciples, so far as French Protestantism is concerned, was Guillaume Farel (1489–1565).[45] Lefèvre in 1507 had been invited by Guillaume Briçonnet (1470–1534), then abbot of Saint-Germain-des-Prés, to come to the abbey to study and teach. Saint-Germain-des-Prés soon became a center of religious studies. Farel came to Paris in 1509 to study at the most celebrated university of Europe and was one of the many students who, probably from curiosity, visited the abbey. Almost immediately a close friendship developed between Farel and Lefèvre which was to last until Lefèvre's death. Farel's conversion to the Reformation was due in large part, if not exclusively, to Lefèvre's influence.[46] Farel became, in the

42. *Quincuplex Psalterium* (Paris, 1509). See "General Introduction," *Luther: Lectures on Romans,* trans. and ed. Wilhelm Pauck, The Library of Christian Classics vol. 15 (Philadelphia, 1961), p. xxxff.

43. According to Pauck, "In his lectures on the Psalms, Luther was so strongly under the influence of these ideas that Faber's mentality was reflected not only in his thoughts but also in his vocabulary" (*Luther: Lectures on Romans,* p. xxxi).

44. *Humanisme et Renaissance,* p. 210.

45. The following material is taken mostly from the exhaustive study *Guillaume Farel,* ed. Comité Farel (Neuchatel and Paris, 1930).

46. See the interesting account in Farel's *Epistre a tous seigneurs et peuples* of 1530 in which he recounts the arresting devotion of Lefèvre, the prediction that

words of John T. McNeill, "Lefèvre's most aggressive pupil, a second-rate scholar and hot gospeler."[47] He left France as early as 1523 and carried on reformatory activity in Switzerland in the French-speaking districts west of Fribourg and Bern. It was this fiery evangelist who first brought Geneva into the Reformation camp, having begun to work there in 1532. And, as is well known, it was Farel who was the instrument "of God's call" of John Calvin to Geneva.

The evangelical movement which grew out of the teaching of Lefèvre was to take two directions. One branch would remain faithful to the Catholic Church, and the reforming activity which took place in the diocese of Meaux under Bishop Briçonnet, along with Gérard Roussel and Lefèvre himself, was a part of this branch. To it also belonged the sister of Francis I, Marguerite d'Angoulême, the great humanist scholar Guillaume Budé (1467–1540), the king's confessor Guillaume Petit, the king's personal physician Guillaume Cop, members of the king's council such as Louis de Berquin, and many others.[48]

The other branch chose to break with the old Church. Farel and Calvin can be numbered among this group. These men who made the break were encouraged by the example of Luther, nurtured and sustained by his writings which were in abundance at Paris by 1520. In 1521, upon the insistence of the Sorbonne, the Parlement issued a decree banning the writings of Luther, and the history of the French Protestant Church after this could

---

the world would soon be renewed, and the account of his own "renewal" which began with Lefèvre's pointing out the inefficacy of merit and the all-sufficiency of grace: "par sa parole me retira de la fausse opinion du merite & m'enseigna que nous n'avions point de merites, mais que tout venoit de grace, & par la seule misericorde de Dieu, sans qu'aucun l'ait merité. Ce que je creu, si tost qu'il me fust dit . . ." (reprint of Farel's *Du vraye usage de la Croix* [Geneva, 1865], pp. 170–71). For a learned account of Farel's conversion, see J. Barnaud in *Guillaume Farel*, pp. 104–10.

47. *History and Character of Calvinism*, p. 131.

48. See esp. the discussion in E. G. Léonard, *Histoire générale du protestantisme*, 3 vols. (Paris, 1961–64), 1:202; also the spirited account in the *Histoire ecclésiastique des églises réformées au royaume de france* attributed to Théodore de Bèze, ed. G. Baum and E. Cunitz, 3 vols. (Paris, 1883–89), 1:10–37. Geisendorf, *Théodore de Bèze* (Geneva, 1949), lists this as one of the works "faussement attribués à Théodore de Bèze" (p. 441).

easily be written as a martyrology. Though Francis I blew hot and cold in his policies toward the "Lutherans" (as they were then called), by the time of his death the new religion was solidly established in France. William Stevenson's judgment is that:

> With the one exception of Brittany, Protestantism was entrenched in every district of France, and was specially strong in the towns, along the great waterways and rivers, in those areas that lay at a distance from Paris or were accessible to foreign influence; . . . Indeed, in Dauphiné and eastern Languedoc the Protestants were actually in the majority.[49]

Under Henry II (1547–59), remembered especially for his infamous *chambre ardente,* stricter and more consistent measures were taken to crush Protestantism. Nevertheless the Protestant religion continued to grow apace, and from his reign date two of the great landmarks of the Huguenot Church, the founding of the first church at Paris in 1555 and the convening of the first National Synod in 1559. And since, at least after the French translation of Calvin's *Institutio* (1541), French Protestantism had become broadly aligned with Calvinism, it is of special interest to inquire into the precise relation of these historic events in the development of the Huguenot Church to Calvin.

It is certain that, having come from their midst, Calvin had a special affection for the French Protestants. His letter to Francis I, prefaced to his *Institutio,* was written on their behalf. He had championed their cause at Ratisbon in 1541. His voluminous correspondence with their leaders portrayed a paternal as well as concerned spirit. And, doubtless, the feeling was mutual. But this ought not to lead one to conclude that Calvin in fact ruled in French Protestantism. The evidence points to the conclusion that at decisive points the French Church went its own way, perhaps consulting Calvin but by no means rendering absolute allegiance to him.

The church established at Paris in 1555 may be characterized as Calvinist in structure. That is, in it there was made the provision for four church offices, preachers, teachers, elders and deacons, as these were set forth in Calvin's *Ordonnances ecclesi-*

49. *The Story of the Reformation* (Richmond, 1959), pp. 91–92.

astiques of 1541. Nevertheless recent writers, and especially the late Émile Léonard in his perceptive chapter entitled "L'adaptation française du calvinisme," have maintained that this first Huguenot church did not take Calvin's Genevan church for its model, but rather patterned itself after the church at Strasbourg.[50] While this is perhaps not surprising, since it is fairly certain that Calvin himself derived his ideas of church government from Bucer during his stay at Strasbourg,[51] Léonard and Febvre maintain that there were significant differences between the Genevan church of 1555 and the Strasbourg church. S. Mours, in his exhaustive study of the French Reformed churches, lists no less than 51 congregations in existence before 1555.[52] It is likely that these congregations looked to Strasbourg for guidance. Indeed, the *Histoire ecclésiastique* informs us that the *"Lutheriens de Meaux"* had thoughtfully visited and considered the French church at Strasbourg and had patterned their church after it.[53] It appears reasonable, therefore, that upon its establishment in 1555 the Paris church should draw upon the tradition already established in France, a tradition which owed its form to the church at Strasbourg. In doing this the Paris church indicated its independence of Calvin and Geneva.

This independence from Calvin is evidenced in other ways as well. Robert Kingdon has shown in his detailed and scholarly study that in the years 1555–62 Geneva supplied France with at least eighty-eight pastors.[54] One might well expect that these men, trained in Geneva, would demonstrate an irrevocable allegiance to the principles advocated by Calvin. Whatever may be

50. See Léonard's *Histoire générale du protestantisme*, 2:82–149; also Febvre, *Au coeur religieux de XVIᵉ siècle*, pp. 251–67, for the authority cited by Léonard.

51. Bucer studies, becoming more and more common, have established beyond doubt Calvin's reliance upon Bucer at many points, perhaps especially church government. See François Wendel, *L'Eglise de Strasbourg* (Paris, 1942), pp. 237–41, and Wilhelm Pauck, "Calvin and Butzer," in *The Heritage of the Reformation*, rev. and enl. ed. (Glencoe, 1961), pp. 85–99.

52. *Les Eglises réformées en France* (Paris and Strasbourg, 1958), pp. 56–107.

53. 1:67. In this account the Strasbourg church is said to have been "dressée" by Calvin, but Wendel's study shows this to be incorrect; see esp. pp. 189ff.

54. *Geneva and the Coming of the Wars of Religion in France, 1555–1563* (Geneva, 1956), preface and *passim*.

the reason, such does not seem to be the case. Calvin was un-yielding in his opposition to armed insurrection unless a revolt were to be led by "lesser magistrates."[55] Yet many of these pastors involved themselves in the celebrated incident known as "La Conjuration d'Amboise."[56] The plot was opposed by Calvin from the first,[57] but this did not seem to deter the plotters. It is true that Calvin's more radical associate, Theodore Beza, may well have been involved,[58] but this hardly implicates Calvin. It is

55. One of many indications of this is found in *Institutio*, IV.xx.25: "Verum si in Dei verbum respicimus, longius non deducet, ut non eorum modo principum imperio subditi simus qui probe, et qua debent fide, munere suo erga nos de-funguntur: sed omnium qui quoquo modo rerum potiuntur, etiamsi nihil minus praestent quam quod ex officio erat principum" (*OS*, V.495.27ff).

56. See Henri Naef's *La Conjuration d'Amboise et Genève* (Geneva and Paris, 1922), a remarkably detailed study, the scholarship of which is first-rate, the pre-suppositions debatable. See also R. M. Kingdon's judicious analysis in *Geneva and the Coming*, pp. 68–78. In the most recent full-scale study on the Amboise con-spiracy, N. M. Sutherland's "Calvinism and the Conspiracy of Amboise," *History* 47 (1962) 111–38, the case is made for the non-involvement of Huguenot ministers in the plot. I am unable to accept this argument for it assumes, in my opinion, too great an idealism in the ministers.

57. See his letter to Sturm of March 23, 1560, *CO*, 18:38–39, his letter to Bullinger of May 11, 1560, *CO*, 18:84ff., and his detailed disavowal in a letter to Coligny of April 16, 1561, *CO*, 18:425–31. See also the account in Naef, *La Con-juration*, pp. 151–63. Naef wonders why Calvin did not do more to prevent this incident (pp. 162–63). This presupposes two things which are open to question: (1) that Calvin felt it his duty to exert pressure in such circumstances; (2) that the French ministers would have listened if he had issued a storm of protest. We know that he had counselled the leaders of the movement not to proceed with the plan and they had summarily disregarded his advice (see the letter to Coligny, opening pars., *CO*, 18:425–26).

58. Kingdon, *Geneva and the Coming*, pp. 69ff; Naef, *La Conjuration*, pp. 163ff. See also Kingdon's important article, "The First Expression of Theodore Beza's Political Ideas," *ARG* 46 (1955), 88–100. It would seem clear that Beza's stand on the theories of resistance was much more radical than Calvin's. One can hardly overemphasize the radical nature of the teachings in this treatise of Beza's (*De haereticis a civili magistratu puniendis libellus* [Geneva, 1554]) which Kingdon has analyzed in *ARG*. It is certain that on this subject Calvin and Beza were not in accord. Elsewhere Kingdon even speculates that with regard to the Amboise Conspiracy "Beza-Morel ideas triumphed over Calvin's objections in the Company [of Pastors] meetings" (*Geneva and the Coming*, p. 72). It is my belief, which I will develop further, that this is by no means the only topic on which Calvin and Beza differed sharply, that there was considerable divergence in their theologi-cal program as a whole, especially evident in methodology. Kingdon's provocative *Geneva and the Consolidation of the French Protestant Movement, 1564–1572*

further true that Calvin later helped raise funds to support the
wars of religion, as Kingdon proves,[59] but his somewhat prag-
matic activity was carried on in relation to a war he regarded as
led by "lesser magistrates" (Condé and Coligny). It was far removed from the clandestine activities of many of the French
ministers.[60] One simply cannot avoid the conclusion that they
did not follow Calvin's teaching on this matter very faithfully.[61]

Perhaps most significant of all is the independence from
Geneva demonstrated by the French ministers at their first National Synod, held secretly in Paris May 25–29, 1559.[62] Accord-

---

(Geneva and Madison, Wis., 1967) indicates that Beza exercised much more of an
iron control over Geneva than Calvin had. Some of Calvin's closest friends, in fact
(e.g. Jean-Raymond Merlin and Nicolas Colladon) were deposed for opposing Beza.

59. *Geneva and the Coming*, pp. 115ff.

60. This work of Calvin on behalf of the warring Huguenots appears to
render credence to the interpretation of some reputable scholars who regard him
as an opportunist: Pierre Imbart de la Tour, *Les Origines de la réforme*, 4 vols.
(Paris, 1905–35), 4:185–93; Naef, *La Conjuration*, pp. 69–81, and Kingdon, *Geneva
and the Coming*, p. 112. I myself am not convinced. Calvin had consistently taught
that resistance was possible through "lesser magistrates" (*Institutio*, IV.xx.31) and
Condé's involvement supplied this.

61. In his intriguing *The Revolution of the Saints* (Cambridge, Mass., 1966)
Michael Walzer attempts, unsuccessfully I believe, to show Calvin as the source of
such political activity. While he presents evidence of having read widely in Calvin,
his interpretation of Calvin as essentially a political figure who saw a repressive
state as the means to his religious program simply cannot be accepted. He evidently regards it as "the only way of explaining his [Calvin's] achievements at
Geneva and of revealing the sources within his thought of that radicalism that
continually burst forth among his followers" (p. 46), but his mistake may lie in
assuming that they must be explained as originating in Calvin himself. Can it be
assumed with propriety that "Huguenot ministers deferred on all important matters to Calvin's opinion . . ."? Is this not a striking example of the problem which
has bedeviled Calvin research for so long—the attempt to interpret Calvin via the
historical movement known as Calvinism? In any case, Walzer is surely wide of the
mark when he sees Calvin as "always and insistently concerned with obedience, but
not with reconciliation" (p. 45), or when he sees Calvin's concept of the Church
as "a coercive institution designed to bring men into the 'obedience of the gospel,'
which is to say: not to open them for grace, but to expose them to command"
(p. 51). While one may agree with J. E. Neale and Robert Kingdon that organization in French churches was decisive, to push this to Walzer's extreme is to seriously
distort Calvin's thought.

62. The date given in both collections of the proceedings of the French synods:
J. Aymon, *Tous les synodes nationaux des eglises reformées de France*, 2 vols.
(La Haye, 1710), 1:98; and J. Quick, *Synodicon in Gallia reformata*, 2 vols. (London,

ing to the *Histoire ecclésiastique,* it was at a small gathering (synod?) at Poitiers near the end of 1558 that the idea of a national synod was broached. The minister Antoine de la Roche-Chandieu was charged with communicating with the Paris church to see about the possibility of drawing up a confession and discipline. Evidently Chandieu contacted the Parisian minister François de Morel, who was favorable to the proposal. It seems that a date was fixed for the convocation of a synod, so de Morel in turn wrote to Calvin, addressing the letter to Nicholas Colladon.[63] In the letter, de Morel sought Calvin's advice concerning the proposed synod and perhaps asked him to prepare a confession of faith for the French Church.

It has been commonly accepted that Calvin "was far from sharing the opinion of the necessity of a confession . . ."[64] It does need to be recognized that Calvin never responded to de Morel's letter.[65] However, we can be quite sure Calvin never saw this letter, for he begins his own of May 17 with the words, "How unfortunate that we have not been advised sooner of your synod which is so close at hand!"[66] In any case, this letter of May 17 is in response to a second letter of de Morel's dated April 25, a letter which shows that de Morel is somewhat upset over Calvin's

---

1692), 1:91. The *Histoire ecclésiastique* gives 26–29 May, but this seems to be inaccurate. Our discussion will not consider the discipline adopted at the 1559 synod at Paris, but as Pannier notes, Calvin certainly was not its author (*La Confession de foi,* p. 104). The material that is included here is designed to contest the popular idea, as expressed by Preserved Smith, that the *confessio Gallicana* set forth "in forty articles the purest doctrine of Geneva" (*Reformation in Europe,* p. 162).

63. Pannier, *La Confession de foi,* says: "Nicolas Colladon est un des hommes qui ont vu le plus souvent Calvin pendant les dernières années de sa vie . . ." (p. 86). The following account relies quite heavily on Pannier's learned treatise.

64. *Histoire ecclésiastique,* 1:200 n3.

65. Baum and Cunitz think the letter never reached Calvin but was lost en route (*ibid.,* 1:200 n1). Pannier thinks Calvin's severe illness of late 1558 and early 1559, or perhaps Colladon's ill-will towards the idea of a French confession, accounts for Calvin's silence at this critical period in the life of the French Church (*La Confession de foi,* pp. 86–7). In any case, note that though they had no response from Calvin, the plan to hold the synod does not seem to have been at all affected.

66. "Utinam de proximo vestro conventu maturius fuissemus admoniti" (*CO,* 17:525).

lack of response to his first letter.[67] Calvin in turn is very forthright about his displeasure over their idea of drafting (or is it
publishing?) a confession. He expresses himself thus: "Some are
strongly declaring the urgency of setting forth this confession.
However, we have angels and men as our witnesses that this
ardor is displeasing to us at this time. . . . I very sharply regret
seeing you in such a state of affairs."[68]

Though he doubted they would arrive in time, Calvin sent
three ministers to aid in the deliberations of the synod. It may
be that he also hurriedly drew up a confession which he sent
with these ministers. We know from a letter of de Morel's of
June 9 that the ministers did arrive in time to participate in the
synod, though one of them, des Gallars, could not attend because
of illness.[69] The letter has been thought also to give a clue to
the authorship of the basic part of the confession, for de Morel
writes: "We have thought it necessary to add some articles to
your confession of faith. The other articles we have adopted
with very little change."[70] This passage is thought to be quite
enlightening, especially with regard to the authorship of the confession. It has been thought quite safe to assume, with the editors
of the *Calvini opera* as well as those of the *Opera selecta,* that
the confession published in thirty-five articles in 1559 is the
confession drafted by Calvin.[71] And the editors of the *Calvini
opera* have pretty well established that this confession incorporates large portions of the 1557 confession, the *Confessio ecclesiae parisiensis,* which they attribute to Calvin. However,
there are at least three considerations which cast some doubt
on the accepted account of this whole relationship, as well as on

67. "Postrem[is] literis quas ad *Colladonium* nostrum dederam obtestabar ut
sententiam vestram de conventu pastorum celebrando, confessionis fidei scribendae
causa, nobis significaretis, viros etiam duos petebamus nobis subsidio tot gregibus
agendis. *Qua de re sicuti de multis aliis ne lineam quidem responsionis ac-
cepimus"* (*CO,* 17:505–6. Emphasis added).

68. "Si confessionis edendae tam pertinax quosdam zelus sollicitat, tamen angelos
et homines testamur ardorem hunc nobis adhuc displicere. . . . Tantopere apud
vos trepidari valde mihi dolet . . ." (*CO,* 17:526).

69. In *CO,* 17:540–42.

70. "Confessioni vestrae nonnulla visum est addere, perpauca vero commutare"
(*CO,* 17:540).

71. *CO,* 9:739–51; *OS,* II.310–24.

the strict relation of the official confession to the thought of Calvin.

In the first place, a recent article by Jacques Poujol in the *Bulletin*[72] presents evidence that there was a confession circulating in France before the synod of 1559, indeed before Calvin ever penned his letter to the synod. Poujol quotes from a letter of the English Ambassador to France, Nicolas Throckmorton, to the English Secretary of State. The letter is dated May 15, 1559. The critical passage is as follows:

> I have learned that about 15,000 people, of the provinces of Gascogne, Guyenne, Anjou, Poitou, Normandy, and Maine have subscribed a confession similar to that of Geneva. This confession they intend soon to present to the king. Among these people were many of importance. In the same circles it is said that as soon as they have presented this confession to the King the Church will be forced to receive his assurance that they will be completely wiped out.[73]

If one adopts this account as factual then perhaps two conclusions are necessary. Doumergue may in fact be right, for one, in his interpretation that Calvin did not oppose the drafting of a confession, only its *publication*.[74] It seems that the correspondence between Calvin and de Morel quoted above may well substantiate this thesis, for when Calvin writes that he is displeased that some are insisting on setting forth (*edendae*) a confession, he most likely refers to the intention of publishing a confession and presenting it to the king.[75] This interpretation is strengthened even further when one recalls Calvin's strong aversion to any political stand which might be taken by the French Protestants. He doubtless knew that such a move would make inevitable the repercussions mentioned in Throckmorton's letter and wanted this to be avoided. Moreover, when de Morel writes

---

72. "L'Ambassadeur d'Angleterre et la Confession de Foi du Synode de 1559," *Bulletin* 105 (1959), pp. 49–53.

73. Quoted, *ibid.*, p. 49.

74. Emile Doumergue, *Jean Calvin*, 7 vols. (Paris, 1899–1927), 7:202.

75. For the same interpretation, but without Throckmorton's correspondence as substantiation, see L. Joubert, "Les Années décisives de la Réforme française 1559–1562," *Etudes théologiques et religieuses* 34 (1959), pp. 213–38, esp. pp. 221–22.

and assures Calvin that "the confession, established by unanimous vote, will be retained in the archives of each church, and will not be presented to the magistrates or the king unless some church finds itself in extreme circumstances,"[76] is he not answering the cause of Calvin's expressed displeasure?

A second consideration, perhaps made necessary by careful recognition of Throckmorton's correspondence, is more important yet for our purposes. That is, that the document upon which the Confession of 1559 is based may not have been one drafted at the last moment by Calvin. In any case, even if he did send a confession to this synod, they had another upon which to draw. Was this perhaps a document drawn up by the Poitiers "synod"? Or is it the *Confessio ecclesiae parisiensis* of 1557? And if it is the latter, is that document itself not a product from within French Protestantism rather than exclusively Calvin's? It may be overly ambitious to claim, with Pannier, that "it is an error that it has been published among the works of Calvin,"[77] yet Calvin's participation (if any) may have been minor. His approval of the document certainly does not demand that he be its author. The title "Confession of the Church of Paris" suggests French origins. In any event, the existence of the confession mentioned by Throckmorton, apparently complete enough that the French pastors considered it a worthy statement to present to the king, seems to be evidence of more independence from Calvin than is commonly recognized.

A third consideration which reflects this independence is de Morel's very statement, ". . . we have thought it necessary to add some articles to your confession." Even if one accepts the conclusion of the editors of *CO* and *OS* that Calvin was the author of a thirty-five article confession, still the first six articles of the official document are generally recognized as the work of the pastors at the Paris synod. And these six articles, it is necessary to emphasize, are quite significant additions. They comprehend the doctrine of God, the knowledge of God (how He has revealed himself), the canon, the authority of the Bible, and

76. *CO*, 17:540.
77. *La Confession de foi*, p. 83. Pannier's conclusion is shared by the editors of the *Opera selecta*, who do not include the confession in their collection.

the doctrine of the Trinity. Moreover, they are decidedly more scholastic than the rest of the document. This may be seen in article one, where there is a long list of God's attributes, a characteristic of medieval or seventeenth-century theology but not typical of Calvin. Or again this may be seen in the second article, which seems to present the difference between the revelation of God in nature and the revelation in his Word as simply a difference in degree. That is, the only distinction between these two revelations is that God is manifested "more clearly through his Word."[78] This was to become a matter of great importance in the seventeenth century, but as it stands in this document it would not have been condoned by Calvin without a statement concerning man's inability to comprehend God's revelation through his works.

A fourth consideration which helps point up the independence of French Protestantism from Calvin is somewhat less clear cut, but nevertheless appears to be indicative of a trend. We have seen that Calvin seemed to be particularly concerned over the publication of the confession of French Protestantism and that de Morel assured him their confession would not be published unless a church found itself in desperate circumstances. This promise of de Morel was not kept. Evidently those who were insisting on publishing the confession prevailed, for as Pannier notes it was published in 1559.[79] But the interesting factor is that, also in 1559, there were at least two publications of the text of thirty-five articles, neither of which gives the place of publication. Does this not point up a bit of intrigue? One can easily read into this that Calvin, learning that the confession adopted by the Paris synod was going to be published, and not being happy with either this spirit of independence or the confession as it stood, quickly published a version of which he approved. Our suspicion of intrigue is perhaps further validated by the fact that the confession of forty articles never appeared with Geneva as the place of publication during Calvin's lifetime, though the version with thirty-five articles did in 1562. Moreover, there is another factor in this story which tends to substan-

78. "plus clairement par sa parole" (OS, II.310.37–38).
79. La Confession de foi, p. 127ff.

tiate the claim that the French Protestants jealously guarded
their independence; namely, that the title of the version with
thirty-five articles alreadys reads *Confession de foy faicte d'un
commun accord par les EGLISES qui sont dispersees en France,*
whereas the version with forty articles has for its title *Confession
de foy faicte d'un commun accord par les FRANÇOIS qui de-
sirent vivre selon la pureté de l'evangile de nostre Seigneur Jesu-
christ.*[80] It is of course true that Calvin was himself a Frenchman,
so that this variance in title should perhaps not be pressed too
strongly. At the same time, if our theory is true it would help
explain why the confession of thirty-five articles was ever printed
at all.

The Huguenots did present their confession of faith to King
Francis II in the spring of 1560. The increased persecution evidently foreseen by Calvin followed. Pannier contends that only
the good graces of the chancellor, Michel de l'Hôpital, saved
France from the establishment of the Inquisition.[81] The Huguenots, spurred on by the Guise-family control of the early
years of Francis II, developed increasingly political aspirations.
In the end they decided to take up arms, a move generally deplored by Calvin, though he may have been somewhat mollified
by the Huguenot pretext that this was being done to guard
against foreign invasion. Catherine de Medici evidently made
a genuine attempt to pacify an increasingly threatening situation
by her religious-toleration edict of January, 1562. Ironically,
the edict only hastened the coming of the wars of religion, for
it emboldened the Huguenots and embittered the Guises. For
our purposes it is perhaps sufficient to note that the wars lasted
at least until 1598, if not until the siege and fall of La Rochelle
in 1628 under the direction of Richelieu.

This time of devastating civil strife was not conducive to the
development and elaboration of theology. There was, then, in
France little development beyond that found in the confession
of faith. In the realm of political thought, however, there was
a spate of literature devoted to the theory of resistance and ex-
emplified in the famous *Vindiciae contra tyrannos* by "Junius

80. *Ibid.,* pp. 127–28. The capitals are added.
81. *Ibid.,* p. 133.

Brutus."[82] The revolutionary teaching of this book, that tyrants must be resisted, is another instance of the *"adaption française du calvinisme."*[83]

It was around the year 1600 that French Protestants were once again free to devote primary interest to theological matters, to an exchange of theological ideas with the rest of international Calvinism. By this time the major part of international Calvinism had replaced with a quite different theological expression and spirit the humanistic orientation which characterized most of the early reform movements. The phenomenon many have called Protestant scholasticism had set in.[84] Though this term for the phenomenon has been widely adopted, few, if any, have

82. Edinburgh (in reality Basle), 1579. There was a French translation entitled *De la puissance légitime du prince sur le peuple et du peuple sur le prince* (Basle, 1581). This treatise is generally thought to be the work of either Languet or du Plessis-Mornay.

83. Léonard, *Histoire générale du protestantisme,* 2:82–149.

84. This term has come into quite general use as an "umbrella" under which most of 17th-century Protestantism is gathered. It was used as early as 1882 by Charles Beard in his scintillating Hibbert lectures now available in paperback under the title *The Reformation of the 16th Century* (Ann Arbor, 1962); see esp. pp. 262–99. Ernst Troeltsch in his brilliant *Vernunft und Offenbarung bei Johann Gerhard und Melanchthon* (Göttingen, 1891) describes the phenomenon and pinpoints its emergence in Protestantism in the writings of Melanchthon. The thesis on which it rests has stood the test of time and has been followed by most scholars. (I shall suggest that it needs some revision as far as Reformed scholasticism is concerned.) Two recent works dealing with Protestant scholasticism are, for Lutheranism, Robert Scharlemann, *Aquinas and Gerhard: Theological Controversy and Construction in Medieval and Protestant Scholasticism* (New Haven, 1964), and, for Reformed Protestantism, the introduction to John W. Beardslee III, ed. and trans., *Reformed Dogmatics* (New York, 1965). Throughout this study I have juxtaposed this "Protestant scholasticism" and (since I have dealt mainly with France) "French humanism." The actual picture is of course not so neat, the distinction between these two expressions not always (if ever!) clear-cut. Most of the Protestant scholastics were influenced by the humanist ideal; as Kristeller notes for the movements in general, "all kinds of adjustments and combinations between humanism and scholasticism were possible and were successfully accomplished" (*Renaissance Thought: The Classic, Scholastic, and Humanist Strains* [New York, 1961], p. 116). Nevertheless there was a distinctive orientation to each which will be described in the following pages for scholasticism and in chapter 3 for humanism—orientations fundamentally at odds and which in the heat of religious controversy came to the fore. I do not wish to divide all of Reformed Protestantism into two warring camps (for in the early years the distinction was not readily apparent), but to understand later struggles one must be aware of these opposing trends.

attempted a definition. There is good reason for this because, like Puritanism, Protestant scholasticism is more a spirit, an attitude of life, than a list of beliefs. For this reason it practically defies precise definition. The term will be used in this study to refer to at least four more-or-less identifiable tendencies: (1) Primarily it will have reference to that theological approach which asserts religious truth on the basis of deductive ratiocination from given assumptions or principles, thus producing a logically coherent and defensible system of belief. Generally this takes the form of syllogistic reasoning. It is an orientation, it seems, invariably based upon an Aristotelian philosophical commitment and so relates to medieval scholasticism. (2) The term will refer to the employment of reason in religious matters, so that reason assumes at least equal standing with faith in theology, thus jettisoning some of the authority of revelation. (3) It will comprehend the sentiment that the scriptural record contains a unified, rationally comprehensible account and thus may be formed into a definitive statement which may be used as a measuring stick to determine one's orthodoxy. (4) It will comprehend a pronounced interest in metaphysical matters, in abstract, speculative thought, particularly with reference to the doctrine of God. The distinctive scholastic Protestant position is made to rest on a speculative formulation of the will of God.

This new outlook represents a profound divergence from the humanistically oriented religion of John Calvin and most of the early reformers. The strongly biblically and experientially based theology of Calvin and Luther had, it is fair to say, been overcome by the metaphysics and deductive logic of a restored Aristotelianism. Luther in particular had struck out bitterly against Aristotle's corrupting influence in theology, professing himself to be grieved "to the heart that this damned, conceited, rascally heathen has with his false words deluded and made fools of so many . . ."[85] Calvin, as a classical scholar in the humanist mold, was less vehement about Aristotle but in general successfully rejected Aristotelian philosophical influence in his theologizing.

In fact, a proper appraisal of the *nature* of Calvin's theological program shows a striking absence of those features we have listed

85. *Three Treatises* (Muhlenberg, 1960), p. 93.

as characteristic of Protestant scholasticism.[86] In particular one needs to underline the fact that his major theological effort, the *Institutio,* is by no means meant to be an end in itself. It is, as the preface makes abundantly clear (both the preface to the Latin edition and the prefatory "Subject Matter of the Present Work" drafted for the French edition), designed to be an aid in the reading of the Scriptures.[87] Thus Rist is absolutely correct in saying that for Calvin, "Christian doctrine is contained in the Holy Scriptures, not in dogmatics, and this is why theology can only be an echo of the biblical text, returning to it constantly but not permitted to add anything to it."[88]

Just as the purpose of Calvin's theologizing is to provide a key for the understanding and use of Scripture, so the key to understanding Calvin's *Institutio* is to recognize his attempt to be utterly faithful to the scriptural record. His theology is, as Dowey has noted, entirely meant to be a "theology of the Word."[89] He consistently rejects any modification of the force of a scriptural passage because it may be somehow offensive to reason.[90] At the same time he neither feels compelled to har-

86. The best exposition of the nature of Calvin's theology is now the remarkable article by Gilbert Rist, "Modernité de la méthode théologique de Calvin," *RTP* 1968, no. 1, pp. 19–33. The following discussion owes much to this brilliant exposé.

87. See these in *OS,* III.5–8, *passim.* Especially pertinent is the following passage from the Latin preface: ". . . hoc mihi in isto labore propositum fuit, sacrae Theologiae candidatos ad divini verbi lectionem ita praeparare et instruere, ut et facilem ad eam aditum habere, et inoffenso in ea gradu pergere queant;" (III. 6.18–21).

88. "Méthode théologique de Calvin," p. 21.

89. Edward A. Dowey, Jr., *The Knowledge of God in Calvin's Theology* (1952; reprint ed., New York, 1965), p. 3.

90. This is always his reply to those who attack his doctrine of predestination. See "De aeterna Dei praedestinatione," where he often calls his opponent "our human reasoner" (*CO,* 8:249–366), his "calumniae nebulonis de occulta providentia Dei cum responsione" (*CO,* 9:269–318), and his "Response a certaines calomnies et blasphemes" (*CO,* 58:201–6). Perhaps of these the treatise on God's secret providence is the most vehement. In one of many pertinent passages he says: "Readers of any discernment will appreciate the value of your discourse, about the nature of the true God, when they observe that in all inquiry upon the subject, you make common sense the starting point. The existence of God it is true was admitted by all nations and ages; since the principle and seed of this knowledge was naturally implanted in the mind of man. But how shall reason define what God is, when

monize all elements of his teaching[91] nor ever allows for any speculative remarks regarding God's hidden purposes. Indeed, if there is a persistent theme in Calvin it is that God's ways and thoughts are incomprehensible to man without special revelation.[92] His theology then is an expression of faith and complete trust in God, written by a man of faith to encourage and aid the faithful of God. As such the rational dimension is clearly subordinated to the religious. In this program theology is designed not to meet the demands of a rationally acceptable and defensi-

---

with all her perspicacity, she can do nothing but turn the truth of God into a lie, thereby adulterating all the knowledge and light of true faith and religion? The Holy Spirit commands us to become fools, if we would be disciples of the heavenly doctrine; inasmuch as the natural man is unable to receive or taste aught of it. You on the other hand would have the human faculty decide on the mysteries of God; and reason, which in its blindness, utterly extinguishes the divine glory, you not only set up as a guide and mistress, but presume to prefer it to Scripture itself. . . . I maintain that the wisest men are blinded by their own pride, and never even taste the heavenly doctrine, till such time as they become fools, and commanding their own notions to be gone, devote themselves in meek simplicity to the obedience of Christ. For human reason is utterly undiscerning, and human acuteness stupid, in the mysteries of God" (from James Lillie, trans., *On Secret Providence* [New York, 1840], pp. 106–7, 116; see *CO,* 9:313ff). For Calvin's utter faithfulness to the biblical text, see Joseph Haroutunian's "General Introduction" to *Calvin: Commentaries,* The Library of Christian Classics, vol. 23 (Philadelphia, n.d.), pp. 15–50.

91. A prime example we shall discuss further—Calvin's teaching of the double will of God, God's revealed will and secret will. Sebastian Castellio, former rector of the Genevan Academy and opponent of Calvin's conservatism, attacks Calvin at this point, charging that his position is contrary to Scripture, as in Malachi 3:6 and James 1:17, which teaches the immutability of God. Calvin's venomous reply is, essentially: "In fact it is true that one ought not seek God's will except in Scripture, but what this swine of a character does not realize in his rooting up of everything with his snout is that while the faithful are cultivating reverence and sobriety the secret judgments of God are not cancelled. It is one thing to regard with modesty of faith this profound subject, quite another obstinately to reject it *just because it overwhelms man's reason*" ("Responsio ad calumnias nebulonis de praedestinatione" *CO,* 8:263. Emphasis added).

92. Passages of this nature are legion; a brief, characteristic exposition can be found in the second sermon of "Treze Sermons de M. I. Calvin, Traitans de l'election gratuite de Dieu en Iacob, et de la rejection en Esau," *CO,* 58:31–44, *passim.* See also his expositions on predestination or the will of God (*CO,* 8:85–140, 249–366; 9:253–318; 33:239ff.; 49:18off.; 51:147ff.; 271–302; 58:17–206; *OS,* III.219–27; IV.368–432; etc.).

ble system but to assist the faithful in understanding God's revelation. If man's reason is offended by any of this revelation
Calvin always answers that we are not to debate with God but
to worship him,[93] to submit ourselves in obedience to what God
has deemed necessary that we know.[94]

Calvin teaches that this licit knowledge of God, which is since
the fall of man available only in the words of Scripture, is itself
also not scientific knowledge but religious in character. It is not,
for example, designed to teach us a certain number of propositions about God, but rather how man may unite with God's
purposes. We are to know not what God is in himself but what
he is *erga nos,* what he has revealed to us. Though he firmly
asserts that this revelation is the scriptural record, he teaches
that even here we are dealing not with scientific knowledge but
with saving knowledge. The Scripture becomes a source of this
knowledge only for the man of faith, for the man in whom the
Holy Spirit works. Thus, as many have noted, Calvin establishes
a necessary relationship between Word and Spirit.[95] The knowledge one derives from the Word is useless without its application
to our minds and hearts by the Spirit. He is not saying that there
is no knowledge apart from the work of the Spirit, just that such
knowledge is "barren and ineffectual."[96] That is, he recognizes
the validity of objective knowledge, in fact even argues for its

93. E.g. *CO,* 58:35: "Il ne faut point que nous entrions en plus grande dispute,
sinon d'adorer avec estonnement le conseil secret de Dieu, . . ."

94. E.g. *CO,* 58.34: ". . . cognoissons que nostre Seigneur nous enseigne que
nous ne pouvons faillir d'escouter et d'ouvrir les aureilles pour nous enquerir de
ce qu'il lui plaist que nous sachions: mais gardons-nous de passer plus outre: car
il n'y a rage si grande ne si enorme, que quand nous voulons plus savoir que Dieu
ne nous monstre. Et au reste, nous aurons beau travailler, appliquons-y tous noz
sens et toutes noz estudes: où est-ce que nous parviendrons? Ce sera nous fourrer
tousjours tant plus avant au labyrinthe, sinon que nous aions la conduite de Dieu
pour nous esclairer. Gardons donc ce moien: c'est d'escouter ce que Dieu nous
propose: et si tost qu'il ferme la bouche, que nous aions tous noz sens enserrez et
captifs, et que nous n'entreprenions pas de plus savoir que ce qu'il nous aura
prononcé."

95. See, for example, Wilhelm Niesel, *The Theology of Calvin,* trans. H. Knight
(Philadelphia, 1956), p. 24ff.; François Wendel, *Calvin,* trans. P. Mairet (New York,
1963), p. 157ff.; Dowey, *Knowledge of God in Calvin's Theology,* p. 117ff. (excellent); and Rist, "Méthode théologique de Calvin," pp. 24–28.

96. "Sermons sur II Timothée," *CO,* 54:285.

necessity, but such knowledge is not the stuff of theology. Theological knowledge is faith's knowledge.[97]

While this conjunction of Word and Spirit is, to use Rist's phrase, the *"fondement de la théologie,"*[98] Calvin reveals his primarily religious interest by going yet further. It is not in fact the scriptural record itself to which faith is attached, but rather Christ.[99] The words of a book could never suffice to bridge that awful gulf which separates man from God. Faith could never originate from confrontation with a book, and besides, not every passage of Scripture is conducive to the production of faith.[100] Man needed a mediator to bridge the gulf between the fearsome majesty of God and the smallness and limitations of sinful man.[101] This mediator was the God-man Jesus Christ in whom God accommodated himself to our capacity.[102] And faith needed as its object a demonstration of God's mercy and fatherly concern —for "upon grace alone can man's heart repose."[103] This too was found in Jesus alone, who by his Incarnation assured us that "we are the children of God," since he became body of our body, flesh from our flesh, and bones from our bones.[104]

Further, we can say that even Christ as he is in himself, in his essence, is not the proper object of faith.

97. See Dowey, *Knowledge of God*, p. 153ff.

98. "Méthode théologique de Calvin," p. 24.

99. ". . . faith rests in Christ alone, all the promises of God being in Him . . ." (*CO*, 7:600). See also the impressive battery of quotations gathered by Dowey (*Knowledge of God*, p. 158), and the discussion in E. David Willis, *Calvin's Catholic Christology* (Leiden, 1966), p. 109ff. (particularly valuable). Willis shows that the sticky question of "natural theology" in Calvin can perhaps be resolved when one recognizes that Calvin taught a double mediation of Christ—mediation as reconciliation, but also mediation as sustenance of the universe. Thus a possible knowledge of God through contemplation of "nature" as taught by Calvin would still be christologically mediated. See esp. his pp. 67–71.

100. *Institutio*, III.ii.7. *OS*, IV.15.17ff.

101. These sentiments are repeatedly set forth by Calvin; e.g. *Institutio*, II.vi.1–4, especially section 4, where men are referred to as "grubs crawling about on the earth" (*OS*, III.325.20–22). See also his *Commentary on John* 5:22: "Since all our senses fail when we desire to reach God, Christ, the visible image of the invisible God, is portrayed before our eyes" (see the whole passage, *CO*, 47:112).

102. *Institutio*, II.vi.4, where Calvin quotes Irenaeus. *OS*, III.325.41–326.3.

103. *Institutio*, III.ii.7. *OS*, IV.16.4.

104. *Institutio*, II.xii.2. *OS*, III.438.27–439.1.

Indeed, faith should not cling only to the essence of Christ, so to say, but should pay heed to his power and office. For it would be of little advantage to know who Christ is unless the second point is added of what He wishes to be towards us and for what purpose He was sent by the Father.[105]

It is the work of Christ in which he takes away the sin of the world by his death that Calvin calls Christ's chief office.[106] Thus it is Christ's reconciling work which properly is the object of faith. It is Christ as the "good news," the Gospel, the Christ who represents the promises of God as our redeemer, to which faith must look.[107] And we may further say that Christ is not only central for Calvin's doctrine of faith, but we may claim without equivocation that the whole of Calvin's theology is directed to this end, that is, is christocentric.[108]

This brief look at Calvin's religious thought should make it clear that his whole theological program is at odds with the orientation of scholasticism as it has been characterized above. In general we must say, however, that scholasticism, not Calvin's theology, prevailed in Reformed Protestantism. We are not here prepared to judge why Reformed theology developed as it did but only to recognize the phenomenon itself.[109] Men like Mar-

105. Comments on John 1:49, *Commentary on the Gospel According to St. John*, trans. T. H. L. Parker, vol. 4 of *Calvin's New Testament Commentaries*, ed. D. W. and T. F. Torrance (Grand Rapids, 1959), p. 43.

106. *Commentary on John* 1:29; *CO*, 47:25–26.

107. ". . . since all the promises of God are gathered together and confirmed in Christ, and are, so to speak, kept and accomplished in him, it appears without doubt that Christ is the perpetual object of faith. And in that object, faith contemplates all the riches of the divine mercy" (from *Instruction in Faith* [*1537*], tr. P. T. Fuhrmann [Philadelphia, 1949], pp. 38–39).

108. Niesel has stressed (perhaps overstressed) this point in *The Theology of Calvin, passim*.

109. The old idea, still present to some degree, was that Calvin's formulations did not satisfy the polemic situation and that a more absolutist theology had to be developed to effectively combat the Roman Catholics. Ernst Troeltsch's thesis that the very nature of Protestantism was responsible for this development in Lutheranism is also probably applicable to the Reformed (see his *Vernunft und Offenbarung bei Johann Gerhard und Melanchthon*). Troeltsch's thesis is developed by most of recent scholarship in one way or another; see the works of Paul Althaus, Ernst Bizer, Walter Kickel, and Peter Petersen listed in the bibliography; also note 84 above.

tyr, Zanchi, Beza, Antoine de Chandieu, and Lambert Danaeus represent this divergence from a theology which had been carefully constructed by Calvin to represent faithfully the scriptural teaching, and so usually presented a certain tension or balance of doctrines. The practice of these men was to fasten on one element of Calvin's teaching, isolate it, and then stress that element to the exclusion of another and qualifying teaching, thus producing a rationale for the *sui generis* existence of the element isolated. In this way the tension or balance of doctrines as presented in Calvin was destroyed. By the dawn of the seventeenth century the resultant scholasticism reigned in all the leading Reformed academies outside France.

Of these men it was probably Beza who was most influential, and for this reason one may lay much of the blame for scholasticism at his feet. His very influential position as professor of theology at, and unquestioned supervisor of, the Genevan Academy gave him uncommon opportunity to direct the theological program of the Reformed Church. It was he who was responsible for the return to Aristotelian philosophy as the basis of the Genevan curriculum in logic and moral philosophy.[110] As is well known, it was Beza who refused the humanist Peter Ramus a teaching post at the Genevan Academy because of Ramus' anti-Aristotelian program.

Though it is not generally recognized, the evidence indicates that the prime source of this new trend toward Aristotle and eventually Protestant scholasticism was the Italian Aristotelians. It therefore comes as no surprise that in volume 4 of the recently printed *Correspondance de Théodore de Bèze* there is a letter in which Beza requests a work by the Aristotelian Pietro Pomponazzi.[111] The editors of his correspondence interpret this as

110. See Kingdon, *Geneva and the Consolidation*, pp. 18, 120; Charles Waddington, *Ramus, sa vie, ses écrits, et ses opinions* (Paris, 1855) p. 225ff.; Borgeaud, *L'Académie de Calvin*, p. 112ff.

111. Meylan, Dufour, and Tripet, eds., vol. 74 of Travaux d'Humanisme et Renaissance (Geneva, 1965), entry 282, pp. 182–83. Beza had had contacts with Aristotelianism long before this, and it may be that Peter Martyr and Girolamo Zanchi in particular, both Italian Aristotelians, had influenced him. Robert Kingdon in his review of vol. 4 of *Correspondance* in *BHR* 30 (1968), 385–87, suggests that Beza may have gotten his Aristotelianism from Martyr.

corroboration of the claim that Beza was one of the first of the Protestant scholastics.[112] Certainly it offers substantiation to Bizer's argument that in Beza reason and Aristotelian logic were elevated to a position equal to that of faith in theological epistemology, for in this work that Beza requests, Pomponazzi had demonstrated how reason and logic could and should be made integral to the science of theology.

Suspicion of Beza's scholastic orientation and his role in leading Reformed Protestantism in that direction receives almost decisive corroboration in Walter Kickel's *Vernunft und Offenbarung bei Theodor Beza*.[113] This carefully documented and developed study is the first major treatise to deal with Beza's thought. If for no other reason it merits careful consideration. Kickel's conclusions regarding Beza's scholasticism are probably overdrawn, since he seems to have considered only those writings of Beza which pertain to systematic theology, an approach which would be apt to lead one to conclude that Beza was overly concerned with systematization. Moreover, the divergence from a Calvin-like theology was certainly more gradual and less apparent (at least to sixteenth-century Calvinists) than Kickel's study suggests. Nevertheless, in spite of such reservations, only the most reluctant can any longer doubt after Kickel's detailed evidence that Beza's whole theological program shows a serious departure from that of Calvin.

In particular, Kickel's study lends powerful support to the contention that nowhere is the scholasticizing tendency more apparent in Reformed Protestantism than in the discussions of the doctrine of God. Both Beza[114] and Zanchi[115] had once again

112. *Correspondance de Théodore de Bèze*, p. 183n5, and Introduction, p. 9. The claim is that of Ernst Bizer in his very penetrating study, *Frühorthodoxie und Rationalismus* (Zurich, 1963).

113. In the series Beiträge zur Geschichte und Lehre der Reformierten Kirche, vol. 25 (Neukirchen, 1967).

114. See Beza's "chart" of salvation in Heinrich Heppe, *Die Dogmatik der evangelisch-reformierten Kirche*, ed. Ernst Bizer (Neukirchen, 1958), p. 119; also Basil Hall's "Calvin against the Calvinists," G. E. Duffield, ed., *John Calvin*, The Courtenay Studies in Reformation Theology, vol. 1 (Appleford, Abingdon, and Berkshire, 1966), pp. 25ff. Hall's interesting discussion is sometimes so in error as to almost nullify his point. For instance, he claims that Beza distorted Calvin's doctrine of justification by including in it not only remission of sins but also

placed the celebrated doctrine of predestination in their discussions of the doctrine of God, precisely where it was discussed by St. Thomas Aquinas. Calvin, on the other hand, never discussed predestination in this context.[116] In the *Institutio* Calvin discussed this doctrine only when he had completed his exposition of all the soteriological doctrines. While a simple relocation of the doctrine of predestination may not at first sight seem momentous, it in fact is. It makes the most profound difference whether one approaches theology via predestination or simply discusses the doctrine as an implicate from grace.

However, Kickel studies Beza's doctrine of predestination and shows that the divergence from Calvin is much more decisive than this relocation of the doctrine. In the first place he shows that Beza emphasized the rational element while neglecting the religious.

> Beza very strongly extracts the rational side of Calvin's doctrine of predestination to the neglect of its religious side. By doing this his doctrine became singularly rational and free of contradiction. It took on the character of a unified, scientific system. But it lost the multidimensional character of Calvinistic thought and the continuity with the fulness and with the spirit of scriptural revelation. If one wishes to formulate the Beza-Calvin relationship with respect to the doctrine of predestination, he can define Beza's doctrine as the result of a rationalization of Calvin's doctrine.[117]

Kickel then goes on to show further that this rationalization of the doctrine is complemented by its base in the Aristotelian

---

God's acceptance of the sinner as righteous. This is manifestly wrong, for Calvin's doctrine does include both elements; witness Calvin's famous definition of justification in *Institutio* III.xi.2: "Ita nos justificationem simpliciter interpretamur acceptionem qua nos Deus in gratiam receptos pro justis habet. Eamque in peccatorum remissione ac justitiae Christi imputatione positam esse dicimus" (*OS*, IV.183.7–10).

115. See Otto Gründler, "Thomism and Calvinism in the Theology of Girolamo Zanchi" (Th.D. diss., Princeton Theological Seminary, 1963). Recently published in German translation.

116. Perhaps it is even fair to say that Calvin never developed a doctrine of God per se. In any case, he has no section "De Deo," but only "De cognitione Dei."

117. *Vernunft und Offenbarung bei Beza*, p. 159. On p. 167 he calls Beza's doctrine a "one-sided rationalization of Calvin's."

philosophical system. This, he concludes, has far-reaching effects on Beza's whole methodology, his concept of God, and especially his doctrine of predestination.[118] It means that the location of predestination in the doctrine of God is the only logical foundation for Beza's doctrine. Moreover, Kickel shows that the result of this commitment to an Aristotelian philosophical and metaphysical program has serious consequences for the basic orientation of all of theology.

> The result of these Aristotelian influences is the removal of Christ and the Word from their place of centrality in theology and the substitution of a rational system of final causation for christocentricism. . . . We must also admit the judgment that Beza's doctrine of predestination does not conform well to revelation. It perverts not only all statements of God which are essentially statements of faith, but also removes Christ from his place as the foundation stone (*Realgrund*) and criterion of knowledge (*Erkenntnisgrund*) for theology.[119]

Without going into detail we may finally note that Kickel shows that predestination is certainly the *Centraldogma* of Beza, that "The place in theology of the doctrine of justification, as well as the doctrine of the Trinity, the doctrine of the two natures, and the doctrine of the sacraments, is determined by the doctrine of predestination."[120] He goes on to discuss these, showing the philosophical flavor of each as developed by Beza, and thus the basic discrepancy with Calvin's teaching.

Beza introduced other rigid teachings into Reformed theology, among them supralapsarianism,[121] a limited atonement,[122] and

118. *Ibid.*, p. 167.
119. *Ibid.*, pp. 167–68.
120. *Ibid.*, p. 169.
121. *Supralapsarianism* and *infralapsarianism* are terms used in the debate of late-sixteenth- and seventeenth-century Calvinism over the "order" of God's decrees. Supralapsarianism refers to formulation of an order in God's decrees as follows: (1) The decree to elect and save men who are spoken of as "createable." (2) The decree to create man. (3) The decree to permit man to fall. (4) The decree to send Christ to redeem. (Usually one can add here "the elect" for most supralapsarians seem to hold that Christ was sent only for the elect.) (5) The decree to send the Holy Spirit to apply to the chosen of God the redemption to be procured by Christ. Infralapsarianism, on the other hand, formulates the following order: (1) The decree to create man. (2) The decree to permit the fall of man. (3) The decree to elect some of these fallen men and to pass by the rest. (4) The decree to

the immediate imputation of Adam's sin.[123] These all, to some degree, represent a distortion of Calvin's teaching. As the years passed, they became more and more rigidly espoused in international Calvinism.

This was the scholasticism, only partially assimilated by French Protestantism, which ruled in the Calvinist academies at the turn of the century. Reaction to it sprang up in different places and ways. In the Low Countries the reaction took the form of Arminianism. In France it took another form. It was during this time, in the year 1600, that a young Scot from Glasgow arrived on French soil. This young man, John Cameron by name, was to lay the foundation of that system in France which would lead a French reaction to the reigning scholasticism of international Calvinism. It would be a system admirably in accord with the humanistic predisposition of French Protestantism.

Cameron was to develop his program by claiming a return to the theology of John Calvin, and apparently believed that the man primarily responsible for the scholastic bent of Reformed Protestantism was Theodore Beza, for he would oppose Beza at every turn. Indeed, the orthodox theologian Pierre du Moulin ruefully complained that Cameron so controverted Beza that "he might well be called Beza's scourge (*Bezae mastyx*)."[124]

JOHN CAMERON AND HIS THEOLOGY

John Cameron was the inspiration for, and father of, the distinctive teachings of the Academy at Saumur. Amyraut himself

---

provide a redeemer for fallen men. (5) The decree to send the Holy Spirit to apply this redemption to the elect. There is some debate over Calvin's position, but it is my belief that Calvin cannot fairly be thought of as either. First, he steadfastly refused to speculate about the decrees of God and never discussed order in this context. Secondly, the debate is not contemporary with Calvin, and thus it is an anachronism to apply such terminology to him. His most common statement is that God elects men who are fallen, but he does not relate this to any pretemporal sequence of events in the mind of God.

122. *Limited atonement* refers to the teaching that Jesus died for the elect only, that his death was not intended to atone for the sins of all mankind.

123. See Hall, "Calvin against the Calvinists," p. 27.

124. In du Moulin's *de Mosis Amyraldi . . . libro judicium,* as quoted in Pierre Bayle, *Dictionnaire, s.v.* Cameron, Jean; p. 213 of du Moulin's treatise, "Bezae mastyx potest appellari," See also p. 227: ". . . Bezae non meminit, nisi ut eum reprehendat."

often acknowledged his debt to and fondness for Cameron. Writing in 1638 to Théophile Brachet de la Milletière, Amyraut said:

> I declare to you that whatever little I am able to offer in the explanation of theology, I owe this, after the reading of Scripture, to the insights [*ouvertures*] that this great man has taught me. And after the grace that God manifested in giving the knowledge of His saving truth, I bless Him particularly that He has allowed me the close fellowship of this man, who, beyond the other excellent gifts that he had (and everyone has his strengths and weaknesses in this life), I judge that in his time he has not been surpassed in that part of theology which consists in the understanding of the Bible.[125]

This testimony is all the more interesting when we note that Cameron taught at Saumur only three years at most. And this testimony of Amyraut would be equally true if expressed by Daillé, de la Place, Cappel, or many others. What kind of man was this who in three short years could so inspire the sharpest theological minds in France, and, indeed, create at Saumur a theological approach which for more than half a century would challenge many of the teachings of orthodox Calvinism?

To be sure, Cameron is something of an enigmatic figure. There is no substantial scholarly study of his life or work.[126] As

125. *Replique a M. de la Milletiere sur son offre d'une conference amiable pour l'examen de ses moyens de reunion* (Saumur, 1658), p. 203.

126. The best biographical study is Gaston Bonet-Maury's "Jean Cameron, pasteur de l'église de Bordeaux et professeur de théologie à Saumur et à Montauban 1579–1625," *Etudes de théologie et d'histoire* (Paris, 1901), pp. 77–117; printed in English with some revision: "John Cameron: A Scottish Protestant Theologian in France," *The Scottish Historical Review* 7 (1910), 325–45. Most of the biographical material in the following discussion derives from this source. The most extensive theological survey of Cameron remains Robert Wodrow's very antagonistic study: "Collections on the Life of Mr. John Cameron, Minister at Bourdeaux, Professor of Divinity at Saumur, Principall of the College of Glasgow, and Professor of Divinity at Montauban," in *Collections upon the Lives of the Reformers and most eminent Ministers of the Church of Scotland* (Glasgow, 1848), vol. 2, pt. 2, pp. 81–229. Jürgen Moltmann's doctoral dissertation is also of some use here: "Gnadenbund und Gnadenwahl" (Göttingen, 1951), pp. 23–94. See also François Laplanche, *Orthodoxie et prédication: L'Oeuvre d'Amyraut et la querelle de la grâce universelle* (Paris, 1965), pp. 50–57. Walter Rex's recent *Essays on Pierre Bayle* contains valuable material on Cameron's theology and place as a controversialist in the French Church. Of some value are L. Cappel, "Johannis Cameronis Icon," prefaced to Cameron's *Opera*; T. F. Henderson, "John Cameron,"

for contemporary witnesses, one is never quite sure what to believe about him for the simple reason that we have no neutral witnesses. Either he was the object of unqualified admiration or intense dislike. All agree that he was one of the few truly original minds in seventeenth-century Reformed Protestantism. Yet, because this was no century for originality in theology, he was constantly embroiled in controversy, and most of what we know of his life relates to these controversies. It is certainly quite likely that Cameron's contentious nature and fiery temper got him into a great deal of the trouble which plagued his life. Because he was his own worst enemy in this regard and because the bulk of our information derives from his opponents, it is particularly important, if we are to evaluate the man himself properly, to view what information we have critically.

His was, in Walter Rex's words, "a restless, wandering life."[127] He was born in Glasgow about 1580 and matriculated at the university in that city at about the age of sixteen. The curriculum then taught at Glasgow had been established by the "Scots Melanchthon," Andrew Melville, upon his return from the continent in 1574. To understand Cameron's thought and work and to avoid much confusion concerning the philosophical position of the Salmurian theology it is necessary to determine his course of study at Glasgow, for apparently his teaching followed the pattern learned at Glasgow almost without deviation.

Thomas McCrie informs us that the instruction Melville imparted to his students followed this pattern:

> He began by initiating them into the principles of Greek grammar. He then introduced them to the study of Logic and Rhetoric, using, as his textbooks, the Dialectics of his Parisian master, Ramus, and the Rhetoric of Talaeus. While they were engaged in these studies he read with them the best classical authors, as Virgil and Horace among the Latins, and Homer,

---

DNB 8 (New York, 1886), 295–96; D. Irving, *Lives of Scottish Writers* (Edinburgh, 1839), 1:333–46; C. Read, "Cameron," *Encyclopédie des sciences religieuses publiée sous la direction de F. Lichtenberger* (Paris, 1877), 2:561–63; H. M. B. Reid, *The Divinity Principals in the University of Glasgow 1545–1654* (Glasgow, 1917), pp. 170–251; and A. Schweizer, *Die Protestantischen Centraldogmen* (Zurich, 1856), 2:235–39.

127. *Essays on Pierre Bayle*, p. 9.

Hesiod, Theocritus, Pindar, and Isocrates, among the Greeks; . . . Proceeding to Mathematics and Geography, he taught the elements of Euclid, with the Arithmetic and Geometry of Ramus, and the Geography of Dionysius. . . . Moral Philosophy formed the next branch of study; and on this he read Cicero's Offices, Paradoxes, and Tusculan Questions, the Ethics and Politics of Aristotle, and certain of Plato's Dialogues. In Natural Philosophy he made use of Fernelius, and commented on parts of the writings of Aristotle and Plato. To these he added a view of Universal History, with Chronology and the art of Writing. Entering upon the duties of his own immediate profession, he taught the Hebrew language, . . . He then initiated the students into Chaldee and Syriac; reading those parts of the books of Ezra and Daniel that are written in Chaldee, and the epistle to the Galatians in the Syriac version. He also went through all the common heads of Divinity according to the order of Calvin's Institutions, besides giving lectures on different books of Scripture.[128]

While Melville had left Glasgow in 1580 to go to St. Andrews, the curriculum he established at Glasgow seems to have remained almost intact until sometime in the seventeenth century.

The importance of the various elements of this list can hardly be emphasized too strongly.[129] There are several distinctive features in it which deserve more comment than can be given here. Morison mentions "the mastering of Greek grammar in the freshman year, so that Greek authors might be read in the original, the undergraduate study of Hebrew, and the study of History."[130] These all were immensely important in Cameron's

128. *Life of Andrew Melville*, 2 vols. (Edinburgh, 1819), 1:72–74. New critical study of Melville is needed in the light of recent research, especially that on Ramus.

129. In "Gnadenbund und Gnadenwahl," p. 26, Moltmann claims that Cameron learned Ramism (as well as covenant theology) from Abraham Scultetus while at Heidelberg. This is not tenable for many reasons. For one, it would place such formative ideas too late in Cameron's life; also, and in a passage Moltmann himself quotes, W. Rivet informs us: "Joannes Camero Rameam Grammaticum solam puer dicit. Et adolescentulum adhuc Ramae Philosophiae, ipse ego vidi addictissimum. Eam enim cum zelo defendebat . . ." Rivet refers to the time when he was a classmate of Cameron's at Glasgow (1595). See A. Rivet, *Opera* (Rotterdam, 1660), III.897.2.

130. Samuel Eliot Morison, *The Founding of Harvard College* (Cambridge, 1935), p. 134.

development, as we see in him both an unusual mastery of the biblical languages and an unusual sense of the importance of history. But, because the present study is so often to be concerned with the problem of Protestant scholasticism, the description of the philosophical instruction he received is perhaps even more important. Logic was taught from Ramus and not Aristotle, and rhetoric was from Omar Talon, Ramus' close friend and disciple. Moreover, according to one of Cameron's classmates at Glasgow, Cameron as early as 1595 "was addicted to the philosophy of Ramus and defended it with zeal" (see n. 129). However, the fact that Aristotle's writings were used in both moral and natural philosophy suggests that Cameron would not have rejected Aristotle *en bloc*. It is a fact that the theologians of Saumur employed Aristotle frequently, as Amyraut was to say, "in matters of common sense."[131] But they also took the important step of rejecting the validity of Aristotelian logic for theology; that is to say, they did not employ the use of argumentation which deduces one or several conclusions from a given principle. In this they departed from one of the most salient features of the scholasticism of orthodox Calvinism.

Patrick Sharp was principal of Glasgow during Cameron's student years, and from him, most likely, Cameron took another of his favorite teachings—the divine right of kings.[132] Cameron graduated from Glasgow in 1599, having already shown signs that he was "one of the most learned men who ever studied or taught within the University."[133] His brilliance in his studies earned him an appointment as regent in Greek at the university.

131. In the dedicatory epistle to his *Defense de la doctrine de Calvin* (Saumur, 1644), Amyraut says that if in his works one encounters the name of Aristotle "c'est en des choses qui peuvent estre comprises par le sens commun, & sur lesquelles l'experience des mouvemens de vos esprits vous peut faire de fort bons & fort amples Commentaires" (p. 14).

132. See the section on Sharp in Reid, *Divinity Principals in Glasgow*, pp. 106–14. It is also probable that Cameron's parents had episcopal leanings, and he may have learned this doctrine in his home. At least we have Cameron's own testimony that "as a child" he "looked on Kingly majesty . . . with a kind of veneration" (quoted in Wodrow, *Life of Cameron*, p. 157).

133. The judgment of James Coutts in *A History of the University of Glasgow* (Glasgow, 1909), p. 87. Reid notes that Cameron's name stands first in the list of graduates, which means that he was the most distinguished graduate of his year (*Divinity Principals in Glasgow*, p. 171).

He taught there but one year and in 1600 migrated to Bordeaux in France.

France was to become Cameron's arena of activity. His erudition won the admiration of the great humanist scholar Isaac Casaubon, and upon his recommendation Cameron was named professor of Greek and Latin at Bergerac. His reputation grew so fast that he was called to Sedan as professor of philosophy after one year. He taught at Sedan for only two years and was recalled to Bordeaux by the town's Huguenot church, which wanted him for its pastor. He was immediately appointed a travelling scholar, the church bearing part of the expense, and also became tutor to the two sons of one Calignon, chancellor to Henry of Navarre. Cameron spent one year in Paris in Calignon's home, then removed to Geneva, where he studied for two years (1605–6). After two years of hard study at Geneva under Antoine de la Faye, Jean Diodati, and perhaps Charles Perrot,[134] Cameron repaired to Heidelberg where in April, 1608, he presented his *De triplici Dei cum homine foedere theses.*[135]

These theses, as Moltmann has suggested, "are not only the foundation of his theology, but they also became the foundation for the program of the Academy of Saumur." Indeed, we can even say further with Moltmann that "Here were already the discernible roots for the *heilsgeschichtlich* outline of Amyraut's doctrine of predestination."[136] Here Cameron departs somewhat from orthodox Calvinism, distinguishing three covenants instead of the usual two.[137] Moreover, this is one of the first clear-cut

134. See the list of professors in Borgeaud, *L'Académie de Calvin,* pp. 638–39. It is interesting that Cameron remained friendly with the strictly orthodox Diodati. Two letters from Cameron to Diodati have been printed in the *Bulletin* 50 (1901), 159–63.

135. In *Joh. Cameronis S. Theologiae in academia Salmuriensis nuper Professoris, Praelectionum in selectoria quaedam N.T. loca Salmury habitarum,* 3 vols. (Saumur, 1626–28), 3:609–30. Or in his *Opera* (Geneva, 1642), pp. 544–52. I have used the latter edition throughout.

136. J. Moltmann, "Prädestination und Heilsgeschichte bei Moyse Amyraut," *ZKG* 65 (1954), 275.

137. Cameron, or Amyraut for that matter, never speaks of a covenant of redemption as a pact between the Father and the Son in eternity, as did Coccejus and later federal theologians. His three-fold covenant is a development within time and should not be confused with the three-fold covenant which saw the first covenant as a pact between the first two members of the Trinity.

expressions of what was later called "federal theology." Because covenant theology is the foundation of Salmurian theology I shall discuss Cameron's theses at some length.

Implicit in Cameron's discussion is the idea that became quite explicit in Amyraut: "all true religion necessarily consists in some covenant which occurs between God and man."[138] In this sense Cameron is one of the first Reformed theologians to set forth an explicit formulation of covenant teaching as the locus under which all of theology was to be comprehended.[139] And it

138. From thesis 1 of Amyraut's "Theses Theologicae de tribus foederibus divinis" in *Theses Salmurienses,* 4 vols. in 1 (Geneva, 1665), 1:212.

139. The precise source of Cameron's covenant theology is very difficult to determine, due partly to the confusion which surrounds the rise of covenant theology and its various expressions and partly to the somewhat unique character of Cameron's teaching itself. The fact that Cameron's theses on the covenant were delivered at Heidelberg we know is of capital importance. Covenant theology there had begun, in Olevianus (1536–87) and Ursinus (1534–83), to show signs of becoming the ordering principle of theology. Olevianus' *De substantia foederis gratuiti inter Deum et electos* (Geneva, 1585) presents but one covenant, the covenant of grace, and resembles the teaching of Calvin under whom Olevianus had studied. Coccejus testifies in the preface to his *Summa doctrinae de foedere et testamento Dei* that Olevianus was most influential in his own formulation of the covenant. Apparently it was Ursinus, student of Melanchthon and Bullinger, however, who introduced the two-fold covenant which characterized the later development of covenant theology. (See G. Schrenck, *Gottesreich und Bund im älteren Protestantismus,* pp. 63ff., where he discusses "Die dogmatische Konsolidierung der Lehre vom Doppelbund: Gomarus, Polanus, Wolleb, Egli, Wendelin.") In his *Summa religionis christianae* (Nystad, 1584) Ursinus speaks of a *foedus naturae* known to man naturally and requiring perfect obedience in order that eternal life be possible. Schrenck sees this as an incorporation into theology, in the garb of a covenant, of the *lex naturae* teaching of Melanchthon. This became the standard teaching of the covenant theology, though Polanus, or perhaps Rollock, apparently introduced the new terminology of *foedus operum.*
It is uncertain how much of this teaching continued at Heidelberg during Cameron's study there in 1607–8. David Paraeus (1548–1622) and Abraham Scultetus (1566–1624) were the leading professors at the time, but to my knowledge no study has been made of the covenant teaching of either. But then, Cameron need not have depended on the Heidelberg teaching to learn covenant theology. Undoubtedly he was familiar with his fellow-countryman Robert Rollock's *Tractatus de vocatione efficaci* (Edinburgh, 1597). Rollock had made some very sweeping statements concerning the covenant—"the whole of God's Word has to do with some covenant for God does not communicate to man unless it be through a covenant" (ch. 2, *ad init.*). Moreover, Cameron's emphasis upon the conditional covenant suggests a heritage of covenant teaching not common to continental Reformed theology but already very common to the British Isles in Matthew Tindal's writings. Tindal, in the prologue to the Sermon on the Mount, made this condi-

needs to be emphasized that in this explanation of the covenants we find many of the distinctive features of the Salmurian theology.

Using the method of dichotomizing learned from Ramus, Cameron begins by stating that the word covenant (*foedus*) has two meanings in Scripture. "Sometimes it signifies an absolute promise of God, with no condition included, such as the covenant God contracted with Noah."[140] Most generally, however, the meaning of the word covenant is *hypotheticum,* that is, "by it the gratuitous promise of God is indeed signified, yet with the requirement of our duty subjoined . . ."[141] And the distinction of these covenants he bases in a distinction in the love of God. There is a love of God which is primary or antecedent, and the source of anything good in the creature, and there is a secondary or consequent love of God which the creature receives. Upon that love which must be received depends the fulfilling of the requirement of the *foedus hypotheticum.* In this hypothetical covenant God does what he has promised because the creature fulfills the requirement annexed thereto. Yet though God's action is in this way made dependent upon man's response, this response itself proceeds from his antecedent love which produces whatever good there may be in that man.[142] It is this

---

tional element most explicit: ". . . all the good promises which are made throughout all the scripture, for Christ's sake, for his love, his passion or suffering, his bloodshedding or death, are all made to us on this condition and covenant on our part, that we henceforth love the law of God, to walk therein, and to do it, and to fashion our lives thereafter" (p. 131 of his works in the British Reformer series [London, n.d.]). For an extended discussion of this element in early English reformers see L. J. Trinterud, "The Origins of Puritanism," *Church History* 20 (1951), 37ff. The conditional element was very prominent in English Puritanism, and this may have been the source of Cameron's teaching. Cameron departed from the orthodox pattern as well as the Puritan tradition, however, by distinguishing three separate covenants. There seems to have been no precedent for this.

140. ". . . interdum significat promissionem Dei absolutam, sine ulla restipulatione, quale Foedus erat quod Deus cum Noacho . . . iniit, . . ." (thesis 1, *Opera,* p. 544, 1).

141. "eo significari gratuitam quidem Dei promissionem, cum restipulatione tamen sed officii . . ." (thesis 2, *ibid.,* p. 544, 1).

142. "Pendet ista Foederis distinctio à distinctione amoris Dei, est quippe amor Dei erga creaturam unde quicquid est in creatura boni totum promanavit, & est amor Dei acquiescens in creatura, idque ob ea quae non quidem ipsa à se, sed à

foedus hypotheticum which has to do with God's redemptive activity.

Heinrich Heppe contends that in Reformed theology, "To establish the doctrine of the covenant of God with man is, in the first place, to establish the doctrine of God."[143] Evidently following this lead, Moltmann devotes his entire discussion of Cameron's *De triplici Dei cum homine foedere theses* to this problem. Moltmann's main contention is that "we find already, in the definition of the covenant idea and in its application to the doctrine of God and the covenant of grace, Cameron's first step away (*Distanzierung*) from the orthodox tradition."[144] That is, "it is not in the sovereignty and the freedom of God that Cameron bases the grace of the covenant of grace, but in that condescendence and accommodation of God in the humanity (*Menschlichkeit*) and mutuality of partners."[145] However, while we can agree that the whole emphasis in Cameron, at least in the covenant of grace, is on the accommodation of God, we may still wonder if it is proper to make such a sharp distinction between the concepts of sovereignty/freedom and condescendence/accommodation. Moltmann himself makes further and judicious precisions on this subject, pointing out that "It is not, according to Cameron, freedom of choice but rather freedom of spontaneity, an ontological idea of freedom, which determines God's dealings with men."[146] Cameron's position is that God is most certainly free, since he does whatever he desires, but it is true that he cannot contradict his own nature. It is in this sense that Cameron often expressed his belief in both God's omnipotence and freedom.[147]

Deo, quatenus primo illo amore amata fuit, accepit: illum *Primarium* sive *Antecedentem,* hunc *Secundarium* sive *Consequentem,* docendi causâ, appellamus. . . . at in eo Foedere cui annexa est restipulatio, Deus implet quod promisit quia creatura exhibuit quod exigebatur, tametsi quòd Deus ejusmodi Foedus iniit, hoc est, talia praestanti promisit tanta, totum proficiscitur ab amore Dei antecedente" (theses 3 and 4, *ibid.,* p. 544, 1).

143. Heppe-Bizer, *Die Dogmatik der evangelisch-reformierten Kirche,* p. 37.

144. "Gnadenbund und Gnadenwahl," p. 34.

145. *Ibid.,* p. 32.

146. "Prädestination und Heilsgeschichte," p. 277.

147. E.g. in his "Collatio cum Tileno," *Opera,* p. 649, 2: ". . . *potentia* autem

One of the most arresting features of Cameron's doctrine of God is the similarity of many expressions and ideas with nominalist thought, a question Moltmann does not discuss. The *foedus absolutum* and *foedus hypotheticum* seem to suggest the *potentia Dei absoluta* and *potentia Dei ordinata* of Scotus, Occam, and Biel. This is first suggested when we understand Cameron to be teaching that God has restricted himself to a particular way of dealing with his creatures, and the suspicion grows as we read that God's action is dependent on man's fulfillment of a certain condition and that the whole of this teaching is based upon a distinction in God's love as antecedent or consequent. Nevertheless, when this is given careful consideration and Oberman's recent study on Biel[148] used for purposes of comparison, the similarities reveal themselves as more apparent than real. Though the similarity seems strongest as regards the *potentia ordinata* (and does not every covenant theology in some way suggest this teaching of nominalism?), for Cameron the accommodation of God to work in a prescribed manner is not a part of the doctrine of God, not a discussion of how God can or might act, but rather how he did act in procuring redemption. The distinction may be a fine one but I think it is significant. There is, moreover, a radical difference from nominalism, or at least Biel, in Cameron's anthropology, which appears to be the basis of his strong emphasis on God's accommodation. It is certain that he in no way sees man as the *viator* who stands between the beatified and the damned and who is capable of free

---

Dei sit *omnipotentia*, aio omnem operationem quae est à Deo, *quatenus*, inquam *est à Deo*, esse ab *omnipotentia* proindé que & opus quod sequitur operationê pariter assero esse divinae *omnipotentiae* effectum." I have found no place where Cameron expressly uses the term "sovereignty of God" (neither did Calvin), but that does not mean the idea is not there. He discusses the freedom of God in four letters he wrote to L. Cappel, making quite clear that God's freedom is circumscribed only by His nature: ". . . libertas Dei vel à natura, vel à sapientia occulta ipsius dependet, cujus ratio saepenumerò nos fugit" (letter of Dec., 1610, *ibid.*, p. 530, 2). "Sed ego nullam in Deo potentiam resistibilem agnosco, nihil enim conatur quod non possit, aut si id non [facere] potest, sive quia est ἀσύζατον sive quia est ἄδικον non id molitur etiam" (letter of Dec., 1611, *ibid.*, p. 533, 1).

148. H. A. Oberman, *The Harvest of Medieval Theology* (Cambridge, 1963), esp. pp. 30–56.

choice.[149] Rather man, in Cameron's theology, is totally incapable of fulfilling the required condition unless moved by God's grace. And so we can conclude that there is no real affinity with nominalist thought, but that Cameron's distinction between the *foedus absolutum* and *foedus hypotheticum* stems from his rigid adherence to the dichotomization so characteristic of Ramism. At any rate, the *foedus absolutum* does not seem to be of importance or use in his covenant teaching.

As Cameron enters into discussion of the *foedus hypotheticum* he elaborates his innovation in Reformed theology, the threefold covenant. He distinguishes the *foedus naturae,* the *foedus gratiae,* and the *foedus gratiae subserviens* or *foedus vetus.*[150] He maintains that of these three the two principal ones are the covenant of nature and the covenant of grace. He then makes a detailed comparison of the two to show, primarily, that God dealt with unfallen man in justice, requiring of him strict obedience, but now deals with fallen man in mercy, requiring only faith, a faith He himself supplies. Cameron's object in this seems to be to show that there is a progression in the way God deals with man[151] and that the mercy of God ought to be especially emphasized in the *foedus gratiae.* That is, he introduces two elements which he believes will serve as a corrective to orthodox Cal-

149. See *ibid.,* p. 39.

150. Thesis 7, *Opera,* p. 544, 2. Cameron's novelty lies in his making the *foedus subserviens* a distinct covenant. Calvin had regarded it as part of the covenant of grace, the difference being one of *administratio:* "Patrum omnium foedus adeo substantia et re ipsa nihil a nostro differt, ut unum prorsus atque idem sit: administratio tamen variat" (*Institutio* II.x.2; *OS* III.404.5ff). Rollock, on the other hand, identified the covenant of nature and the covenant of law, embracing them both under a *foedus operae* (see his *Tractatus de vocatione efficaci,* ch. 2).

151. The idea of progression is illustrated in many ways and commands Cameron's attention in theses 8–41. For example, regarding salvation through Christ, the covenant of nature points to Christ only *per accidens,* the legal covenant points to Christ directly, for this is its *verus & proprius scopus,* the covenant of grace reveals Him fully. There is, also, a great deal of stress on the two "times" of the covenant of grace: the time of promise and the time of manifestation. Cameron stresses the obscurity of the gospel message during the time of promise (before the Incarnation), but even this obscurity was progressively diminishing: before the law the promise was quite obscure, from the law to the prophets it was a little clearer, from the prophets to John the Baptist, still clearer, during the ministry of John absolutely clear (*operta*) and in Christ fully revealed (see esp. thesis 28).

vinism—a more historical understanding of God's redemptive activity, and an elevation of God's mercy above his justice—hoping thereby to counteract the tendency of the orthodox to give first importance to his justice. Perhaps also he hoped to attempt a solution to this problem which had plagued theologians for centuries, a problem which had been rendered even more acute by the increasingly literal idea of substitutionary atonement in Reformed theology, the problem of the tension of God's mercy and justice.

At this point a few brief remarks need to be made about the *foedus naturae*, since it is under this rubric that one finds the essence of Cameron's thought on natural law and natural theology. Reid contends that his teaching hereon contains the germ of the idea "that the nature of man, so far as concerns his will, remained to a certain extent unimpaired" and so "man was still saveable by his contributory act of will."[152] He apparently bases his contention on the statement by Cameron that this covenant is eternal[153] and "that the knowledge of it was not completely obliterated from the mind of fallen man, since it was made by God to restrain man from sin and to lead him to Christ."[154] Nevertheless a careful analysis of Cameron's teaching fails to reveal any hint of this "heretical" leaning that Reid detects. Rather, what Cameron has done is to make the *foedus naturae* the basis of the natural law idea. That is, for Cameron the idea rests on a covenantal foundation, upon the basis for fellowship established by God with man in the *status integritatis,* before there was need for God's merciful work in Christ.[155] This consisted in simply maintaining a dispensation of strict justice. Of man was required *justitia naturalis;* that is, he was to render unto God "due obedience"[156] and God would deal with him in

152. *Divinity Principals in Glasgow,* p. 176.

153. ". . . foedus Naturae est aeternum" (thesis 46, *Opera,* p. 548, 2).

154. ". . . quod ejus cognitio ex hominis lapsi mente non sit penitus obliterata, factum est à Deo in hunc finem, ut eo esset quo homines cohiberentur, & ad Christum adducerentur" (thesis 50, *ibid.,* p. 549, 1).

155. This placing of the natural relationship of man and God under the covenant differs from the practice of the greater part of Calvinist orthodoxy, who distinguished between the natural relationship and the covenantal relationship. See the discussion in L. Berkhof, *Systematic Theology* (Grand Rapids, 1953), p. 215.

156. ". . . foedus Naturae tantum ad obedientiam debitam lege Naturae, . . .

justice according as man did or did not render this obedience. Indeed, "the end of the covenant of nature is the declaration of God's justice."[157]

Making the *foedus naturae* the basis of God's total relationship with man also places at least part of the question of natural theology within a covenant teaching. Cameron has said that this covenant is written upon everyone's heart. It is this, then, which corresponds to Calvin's *sensus divinitatis* or *semen religionis*. Because of this original covenant engraven on the heart, which Calvin apparently did not call a covenant, man recognizes that there is a God and that he owes obedience to this God. Because this knowledge inflames the heart of man with the desire for the knowledge of God's grace it may be said to lead to Christ. That is, it performs, to a lesser degree, the same function as does the law—it leads man to despair. Yet this is only an accidental function, inasmuch as it was not the original purpose of the *foedus naturae*.[158] In sum, this aspect of the *foedus naturae*, this testimony of God written on our heart, may be thought of as expressing the same thing as does the term *sensus divinitatis* in Calvin. It may perhaps also include what Calvin comprehends under *conscientia*, but this is not so evident in the document under consideration and we know of no place where Cameron specifically devotes himself to this teaching. Nor do we know of any place where he discusses the other part of "natural theology," God's revelation in the universe. Though Amyraut is often

---

obligat" (thesis 46, *Opera*, p. 548, 2). This is reminiscent of the passage in Calvin's *Institutio*, III.vi.7: "Siquidem officiorum inter membra communicatio nihil gratuitum habere creditur, sed potius solutio esse eius quod *naturae lege debitum* negare prodigiosum esset" (*OS*, IV.158.8-11. Emphasis added).

157. ". . . finis Foederis Naturae est declaratio Justitiae Dei, . . ." (thesis 9, *Opera*, p. 544, 2).

158. ". . . non negemus foedus naturae, in hac corruptione naturae nostrae, foederi Gratiae subservire, quatenus hominum animos ejus desiderio inflammat, quod tamen facit per accidens, cùm non sit hic foederis illius scopus, . . . (thesis 7, *ibid.*, p. 544, 2). Also, ". . . Foedus Naturae per accidens homines ad Christum adducit, quatenus ostendit quid homo debeat Deo, & quae non solventem debitum maneat poena, unde ad Mediatorem cogit respicere, cum homo nec solvendo debito, nec ferendae poenae videat se esse parem" (thesis 48, *ibid.*, p. 549, 1).

charged with teaching that there is a saving knowledge of God outside of Christ, this charge is not brought against Cameron even by the hyperorthodox, highly suspicious Wodrow. We can only conclude that Cameron was singularly uninterested in this idea; his whole theology is designed to elevate the covenant of grace, the revelation of God's mercy in Christ.

Before leaving off our discussion of Cameron's covenant teaching we should note again that his making a distinct, separate covenant of the *foedus subserviens* had special significance for Reformed theology and was in fact his novelty *vis-à-vis* orthodox Calvinism. Why should he risk his theological reputation and future in his first published work? The logical answer seems to be, precisely because he intended this as a corrective to the Reformed theology of the day. He apparently disliked a certain legalism into which he considered Calvinism to have fallen, and hoped to remedy the situation. In accord with this desire he formulated his teaching in a way that would point up the opposition of works-righteousness and faith-righteousness. And so he comprehended under this covenant what was usually discussed in terms of "law." That is, the *foedus subserviens–foedus gratiae* opposition was simply the law-gospel distinction of Luther and Calvin. This seems to indicate that justification was the decisive factor in his theology. Cameron evidently thought that the doctrine of justification *sola gratia* had become obscured, and throughout his theses he made a detailed comparison of faith- and works-righteousness.[159] His discussion of the *foedus subserviens* therefore closely approximated Luther's teaching regarding the law. That is, that the theological use of the law, its primary use, is to convict men of their sin so that they take

159. "*Justitia* autem & *Fides* differunt ut *Dare* & *Accipere*, nam Justitia Deo dat, Fides accipit, Justitia sita est in mutuo amore Dei, Fides in persuasione de amore Dei" (thesis 10, *ibid.*, p. 545, 1). Again, ". . . in uno eodemque foro (ut ita loquar) ad hominis justificationem seu absolutionem nequeant concurrere, nam in Justitiae foro, in quo jus dicitur ex Foedere Naturae, vel justus absoluitur vel injustus condemnatur, nec quaeritur directè *an credideris te Deo fuisse carum,* sed, *an amaris Deum,* At in foro Misericordiae non quaeritur primò & propriè *an amaris Deum,* sed *an credideris,* & absolveris si credidisti . . ." (thesis 13, *ibid.*, p. 545, 1).

refuge in Christ.[160] Moreover, the theological use of the law was abolished by the promulgation of the *foedus gratiae*.[161]

This latter idea—that the *foedus subserviens* was only temporary—introduces us to another phase of Cameron's critique of the envisioned legalism of the orthodox. He strikes at the very roots of any idea that eternal life was attainable through the law. Namely, the *foedus subserviens,* as Galatians 4:24 teaches, was a covenant of bondage and not of spiritual deliverance. It promised simply a blessed life in Canaan. Therefore one would not be saved by its observance even if perfect obedience were possible (which it is not). And Cameron even maintains the logical corollary of this: "It is not possible that anyone be condemned by the law unless he is an unbeliever."[162]

Shortly after the publication of these theses Cameron returned to France. He was named co-minister of the Bordeaux Church, serving with fellow-countryman Gilbert Primrose, and served as minister at Bordeaux until his call to Saumur as professor of theology in 1618. While at Bordeaux Cameron wrote a series of four letters to Louis Cappel concerning Christ's atoning work on the cross. These have been analyzed at some length by Wodrow, and by Reid, who summarizes Wodrow.[163] Because the letters deal with a very important aspect in Cameron's theology, his theory of the universal design of Christ's atonement, a brief outline of their content is in order.

160. ". . . quum utrumque foedus adducat ad Christum, . . . foedus Vetus hoc facit per se, est enim ejus verus & proprius scopus. . . . in foedere subserviente Deus jus suum non alio fine exigit, quàm ut homines convicti imbecillitatis suae ad Christum confugiant" (thesis 46, *ibid.,* p. 548, 2). See also thesis 42. Despite the similarity to Luther there seems to be no dependence of Cameron on Luther's writings. Indeed, Cameron even seems to "out-Luther" Luther, for he discusses no other use of the law than as a "killer."

161. ". . . Legis usum (cujus *a custodiâ coercebamur usque ad fidem revelandam*) abolitum: Christo jam crucifixo, mortuo, sepulto, denique in coelum recepto: . . ." (thesis 38, *ibid.,* pp. 547, 2; 548, 1).

162. ". . . *neminem à Lege damnari posse nisi idem incredulus sit.*" Or again: ". . . nemo in illam [condemnation] incurrat nisi qui Christum pro se mortuum esse non crediderit" (letter of Cameron to Louis Cappel, May, 1612, *Opera,* p. 534, 1).

163. Wodrow, "Life of Cameron," pp. 92–106; Reid, *Divinity Principals in Glasgow,* pp. 180–85.

Cameron asserts that election is "a secret of God's wisdom";[164] that the faith which makes us acceptable to Him originates "in God's sheer good pleasure."[165] It is in fact this faith which "renders efficacious the death of Christ, not by any dignity or merit which is in it, but because by it God desires to unite us to Christ our head."[166] Here Cameron has introduced a slight variation to the orthodox explanation of redemption. Namely, he implies that saving faith does not stand in an inevitable cause-effect relationship to Christ's atoning work. Rather, the gift of saving faith *presupposes* a prior satisfaction of God's justice. That is, he opts for a strict historical sequence in the redemptive act: first Christ's death, which placates God's wrath, then the gift of faith, which unites the believing one to Christ.

Such is indeed Cameron's answer to the thorny problem, "In what manner does Scripture declare Christ made satisfaction for all men?" His orientation was too strongly biblical to allow him to accept the "sham explanation of the divines" (Cameron always refers to the orthodox as "the divines")—to interpolate "elect" after each statement that Christ died for all. Cameron, rather, adopts an explanation based on a historical sequence in redemption. And this sequence is in fact present in the divine perfections or decrees. In the first of these letters he reiterates the distinction we have seen him make in the context of his covenant theology—"There is a twofold mercy of God: one antecedent . . . , the other consequent."[167] He then explains his historical-sequence idea in a striking passage:

> Scripture describes the antecedent love of God to us as having in it certain degrees. The first degree is that Christ is given both for Gentiles and Jews (this is understood in the scriptural phrases *every creature, all flesh, the world . . .*) with the condition an-

164. ". . . quod Deus hominem peccato corruptum facit aut non facit membrum Christi, est arcanae Sapientiae, . . ." (letter of Dec., 1610, *Opera*, p. 530, 2).

165. "Unde igitur fides? . . . ex mero scilicet Dei beneplacito," (letter of Dec., 1610, *ibid.*, p. 531, 1).

166. ". . . est enim fides quae mortem Christi reddit efficacem, non ullâ quae ei insit dignitate aut meritò, sed quia Deus voluit nos inseri per eam Christo capiti" (letter of May, 1612, *ibid.*, p. 535, 1).

167. Letter of Dec., 1610, *ibid.*, p. 531, 1.

nexed that they believe in Him. This degree of antecedent mercy is described in that celebrated verse, *God so loved the world* &c. John 3. . . . It is with regard to this first degree of His antecedent love that God is said *to have given Christ for the life of the world, to will the salvation of all,* inasmuch as He truly calls all to repentance, either by the law of Nature, by the written Law, or by the preaching of the Gospel. . . . It is by the second degree of *antecedent* love that God gives faith. This is pointed out in that equally celebrated verse, *No one comes to me unless my Father draws him.* It is with regard to this last degree of antecedent love that He is said to be given for the elect only, and that He wills to save them only.[168]

It is clear, then, that Cameron distinguishes the decree of sending Christ for all men and the decree to give faith to the elect. In another place Cameron explains himself even more concisely:

The first decree has to do with the restoration of the image of God in the creature, but so as to be consistent with God's justice; the second with the sending of the Son who saves each and every one who believes in Him. . . ; the third with rendering men capable of believing; the fourth is to save those who believe. The first two decrees are general, the last two are particular.[169]

It is to be understood that the general (universal) decrees pertain to God's work in Christ, the particular decrees to the application of that work to the believer. Cameron realizes, however, that the decree of God is substantially one, and so bases his distinctions on God's accommodation to our weakness: "All these things are to be understood as said of God in accommodation to the weakness of human nature."[170]

Here, then, is the essence of Cameron's "hypothetical uni-

---

168. Letter of Dec., 1610, *ibid.,* p. 531, 2.

169. "Primum decretum est de restauranda imagine Dei in creatura, salvâ tamen Dei justitiâ. Secnndum [*sic*] est de mittendo Filio, qui servet omnes & singulos qui in eum credunt, hoc est, qui ejus membra sunt. Tertium est de reddendis hominibus idoneis ad credendum. Quartum de servandis credentibus. Priora duo Decreta generalia sunt, posteriora duo specialia" (from the treatise entitled "de ordine decretorum Dei, in negotio salutis humanae, Joh. Cameronis sententia," *ibid.,* p. 529, 2).

170. "Atque haec omnia intelligenda sunt de Deo dicta accommodatè ad infirmitatem ingenii humani" (*ibid*).

versalism." The decree to redeem the world in Christ is first and is universal. Therefore in the work of Christ God has redeemed all men—hypothetically or potentially. The universality of the virtue of Christ's death Cameron illustrates by the shop-worn analogy to the universality of sunlight. "The sun," he says, "shines on all men, but those who sleep or voluntarily close their eyes do not receive its light. Now this is not because of any deficiency in the sun; rather it is the fault of the one who makes no use of this benefit. Accordingly, Christ died for all, but his death makes blessed only those who lay hold of him by faith."[171] He is, he says, in full accord with the formula adopted by the divines: "Christ's death is sufficient for all, but is efficacious strictly for believers."[172] He quickly admits, however, that perhaps his use of the word sufficient is more embracing (*amplius*) than is that of "the divines."

It is hard to see how this teaching could have been regarded as heretical. And it is perhaps significant that it was not so regarded until long after Cameron was dead. There is very little in it which differs from the orthodox expression found in the Canons of Dort. These canons, for example, clearly taught infralapsarianism.[173] Moreover, they repeatedly emphasized that Christ's death was "of infinite value and worth, abundantly sufficient to expiate the sins of the entire world."[174] But then these canons do not reveal the rigid orthodoxy with which they are commonly charged. There is good reason to believe that the presence of the delegates from England, Bremen, and Hesse prevented the adoption of an orthodox document which would have

171. Letter of Dec., 1611, *Opera*, p. 532, 2.
172. ". . . Christum pro omnibus *sufficienter*, pro fidelibus duntaxat efficaciter esse mortuum: . . ." (letter of May, 1612, *ibid.*, p. 533, 2). Cf. p. 534, 2.
173. In chapter 1, section 7, we read that God has "en Jésus-Christ, élu au salut avant la fondation du monde—d'entre tout le genre humain déchu par sa propre faute de sa première intégrité dans la péché et la perdition—une certaine multitude d'hommes, ni meilleurs ni plus dignes que les autres, mais qui, avec ceux-ci, gisaient dans une même misère" (from the recent French edition by Pierre Marcel in *La Revue réformée* 14, no. 3 [1963], 8).
174. In chapter 2, section 3: "Cette mort du Fils de Dieu est l'unique et très parfait sacrifice et satisfaction pour les péchés, d'une valeur et d'un prix infinis, qui suffit abondamment pour expier les péchés du monde entier" (*ibid.*, p. 16).

been more characteristic of such delegates as Bogerman, the moderator, F. Gomarus of Leyden, and J. Diodati and T. Tronchin of Geneva.[175]

It seems quite clear that the orthodoxy of the rigid Calvinists became more and more entrenched as their struggle with Arminianism dragged on. There is, for example, a noticeable narrowing of the front in the later writings of du Moulin—to such a degree, in fact, that it is not difficult to show that in the controversy with Amyraut, du Moulin condemns positions which he himself once advocated. Because of this continuous withdrawal to a more and more defensible position, orthodoxy, with du Moulin in the vanguard, finally brought heresy charges against Cameron's teaching. This was done by du Moulin in a letter to the Synod of Alençon (1637), which synod was hearing the charges against Amyraut. The main thrust against Cameron was that he had reversed the usual order of the decrees of God. That is, the orthodox, to hedge their doctrine of limited atonement, were insisting on a strictly logical connection between the decree of election and the decree of sending a redeemer, with the decree of election preceding that of sending the redeemer. Cameron, as we have seen, reversed these, making the decree to redeem the world primary. Since all were agreed that there was really no time sequence in the decrees, however, this was a purely academic question. Nevertheless, it is interesting that the orthodox were willing, to a large degree, to base their position against "hypothetical universalism" on the order of the decrees.

We have noted that Cameron was called to Saumur in 1618. Rex judges that "Although this event took place in the shadow of the pompous display at Dordrecht, it would be difficult to find an occurrence of greater importance for the history of French Calvinism than the arrival in Saumur of this lively, impatient, temperamental Scot."[176] The event is even more significant when it is remembered that he was called to fill the chair of theology that F. Gomarus had vacated in order to go to Leyden. The contrast between the nature of the theology that

175. For a provocative discussion of the "moderate" teaching of the Dort Canons see Rex, *Essays on Pierre Bayle*, pp. 80–91.
176. *Ibid.*, p. 88.

these two men taught could hardly be more striking. Gomarus was the impeccably orthodox logician and dogmatist, Cameron the restless, original-thinking, broad-minded exegete and theologian. As Rex has said, "Cameron brought to France an antidote to the stultifying rigidity of the post-Dordrecht conservatives."[177] And his inaugural exercises at Saumur clearly demonstrated his versatility and inspiring originality. One was on Matthew 16:18 and pointed up his ability as an exegete and theologian; the other was *De gratia et libero arbitrio* and pointed up his profound philosophico-theological teaching. The latter we shall use below, for it reveals his reformulation of the nature of faith and conversion, the only major point of doctrine which the orthodox challenged during his lifetime.[178]

The contrast between Gomarus and Cameron does not end with a consideration of their theological teaching. Perhaps most significant of all is the fact that Gomarus had no lasting influence on French Protestantism, whereas Cameron's influence was tremendous. Amyraut, who reportedly mimicked even Cameron's accent and pulpit mannerisms, is but one of a host of his devoted disciples. This outstanding success probably owed much to Cameron's gregarious nature. It also lends credence to Cappel's laudatory *Icon* (citing for instance Cameron's readiness to communicate his most intimate thoughts to his students),[179] and tends to discredit the characterizations of him by du Moulin and W. Rivet as a "garrulous windbag," to use Rex's phrase. However, it is possible that Gomarus' lack of influence was due not so much to his personality as to the character of French Protestantism. We have noticed that French theology lagged behind the scholastic theology of the rest of the Continent and that French Protestantism was especially amenable to humanism. These two features combined to produce a milieu in France,

177. *Ibid.*
178. During his ministry at Bourdeaux Cameron's orthodoxy had been challenged regarding the "heresy" of Piscator on the doctrine of justification—that we are justified by Christ's passive obedience only and not his active obedience. Cameron would not sign the orthodox subscription clause, but the matter was dropped because of the inconsequential nature of the teaching.
179. Prefaced to Cameron's *Opera*, p. 3: ". . . volentes à se discere nil celabat, quin facilè quicquid singulare aut reconditùm habuit, iis communicabat."

and especially at Saumur, in which the spirit of the broad-minded du Plessis-Mornay generally prevailed; it was adverse to the dogmatism of Gomarus and favorable to the spirit of inquiry and examination fostered by Cameron.

Cameron had been at Saumur but two years when he was persuaded to engage in debate with Daniel Tilenus (1563–1633), then a professor of theology at Sedan with decidedly Arminian tendencies, on the topic of effectual calling. In Reid's words, "The incident created as much excitement in theological circles as a modern prize-fight does among devotees of sport."[180] The subject agreed upon for debate centered on articles 21 and 22 of the *Confessio gallicana;* that is, illumination by the Spirit, and regeneration. We find in this debate a clear exposition of Cameron's doctrine of faith and conversion, so we shall look at a synopsis of Cameron's position, comparing his other writings with some pivotal passages in this document.[181] Before turning to a discussion of this doctrine, however, it is worth noting that in February, 1622, the theological faculty of Leyden wrote to Cameron about it, expressing their displeasure with his teaching that there is "no other change in the will, either to avoid or seek an object, except that moral change which proceeds from the demonstration of the object and the judgment of the intellect to choose, reject, or prefer that object without any immediate intervention of God on this will, and especially in supernatural matters."[182] They asked therefore that he add a preface to the *Amica collatio* stating that he utterly (*prorsus*) acquiesced to the Dort Canons; and, they ask, would he either elucidate or change any statements which do not "in every particular" conform to these Canons? Cameron, stung by the requests, denied the sentiments as expressed in their letter to be his, and declined both to write the preface and to revise his terminology. There is

180. *Divinity Principals in Glasgow,* p. 206.

181. It is published in his *Opera,* pp. 612–708, under the title "Amica collatio, de gratiae et voluntatis humanae concursu in vocatione et quibusdam annexis, instituta inter Danielem Tilenum, & Johannem Cameronem . . ."

182. ". . . nullam aliam mutationem in voluntate aut concedere, aut requirere praeter moralem illam quae sit ab objecto monstrato & rationis judicio de eo eligendo, aut rejiciendo, aut praeferendo sine ullo influxu Dei immediato, in ipsam voluntatem, praesertim in rebus supernaturalibus" (*Opera,* p. 709, 1).

no question but that Cameron deplored such rigid subscription clauses. The result of his refusal at this point was that the *Amica collatio* appeared, as Reid says, "without the valuable imprimatur of the Leyden Faculty."[183]

As we turn to the doctrine of conversion some preliminary remarks are necessary. It is difficult to understand this doctrine in this century of Protestant scholasticism without some feeling for the importance of the "faculty psychology" of the time.[184] That is, that part of rational man which governed behavior was thought of as having two parts, the intellect and the will. The intellect, the "eye of the soul," both surveyed the data presented and made a judgment concerning it; the will was generally in accordance with the judgment made by the intellect.

As one reads either Cameron's inaugural address of 1618, *De gratia et libero arbitrio,* or the *Amica collatio,* of 1620, he is immediately struck by a theory of epistemology somewhat different from that seen in the orthodox theologians, and the consequently different explanation of the psychology of conversion. The orthodox position stated that both the will and the intellect are to a certain degree autonomous: the intellect has to do with knowing, the will with loving.[185] Man's rational faculties, that is, are carefully parcelled into two very distinct categories. Therefore the work of God in conversion must take two very distinct operations: the illumination of the intellect and the renewal of the will. The Dort Canons express these two operations as follows:

> When God executes his good pleasure in the elect, or when he converts them, he not only sees to it that the Gospel is externally preached to them, and powerfully illumines their intellect by the Holy Spirit so that they comprehend and properly

183. *Divinity Principals in Glasgow,* p. 209.

184. There is a very useful discussion of conversion in Rex, *Essays on Pierre Bayle,* pp. 91ff. The following draws on this account.

185. I.e., du Moulin says: "Duae sunt animae rationalis facultates, Intellectus et Voluntas: illa quae cognoscit verum, haec quae appetit bonum. . . . Per intellectum docti & sapientes, per voluntatem boni et justi perhibemur. . . . Ad intellectum oportet voluntas accedat, Sancti enim non uniuntur Deo sola intellectione sed etiam amore: . . ." ("Theses theologicae de summo bono & beatitudine," *Thesaurus theologicae Sedanensis* [Geneva, 1661], 1:739–40).

discern the things of the Spirit of God, but also by the efficacy
of this same regenerating Spirit he penetrates to the innermost
parts of man, opens the closed, softens the hardened, and cir-
cumcises the uncircumcised heart; introduces new qualities into
the will, which, being dead, he gives life, being evil, obstinate,
and disobedient, he makes good, pliable and obedient; he puts
it to work and fortifies it that it, like a good tree, might produce
good fruit.[186]

Thus in conversion there are two quite separate acts: illumination and renewal. The careful delimitation of the work of grace
on each of these faculties forms the basis for what Geiger calls a
"gross-mechanistischen Theorie."[187]

Cameron introduces a more existential understanding of man,
and the consequences of this move are far-reaching. That is,
Cameron denies that the intellect and will are two somewhat
autonomous faculties. Rather, he says, they are so intimately
connected that we cannot speak of one without including the
other, or, in his words, "the intellect influences and necessarily
leads the will along."[188] So when Cameron talks of conversion
he speaks of the Holy Spirit's action as one, though including
two aspects, illumination and regeneration. And he customarily
speaks of that action as occurring in the intellect, since he understands the will to be necessarily involved in any action on the
intellect. Now, because the orthodox were working on the
hypothesis of *their* understanding of faculty psychology, they
were unable to understand Cameron's teaching concerning conversion. They naturally suspected that he was denying any
"immediate *influxus* of God on the will." This is, to be sure,
the point of the passage quoted above from the letter of the
Leyden theological faculty.

Because Cameron speaks of conversion as occurring in the
intellect, the pivotal word in his conversion vocabulary is *illuminatio,* though he often uses *renovatio* interchangeably with

186. Ch. 3; ch. 4, art. 11.
187. Max Geiger, *Die Basler Kirche und Theologie im Zeitalter der Hochorthodoxie* (Zurich, 1952), pp. 114ff.
188. ". . . intellectus trahit secum & ducit necessariò voluntatem, . . ." ("Praelectiones in Matth. Cap. XVIII, Vers. 7," *Opera,* p. 101, 2).

it.[189] And because Cameron is fearful that the orthodox explanation of conversion reduces man to a mere block of wood, he insists on a distinction which became very important in the Salmurian theology—a distinction between moral and natural ability. He maintains this distinction in order to explain the working of grace on man *as a rational being*. He finds it necessary to make a point of the fact that God accommodates himself to the nature of the human soul in conversion,[190] and that man by nature (that is, because he possesses rational faculties) is capable of responding to the offer of grace. However, because man is corrupted and depraved he will not respond. That is, by his nature he is able, but because corrupt he will not. So Cameron distinguishes a natural ability but a moral inability.

The movement of the will through grace, then, is "ethical, not natural, although fully as efficacious as if it were natural."[191] Moreover, the will itself is free. That is, Cameron here applies to the will the same concept of freedom he employed to declare that God is free—freedom of spontaneity. True, the will is always inclined, either to good or bad, but also, because there is no *coactio*, is perfectly free. It moves as it desires, maintaining its character at all times. It follows that the choice of the object to which the will moves the individual resides in the intellect,

189. I.e., in "Johan Cameronis sententia aliquot ab hinc annis thesibus explicata" he says, ". . . mentis renovatio, voluntatis renovationem producat" (*Opera*, p. 720, 2). In fact, Cameron can use any number of terms interchangeably with *illuminatio*; in thesis 9 of "de gratia et libero arbitrio" he lists creatio, mortificatio, vivificatio, regeneratio, renovatio, . . . conversio, sanctificatio, fidei, poenitentiae donatio, revelatio, [etc.] (*ibid.*, p. 332, 1).

190. ". . . nempe peccatoris conversio, etsi divinum opus sit, tamen ratione ad naturam humani animi accommodata peragitur; non enim Dominus cum hominibus agit perinde ac si stipites essent aut trunci, sed dum eos vult in viam revocare, agit eo modo ac ratione quae decet ejus sapientiam, nempe, ut qui ratione praediti sunt non agantur coeco motu, sed quem ratione potest admittere; rationem autem non hic voco corruptam & depravatam hominis naturam, sed vim intelligendi, quae humanam animam à bellvina distinguit" ("Praelectiones ad Matth., cap. XVIII, vers. 15," *Opera*, p. 145, 2). "Itaque non tam in nos contumeliosi sunt, quàm in Spiritum Sanctum, qui odiosè exclamant, sic hominem statui stipitem, & truncum, & demortuum, sine sensu, sine motu, sine vita" (thesis 30, "de gratia et libero arbitrio," *Opera*, p. 333, 2).

191. ". . . Ethico, non Physico, qui motus tamen sit tam efficax quàm si Physicus foret" (thesis 10, "de gratia et libero arbitrio," *Opera*, p. 332, 1).

not in the will which is always inclined. Therefore in the work of conversion the gospel must first be proclaimed, and then the Spirit, who accompanies the Word, illumines the intellect, enabling it to see the truth that God has accepted the sinner in Christ. Now Cameron maintains that it is impossible for the intellect not to assent to the knowledge of the truth.[192] Or again, it is impossible for the will not to move to what the intellect presents to it as good; that is, since man always seeks his own happiness, it is impossible for the intellect not to choose the perceived good.[193] There is a discernible moral determinism here which Cameron easily correlates with the idea of irresistible grace. In fact it is the basis for Cameron's explanation of this doctrine. Nevertheless, he is able to maintain that the "determination of the human will does not destroy its nature as will, but rather conserves and dignifies it. And this determination is not natural, depending on natural principles, but moral, depending on judgment and reason."[194]

Cameron sometimes employs the term *demonstratio* to characterize the efficacious presentation of the gospel. This *demonstratio* is in fact the power of the Spirit, and it is not possible for the intellect to reject this demonstration. Probably Rex is right when he maintains that one may discern here the seeds of rationalism, for rational demonstration has assumed a rather larger role than in orthodox theology.[195] However, it is also true that Cameron's favorite term is *persuasio,* indeed *persuasio moralis.* "This movement of God is a most powerful, most vigorous, most efficacious persuasion, by which the will is inclined, turned, led,

---

192. ". . . *intellectum non posse non assentiri veritati agnitae, aut verò nondum agnitae assentiri.* Itaque etiam fateantur necesse est, *eum qui agnoverit veritatem non posse non credere*" (*Opera*, p. 343, 1). This brings Cameron very close to the heresy of which he is accused—a doctrine of moral suasion which needs no accompanying *renovatio* of the will.

193. See *Opera*, p. 99, 2.

194. "Itaque ista voluntatis humanae determinatio ejus naturam non destruit, sed conservat & ornat. Neque enim *physica* est, à principiis physicis profecta; sed *ethica*, pendens à judicio & ratione" (thesis 28, "de gratia et libero arbitrio," *Opera*, p. 333, 2).

195. See *Essays on Pierre Bayle*, pp. 9–120, *passim*, but esp. p. 99.

and then irresistibly drawn."[196] He then indicates his reasons for calling it a *persuasio moralis:*

> This movement some call *natural,* others call *moral.* We think it may be more properly called *moral* than *natural.* Not that we would dissent from the intention of those who call it natural, but because this terminology is not only unfavorable to their expressed intent, but also because it renders them extremely liable to misrepresentation. For when one hears the phrase "natural movement," what else can he think of but of *a movement of an animal, such as that of sheep who are led by instinct, or of a stone which falls by a natural impetus unknown to it?* But, the one who calls this persuasion a *moral movement* both cuts short the occasion for misrepresentation and appropriately signifies the matter itself.[197]

Once again, then, he has employed the term *moralis* (or *ethicus*) to emphasize that the movement of God in conversion is accommodated to man as a rational being. Cameron has often been accused of teaching the doctrine of moral suasion in conjunction with Pelagianism. However, this is to misunderstand him completely. He very explicitly makes a distinction between "suasion" and "persuasion":

> Without question persuasion is when the Holy Spirit accompanies the preaching of the Gospel with such power that faith is created, and through this faith the love of God and neighbor and the new life: which grace is neither common nor is it the moral suasion condemned by the Fathers in Pelagius and by the present-day Orthodox in you Arminians, for faith is not in all men.[198]

196. "Motus hic Dei persuasio est, sed potentissima, valentissima, efficacissima, quâ voluntas *inclinatur, flectitur, ducitur, rapitur* denique" ("Praelectio ad Philipp. cap. II, vers. 13," *Opera,* p. 343, 2).

197. "Hunc motum alii *Physicum,* alii *Ethicum* dicunt, nos magis propriè *Ethicum* quàm *Physicum* appellari posse putamus: non quod ab eorum mente, qui Physicum eum vocant, dissentiamus, sed quia eorum menti exprimendae haec vox non modò visa est parùm commoda, sed etiam reddere calumniae vehementer obnoxiam. Qui enim motum Physicum dici audit, quid aliud statim significari putabit quàm *motum brutum, qualis est pecudum, quae appetitu ducuntur, aut lapidum, qui feruntur deorsum impetu quodam naturae, quae sui nescia est?* At, qui *Ethicum motum* persuasionem istam vocabit, & ansam calumniae praecidet, & rem appositè significabit" (*ibid.,* p. 344, 1).

198. From "Johan Cameronis responsio ad praecedentem Viri docti anonymi Epistolam," *Opera,* p. 743, 1.

By this term *persuasio* we are introduced to Cameron's distinctive teaching concerning the nature of faith. Perhaps of all Cameron's innovations the most significant for Reformed theology is his redefinition of faith. It is, of course, intimately tied up with his teaching concerning conversion, and he used the word faith conterminously with the other words in his conversion vocabulary. So it is to be understood that all of the preceding discussion on conversion ought not to be separated from Cameron's doctrine of faith. Faith is discussed separately in order to point up the variances with the orthodox doctrine. In orthodox doctrine faith was, of course, quite distinct from conversion.

The first impression one receives when reading Cameron is of the dynamic and all-embracing character of faith in his theology. In orthodox theology faith had become a rather static concept and, more importantly, had become only one of the heads of doctrine, usually discussed quite far down the line.[199] Cameron attempted to make faith the locus under which all of theology was to be discussed. This is most noticeable in his theses on the covenant where, by making faith the condition of the covenant of grace, he even runs the risk of making God dependent on man. However, this risk he apparently was willing to take, being convinced that there were many things in Reformed theology which he wished to see reformed, as du Moulin reported, hoping to discredit Cameron's memory.[200] At any rate, Cameron suggested that faith sums up the whole word of God.[201]

Cameron also presented a much more dynamic concept of faith than we find in orthodox theology. The orthodox doctrine was generally discussed as made up of three elements: *notitia*, *assensus*, and *fiducia*. And, as we noted was their conversion doctrine, these three elements were related strictly to their un-

199. E.g. in Wollebuis' *Compendium Theologiae Christianae* (trans. by Beardslee in *Reformed Dogmatics*), where faith appears not only after the doctrines of God and christology but even after the sacraments and ecclesiology.

200. Bayle in his *Dictionnaire* (*s.v.* Cameron, Jean) quotes this passage from du Moulin's *Judicio de Amyraldi libro*, p. 211: "Fuit ingenio inquieto, semperque aliquid novi animo volutabat et nominabat, nec dissimulabat inter amicos (quorum ego unus eram) multa esse in religione nostrâ quae cuperet immutata."

201. See *Opera*, p. 60, 1.

derstanding of faculty psychology and the operation of these faculties. We read, for instance, in a treatise from Leyden: "*Notitia* and *assensus* pertain to the work of the *intellect; fiducia* pertains to the work of the *will.*"[202] Cameron, too, discussed faith as consisting of these three elements. He made it quite clear that faith is consonant with rational knowledge.[203] In one place he even defined justifying faith as "a firm assent" to God's revelation of eternal life in Christ.[204] However, he broke through the scholastic precision-making of the orthodox by his more unified concept of man and also, most significantly, produced a different terminology and content for the doctrine of faith—the idea of persuasion. He seldom, if ever, used the term *fiducia*. Rather, *persuasio* was his most frequently used term. In his very first writing he defined faith as the persuasion that we are loved and accepted by God in Christ.[205] And this persuasion is so powerful, so dynamic, that the individual in question is wholly overcome by it. Summing up his comments on Philippians 2:13 ("For God is at work in you, both to will and to work"), Cameron said: "We understand persuasion to be that which accomplishes *both to do and to will.*"[206] We are, that is, so overcome, that faith is created and we serve God by it.

In all his discussion of faith Cameron refused to consider it in the abstract. Faith for him always originated in the work of the Spirit and was the instrument of our union with Christ.[207] The Holy Spirit was the lost person of the orthodox Trinity and Cameron helped correct this by his doctrine.

202. "*Notitia* enim et *assensus* ad *intellectum* pertinent; *fiducia* autem ad *voluntatem*" (from *Synopsis purioris theologicae doctorum et professorum in academia Leidensi*, 6th ed. [Leyden, 1652] ch. 31:14, as quoted in Heppe-Bizer, *Die Dogmatik*, p. 424).

203. ". . . fides praesupponit rationem, non destruit, praesupponit, . . ." ("Praelectiones de ecclesia," *Opera*, p. 311, 2).

204. "*Fides justificans est firmus assensus quem praebemus impulsu Spiritum Sancti omnibus iis quae in verbo Dei vel narrantur, vel promittuntur, speciatim autem promissioni de vita aeterna parta per Christum*" ("Praelectiones ad Matth. XVII, vers. 14," *Opera*, p. 60, 1).

205. See thesis 12, "de triplici dei cum homine foedere," *Opera*, p. 545, 1.

206. "At nos persuasionem intelligimus, quae efficiat & *velle* & *perficere*" (*Opera*, p. 344, 2).

207. "Fides proficiscitur ab illuminatione Spiritus S." ("Amica collatio cum Tileno," *Opera*, p. 612).

Cameron left Saumur in 1621, since under Louis XIII he had lost his privilege as a foreigner to teach in France. He went to London, where he taught theology for a year. King James then appointed him principal of Glasgow, probably because of Cameron's strong royalist position. Cameron spent but one year at Glasgow, unable to get along in the strongly republican atmosphere. He returned to France late in 1623 and spent the last two years of his life there, hoping that the king would grant him permission once again to teach theology. Finally this permission did come, and he taught for a short time at Montauban. Here, in 1625, he was killed by a mob, probably Protestant, because of his royalist stand. These years after his ministry at Saumur were not very profitable, but in his short stay at Saumur he had effected a theological revolution. Upon the foundation laid by Cameron, Moïse Amyraut was to construct his theology.

2

A BRIEF

BIOGRAPHY OF AMYRAUT

THE SOURCES FOR CONSTRUCTING A LIFE OF AMYRAUT are very meagre indeed. In the first place his personal papers have been lost, and for some mysterious reason also the bulk of his correspondence, even that which should appear in the preserved collections of his known correspondents.[1] To be sure, there are a few of his letters available in libraries in Paris, La Rochelle, Leyden, Geneva, and Zurich, but these letters are quite occasional (most relate in some way to the quarrel over universal grace) and they seldom contain information helpful in compiling his biography. Secondly, like Calvin, Amyraut seldom made any autobiographical statements. Here and there references appear in the prefaces and dedicatory epistles of his writings which are at times helpful, but for the most part these are concerned solely with the occasion for the particular writings involved.

For these reasons insights into Amyraut's intimate thought are almost all a matter of individual judgment; Amyraut the man remains largely a shadowy figure. From his conduct in the bitter universal-grace quarrel many implications can be drawn, but they are always subject to qualification, since it is not to be expected that we get a true picture of the man when he is responding to heated charges of heresy and to character defamation.

1. E.g., the correspondence of A. Rivet preserved in the state archives of The Hague, or that of Louis Tronchin in the Archives Tronchin at Geneva. This paucity of Amyraut letters leads one to suspect that they may have been intentionally removed.

Nevertheless, I believe sufficient information is available to allow for some general observations on his character.

Nowhere was the cosmopolitanism of the Amyraldians more evident than in Amyraut himself. Moreri observed that he was "highly esteemed, not only by those of his own communion, but also by some of the highest ranking Catholics (*des plus grands seigneurs catholiques*)."[2] His associations with prominent men are quite evident in the intimacy with which he addressed those to whom his writings are dedicated.[3] Orentin Douen gives some further indications of this urbanity:

> The illustrious professor of Saumur . . . was a close friend of Comminges, governor of the city; of le Goux de Berchère, first president of the parliament of Grenoble, who, consigned to Saumur, saw him twice a week; of Mandet, the intendant of Poitou, who had him to dinner with the archdeacon of Bourges and other ecclesiastics; of the marshall of Brézé, who, in his last sickness asked that he be prayed for in the temple.[4]

We know also that both Cardinal Richelieu and Mazarin paid Amyraut frequent visits. Unquestionably, then, Amyraut was at home with "men of quality." And this may be, in some ways, his most striking characteristic. He had an unusual ability to represent and communicate the position of Reformed Protestantism to the nobility, even when that nobility was strongly Roman Catholic. To do this Amyraut had to have had to an unusual degree the qualities of moderation and largeness of spirit, qualities which are strikingly prominent in the other areas of his life and work.

His work as a theologian, too, was infused with the same broad and irenic spirit, both in his relations with churchmen of other confessions and in his work within the Reformed Church. In the first respect, he was a spirited advocate of Church union with the Lutherans and composed two substantial treatises upon this

2. Louis Moréri, *Le Grand Dictionnaire historique* . . . , 10 vols. (Paris, 1759), 1:495.

3. These persons have been identified wherever possible in the bibliography. See also the more complete identification in the bibliography of Roger Nicole's "Moyse Amyraut and the Controversy on Universal Grace. First Phase (1634–1637)" (Ph.D. diss., Harvard University, 1966).

4. *La Révocation de l'édit de Nantes à Paris*, 1:20.

topic.[5] In the second respect, the very nature of his teaching revealed his spirit. Though his teaching remained faithful to the Reformed confessions, it may well be thought of as an attempt to remove the harsh features of orthodox Calvinist dogma. Certainly his attempt to reformulate the doctrine of predestination falls, at least to some extent, under such an interpretation.

His broadmindedness is also displayed in his legendary *charité fraternelle:* "During the last ten years of his life Amyraut distributed to the poor, without distinction of religion, his salary as minister."[6] It goes without saying that this was a demonstration of liberality quite unheard of in Amyraut's time.

His writings witness that he was a man of sound learning, especially well versed in Latin and the biblical languages and unusually sensitive to the contemporary situation. Occasionally we see flashes of originality of thought, and in some instances evidences of a penetrating mind. In general, however, his thought appears to be neither extraordinarily profound nor incisive. Though he apparently had a real ability to see all facets of an issue, a trait which set him apart from many of his contemporaries, he was often outclassed by friend and foe alike when it came to sheer native intelligence, profundity of thought and dialectical rigor. He had therefore to rely on long hours of diligent study, and he relied heavily on the insights of Cameron. Yet despite a heavy style annoyingly cluttered with appositional phrases, his writing exhibits a freedom and independence of spirit and thought which makes it refreshing reading when compared with that of most of his Protestant contemporaries. His sermons are only mediocre, though always attuned to the situation at hand and spiced with interesting analogies and illustrations usually taken from classical literature. Perhaps the one respect in which he possessed extraordinary gifts was in his ability as a teacher. This is to some extent an hypothesis since, at least in his case, there is no sure way to document such a claim. Nevertheless we do know that the *proposants* left Saumur wholly devoted to the Amyraldian theology, and that seldom did one leave Saumur and turn against this theology.

5. See Richard H. Stauffer's excellent *Moïse Amyraut: Un Précurseur français de l'oecuménisme* (Paris, 1962). Further remarks on Stauffer in appendix 2.
6. Douen, *La Révocation,* 1:20.

As we turn to an account of what we are able to construct of Amyraut's life, we are to a great extent dependent on two sources. The first of these is the famous article in Pierre Bayle's *Dictionnaire*.[7] Bayle reportedly received his information from Amyraut's son, and his article has been the basis of almost all biographical remarks about Amyraut. It has proved to be substantially accurate insofar as it can be checked and is therefore used frequently in the following account.

The second source we now have for biographical information about Amyraut is Father Laplanche's reconstruction of his life[8] based on the available manuscript letters, on the archival materials relating to the Saumur Academy, on the various prefaces to his works, and sometimes on the works themselves, where material could be found. I have freely used Laplanche's account, indeed, relied on his entire study, since his work is a detailed history of the *querelle de la grâce universelle,* a quarrel which had its origin in Amyraut's writings and which had its main course in relation to Amyraut himself, and which therefore, in my judgment, cannot be separated from an account of Amyraut's life. The reader should be advised, however, that the account of the quarrel here will be severely compressed, and so the work of Laplanche is recommended if further information is desired on any particular. It should also be explained that the following narrative will give special attention to Pierre du Moulin and his opposition to Amyraut, since he was Amyraut's outstanding opponent among those most closely related to the French Church. Du Moulin will also serve as our example of orthodox Calvinism in the following chapters on the Amyraldian theology.

Early Life and Work

Amyraut was born at Bourgueil, not far from Saumur, in September, 1596. Very little is known of his parents, though Bayle reports that it was a "good and old family, originally from

7. *Dictionnaire historique et critique, s.v.* Amyraut, Moïse. Also worth mention is Célestin Port, *Dictionnaire historique, géographique, et biographique de Maine-et-Loire,* 3 vols. (Paris & Angers, 1878), *s.v.* Amyraut, Moïse.

8. *Orthodoxie et prédication: L'Oeuvre d'Amyraut et la querelle de la grâce universelle* (Paris, 1965), pp. 58–83.

Orléans."[9] Bayle also reports that Amyraut was sent to the University of Poitiers to study law, that he studied fourteen hours a day, and that at the end of one year took his *licences*.[10] That was apparently the year 1616. At this juncture of his career the minister at Saumur, Samuel Bouchereau, challenged him to undertake the study of theology. Amyraut thereupon began a study of Calvin's *Institutio* and upon its completion decided for theology. He succeeded in talking his father into this change of careers, "although with difficulty," Bayle notes, and enrolled at Saumur. The exact date of his enrollment at Saumur is not known, but it was probably sometime in 1618, the year Cameron arrived there as professor of theology. We have already seen that Amyraut felt himself deeply indebted to Cameron. In fact, Cameron is the only one of Amyraut's professors mentioned in his writings. And Laplanche is correct in saying that the influence of Cameron is "the only positive information that we have regarding the intellectual formation of the future theologian of Saumur."[11]

Amyraut's course at Saumur is of unknown duration. Bayle records that he was a *proposant* for a "very long time." According to a document published in the *Bulletin* by Jacques Pannier, Amyraut sought permission at the provincial synod of Loudun in 1623 to take a church in that province, or wherever God might call him.[12] This would mean that he was a student for about five years. But it would also leave us all the more in the dark concerning his activities from 1623 to 1626, for his request was not granted by the Loudun synod.[13] Pannier speculates that he may have served as temporary supply pastor at

9. *Dictionnaire, s.v.* Amyraut.

10. *Ibid.* Célestin Port was unable to find any evidence of this law training either in the University records at Poitiers or in Amyraut's writings themselves. If Bayle's account is correct, however, it would put Amyraut at Poitiers at the same time as Descartes. There is no mention of Descartes in Amyraut's writings.

11. Laplanche, *L'Oeuvre d'Amyraut*, p. 59. See also Nicole, "Moyse Amyraut and the Controversy," p. 30.

12. *Bulletin* 74 (1925), 491.

13. Bayle's account placing Amyraut at Saint-Aignan-du-Maine as minister for eighteen months after he left Saumur is apparently in error. The document cited in the preceding note mentions that Amyraut's nephew, Abel, was sent to Saint-Aignan as minister.

Saumur till mid-1624; also that from 1624 to 1626 he may have ministered in the household of Clermont d'Amboise.[14] The only fact of this period of which we can be reasonably sure is that he succeeded Jean Daillé as minister at Saumur in July, 1626.[15] So, of the years 1618–26 we have very little information. Amyraut does mention in the preface to one of his writings that during part of 1620 he was in Leyden, where he met and established a friendship with André Rivet.[16] And it is interesting that even at this early date, as he relates, he undertook the defense of Cameron's teaching against the misgivings of the Leyden theologians.

At the time, or shortly after the time, that he was installed as minister at Saumur, Amyraut began lecturing on theology at the Academy. From this moment until his death Amyraut was to dominate the Academy at Saumur. Evidence of this is seen from the very beginning, for one year after he began teaching he became rector. Apparently he served in this post at least until 1631.[17] Bourchenin says he was rector four different times.[18] Moreover, during this time he was assigned, along with Cappel and Bouchereau, to oversee the publication of Cameron's *Opera*.

Sometime during this period Amyraut married Elisabeth

14. A supposition apparently based on the fact that two of Amyraut's earliest writings, which date from 1625, were dedicated to "Madame de Clermont d'Amboise." They were entitled *Cent cinquante sonnets chrétiens* and *Hymne de la puissance divine* and were published at Paris by Pierre des Haies. Both are rather amateurish attempts at poetry and are not important to the understanding of his theology (if we are to follow the account in E. and E. Haag and Henri Bordier, *La France protestante*, 6 vols. [Paris, 1877–92], 1:190–91). Despite extensive correspondence with libraries abroad and in this country I have been unable to locate either work.

15. At least Adrien Daillé asserts that his father arrived at Paris to become co-minister of the great Charenton church in July, 1626, and we know that Amyraut succeeded Daillé at Saumur (see A. Daillé, *Abbregé de la vie de Monsieur Daillé* [Quevilly, 1670], p. 15).

16. "Ad reverendos viros, ecclesiarum in gallia reformatarum pastores, Mosis Amyraldi apologetica praefatio," *Specimen animadversionum in exercitationes de gratia universali* (Saumur, 1648), p. 29ff. Professor Nicole of Gordon Divinity School also informs me that Amyraut's name is entered in the register at the Leyden Academy; Amyraut apparently studied at Leyden for at least one semester.

17. Laplanche, *L'Oeuvre d'Amyraut*, pp. 76n21, 77n25.

18. P-Daniel Bourchenin, *Etude sur les académies protestantes en France au XVIe et au XVIIe siècle* (Paris, 1882), p. 463.

Aubineau, daughter of an *ancien* of the Saumur church.[19] They had two children, a daughter born in 1629 and a son, Moïse, born in 1631. The daughter, Elisabeth, died in 1645; the son fled to England at the time of the Revocation and became a professor at Oxford University.

The year 1631 was especially eventful in Amyraut's life. First, on July 28 both Cappel and Amyraut, who had been teaching part-time in the Academy as well as serving as pastor to the Saumur church, submitted their resignations as professors, because of the excessive amount of work entailed. The academic council, however, rather than accepting these resignations, appointed both to be full professors and at the request of the two men agreed to allow them to occupy one chair, the duties being equally distributed. Their nomination was confirmed by the provincial synod of Loudun in August, and by the national synod of Charenton on September 1. Amyraut's career was now determined. Until death he would remain at Saumur, charged with the dual responsibility of minister and professor. Moreover, he would serve as principal of the Academy from 1641 to 1664.

Secondly, in 1631 Amyraut was deputed to the national synod of Charenton. It was customary that each national synod would depute one of its members to present to the king a list of grievances concerning various infractions of the Edict of Nantes. The delegate was required to kneel as he submitted this document to His Majesty. However, Amyraut felt that the requirement of kneeling was in itself an infraction of the Edict and so brought the matter to the attention of the synod. The synod adopted his suggestion that no discrimination between Protestant and Catholic should be tolerated and promptly appointed him as delegate to carry out this change of policy. But since each national synod was attended by a commissioner of the king, when Amyraut arrived at Monceau, where the king was holding forth, he learned that the king knew of the plans and had already decided that nothing would be changed. Amyraut nevertheless insisted that he be admitted before the king, and that he be allowed to stand while addressing him even as the Roman Catholic churchmen were. The king did not relent. For fifteen days

19. Laplanche, *L'Oeuvre d'Amyraut*, p. 60.

Amyraut respectfully submitted his request. Finally Cardinal Richelieu, hearing of the spirit of this minister, decided to see him and talk him out of his design. Amyraut forcefully countered each of Richelieu's arguments and was finally granted his audience with the king in the manner he had requested. Bayle, whose account we follow here, mentions both that Amyraut's address before the king was immediately printed in the *Mercure français* and that by his moderate yet firm position Amyraut won the lasting admiration of Cardinal Richelieu.[20]

Amyraut was probably responsible, at least in part, for another interesting measure taken by the 1631 Charenton synod. This had to do with the relationship of the Reformed to those of the Lutheran communion. We have mentioned that Amyraut was an advocate of union with the Lutherans, and we shall see later in this chapter that he wrote two substantial treatises on the subject. At this synod the record reads that action was taken that the "Faithful of the Augustane Confession . . . may be, without abjuration at all made by them, admitted unto the Lord's table with us" and, moreover, "as Sureties may present children unto Baptism."[21] David Blondel in his *Actes authentiques* adds that marriage between members of the two communions was also permitted.[22] Exactly what part Amyraut played in this cannot be determined, but we know that his good friend Blondel wrote the article[23] and that he himself was in full accord with such sentiments.

Again, 1631 was the year of Amyraut's first major publication. This work, entitled *Traitté des religions contre ceux qui les estiment toutes indifferentes*,[24] was an apology of the Christian

20. *Dictionnaire, s.v.* Amyraut.

21. Quick, *Synodicon*, 2:297. See also Aymon, *Tous les synodes*, 2:500–501, and Stauffer, *Un Précurseur français de l'oecuménisme*, pp. 14–16.

22. *Actes authentiques des eglises reformées de France, Germanie, Grande-Bretaigne, Pologne, Hongrie, Pais-Bas, etc. touchant la paix et charité fraternelle que tous les serviteurs de Dieu doiuent sainctement entretenir avec les protestants qui ont quelque diversité, soit d'espression, soit de méthode, soit mesme de sentiment . . .* , (Amsterdam, 1655), p. 8.

23. Blondel himself says he wrote the "decret" (*ibid.*, p. 9).

24. Published at Saumur. There was a second edition somewhat enlarged (Saumur, 1652) and an English translation of this second edition entitled *A treatise concerning religions, in refutation of the opinion which accounts all indifferent* (London, 1660).

religion against the doctrine of indifferentism. It also seemingly was an apology for the Reformed faith against the philosophical position of the Roman Church in the Protestant-Catholic controversy. Richard H. Popkin, in a recent penetrating study, has shown that Catholic apologists rapidly adopted a "new Pyrrhonism" in their intellectual battle with the French Protestants, a technique devoted to "destroying all human claims to rationality through scepticism."[25] This scepticism, which issued in a radical fideism, was propounded in Montaigne's *Essais,* in Father Pierre Charron's *Les Trois Véritez* and *La Sagesse,* in François Veron's many writings—perhaps chiefly his *Méthodes de traiter des controverses de religion*—and even in some of the formidable du Perron's writings. It was employed with great success, especially by Veron in his many conferences with Protestant leaders, since it was applied indiscriminately to Protestant positions, engulfing them in sceptical difficulties.

Such is the background against which this first writing of Amyraut's must be portrayed. There is no room here to subject it to critical analysis. Nevertheless it is clearly, from this, a quite remarkable defense of the integrity of man's rational faculties even in matters of religion inasmuch as God has accommodated himself to man in His revelation. It reveals more than any of Amyraut's writing the latent rationalism of his thought.

It was to be expected that in 1631 or 1632 Amyraut would have sustained the examination that would formally mark his installation as professor at Saumur. This was not accomplished however until 1633, probably because of a serious illness which he contracted sometime during this period. We know that on August 1, 1632, he recommended his children to God's care and to that of their mother, thinking he was soon to die (*"au lit de la mort"*).[26] It is perhaps appropriate to note here that Amyraut apparently suffered from chronic ill health, there being frequent mention of his infirmities in his writings and letters.[27]

25. *The History of Scepticism from Erasmus to Descartes* (Assen, 1960), p. 67. See also Popkin's useful article "Skepticism and the Counter-Reformation in France," *ARG* 51 (1960), 58–86.

26. According to a document printed in the *Bulletin* 11 (1862), 7. See also Laplanche, *L'Oeuvre d'Amyraut,* p. 77n31.

27. See Laplanche, *L'Oeuvre d'Amyraut,* p. 61.

In 1633, then, Amyraut, along with Cappel and Placeus, sustained his examination and delivered the *thèse inaugurale* which marked his official installation in the chair of theology at Saumur. His inaugural address was delivered June 14 and was entitled *Theses theologicae de sacerdotio Christi.*[28] In spite of his own evaluation of this address,[29] it immediately received high praise. In his theses Amyraut laid the foundation for a strongly christocentric theology. He went so far as to say that while we can call the whole of the revelation of the Bible Christian, this nomenclature is more properly used when it refers to the revelation of Christ himself.[30]

In 1634 Amyraut innocently precipitated what was to become, in Bayle's words, "a kind of civil war among the Protestant theologians of France."[31] That is, in this year he published his *Brief Traitté de la predestination et de ses principales dependances*[32] which initiated the controversy over universal grace. From this time on the story of his life is pretty much the story of this controversy.

According to Bayle's account Amyraut wrote the *Brief Traitté* for a very special purpose. The circumstances which occasioned it serve to reveal the character of Amyraut as well as to instruct us concerning the somewhat extraordinary character of its teach-

28. Published the same year at Saumur. They are also to be found as the second entry in the famous *Theses Salmurienses* (Saumur, 1641, 1653, 1664, 1665; Geneva, 1665).

29. In a letter to André Rivet dated June 1 Amyraut says he is sending him the inaugural theses of all these men even though "elles ne le méritent pas, en ce qui y est du mien. Car, outre mes autres défauts, les longues et continuelles infirmités desquelles Dieu me visite, m'empêchent de suppléer par ma diligence ce qui manque d'ailleurs" (as quoted in Laplanche, *L'Oeuvre d'Amyraut*, p. 78n34).

30. "Doctrine coelestis in Verbo Dei revelata, est illa quidem tota & appellari potest Christiana. . . . Eam tamen nomenclaturam doctrina quae propriè de ipso Christo est suo quodam jure sibi vindicare videtur" (thesis 1, p. 1 of the 1633 ed.). This remarkable thesis also speaks to Amyraut's doctrine of Scripture, for while he would probably have agreed that Christ is the focal teaching in Scripture he also clearly implies that there is much which does not refer to Christ and is therefore not properly "Christian." It is interesting, also, that almost all the thesis' documentation from Scripture is from the book of Hebrews, the book which remained his favorite throughout life and the source of texts for the largest corpus of his sermons.

31. *Dictionnaire, s.v.* Amyraut.

32. Saumur, 1634; with some revision, Saumur, 1658.

ing. Amyraut, who all his life maintained excellent relations with the ecclesiastics of the Roman communion, had been invited to dine with the Bishop of Chartres, abbot of Bourgueil, along with a gentleman of some rank *("un homme de qualité")*.[33] This gentleman was, according to Amyraut himself, "filled with horror by the doctrine of predestination as taught in our churches," and regarded it as "contrary to the nature of God and His gospel to say that He created the greatest part of mankind with the express purpose of damning them."[34] Amyraut was able, apparently, to remove these misgivings by his explanation of the matter. So, Amyraut says, "those to whom it was particularly beneficial that he remain in our communion, and fearing that the sinister impression given him by some preachers in the Roman communion concerning our belief at this point would scandalize him, implored me insistently that I remedy the situation by writing a clarifying treatise on the matter."[35]

These considerations make more understandable the following passage in Amyraut's *Brief Traitté:*

> The reasons which prompted me a while ago to write this short treatise on predestination made it expedient that it be very brief and did not allow me to write in another manner nor in another language than French. And so one should not look here for profound speculations such as is the nature of those produced in the schools when such and like matters are treated. My intention has been only to extricate this doctrine, which is so often judged difficult and thorny, from the subtlety of controversy, where more often than not the heat of controversy alters the spirit, and the prejudices of the disputants hinder the functions of the intellect from furthering the practice of piety or from contributing to the edification and consolation of the conscience. And I have not touched upon some matters commonly disputed except insofar as my faulty judgment hindered my design.[36]

33. According to Bayle a "catholique romaine de qualité" (*Dictionnaire, s.v.* Amyraut). However, Amyraut says that this individual had "nouvellement venu en nostre profession" (preface to *Six Sermons* [Saumur, 1636]).

34. Preface to *Six Sermons,* [pp. i–ii].

35. *Ibid.,* [p. ii]. Bayle reports that the gentleman himself, being greatly impressed by Amyraut's explanation of these matters, requested that he publish a book in which his clarifications would be set forth (*Dictionnaire, s.v.* Amyraut).

36. "Epistre au lecteur," *Brief Traitté,* 1634 ed., [p. i]. This prefatory epistle was not reprinted in the 1658 edition.

It seems quite likely that the "subtlety of controversy" which Amyraut here mentions refers most particularly to the supralapsarian-infralapsarian debate within Reformed scholasticism and the related disagreement over the order of the decrees. Moreover, it is not unlikely that the revulsion of the gentleman mentioned as the occasion for this treatise was indeed shared by Amyraut himself. Amyraut was most assuredly opposed to any scheme which seemed to teach that God created in order to have an object for his wrath. Perhaps one of the most significant of his remarks in his account of the composition of the *Brief Traitté* is a notation that he "judged that the best method of explaining this doctrine would be to represent it in a manner which, without doing violence to the justice of God or to His liberty, would render His mercy superlatively commendable (*souverainement recommandable*)."[37]

It is not our purpose here to give an analysis of the *Brief Traitté,* a task which has been done and done well by Schweizer, Geiger, Nicole, and Laplanche. It should be noted, however, that its most debated teaching was the affirmation that God sent his Son into the world to redeem all men provided that they believe. That is, as we have seen in Cameron, there is an antecedent will of God which extends salvation to all men but which becomes effective only as it is appropriated by faith.

The *Brief Traitté* did precipitate a "civil war" within Reformed Protestantism. Stiff opposition to its teachings developed outside of France in Geneva, Bern, Leyden, Groningen, Franecker, and Sedan, and within France was especially strong in the provinces which bordered on the Low Countries and in the provinces of Poitou, Saintonge and Bas-Languedoc. In an attempt to appease the growing opposition Amyraut published *Six Sermons de la nature, estendue, necessité, dispensation, et efficace de l'evangile.*[38] These are very important as an exposé

37. Preface to *Six Sermons,* [p. iii].

38. Saumur, 1636. Though the title page gives the date 1636, they may have been published late in 1635. Already by February 8, 1636, the Parisian pastor Michel le Faucheur had written to Theodore Tronchin at Geneva, "Je croy que vous avez veu [leu?] les Sermons de Mons. Amyraut, & les esclaircissements qu'il donne sur quelques expressions nouvelles & fascheuses qui se trouvent en son livre de la Predestinaôn . . ." (Archives Tronchin, 27:183. MS). The time span

of the basic positions of Amyraldianism. In actuality they are six short, systematic, theological treatises designed as an explanation and defense of his teachings in the *Brief Traitté*. To these sermons Amyraut prefaced a 75-page *Eschantillon de la doctrine de Calvin* wherein he sought to show that his doctrine was a faithful reproduction of Calvin's theology. These two pieces, however, failed to satisfy the orthodox. Rather, they increased the already considerable feeling of misgiving, and so the "civil war" erupted in earnest.

One may be fairly sure that the main source of this opposition was the intractable Pierre du Moulin. Du Moulin was one of the most learned men of his age in Reformed Protestantism, probably more capable than Amyraut. And though his learning was encyclopedic he was, as Rex notes, "nothing if not traditionalist."[39] He was in fact a great devotee of the restored Aristotelianism and began his career as professor of philosophy at Leyden. His first published work was entitled *Elementa logicae*,[40] and was simply a condensation of Aristotle's *Organon*.[41] Although there was nothing of significance upon which du Moulin did not write, this was his most successful work; he himself noted in his autobiography that it had been printed thirteen times.[42] His Aristotelianism, added to his traditionalist orientation, makes him a premier example of the Protestant scholasticism of this century. And perhaps more than anything else he should be remembered for his relentless efforts to root out any hint of heresy within the Reformed tradition. He was moderator of the synod of Alais of 1620 and was largely responsible for both its action making the Dort Canons binding on

---

is not so great that it would rule out an early 1636 publication date, but since it is about a three-week trip from Saumur to Geneva and since le Faucheur knew they had arrived in Geneva by some means it seems likely they were published sometime in December, 1635.

39. *Essays on Pierre Bayle*, p. 20.

40. Leyden, 1596. There are French and English translations of this work.

41. E.g., a comparison of Aristotle's 4th chapter (Categoriae) with the 3rd chapter of du Moulin's treatise ("Denombrement des dix Categories") shows that du Moulin not only slavishly repeated the Aristotelian categories but also repeated the very examples Aristotle had used to illustrate them.

42. As cited in Haag-Bordier, *La France protestante*, 5:808.

the French churches and for the strict subscription clause relative to those Canons. Indeed, according to O. Douen, he was accused by the *modérateur adjoint,* Laurent Brunier, of usurping *"une autorité papale"* in order to assure the adoption of the Dort Canons.[43]

Du Moulin was, moreover, contentious and often uncharitable in his attempts to ensure the strict orthodoxy of the Reformed Church. He had, for instance, written and submitted for publication his *Anatome Arminianismi,* which congratulated the Dort deputies on their condemnation of the Arminian *"heretiques, sectaires, monstres, hardis blasphémateurs,"* and *"insolents coquins,"* before the Dort synod began![44] And not a little of this contentious and rude spirit is evident in the Amyraut controversy.

By late 1635 or early 1636 du Moulin was circulating in manuscript his *Examen de la doctrine de MM. Amyrault & Testard.*[45] It was evidently composed sometime after the publication of the *Six Sermons* of Amyraut, for many of its comments refer to these, and was a violent attack on Amyraut and the less able P. Testard (1599–1650), pastor at Blois. Testard, too, had been a student of Cameron at Saumur. In 1633 he had published his *Eirenikon, seu Synopsis doctrinae de natura et gratia,* a work with some rather damaging passages on natural theology. Du Moulin accused both of these men of Arminianism and in an incendiary preface cleverly compared the way Arminianism arose in the Netherlands with the situation then in France.

Extremely interesting and significant is the fact that du Moulin's first two chapters have to do with "the order of the decrees on predestination held in the Reformed Churches" and "how the Arminians have reversed this order." He shows clearly that he understands the Reformed teaching to be infralapsarian,

43. *La Révocation de l'édit de Nantes à Paris,* 1:275.

44. See Haag-Bordier, *La France protestante,* 5:814. This treatise of du Moulin was printed at Leyden in 1619. It was immediately translated into English under the title *The Anatomy of Arminianism* (London, 1620).

45. Amsterdam, 1637. Du Moulin had hoped to print this *Examen,* but left the matter up to the Alençon synod. The synod apparently judged that it ought not be printed for it was not, until pirated by the Arminian, de Courcelles. Laplanche has an especially good analysis of this work in *L'Oeuvre d'Amyraut,* pp. 118–27.

since the proper order of decrees, he says, is: (1) God has determined to elect some from the corrupt mass of mankind; (2) God has determined to send his Son to ransom those whom he has elected; and (3) God has determined to give faith to his elect. The Arminians, however, reverse this order and hold the following: God has determined (1) to send his Son in order to save all mankind; (2) that whoever believes will be saved; (3) that He would give to all men sufficient grace so that they might believe; and (4) that He will elect those he foresees will have faith.[46] After setting forth these two conceptions of the order of the decrees, du Moulin makes explicit what one would expect from his placing his discussion of the decrees first in his book, namely, that "This order of the decrees is the foundation upon which the whole of Arminianism rests and all of their errors result from it."[47]

Du Moulin then lists the three principal errors of Arminianism which result from their faulty conception of the order of the decrees. Since almost all of the subsequent discussion in his *Examen* is concerned with refuting Amyraut and Testard in terms of these three "errors" we shall quote du Moulin's account at this juncture:

> From the first decree which supposes that God has an earnest desire to save all men, and that He has an equal love towards all men since all are equally His creatures, it necessarily follows that God has been frustrated in His intention, that His purpose has not come to fruition . . . From this it also follows that Jesus Christ died equally for all men, as much for Judas as for Saint Peter . . . And from the third decree, by which God has determined to give all men sufficient grace to believe, it necessarily follows that those to whom the Gospel is not preached have a sufficient grace, and that there is opened a way to salvation without knowing Jesus Christ nor His death.[48]

To these three points du Moulin returns again and again in the ensuing discussion which he divides into seven "*controverses*":

46. *Examen de la doctrine de MM. Amyrault & Testard,* pp. 1–3.

47. *Ibid.,* p. 3. See also the conclusion (pp. 96–97) where he again says that all of the theology of Amyraut and Testard is related to their novel ordering of the decrees.

48. *Ibid.,* p. 3.

(1) Concerning the conditional decrees of God; (2) Concerning the general and conditional election of all men; (3) Concerning the nature of God and the immutability of His counsels, and concerning His justice, goodness and freedom; (4) Concerning the death of Christ and its efficacy; (5) Concerning salvation without knowing Christ; (6) Concerning the universal grace that God gives to all men in order that they might come to salvation, and concerning the natural ability (*forces naturelles*) of man and his inability (*impuissance*); and (7) Concerning Calvin and his authority. Of these seven *controverses* only the second parts of numbers 3 and 6, and number 7, are not comprehended under the three "errors" quoted above.

Du Moulin's basic complaint regarding Amyraut's treatment of God's justice, goodness, and freedom is that, rather than resolving any difficulties, it in fact creates more. Du Moulin feels that for one to say God sent his Son to die for all men upon condition of faith, which condition is impossible for man, is to represent God more unworthily than by saying He sent Christ only for the elect. It does seem, however, that du Moulin is especially concerned with Amyraut's deemphasis of God's justice, with Amyraut's position "that God in the work of redemption has declared his mercy properly and by itself, but his justice only by accident."[49] This is, I believe, a basic point of differentiation between Amyraut and the orthodox and one which deserves detailed investigation.

Du Moulin's point in controversy number 6 is that the distinction between moral and natural ability is a novel doctrine in Reformed theology and, since it serves no useful function nor has any basis in fact, ought to be rejected. His controversy in number 7 is especially interesting. He notes that Amyraut is the first in the Reformed communion to quote Calvin *"en ses prédications"*[50] and so "to degrade the truth of the evangelical

49. *Ibid.*, p. 47. "Dieu en l'oeuvre de la redemption a declaré sa misericorde par soy mesme, mais sa justice seulement par accident."

50. In this du Moulin may be in error, for there was at the turn of the century a great deal of citation from the pulpit of authorities other than the Bible. See Quick, *Synodicon,* 1:228 (ch. 3, no. 4 of the Synod of Gap) where explicit mention is made of the reading of the Fathers and the glosses of the schoolmen. It is clear that du Moulin is right, however, in that the citations from any source other than the Bible were forbidden at that time.

pulpit."[51] His objection is that by so doing Amyraut renders credence to the Catholics' claim that the Reformed are "Calvinists." But in a striking passage du Moulin perhaps reveals that this prudential consideration is not his primary worry after all. For he asks, If Amyraut is permitted to use Calvin in the pulpit, "why not also Martyr, Zanchius, or Beza, who have not been inferior to Calvin in their teaching?"[52] Does this not, we may well ask, reveal a prime difference between Amyraut and the orthodox? Does it not clearly point to the affinity of the orthodox with these more scholastic divines, whereas Amyraut's affinity is in fact with Calvin himself? In any case, it cannot be mere coincidence that du Moulin mentions the three early reformers who most evidently inclined toward the budding Protestant scholasticism.

Another treatise controverting the teachings of Testard and Amyraut was written in 1636, this one by André Rivet of Leyden.[53] Rivet was the brother-in-law of du Moulin, and it is probable that he was urged to write by du Moulin. He had been a friend and frequent correspondent of Amyraut, and the latter was deeply hurt by this attack designed to bring about his condemnation at the next national synod. The tone of Rivet's work is much less hostile than that of du Moulin. One is also impressed by Rivet's sensitivity to the most important issues in Amyraut's *Brief Traitté*. Whereas du Moulin's attack is broad and scattered and often based on a misunderstanding of what Amyraut wrote, Rivet's attack is precise and discerning of what appear to be the vulnerable points of Amyraut's position. In brief, Rivet considers Amyraut orthodox on most points but thinks he has expressed himself exceedingly poorly;[54] he does, however, question Amyraut's interpretation of Calvin (chs. 3–4) and is quite distressed over Amyraut's explanation of the operation of grace in conversion (chs. 6–7). An almost identical complaint had been lodged against Cameron by Rivet and his col-

51. *Examen de la doctrine de MM. Amyrault & Testard*, p. 99.
52. *Ibid.*
53. *Andreae Riveti . . . synopsis doctrinae de natura et gratia.* Not published until 1648, but circulated in manuscript in France from 1636. It was also sent by Rivet to the national synod of Alençon in 1637.
54. E.g., on the matter of the order of the decrees (chs. 1 and 2) and on the idea of salvation without the knowledge of Christ (ch. 5).

leagues in 1620. It is perhaps indicative of Rivet's perspicacity that he conceived one of the greatest dangers of Amyraldianism to be in its explanation of conversion, the point at which some followers of Amyraut did in fact compromise Calvinist theology.

Despite the stinging attack by du Moulin described above, Amyraut's next publication was a letter written in late 1636 to one Théophile Brachet de la Milletière, in defense of du Moulin.[55] From this letter we learn that de la Milletière had charged du Moulin with trying to split the Reformed Church by attacking Amyraut and Cameron. Amyraut shows that he still cannot believe that du Moulin is really opposed to him, and reproves de la Milletière for trying to aggravate the difference between the two of them.[56] The letter is very interesting, then, inasmuch as it points up Amyraut's conciliatory spirit as well as the tendency of the Reformed to close ranks quickly if they envision their differences to be weakening their position *vis-à-vis* the Roman Church.

THE HERESY TRIAL AT ALENÇON

In 1637 Amyraut's first and most serious heresy trial took place, this at the national synod of Alençon, May 27–July 9. It is quite plain that there was a great deal of elaborate planning leading up to this synod. The orthodox had organized their forces and were well ready to present an overwhelming case against Amyraut. The Amyraldian teachings had been condemned at various provincial synods preliminary to the national synod.[57] The writings of du Moulin and Rivet mentioned above

---

55. *Lettre de Monsieur Amyraut, a Monsieur de la Milletière. Sur son escrit contre Monsieur du-Moulin* (Saumur, 1637). Signed Dec. 26, 1636.

56. However, Amyraut's purpose is not wholly the defense of du Moulin, for the last half of the letter (pp. 31–62) is an attempt to rescue Cameron from la Milletière's representation. He says: "Mais ce que m'a autant qu'aucune chose estonné, attristé, & puis qu'il faut que je vous le die, offensé, est cette injurieuse defense du nom de Monsieur Cameron, en laquelle, soubs ombre de loüange, vous l'accusés d'ignorance, eventés les plaintes que vous dites qu'il vous a faites à l'oreille, de ce que ses collegues au ministere ne luy donnoyent pas assés de liberté: & prononcés hardiment qu'il a eu le mesme dessein que vous avés, & qu'il n'a esté empesché d'y mettre la main que par la crainte des censures qui ne luy eussent pas manqué de la part des Ministres" (pp. 31–32).

57. See du Moulin's letter to the Synod (Quick, *Synodicon*, 2:411).

were sent to the synod. Apparently two other violent treatises were also sent, though anonymously.[58] Letters were presented to the synod from Geneva,[59] the Dutch academies,[60] Rivet,[61] and du Moulin.[62] All of these are quite moderate in tone, except for du Moulin's, which expressed the belief that a simple restriction placed upon these men would not be enough; that they should be condemned.[63] Moreover, the moderator chosen was Basnage, a strict orthodox. Indeed, he, breaking precedent, preached at the opening of the synod.[64]

58. In Quick, *Synodicon*, 2:361, we learn that Amyraut requested that the author of these two books, the *Antidote* and *Les Ombres d'Arminius*, be required to explain his actions before the synod. I have not found a trace of either treatise.

59. In Quick, *Synodicon*, 2:397–404, and Aymon, *Tous les synodes*, 2:604–14. This long letter is signed by Diodati, Tronchin, Chabrai, Prevot, and Pauleint, and dated April 26, 1637. Its moderate tone shows that the letters written by Daillé, Mestrezat, and the other Parisian pastors to Geneva defending Amyraut and the orthodoxy of his doctrine had not been in vain. For instance, in Quick's version: ". . . we were somewhat comforted in our Spirits, by the Advice given us, That these upstarted Opinions were not at so great a distance from the Truth as was first reported, . . ." (2:401).

60. These included Leyden, Franeker, and Groningen. The letters were appended to Rivet's *Synopsis doctrinae de natura et gratia* as letters of approbation. The Leyden letter was signed by Polyander, Wallaeus, Thysius, and Triglandus; the Franeker letter by Bogerman, Schotanus, and Maccovius; the Groningen letter by Alting and Gomarus. The Leyden letter is available in Quick, *Synodicon*, 2:405, Aymon, *Tous les synodes*, 2:614, and Rivet's *Opera*, III.851,2; the Franeker letter in Quick, 2:406–7 and Rivet's *Opera*, III.851,2; the Groningen letter in Quick, 2:407–8, and Rivet's *Opera*, III.852,1–2.

61. Found only in Rivet's *Opera*, III.871,1–873,1.

62. In Quick, 2:408–11, and Aymon, 2:615–19. It is basically a defense of his *Examen* and of the motives which inspired its composition. Du Moulin complains that the accusations being passed around that he is contentious are simply not true: "I went about this Work with a great deal of Grief, having nothing that lay heavier upon my heart, or was more contrary to my Temper, than to contend with my Brethren in the Work of the Lord; . . ." But, he says, "I saw the Evil to be so great, and its consequences so dangerous, that I counted my self bound in Conscience to defend the Cause of God, and to endeavour to discover the very bottom of the Imposture, and the hidden Nature of it" (Quick, 2:409).

63. He says: "For if you should content yourselves with a meer allaying of these Controversies, and an Imposal of Silence on both Parties, you will leave the Spirits of Men in suspence, and put Error in the same Rank and Degree of Reputation with Truth; and Foreign Churches and Universities, who have been concerned for these new Notions, and will take your Silence, not for a condemnation of Them, but of the Truth" (Quick, 2:411).

64. See the important document, "Journal sommaire de ce qui s'est passé au

This sermon was most certainly in bad taste. The text chosen was II Corinthians 11:3: "I am afraid that as the serpent deceived Eve by his cunning, your thoughts will similarly be corrupted to some degree, being turned from the simplicity which is in Christ." And, as the writer of the *Journal sommaire* notes, "he spoke in such a way that even though he did not use Testard's and Amyraut's names, not only all the members of the synod but even most of the townsfolk (*ceux du lieu*) understood easily that it was to these two he was referring and that against them all these things were said." Later, when Amyraut accused Basnage of bad faith and of trying to prejudice the synod's thinking, Basnage denied that he had composed the sermon with Amyraut and Testard in mind. However it is quite clear that the judgment of the writer of the *Journal sommaire* is correct. Perhaps the most positive evidence of this is the use Basnage made of the idea that those who would try to introduce new dogmas would say that they were simply following new *méthodes,* precisely the argument being used by the Amyraldians.[65]

On the other hand, the supporters of Amyraut and Testard were not idle either. Michel le Faucheur sent a letter to the synod on behalf of the Charenton pastors, a brilliant defense of Amyraut and plea for moderation. Laplanche judges this letter to be "perhaps the most remarkable piece of the whole history of

synode national d'Alençon commencé le jeudy 28 may 1637, sur l'affaire de MM. Testard et Amyraut, recueilli chacun jour, par P.D.L.S.D.S.," *Bulletin* 13 (1868), 42.

65. *Ibid.,* p. 43. Mestrezat had written to du Moulin on February 8 of this year that "ces differens ne sont que de methodes & façons de parler" (Archives Tronchin, 38:59. Copy). The "Résultat d'une synode provincial de l'Ile-de-France tenu a Charenton touchant le différend de MM. du Moulin et Amyraut, etc." after expressing its opinion on the controverted doctrines, stated: "Ensuite de cecy, le synode jugeant que le différend n'estoit pas de la substance de la doctrine, mais de la méthode et tradition et des expressions, ou de choses peu importantes, et suivant l'exemple de prudence et de charité du synode de Dordrecht, . . ." etc. (*Bulletin* 7 [1858], 410). Or again, following this provincial synod, Daillé wrote to Theodore Tronchin at Geneva as follows: "Vous scauvez par autre voie ce qui s'est passé en nre Synode sur l'affaire de M. Amyraut; Toute la Compagnie a unanimement esté d'advis que cette ne regarde que la methode, les expressions, & la traditive, & quelques choses legeres, & non le fonds de la doctrine salutaire . . ." (March 31, Archives Tronchin, 8:193. MS in Daillé's hand).

the quarrel over predestination.''[66] Moreover, the co-minister of Testard at Blois, Vignier, also addressed a letter to the synod, along with an apologetic treatise on Testard's teaching. Nevertheless, there can be but little doubt that the Amyraldians had none of the organization exhibited by the orthodox, and it is remarkable indeed that the orthodox did not succeed in their design.

It is of more than passing interest to note the teachings of Amyraut singled out for discussion at the synod. According to the account of the *Journal sommaire* there were four main teachings discussed at length. These were, respectively, (1) the order of the decrees, June 17; (2) the sending of Jesus Christ for all universally and Amyraut's doctrine of the conditional decrees, June 18–19; (3) the universality and sufficiency of the grace presented to all, June 22; and, (4) original sin and moral and natural ability, also June 22. These were the principal "errors" attacked by du Moulin and in the same order, so one may be fairly sure the discussion followed du Moulin's *Examen*. Before describing briefly Amyraut's defense at these various points, perhaps it is worthwhile to notice the somewhat peculiar division of points 2 and 3. Both refer to the universality of the atonement, the first having to do, apparently, with God's intent in sending Christ; the second with the actual universality and sufficiency of Christ's work. This order suggests that the synod agreed Christ was sent for all. Therefore an extra session had to be devoted to a consideration of how this might be maintained, since all men in fact are not saved.

---

66. *L'Oeuvre d'Amyraut,* p. 153. The letter is printed in the collection *Lettres de Messieurs Le Faucheur et Mestrezat, escrites sur les diverses methodes qu'employent les orthodoxes pour expliquer le mystere de la predestination & le dispensation de la grace; avec les actes dressez sur ce sujet dans les synodes nationaux d'Alençon, tenu l'an 1637, & de Charenton, l'an 1644* (n.p., n.d.). It is interesting to note just how Le Faucheur defends Amyraut's orthodoxy: ". . . ayant trouve par la lecture des escrits de nosdits freres les sieurs Amyraut & Testard, qu'ils enseignent sur tous les poincts controversez en cette matiere, côme sont ceux de l'Eslection gratuite de Dieu, de l'efficace de sa grace en la conversion des Esleus, de la certitude de la foy, & de la preservance des Saincts, le mesme chose qui est enseignée en toutes nos Eglises, & qu'en ces choses ils soustiennent fort puissamment la saine doctrine, tant contre les Arminiens, que contre ceux de l'Eglise Romaine" (p. 24).

After these rather lengthy discussions, a committee of seven was designated to sift through the material and report back to the full assembly with suggestions. De l'Angle, minister of Rouen and nephew of du Moulin, served as chairman of this committee.[67] He reported that there was basic agreement regarding the committee's judgment of the disputed teachings but admitted that there was some *"dissentiment"* over the "proper ways and means by which we would oblige these men to express themselves as we do, and over the terms that we would use to frame the articles."[68] After this report was read Amyraut and Testard were asked to explain their teaching on the points previously debated at length.

It is a curious fact that the acts of the synod, as they appear in either Quick or Aymon, do not record any *sui generis* response of Amyraut and Testard upon the question of the order of the decrees. Nor is there any indication in either of these accounts of why this should be so. Perhaps the silence is in itself indicative of the judgment of the synod. Was it perhaps agreed upon that the academic nature of this question—since all agreed one cannot use time-sequence concepts as a measure of the actions of the Infinite—ruled it out as a measuring stick for one's orthodoxy?

On the question of universal grace quite the reverse is true. Here we have an extended account of the defense of these two men. They had recourse to the formula we saw Cameron using, namely, "That Jesus Christ died for all Men sufficiently, but for the Elect only effectually."[69] Therefore "his Intention was to die for all Men in respect of the Sufficiency of his Satisfaction,

---

67. At least so de l'Angle reports in a letter to A. Rivet: "Le synode prit resolution de nommer sept Deputéz pour examiner leurs Doctrines, & adviser aux moyens d'empescher le trouble dans nos Eglises. Je fus l'un des sept, avec Mons. Daillé, & eus l'honneur de presider en cette petite assemblée" (letter dated July 5, 1637, Rivet's *Opera,* 3:828).

68. *Ibid.* This account, like all others that we have of this affair, is quite colored by the prejudice of the writer. Certainly we know that Daillé would not have been in accord with the judgment of "heterodoxy" that de l'Angle mentions. Nor can it be supposed that de l'Angle is accurate in representing the judgment of the committee as such, for there is no sign of that idea in the report made to the full synod.

69. Quick, *Synodicon,* 2:354. Cf. Aymon, *Tous les synodes,* 2:572-73.

but for the Elect only in respect of its quickning and Saving Virtue and Efficacy."[70] Then the account goes on to note that this distinction was insisted upon precisely because it was thought that to say Christ did not die for all would be to say that God planned to exclude the reprobate and these would then not be without excuse:

> So that those who are called by the Preaching of the Gospel to participate by Faith in the Effects and Fruits of his Death, being invited seriously, and God vouchsafing them all external Means needful for their coming to him, and showing them in good earnest, and with the greatest Sincerity by his Word, what would be well-pleasing to him, if they should not believe in the Lord Jesus Christ, but perish in their Obstinacy and Unbelief; this cometh not from any Defect of Virtue or Sufficiency in the Sacrifice of Jesus Christ, nor yet for want of Summons or serious Invitations unto Faith or Repentance, but only from their own Fault.[71]

The record tells us that the assembly was "well satisfied" with this explanation; "nevertheless they decreed, that for the future, that Phrase of Jesus Christ's dying *equally* for all, should be forborn, because that term *equally* was formerly, and might be so again, an Occasion of stumbling unto many."[72]

As to the question of the conditional decrees, Laplanche has properly noted that "as the pastors of Charenton had seen for a long time, the quarrel at this point had to do above all with the vocabulary used."[73] So Amyraut and Testard explained that by this terminology they understood and meant nothing more than the will of God as revealed in his Word. That is, the will which gives life to whoever would believe. They explained that the term "conditional" was used only as an anthropomorphism. Amyraut further averred that he never used the phrase "universal or conditional predestination" otherwise "than by way of Concession, and accommodating it unto the language of the adversary."[74] He agreed that if there were objections to the

70. *Ibid.*
71. Quick, *Synodicon*, 2:354. Cf. Aymon, *Tous les synodes*, 2:572–73.
72. *Ibid.* The 1658 edition of the *Brief Traitté* does, in fact, drop most of such terminology.
73. *L'Oeuvre d'Amyraut*, p. 160.
74. Quick, 2:355. Cf. Aymon, 2:574.

phrase "universal or conditional predestination" he would not use it in the future. Moreover, Testard and Amyraut at this juncture also made indirect reference to the idea of the order of decrees when they agreed that the will of God was but one eternal act. And they agreed not to speak of God as having "vehement Desires of things which he hath not."[75]

Both Quick and Aymon record the response of Amyraut at this point to a discussion of the problem of "natural theology"— that is, the possibility of salvation apart from Christ. This discussion, not readily apparent from the account in the *Journal sommaire,* was evidently part of the discussion of original sin. Laplanche thinks it the *"plus délicat"* point of all,[76] but we find no evidence of this. It is true that du Moulin had charged Amyraut with teaching a doctrine of salvation without knowing Christ, but even André Rivet did not believe this to be true.[77] However there is a short explanation recorded on this point, both Amyraut and Testard agreeing that because of man's natural blindness it was impossible for him to be converted in this way. After this Amyraut was asked to explain his use of the term "faith" in the sense of a knowledge of God obtained through a contemplation of his works. This was a much more serious charge and one which had some basis. Amyraut admitted that Paul had simply called this the knowledge of God. He was instructed to rectify his misuse of theological language at this point.

After these two questions relating to natural theology Amyraut and Testard had to answer for their distinction between natural and moral ability. That is, they were required to explain their teaching that man has the natural ability so that he *can* respond to the offer of grace but that he *will* not inasmuch as he is morally corrupt. In answering they conceded that it would be possible to call this inability natural, since it is in us from birth, but that it would perhaps be more precise at times to call

75. *Ibid.* At this point, at least, Amyraut did not adhere very faithfully to these restrictions, for he later affirmed in the strongest terms God's desire that all be saved.

76. *L'Oeuvre d'Amyraut,* p. 161.

77. See his 4th chapter in *Synopsis doctrinae Mosis Amyraldi* (Rivet, *Opera,* III.842,1,2). Alexander Schweizer says of this charge, "Hier ist Amyraut unstreitig nicht recht verstanden" (*Die Protestantischen Centraldogmen,* 2:323).

it "moral," since man is willful and obdurate in his sinful state. The synod approved this explanation.

This was apparently the final explanation required of the two men. They were at last judged to be orthodox and "honourably dismissed to the Exercise of their respective Charges."[78] In order to keep them in check and to assure that such quarrels would not again spring up, certain regulations were passed. Pastors and professors were forbidden upon "Pain of all church-censures, yea, and of Deposal from their ministry"[79] to descant on, in the pulpit or by writing, *les questions curieuses* which could cause scandal. Moreover, they were not to use new expressions which could be interpreted in a bad sense, nor dispute upon such questions, nor propose new matters in their *scolastique*.[80] And finally, it was resolved that the previous ruling that all writings must be submitted to provincial readers before publication was to be strictly observed, and that every six months the theses to be maintained at the academies must be sent to provincial examiners.

The accounts of Quick and Aymon read as though this all went smoothly. From the account of the *Journal sommaire*, however, we may conclude that these specific regulations were not so calmly received. The *Journal sommaire* mentions that Amyraut objected to the illustrations of the *"questions curieuses,"* namely the phrase which read "As is this concerning the nature of the blessedness proposed by the legal covenant considered precisely, and of the sufficiency of Providence to lead men to repentance and salvation."[81] At this point Amyraut's objection was entertained and the phrase was removed from the regulations. It is mentioned, however, that even with this removed Amyraut acquiesced and made the promise required only with *"mescontentement"* at seeing himself so strongly pressed (*fort pressé*), both with regard to the words "upon pain of deposition" and because no allowance was made in case a foreigner should write against him on these matters.[82]

78. Quick, 2:357. Cf. Aymon, 2:576.
79. *Ibid.*
80. Aymon, 2:567. Cf. Quick, 2:349–50.
81. "Journal sommaire . . . ,"*Bulletin* 13 (1868), 60–61.
82. *Ibid.*, p. 61.

It is certain that Amyraut barely escaped being deposed and having his writings condemned. In fact, the opposition was so formidable that it seems unbelievable that he was not condemned. Practically all of the great Reformed academies had declared against him, as well as most of the esteemed professors of Reformed Protestantism. It is very likely that only his own province (Anjou) and that of the Ile-de-France supported him, though Burgundy and Servennes apparently counselled moderation. We know that the provinces of Normandy, Saintonge, Poitou, Basse-Guyenne, Bas-Languedoc and Haut-Languedoc opposed him openly.[83] With this strong and organized opposition how is it that Amyraut escaped condemnation and deposition?

Laplanche speculates that what saved Amyraut and Testard was, "besides the skillfulness of their explanations, the support of the Parisian ministers."[84] Doubtless this was of some importance, but we must remember that of these five ministers only Daillé attended the synod. De l'Angle, in the letter cited above, gives the reason as frankly prudential: the fear of a schism in the Church and the destruction of its most flourishing academy.[85] This was undoubtedly a very important factor. But could not the "French motif" that we have observed in the early years of the French Church have been an equally significant factor? Amyraut was, as Pannier has noted, a *French* theologian if ever there was one;[86] it is very possible that the battery of letters and treatises from outside the kingdom worked against the design for which they were intended. And finally, it is reasonable to presume that Basnage's violently antagonistic opening sermon led some of the deputies to feel that Amyraut and Testard were not being treated fairly, and thus to take every precaution to assure a fair judgment.[87]

WORK AND CONTROVERSY AFTER 1637

In the years immediately following his heresy trial at Alençon Amyraut followed up an earlier letter to Théophile Brachet de

83. See Laplanche, *L'Oeuvre d'Amyraut*, p. 148.

84. *Ibid.*, p. 163.

85. In Rivet's *Opera*, III.828.

86. See his "Actualités" regarding Amyraut in the *Bulletin* 74 (1925), 494–501.

87. It is interesting that Basnage objected to the phrasing of the final *"règlement"* and requested a change. Although a previous request by Amyraut for revision had been honored, Basnage's was not.

la Milletière by composing a full length book in refutation of de la Milletière's writings on behalf of church union with the Roman Catholics. De la Milletière, a one-time friend and disciple of Cameron, is a very curious figure. In his early years he was attached to the Reformed communion and in 1628 was condemned to death as an agent of the Duc de Rohan. He spent but four years in prison and came out "with a pension of one thousand *écus* and wholeheartedly devoted to Richelieu."[88] Apparently in prison he underwent a change of heart, for the Reformed never accepted his views thereafter. Already in 1628 he had published a letter to a Reformed pastor, on union of the Reformed and Catholic communions.[89] Thereafter treatises by de la Milletière on such a union were legion.[90] In 1636 he published his *Christianae concordiae inter catholicos et evangelicos in omnibus controversiis instituendae consilium, unà cum elucidatione primariae controversiae de fidei per Christi gratiam dono et divinâ predestinatione,* in which he tried to reconcile all of the differences between Protestants and Catholics. He sent this book "not only to most of the churches and academies of France, but even to the academy of Geneva . . ."[91] Daillé was officially charged to refute it, though it was also answered by du Moulin, A. Rivet, and Jean Mestrezat. After many warnings, de la Milletière was officially excommunicated by the synod of Charenton in 1645. He was also rejected by the Catholics and died a very disillusioned man.

Amyraut answered him at length early in 1638 in two writings: *De la justification contre les opinions de Monsieur de la Milletiere* and *Du merite des oeuvres contre les opinions de Monsieur de la Milletiere.*[92] To this latter work Amyraut prefaced a lengthy reply to a response de la Milletière had made to his book on justification.[93] Both writings are very interesting in the light

---

88. Douen, *La Révocation de l'édit de Nantes à Paris,* 1:175. See also Haag-Bordier, *La France protestante,* 3:61ff.

89. *Lettre a M. Rambours, ministre du sainct evangile pour la reunion des evangeliques aux catholiques* (Paris, 1628).

90. Haag-Bordier list some 16 (*La France protestante,* 3:62ff).

91. *Ibid.,* 3:63.

92. Both published at Saumur. *De la justification* in February, *Du merite des oeuvres* in April.

93. De la Milletière's treatise was entitled *Admonition a Monsieur Amyraut de*

of Amyraut's own ecumenical spirit. We know that he regarded the split in the Church as scandalous. Because he felt de la Milletière's proposals were "very disadvantageous to the doctrine of the gospel," however, he clearly enunciated the principle of continued separation: " . . . in religion union is not desirable except in matters which are either good or, at least, are tolerable to our conscience."[94] He then went on to indicate that he did not feel the Reformers were in error in separating themselves from the Roman Church. This is, of course, not a surprising position for a Reformed theologian. However, it is significant that Amyraut believed he could best defend the Reformation and best convince de la Milletière of the "weakness and vanity"[95] of his position at one particular point—the doctrine of justification. Amyraut's choice of topic is all the more arresting inasmuch as none of the other Reformed theologians who had refuted de la Milletière had chosen to do it on this ground.[96] Laplanche thinks that Amyraut's motive in entering into this controversy was to ingratiate himself with the orthodox.[97] While I do not subscribe to this thesis, it would not, even if true, diminish the point being made here. The point is, Amyraut believed that the major difficulty in proposing union with the Roman Church was precisely on the topic of the doctrine of justification.

A second significant factor apropos of these two treatises is that they were written in refutation of one who claimed continuing allegiance to the Reformed communion. While Amyraut's argument was that de la Milletière had wholly adopted the Roman Catholic position on justification, we wonder if Amyraut was not at the same time in fact dealing a back-handed blow at the orthodox Calvinist teaching on this doctrine. Our

---

sa contradiction manifeste avec Monsieur Mestrezat & Monsieur Testard, sur le noeud de la matiere de la justification (Paris, 1638).

94. *De la justification*, [p. iii]. In this context the adjective "good" signifies "in accord with the doctrines of the gospel."

95. *Ibid.*, [p. iv].

96. It is true that Mestrezat later wrote against de la Milletière on this point, but only as a result of the controversy which arose over Amyraut's treatise on justification.

97. *L'Oeuvre d'Amyraut*, p. 168.

suspicion at this point is bolstered by the fact that de la Milletière's response immediately after the publication of the treatise on justification attempted to show that Amyraut's teaching was at variance with other Reformed theologians, especially Mestrezat and Testard.[98] At least we can say that the radical distinction between works-righteousness and faith-righteousness underlined by Amyraut in both these treatises is unique at this time in seventeenth-century Reformed theology.

The controversy continued between de la Milletière and Amyraut. The former published a *Response à M. Amyraut* . . . in which he suggested a friendly debate upon these matters.[99] Amyraut apparently refused to dispute him in public debate, but in May, 1638, published a lengthy reply to de la Milletière setting forth his views on efficacious grace.[100] In this work Amyraut gave a clear exposition of his understanding of the operation of the Holy Spirit in conversion.

The next major treatise of Amyraut was a defense of Calvin's doctrine of election and reprobation.[101] He undertook this work, as he avers, in answer to an anonymous treatise written in English, and translated into Latin, wherein the position is taken that the doctrine of reprobation is a novel doctrine and makes God a tyrant.[102] In this writing Amyraut clearly identifies his

98. De la Milletière, *Admonition a Monsieur Amyraut* . . . I suspect that he chose Mestrezat and Testard because he knew their positions best, and not because of any deviation in their teachings on justification.

99. Paris, 1638.

100. *Replique a M. de la Milletiere sur son offre d'une conference amiable pour l'examen de ses moyens de reunion* (Charenton, 1638).

101. *Defensio doctrinae J. Calvini de absoluto reprobationis decreto* (Saumur, 1641). French trans., augmented, *Defense de la doctrine de Calvin. Sur le sujet de l'election et de la reprobation* (Saumur, 1644).

102. Professor Nicole has established this as the English Arminian Samuel Hoard's *God's Love to Mankind Manifested by disproving His absolute Decree for their Damnation* (London, 1633, 1658, 1673). On Hoard see *DNB* 27:23–24. I have found no trace of the Latin translation mentioned by Amyraut. In England Hoard's treatise was answered by both the orthodox supralapsarian William Twisse, moderator at the Westminster assembly of divines, and by the near-Amyraldian John Davenant, Bishop of Salisbury (see Davenant, *Animadversions written by the Right Reverend Father in God John, Lord Bishop of Sarisbury, upon a Treatise intituled Gods Love to Mankind* [Cambridge, 1641]; Twisse, *The Riches of God's Love unto the Vessells of Mercy, consistent with his absolute hatred or reprobation of the Vessells of Wrath* [Oxford, 1653]).

own teaching with that of Calvin. Of all his writings, this is the most important in demonstrating the distinctives of Amyraldianism as compared to the scholastic orientation of the orthodox. Here Amyraut produces passage after passage from Calvin in support of his own teachings. Of capital significance, he argues forcefully that his anonymous opponent has misrepresented Calvin, and defends Calvin's doctrine at length showing this, but does not undertake the defense of Beza and orthodoxy. In fact, as will be shown later, Amyraut implies that he is unwilling to defend the positions being combatted by Hoard. Again, if comparison is made of the replies to this book by Amyraut and the orthodox William Twisse, a most striking dissimilarity in theological orientation becomes apparent. Though he was an adversary of the Puritan John Cotton, who was using arguments very similar to Amyraut's, and though he doubtless knew of Amyraut's work, Twisse's argument is wholly and simply a defense of orthodox teaching developed according to the logic of orthodox formulations. Twisse makes less than half a dozen references to Calvin, and these very occasional in nature, even though his volume is a very prolix one of more than five hundred folio pages.

Interestingly, Amyraut's *Defensio* is a forthright and natural development of his own teaching in the guise of Calvin. Therefore Laplanche correctly notes that "the work resumed the theories already maintained in the recent publications of Amyraut."[103] Laplanche goes on to notice the following interesting features:

> The expressions condemned by the Synod are not found, but the doctrines dear to Amyraut all reappear: the universal extent of redemption and of the promises of salvation (chapters I and IX); moral inability in conversion (chapter VIII), the twofold will of God considered either as lawgiver (*législateur*) or as father (chapters VIII, IX, and XVI), the theoretical possibility of faith for those who have not heard the Gospel (chapter XII), the action of grace through illumination of the understanding.[104]

103. *L'Oeuvre d'Amyraut*, p. 169.
104. *Ibid.*

Surprisingly enough, this writing was received quite favorably by the orthodox. Indeed, Amyraut later reprinted part of a letter from Rivet applauding the work.[105]

Though there is evidence that the *Defensio* was generally well received, apparently this sentiment was not universal. Laplanche reports that the provincial synod of Poitou in 1643 refused, in effect, to admit to the ministry three recent graduate, of Saumur.[106] This upset Amyraut immensely and he wrote to Rivet, who was a native of this province, begging him to use his influence to help alleviate the situation: "Not to receive men who are not accused of incompetency, for they have been pronounced capable, and who will sign the Confession of Faith and all the regulations of our national synods, is, it seems to me, to run headlong into schism."[107] Apparently this situation was cleared up, for there is no reference to it at the next national synod. However, it does show that at least some of the orthodox opposition to the Amyraldian theology was not content to accept the verdict of Alençon.

It was this affair which precipitated the translation of the *Defensio* into French. The registers of the Academic council at Saumur determined, among other things, that this writing of Amyraut "will be put by him into French without change, but only augmented by passages and testimonies of our first and most celebrated theologians of the Reformation."[108] The translation appeared in 1644 with an impressive battery of passages from the early reformers supporting his teachings, especially from Bucer, Musculus, Bullinger and, of course, Calvin.

Amyraut published another polemic piece in 1641, this one opposing the fideism of Roman Catholic theologians. The book was entitled *De l'elevation de la foy et de l'abaissement de la raison, en la creance des mysteres de la religion,* a title stating his opponents' position.[109] In actual fact the point of the book

105. See the dedicatory epistle in Amyraut's work of 1645, *Dissertationes theologicae quatuor* (Saumur).

106. *L'Oeuvre d'Amyraut*, p. 173. Laplanche gives a valuable and extended account of this incident, pp. 172–74.

107. As quoted in *L'Oevre d'Amyraut*, p. 174.

108. *Registre de l'academie*, f. 133, as in *L'Oevre d'Amyraut*, p. 174.

109. Amyraut characterizes the Catholics as maintaining that "pour estre bon

was to show the folly of abandoning reason in matters of faith, for to have faith necessarily implies a rational act. This is, to be sure, Amyraut's most rationalistic writing.[110] Yet while there can be no denial of the rationalistic spirit of this treatise, one must take note of Amyraut's admonitory statements regarding the possible abuse of reason in theology. It is well, too, to compare this treatise with his other, more characteristic, writings before labeling him a rationalist.

It was in 1644 that Amyraut published the first of his paraphrases on the Scripture, the *Paraphrases sur l'epistre aux Romains*. Before he was through he would publish paraphrases on all of the books of the New Testament, except the Synoptic gospels and the Book of Revelation, as well as on the Psalms. These paraphrases are interesting for several reasons. For one, he mentions them first in a later work when commenting on where his dogmatic teachings may best be found.[111] Also, they were published anonymously and, more importantly, were based not upon the Protestant Bible of Olivétan but upon the Louvain edition of the Roman Church. Doubtless this edition was used to give the paraphrases a wide audience among those of the Roman Catholic communion, but the choice may also indicate that Amyraut was not happy with Olivétan's translation.

It was also in 1644 that Frederich Spanheim the elder (1600–1649), recently removed from Geneva to Leyden, prepared some theses against universal grace to be used in a public disputation.[112] Amyraut considered himself under attack and composed four dissertations in defense of his own position: *De oeconomia trium personarum in operibus Divinis, dissertatio; De jure Dei*

---

chrestien, en ce point [transubstantiation] comme en quelque autres, il faut entièrement renoncer à nostre intelligence" (preface, p. xvi).

110. Sabean and Rex have made the most of it in their respective studies: David W. Sabean, "The Theological Rationalism of Moïse Amyraut," *ARG* 55 (1964), 204–16 *passim*, and Rex, *Essays on Pierre Bayle and religious controversy*, pp. 99–109.

111. *In symbolum apostolorum, exercitatio* (Saumur, 1663), p. 5.

112. *Disputatio de gratia universali* (Leyden, 1644). For biographical information on Spanheim the best account is A. Archinard, "La famille des Spanheim," *Bulletin* 12 (1863), 96–101, an article originally prepared for the *PRE* but because it was drastically shortened by the editors, submitted to the *Bulletin*.

in creaturas, dissertatio; Doctrinae de gratia universali, ut ab orthodoxis explicatur, defensio; and *Doctrinae de gratia particulari, ut a Calvino explicatur, defensio.* These he published in 1645 under the title *Dissertationes theologicae quatuor.*[113] With these publications the old quarrel over universal grace erupted with new fury. Laplanche observes that the "new and violent polemics" soon degenerated to a quarrel of personalities. "Each party regards itself calumniated by the other and accused of dishonesty."[114]

Amyraut's *Dissertationes* had barely come off the press when he had to leave Saumur to attend the national synod of Charenton, held from December 16, 1644, to January 26, 1645. At this synod the Saumur theologians were to suffer a crushing defeat.

We have noticed that the decision of the Alençon synod was not well received by the orthodox, and that particularly in the province of Poitou there was considerable continuing opposition to Amyraldianism. The news that another national synod was granted permission to meet was the signal for a new flurry of activity from this opposition. André Rivet, who had written the letter to Amyraut approving his *Defensio,* wrote to Paul Ferry, minister at Metz, revealing his continuing distress over the Salmurian doctrines. He had thought, he said, that Alençon had delivered a *grand coup* to the "evil of Paris and Saumur," but apparently it had "only irritated the matter."[115] He felt that "If this assembly does not provide a vigorous remedy for this situation, there is danger of a schism in our churches" and mentioned that he had "done what he could" to provide this remedy.[116] His doing "what he could" referred to two letters he had addressed to the synod urging action against Saumur. Letters had also been sent from the Leyden academy and from Geneva.

---

113. For an interesting, pro-Amyraut, account of this renewal of hostilities see the letter of Valentin Conrart to André Rivet of March 18, 1645, in R. Kerviler and E. de Barthélemy, *Valentin Conrart* (Paris, 1881), pp. 268–72.

114. *L'Oeuvre d'Amyraut,* p. 180. Laplanche has the fullest account of the renewed hostilities, pp. 180ff. For Amyraut's own account see his *Apologie de Moyse Amyraut contre les invectives de Mr de Launay* (Saumur, 1657), pp. 14ff.

115. Letter of December 23, 1644, partly reproduced in Laplanche, *L'Oeuvre d'Amyraut,* p. 186.

116. *Ibid.*

This time opposition was developed not only against Amyraut and his universalist teachings but also against his colleague Josué de la Place and his doctrine of mediate imputation, set forth in the latter's *De statu hominis lapsi ante gratiam*.[117] The charges brought against Amyraut, which were grounded on the contention that he had violated the regulations of the Alençon synod, were quickly dismissed, even though both his *Defensio* and the *Dissertationes* probably did violate these regulations. The account in Quick reads that the synod, "judging it best to bury in the Grave of Oblivion all those reciprocal Complaints brought in from all Parties, hath, as formerly, dismissed the said Sieur *Amyraud*, with honour to the Exercise of his Professorship, wherein he is exhorted to employ himself with Courage and Cheerfulness."[118] Moreover Amyraut asked permission to defend himself in case attacked from outside the country. He was granted permission to petition the provincial synod of Anjou in this matter if occasion arose.

However, de la Place's doctrine of original sin was not so honored. The orthodox divines had very tenaciously fastened on the federal headship idea appurtenant to the covenant theology. Under this understanding of theology the doctrine of original sin had undergone a refinement not found in Calvin. That is, the orthodox teaching was that of immediate imputation: each of the children of Adam, since Adam is his federal representative, is responsible for Adam's transgression as he participated *in actu*. This means that each individual is condemned before God prior to any personal depravity, that each is guilty before he is a participant even in hereditary sin. De la Place simply made the inherent depravity received by virtue of each man's association in a corrupted race the basis, indeed the only basis, for condemnation. That is, natural depravity precedes guilt. The synod did not name de la Place in its deliberations, so the censure it delivered was not as pointed as it might have been. Nevertheless we read the following words:

> This Synod condemneth the said Doctrine as far as it restraineth the Nature of Original Sin to the sole Hereditary Corruption

117. Saumur, 1640.
118. *Synodicon*, 2:455.

of *Adam's* Posterity, to the excluding of the Imputation of that first Sin by which he fell, and interdicteth on pain of all Church-Censures all Pastors, Professors, and others, who shall treat of this Question, to depart from the common received Opinion of the Protestant Churches, who (over and besides that Corruption) have all acknowledged the Imputation of *Adam's* first Sin unto his Posterity. And all Synods and Colloquies, who shall hereafter proceed to the reception of Scholars unto the Holy Ministry, are obliged to see them sign and subscribe this present Act.[119]

This condemnation of de la Place's views was a stunning blow to the Saumur Academy. Many protests and appeals were tendered to various provincial synods but no action was taken. Meanwhile Amyraut himself was embroiled in bitter controversy. "At Leyden," Laplanche notes, "Spanheim was preparing an enormous work against Amyraut: this would be, he thought, the *machine de guerre* destined to crush definitively Saumur."[120] Amyraut was also involved in some bitter exchanges with André Rivet which broke their till-then friendly relationship.

The quarrel with Rivet was brought to the fore when Amyraut dedicated to him the *Dissertationes quatuor*. Rivet was upset by this, especially since Amyraut seemed so sure Rivet approved his doctrine. A second incident then brought about a complete falling out. Amyraut heard that Rivet had communicated to the Westminster assembly the manuscript of the *Synopsis,* which had been sent to the Alençon synod in 1637, with the apparent hope that the Westminster divines would condemn Amyraldianism. When accused by Amyraut of this, Rivet stoutly maintained his innocence. It turned out that Rivet's nephew, Pierre du Moulin's son Louis, probably had at least given it to Twisse. At any rate, though the assembly confirmed that they had not heard from Rivet, Amyraut never fully believed Rivet when he protested his innocence in the matter, and their relationship became very strained.[121] Laplanche is certainly right when he notes that because of this Rivet lost his usual modera-

---

119. *Ibid.*, 2:473–74.
120. *L'Oeuvre d'Amyraut,* p. 189.
121. For a more complete survey of this unhappy incident see Laplanche, *L'Oeuvre d'Amyraut,* pp. 189ff.

tion. This is seen in his encouragement of Spanheim's plan to "crush" Amyraut, but perhaps even more so from another incident. In 1646 Amyraut lost his only daughter, and to console his wife he wrote a little treatise on the life after death, a treatise later printed.[122] In a letter to Sarrau, one of the king's counsellors, Rivet made the acerb and rude remark that "His wife would need to be well versed in philosophy to draw consolation from that."[123] Such a remark is so unlike Rivet that it points up the bitterness of the "civil war" in Reformed Protestantism.

This renewed and increasingly vindictive quarrel over universal grace also saw an enormous waste of printer's ink. Spanheim's intended *coup de grâce,* his answer to the dissertations on universal and particular grace in Amyraut's *Dissertationes quatuor,* turned out to be three extremely prolix Latin volumes of more than twenty-six hundred pages![124] Spanheim had shown himself to be a very abusive controversialist in his tirades against the Anabaptists, and this reply to Amyraut in no way detracted from that reputation. The tone is mordacious, sometimes insulting. The argument is unbelievably pedantic, repetitious, and rambling, ranging from Amyraut's Latin grammar and vocabulary to his Pelagian tendencies.

Amyraut proceeded to obtain permission from the provincial synod of Anjou in 1646 to answer Spanheim.[125] His actions show that he was nevertheless reluctant to avail himself of this synodal authorization. He sought first to have the pastors of the province of Saintonge serve in the role of mediators, and attended their provincial synod with this end in view. Nothing came of this attempt at reconciliation, so Amyraut sought another medium. In 1645 the king of Poland, Ladislas VII, had tried one of his many efforts at union by calling a colloquy at Torun composed of Lutherans, Reformed, and Catholic theologians. The Calvinists prepared a confession for this, known as the Confession

122. *Discours de l'estat des fideles apres la mort* (Saumur, 1646). This little work saw two more French editions (1648 and 1657) as well as translations into English and German.

123. Quoted in Laplanche, *L'Oeuvre d'Amyraut,* p. 193.

124. *Exercitationes de gratia universali* (Leyden, 1646).

125. See the text of this ruling in Laplanche, p. 200. The following discussion draws heavily on his account.

of Thorn. It taught that Christ died for all. Amyraut learned that Guillaume Rivet approved this confession and so asked him to communicate a proposition to Spanheim: If Spanheim would declare himself in accord with this confession Amyraut would halt his response to the *Exercitationes,* the first part of which was already being printed. Spanheim refused to accept the proposition, but Amyraut was still reluctant to have his response published.

Hoping to pacify his opponents by a statement of his orthodoxy Amyraut published two treatises in quick succession: the *Fidei Mosis Amyraldi circa errores arminianorum declaratio*[126] and *Disputatio de libero arbitrio.*[127] In the former he asserts his fundamental opposition to the Arminian teachings. He thinks "All the matters which the Orthodox and the Arminians dispute relate to these five principal points." He lists (1) the nature and extent of man's corruption; (2) the nature and basis of election and reprobation; (3) the nature of the efficacy of grace; (4) the perseverance of faith; and (5) the nature and extent of Christ's redemption, and of the grace offered and communicated in consequence.[128] To each of these he asserts his orthodoxy and refers to the various places in his published writings where his sentiments are set forth. In three succeeding chapters he treats of the problem of the salvation of the heathen, universal redemption, and his distinction between moral and natural ability, the three points he apparently regarded as most unacceptable to his opponents.

The second of these treatises designed to pacify his opponents Amyraut dedicated to one of them, Jean de Croi, minister at Béziers. In this writing Amyraut demonstrates at length his teaching on free will, namely, that the will is never to be thought of as *in equilibrio* but rather as inclined. In this inclined disposition it chooses freely what it desires. Because it is corrupt, however, the will can never choose the good; indeed, it is totally impotent in salvation unless renewed by God's Spirit.

126. Saumur, 1646. The first chapter was translated into French and published under the title *La Creance de Moyse Amyraut sur les erreurs des Arminiens* (n.p., n.d.).
127. Saumur, 1647.
128. Pp. 2–5.

In addition to these two published treatises, Amyraut wrote long letters to Irminger of Zurich and André Rivet in defense of his teaching on universal grace.[129] At the same time he was working on two other publications of note. One was a first treatise on church union with the Lutherans, *De secessione ab ecclesia romana deque ratione pacis inter evangelicos in religionis negotio constituendae, disputatio*.[130] Even in this Amyraut addressed himself to the predestination question, explaining it in his customary terms and hoping this explanation would remove the difficulty that Lutherans had with Reformed teaching on this point.[131]

The second publication was his *Apologie pour ceux de la religion sur les sujets d'aversion que plusieurs pensent avoir contre leur personne et leur religion*.[132] In this Amyraut asserted the absolute loyalty of the Reformed communion to the king, and denounced any political aspirations his communion may have once had. This offended the Reformed community at and around La Rochelle, for the Reformed in this region were still very sensitive about the siege of La Rochelle of 1628, and particularly about the lack of support from other Reformed regions. One of the pastors at La Rochelle, Philippe Vincent, wrote a short-tempered letter to a Protestant nobleman at Saumur, l'Amiral de Bouilly, in which it is plain that he interpreted Amyraut's book to be an attack against the province of Saintonge because of the opposition of its ministers to Amyraldianism. Moreover, in this letter, reproduced at some length in Laplanche,[133] Amyraut is charged with the sole responsibility for

---

129. The former in MS copy in the Archives Tronchin, fol. 130; the latter lost, but reproduced in part in a response made to it by Spanheim and published in Rivet's *Opera*, III.852,1–896,2. As this response indicates, the letter was written at the end of October, 1645.

130. Saumur, 1647. Reprinted some years later, probably in Germany, with the same format as the Saumur edition except for an "epistola lectori" (n.p., n.d.). See Stauffer, *Un Précurseur français de l'oecuménisme, p. 16n21*. Haag-Bordier, *La France protestante*, 1:199, also lists a German translation which appeared in 1649, published at Cassel. Stauffer has analyzed this treatise with precision.

131. Stauffer, *Un Précurseur français de l'oecuménisme*, pp. 25ff. Amyraut's section on predestination in *De secessione* is ch. 7, pp. 156–91.

132. Saumur, 1647.

133. *L'Oeuvre d'Amyraut*, pp. 205–6.

the quarrel within French Protestantism, both in its inception and in its recrudescence at that time. Vincent also mentions that students from Saumur would not be welcome in the province of Saintonge.

In the face of the failure of all of his attempts at reconciliation, and in the light of the continued opposition to his teaching, Amyraut decided to respond to Spanheim's *Exercitationes*. Doubtless this resolve was furthered, as he avers, by the fact that the two Rivets had insisted to the assembly of the provincial synod of La Rochelle in 1647 that its members read and disseminate Spanheim's book. So sometime early in 1648 Amyraut sent to press his *Specimen animadversionum in exercitationes de gratia universali*. To this he attached a 113-page "ad reverendos viros, ecclesiarum in gallia reformatarum pastores, Mosis Amyraldi apologetica praefatio," in which he gave his version of the quarrel from 1634 to 1648.

Herein he stated that he and the orthodox were at odds on three basic doctrines: the universality of God's will to save, the universal intent of Christ's redemptive act, and the sufficiency of the external call. In the work proper, which, like Spanheim's, was haughty and caustic in tone, Amyraut addressed himself to these three problems under two basic divisions—*"de gratia specialis"* and *"de gratia universalis."* In the face of Spanheim's pedantic attack Amyraut emphasized with renewed vigor the various teachings dear to him. This resulted in some rather bold statements regarding his doctrines which need to be presented in relation to a corollary teaching to properly represent his thought. It was, therefore, easy to take the statements out of context and allege his affinity with Arminianism. But, as Laplanche has noted so well, though the content of the work proper was easily assailed, "the apologetic preface of Amyraut aroused even more violent reactions, for his adversaries naturally contested the veracity of that account."[134] There can be little doubt but that the feeling against Amyraut reached its peak during these years of 1648 and 1649. Formidable and violent opposition was voiced from Geneva, Bern, and Zurich in Switzerland, from Leyden and Breda in the Netherlands, from Sedan, and from many of

134. *Ibid.,* p. 209.

the provinces within France, notably Poitou and Normandy. A thorough discussion of this opposition would take too much time and space for our purposes, so we shall but outline the quarrel, referring the reader to the account in Laplanche for a more detailed presentation.[135]

Most likely the first response came from Spanheim, who published a very long letter written to Matthew Cottière, minister at Tours in Touraine.[136] There is nothing new in this letter except the tone, which is unbelievably mild for Spanheim. Another response, somewhat more violent, appeared when Isaac Chabrol, minister at Thouars in Poitou, published a letter sent him by P. Vincent of La Rochelle.[137] Vincent had been embittered by Amyraut's *Apologie,* which he interpreted as an attack upon the Protestants of La Rochelle, and in his letter charged Amyraut with falsifying the historical facts of the controversy. André Rivet also evidenced his displeasure with this preface of Amyraut's by publishing a collection of letters challenging Amyraut's interpretation of the facts.[138] This collection included the letters of Spanheim and Vincent, plus a letter of Rivet himself to his brother Guillaume and a letter of this latter to Theophilus Rossel, minister at Saintes in Saintonge.

In addition to these letters there appeared a spate of polemic treatises. Pierre du Moulin was as usual the most violent and also the most productive. In 1648 he published a revised edition of his *Examen* entitled *Esclaircissement des controverses Salmuriennes.*[139] It corresponds very closely to the *Examen,* though three new sections have been added: one which relates to the legal covenant in Amyraut's teaching, another on the decree of God to save all men, and a third in which he gives a running

135. *Ibid.,* pp. 211–34.

136. *Friderici Spanhemii epistola ad virum clarissimum Matthaeum Cottierium super concilationem controversiae de gratia universali* (Leyden, 1648).

137. I have found no trace of the original edition of this letter; we know of its existence through the collection of letters published by André Rivet cited in the following note.

138. *Andreae Riveti et Gulielmi fratrum epistolae apologeticae ad criminationes et calumnias Mosis Amyraldi, in praefatione virulenta, ad reverandos ecclesiarum reformatarum in gallia pastores, praefixa animadversionibus de gratia universali* (Breda, 1648).

139. Leyden, 1648.

commentary on the responses of Amyraut and Testard before the Alençon synod in 1637. This particular treatise is probably the most instructive analysis of Amyraldianism produced in the whole controversy, for it notes briefly and in clear style all of the matters at issue in the debate. Du Moulin also replied directly to the *Specimen* of Amyraut with two even more violent treatises than the *Esclaircissement*. The first of them, the *Petri Molinaei de Mosis Amyraldi adversus Fridericum Spanhemium libro judicium*,[140] contains little new argumentation, though it stresses even more strongly Amyraut's alleged Arminianism. We have seen that in his *Specimen* Amyraut expressed himself on several occasions in ways that could easily be misunderstood if not kept in context. Du Moulin, never one to pass up such an opportunity, took full advantage of this opening. He prefaced to this treatise two pages of "extracts" from the *Specimen* of Amyraut which were lifted from their context, and their meaning distorted.[141] Apparently, however, du Moulin thought this an effective weapon, for one year later he published a short treatise, the *Articuli fidei Amyraldianae ex Mosis Amyraldi libris. Praecipue vero ex ejus libro adversus Fridericum Spanhemium fideliter et ad verbum excerpti*,[142] which was wholly devoted to this sort of thing. It is a classic example of misrepresentation and dishonest scholarship. Laplanche cites but one of many examples: "The theologian of Saumur had not written, *Christus potuisset peccare si voluisset*, but *Impossibile fuit Christo peccare, non quod peccare non potuisset si voluisset, sed quia id non voluit, neque vero fieri potuit id ut vellet*."[143] Du Moulin also wrote a short-tempered response to his nephew, Samuel de l'Angle, minister at Rouen;[144] Laplanche briefly describes it and says that herein du Moulin unbelievably "pushed his criticisms further than ever before."[145] He accused Amyraut of secretly preparing

140. Leyden, 1649.
141. Pp. ii-iii.
142. Rotterdam, 1649.
143. *L'Oeuvre d'Amyraut*, p. 219.
144. *Réponse de Pierre du Moulin à une lettre de Samuel de Langle, pasteur de l'eglise de Rouen. Où est contenue un sommaire de la doctrine de Monsieur Amyraut* (n.p., n.d.).
145. *L'Oeuvre d'Amyraut*, p. 220.

a reunion with the Roman Catholic Church and assailed Amyraut's treatise of 1649, *De la vocation des pasteurs*,[146] in which Amyraut had mentioned that the Roman Church conserved the fundamental doctrines of Christianity.

At the same time, the Rivet brothers both published substantial treatises against Amyraut. André finally published the *Synopsis doctrinae Mosis Amyraldi*,[147] which had been circulating in manuscript since 1636. Guillaume composed a large work entitled *Vindiciae evangelicae de justificatione et annexis ei capitibus*,[148] an attempt to show that Amyraut's doctrine of justification was in essence Roman Catholic, an incredible position to anyone who had read Amyraut's *De la justification* of 1638.

Still another work was published by George Reveau, a layman of La Rochelle. In 1649, under the pseudonym of G. Vellius, his *Ad pamphilium centinaeum . . .* appeared.[149] This was the result, according to Blondel, of the encouragement of P. Vincent.[150] Spanheim, too, was busily engaged in drafting a refutation of Amyraut's *Specimen* when death came. The work was edited and published by his son Ezéchiel in 1649 under the title *Friderici Spanhemii vindiciarum pro exercitationibus suis de gratia universali partes duae posthumae adversus specimen animadversionum Mosis Amyraldi*.[151] A. Rivet drafted a preface for this work.

We should notice at least briefly the ferment in Switzerland over Amyraldianism.[152] In 1645 the Bern government had forbidden the academic council of Lausanne to send the students of Vaud to Saumur. There was a great deal of unrest at Basel and Zurich; the lengthy apologetic letter of Amyraut to Irminger of Zurich has already been mentioned. In Geneva the successor to Spanheim, Alexandre Morus (1606–70), espoused Amyraldianism. His presence brought the matter to a crisis by 1647.

---

146. Saumur, 1649. This important work is basically designed to show the apostolic succession in the Reformed Churches.
147. Amsterdam, 1649.
148. Amsterdam, 1648.
149. Leyden, 1649.
150. *Actes authentiques*, pp. 40–41.
151. Amsterdam, 1649.
152. For fuller discussion see Laplanche, *L'Oeuvre d'Amyraut*, pp. 221–29.

The role of Geneva until this time had been largely that of peacemaker, inasmuch as the Genevan professors counselled the warring parties not to publish upon the debated issues.[153] On August 6, however, the *Vénérable Compagnie* ordered that a ministerial candidate "will be required to profess that he not only will teach nothing which does not conform to the Word of God, the Confession of Faith of the churches of France, Switzerland, and the teaching of our catechism, but also that he will not introduce any novelty, whatever it might be, but will hold himself to the purity, simplicity, and orthodoxy of the doctrine as it has been previously practiced and as it has been taught in this church." The new prescription then went on to say that the candidate would be required to give *promesse expresse* that "he would teach in accordance with what has been determined at the synod of Dort, the synods of France to the present time, and particularly that he would reject this novel doctrine of the universality of grace and of the non-imputation of Adam's first sin . . . "[154] These requirements, of course, in effect declare that no student from Saumur would be welcome in Geneva.

This action was rendered even more restrictive in 1649. Morus

153. Their enjoinders to silence were directed primarily to the Saumur theologians; e.g., Spanheim had been encouraged to write his book against Amyraut at the same time that a letter was sent to Cappel asking the Saumur theologians to refrain from writing. See J. Gaberel, *Histoire de l'église de Genève*, 3 vols. (Geneva, 1855–62), 3:117.

154. According to an "extrait du Registre de la V. C. du 6 Aoust 1647," Archives Tronchin, 38:66. MS. Because to my knowledge this extract has not been printed elsewhere I shall give the major part of it: "Estant question du pourvoi d'un en l'Eglise . . . [il] a este proposé s'il ne seroit pas expedient d'adjouster à ce qui est du reiglement pratique ci devant en l'Election des pasteurs, si avoir que celui qui sera esleu sera obligé de professer non seulement de n'enseigner chose qui ne soit conforme à la parole de Dieu, à la confession de la foi des Eglises de France, de Suisse et de la doctrine de nostre Catechisme, mais mesmes de n'apporter aucune nouveauté, que le quelle soit, ains se tenir à la purété, simplicité, et solidité de la doctrine comme il a esté ci devant pratiqué, et selon qu'on a enseigné en cette Eglise. Sur ce a este advisé, qu'on tirera promesse expresse de celui qui sera appellé au st ministere, lors qu'il sera introduit a la Compe outre l'ordinaire, qu'il enseigneroit conformément à ce qui a esté arresté au synode de Dordrect, les synodes nationaux de france jusques à present, et particulierement rejetteroit cette nouvelle doctrine de l'universalité de la Grace, et de la nonimputation du premier peché d'Adam, comme elle est aujourdui enseignée par quelques uns de dela et d'ici, qui a causé du trouble en diverses Eglises de france."

had apparently decided that it was best for him to leave Geneva, and requested of the *Vénérable Compagnie* a certificate of orthodoxy. On June 1 this body drew up a detailed formulary which Morus was required to sign before he could receive his certificate of orthodoxy. This formulary had five heads relating to (1) the imputation of Adam's sin, (2) predestination, (3) redemption, (4) the disposition of men to grace, and (5) the covenant of the law and its promises.[155] Each head was composed as were the Canons of Dort with a positive statement of orthodox teaching followed by a listing of the erroneous teachings which were to be rejected. Not only did Morus have to sign these, but they had to be subscribed by all the pastors. Each had to sign the subscription clause which read, "So I think and so I will teach. I will teach nothing contrary to this, either publicly or privately."[156]

It is clear from all of this activity that the "civil war" was waxing hotter and hotter. Though Amyraut deemed it wise to answer only the two letters from French pastors, those of G. Rivet and Vincent,[157] there was considerable fear that all of this would lead to a schism in the French Church. However, at this juncture Henri-Charles de la Trémouille, Duke of Thouars and Prince of Tarente, intervened and arranged for a meeting at Thouars between Amyraut and his major opponents from within France, Guillaume Rivet, P. Vincent, and three ministers from the province of Poitou.[158] Either by diplomacy or by authority,

155. These may be found in Latin in Schweizer, *Die Protestantischen Central-dogmen*, 2:463–66; in French, in manuscript, in the Archives Tronchin, 38:52–54, 68–69.

156. "Sic sentio sic docebo et nil contrarium hisce docebo, vel publice vel privatim" (as quoted in Gaberel, *Histoire de l'église de Genève*, 3:123).

157. *Ad reverendi viri, G. Riveti, ecclesiae Talleburgensis pastoris, responsoriam epistolam, Mosis Amyraldi replicatio* (Saumur, 1649), and *Adversus epistolae historicae criminationes, Mosis Amyraldi defensio. Ad reverendum virum, D. Chabrolium, Thoarsensis ecclesiae pastorem* (Saumur, 1649). In the latter, Amyraut reproduces portions of some interesting letters from the early days of the quarrel.

158. 1620–72. The prince was a military man who had spent some years fighting for the House of Orange in the Netherlands, and whose primary concern in effecting this reconciliation no doubt was to unite forces of the Reformed in the event an opportunity should arise to take up arms once again. According to

to use Laplanche's words, the prince arranged a peace which, as far as Amyraut himself was concerned, effectively consummated the universal grace quarrel. There was, of course, no resolution of the doctrinal differences, but by the Acte de Thouars, signed on October 16, there was an agreement not to write again on the disputed topics.[159] Later André Rivet also joined in this agreement and answered very cordially a peace-seeking letter by Amyraut. With Spanheim dead, all of the main protagonists in the quarrel were now sworn to silence except for the most violent of all, du Moulin. According to a letter of Conrart to A. Rivet, dated January 21, 1650, du Moulin had at first responded favorably to the attempts made to have him also join in the terms of the Acte de Thouars. However, Conrart also mentions that all the principals in the matter were "extremely astonished" that du Moulin had apparently changed his mind and wanted to publish another book against Amyraut.[160] Conrart therefore urges Rivet to dissuade du Moulin and, above all, not to aid him in the publication of any new works on these matters. It may well be that Rivet did prevail upon du Moulin, for in 1655 a reconciliation between him and Amyraut was effected.[161]

In 1650 Amyraut had occasion again to demonstrate his royalism. He, as most of Europe, was scandalized by the beheading of Charles I by Cromwell's army in 1649. Because Charles' wife was the late Louis XIII's sister, France was especially incensed by this unnecessary act. Amyraut made the most of the situation and composed a treatise entitled *Discours sur la souveraineté des rois*[162] in which he made a bitter denunciation of this regicide and reaffirmed the loyalty of the Protestants to the monarch. Apparently he ingratiated himself with the court by this writing,

---

Vincent the ministers were Jacques Rançonnet, Jean Masson, and Isaac du Soul. (*Lettre de Mr Vincent a Mr Rivet* . . . [n.p., 1649], pp. 2–3, Archives Tronchin, 8:210).

159. The act and the various letters which relate to it were published, and may be found in the Archives Tronchin, 8:215–16, appended to the letter of Vincent mentioned in the preceding note.

160. Letter in Kerviler and de Barthélemy, *Valentin Conrart*, pp. 528–32.

161. Letters exchanged between Amyraut and du Moulin on this occasion were printed and may be found in the Archives Tronchin, 8:220ff.

162. Paris, 1650.

for some two years later the court sojourned in Saumur for about a month. During this time, according to Bayle's account, Mazarin sought out Amyraut and the two men had several lengthy and cordial talks.

In 1653 Amyraut again showed his displeasure with the English Independents in his publication on church government, *Du gouvernement de l'eglise contre ceux qui veulent abolir l'usage & l'autorité des synodes*.[163] Predictably Amyraut demonstrated his attachment to the presbyterial form of church government.

In 1652 Amyraut had published the first volume of the work which was to occupy most of his energy for this whole decade, *La Morale chrestienne*. The sixth and final volume was published in 1660.[164] This, his largest work, was the first major attempt within Reformed Protestantism to produce an ethical system. The ethical concern shown in the massive undertaking is quite instructive of the emphases of Amyraut's theology. It is interesting to note that the opposition which Amyraut saw between the covenant of the law and the covenant of grace renders a rather dynamic force to his discussion of the *morale* of Moses and Christ, which he interprets as being two quite different emphases.

Though he was no longer actively involved in the universal grace controversy, these years saw Amyraut involved in other controversies. In 1651 Pierre de Launay,[165] an elder (*ancien*) in the Charenton Church and a defender of Amyraut's views on universal grace, published his *Paraphrases et exposition sur l'apocalypse* in which he espoused a strict millenarianism. In 1654 Amyraut published *Du regne de mille ans*.[166] He does not directly attack de Launay, indeed he later avers that he wrote it

163. Saumur, 1653; 2nd ed., Saumur, 1658. For an analysis see Rimbault, "Un Traité d'Amyraut: Du gouvernement de l'église," *Etudes théologiques et religieuses de la faculté de théologie protestante de Montpellier* 28 (1953), 157–79.

164. Each volume contains about 800 pages. The work was dedicated to Monsieur de Villarnoul, son of du Plessis-Mornay.

165. 1573–1661. De Launay had a great reputation as a Semitic scholar. He was an Amyraldian during the early years of the quarrel over universal grace.

166. Saumur, 1654; reprint, Leyden, 1655.

in such a way that it would not be so interpreted, but he does refute the chiliastic position. De Launay was very upset that his old friend would react thus to his teaching and answered this book of Amyraut, on the way accusing Amyraut of a contentious spirit. The quarrel became very bitter and lasted at least until 1657. Amyraut published two more pieces relating to it.[167]

Through these years Amyraut was also involved in a painful contention, to use Professor Nicole's phrase, within the Saumur church with his colleague Isaac d'Huisseau.[168] D'Huisseau had suffered for some time from ill health and had frequently been unable to discharge his duties. After several periods of recuperation he had invited a young divinity student and protégé to Saumur to carry on some of the ministerial functions. This had not been cleared with the consistory, and d'Huisseau's project was forbidden when they heard of it. A nasty situation developed when two parties formed, one led by d'Huisseau and the other by Amyraut. In 1656 the church of Saumur relieved d'Huisseau of his duties. After many provincial synods had heard the matter and had not been able to resolve it, the national synod of Loudun in 1659 finally restored calm to the situation. Both parties were judged to be in the wrong and d'Huisseau was restored to his position on condition that no new health problems arise within a six-month probationary period. There is an anonymous writing entitled *Pieces authentiques et decisives de la question à qui doiuent estre imputés les troubles de l'eglise reformée de Saumur,* almost certainly edited by Amyraut.[169]

Amyraut was increasingly plagued by ill health during these years.[170] In 1658 he went to Paris to see Mazarin in order to acquire permission to hold a national synod, and while there visited the *eaux de Bourbon,* seeking relief from his infirmities.

167. *Replique au livre de Monsieur de Launay sur le regne de mille ans* (Saumur, 1656), and *Apologie de Moyse Amyraut contre les invectives de Mr de Launay* (Saumur, 1657).

168. See *Encyclopedia of Christianity,* s.v. "Amyraut, Moïse."

169. Saumur, 1659.

170. See his letter, signed September 4, 1654, "A Monsieur Monsieur de Superville, Docteur en Medicine a Nyort," prefaced to his *Sermon sur ces paroles du chapitre douzieme de l'epistre aux Hebrieux,* 2d ed. (Saumur, 1656).

This was the occasion for his publishing a discourse upon these waters in which he compared their healing effect with that of the gospel.[171]

In 1659 Amyraut was delegated to the national synod of Loudun, the last of the French national synods. Here again complaints were brought against his doctrine and against Daillé, the moderator of the synod, by the province of Saintonge and Lower Languedoc. Both, however, were judged free of fault and were "exhorted to continue in their Faithful Imployment of those rich Talents, which God hath bestowed upon them to the advancement of his Glory, and the edifying of his Church."[172] The condemnation of de la Place's views on the imputation of Adam's sin was also somewhat softened at this synod. Amyraut was entrusted with publishing a correct edition of the discipline, but he apparently did not live to complete it.

In this year Amyraut also published his *Discours sur les songes divins dont il est parlé dans l'escriture*.[173] In 1661 he published the biography of François de la Nouë,[174] a project he had had in mind for some years. And in this same year he published a lengthy *De mysterio trinitatis, deque vocibus ac phrasibus quibus tam in scriptura quam apud patres explicatur, dissertatio*,[175] a work pointing up his idea of progressive revelation, with successive chapters on revelation of the mystery in nature, in the Old Testament, and in the gospel.[176] His argument in this is that the Trinity cannot be learned from the dispensation of nature, that it is a very obscure doctrine in the Old Testament, and that in the New Testament it is clearly revealed.

In the last two years of his life Amyraut returned to more dogmatic topics. In 1662 he published an *In orationem dominicam exercitatio* and in 1663 an *In symbolum apostolorum exercita-*

171. *Discours chrestien sur les eaux de Bourbon* (Charenton, 1658). Dedicated to the celebrated doctor of Gyen, Amyot.

172. Quick, *Synodicon*, 2:554.

173. Saumur, 1659. English trans. by J. Lowde (London, 1676).

174. *Vie de François de la Nouë, depuis le commencement des troubles religieux en 1560 jusqu'a sa mort* (Leyden, 1661).

175. Saumur, 1661, 546 pages.

176. Chapters 3, 4, and 5. Moltmann, in "Gnadenbund und Gnadenwahl," considers this an important work and uses it quite extensively.

tio.[177] At the same time he was working on a treatise which he planned to entitle *Théologie française.*[178] Unfortunately we have no trace of this, though Laplanche has reproduced some comments on it by du Bosc of Caen, an Amyraldian. "I have profited greatly from reading this work," testified du Bosc, "and I have found in it very many rare, solid (*fortes*), and ingenious things, and throughout a very exalted and free atmosphere peculiar to the author,"[179] but du Bosc goes on to reproach Amyraut for his method of following the Bible step by step. This is probably meant as a comment on what we would consider Amyraut's methodology—his historical rather than dogmatic approach to theology. We can only regret then that Amyraut did not live to see this *Théologie française* through to publication. He died on January 13, 1664.

177. Reprinted together in a volume at Utrecht in 1767.
178. There is a manuscript copy of notes for a treatise of this title at the Bibliothèque de l'Arsenal, but Professor Nicole assures me that the quality of work is so poor that it could not be the work planned by Amyraut.
179. As quoted in Laplanche, *L'Oeuvre d'Amyraut*, p. 71 and ff.

3

AMYRAUT'S THEOLOGY
IN ITS HISTORICAL SETTING

W E HAVE OBSERVED that there is no treatise from Amyraut which might be called a systematic theology. More important, what we do know about the *Théologie française* he proposed to write suggests that even this would not have been a systematics in the style of St. Thomas' *Summa,* or even of Calvin's *Institutio.* And it is important to recognize that the treatises we have from Amyraut indicate that he was quite unique in his tradition in this century, for he shows all signs of not having had any interest in constructing a systematized and ordered body of theological material. Indeed, it is not too much to say that if a novice in seventeenth-century Calvinist theology were to sit down and read a representative volume of orthodox Calvinism and then proceed to read a volume of Amyraut, the most obvious disparity he would notice would certainly be in approach, in methodology. It is a commonplace that the orthodox writings of the period are, almost without exception, characterized by two features. First, their theologies are basically composed of a body of systematized material, which systematization has been carried out by deductively moving to the specific doctrine at hand from a general principle—a general principle which may or may not have been derived from Scripture, and which often has its starting point in the decree of God. Second, the orthodox theologians seem to be so preoccupied with producing dogmatics from a

corpus of once-and-for-all revealed material that there is an almost total lack of appreciation for the idea of history and of
movement in history.[1] But Amyraut, as Moltmann notes, "In
place of the orthodox analytical development of the *decretum absolutum* substituted not only a new systematic, but also a new
theologico-historical approach."[2] We turn to a consideration of
this.

The Rapport of Salmurian Theology with Humanism

The strong influence of humanism in, indeed the predomi-
nantly humanistic orientation of, French Protestantism have
been stressed in chapter 1. In the seventeenth century this tradition lived on most vigorously, it appears, at the Saumur Academy[3] and did not survive in the other Reformed academies of
the period, a point of capital importance. This consideration
carries with it major implications for the theology developed at
Saumur in its relation to that taught at the other Reformed
schools, and so demands further clarification.

The term *humanism* has been variously and ambiguously used
in the past, and it seems important that we define at least in a
general way what is meant by its use here. Such a definition is
extremely difficult, as is a definition of the term *Protestant scholasticism*. Humanism, too, is basically a spirit, an attitude toward
life. In general the humanist ideal was practical rather than
philosophical, moralistic or ethical rather than metaphysical or
speculative, and interested in a reasonable, broad-minded pursuit
of truth rather than in a logical, precisely defined construction of
a system of truth. With this general characterization in mind we
can proceed to at least a working definition. In this definition we
will follow what the humanists themselves meant when they used
the term. Paul Kristeller shows that the *studia humanitatis* "was

---

1. K. Barth in *Church Dogmatics*, IV.i.2, designates the orthodox systematics
"static" as opposed to dynamic (p. 58 of the English trans.).
2. "Prädestination und Heilsgeschichte bei Moyse Amyraut," p. 275. See also
p. 287: "Gegenüber dem dogmatischen Apriorismus des orthodoxen Calvinismus
entwickelt sich in Saumur ein heilsgeschichtlicher Aposteriorismus, ein historisier-
ender Offenbarungsempirismus."
3. First emphasized by the ever-perceptive Hans Emil Weber, *Orthodoxie und
Rationalismus*, 2:135.

understood to include such subjects as grammar, rhetoric, poetry, history, and moral philosophy."[4] It should be added that the models followed in this program of studies were those of classical literature. That is, the humanists were men interested in the "humanities," if we may use the term, and who had recourse to antiquity for their authority. Moreover, as Kristeller further suggests, they "on the whole were neither good nor bad philosophers, but no philosophers at all."[5] For the most part the humanists were content to leave philosophy, at least logic and metaphysics, to the other branches of the Renaissance which Kristeller identifies as the Platonists and Aristotelians.[6] Thus in our use of the term, humanism refers primarily to that distinctive element in the Renaissance movement which generally avoided philosophy, metaphysics, logic, and a body of systematized "truth" but which positively stressed ethics, practicality, and reasonableness, and showed prime interest in a program of studies which we may call the humanities. The frame of reference was always the authority of the writings of antiquity; the prime goal, to produce the cultured, cosmopolitan man, the man who would be useful and influential in society.[7]

However, since Ramus, for example, is well known for his work in logic even though a humanist, perhaps the humanists' relation to logic needs further comment. It is true, of course, that the humanists did do some work in the field of logic or, again

---

4. Paul O. Kristeller, "The Moral Thought of Renaissance Humanism," in his *Renaissance Thought II: Papers on Humanism and the Arts* (New York, 1965), p. 24.

5. "Humanism and Scholasticism in the Italian Renaissance," in his *Renaissance Thought: The Classic, Scholastic and Humanistic Strains*, p. 100.

6. *Renaissance Thought, passim.*

7. Essentially I agree with Hanna Gray's contention that the rhetorical concern was paramount for the humanists ("Renaissance Humanism: The Pursuit of Eloquence," *JHI* 24 [Oct.–Dec., 1963], 497–514). However, I have not made this an element of my working definition because this aspect of the humanists' program is more or less nullified as a distinctive when one is dealing with Protestant ministers as I am here. From the very first one of the essential features of the Protestant Reformation was a particularly strong emphasis on the proclamation of the Word of God, on preaching. This has remained to our day the central part of the Protestant worship service. Thus to emphasize "the pursuit of eloquence" in this study in order to distinguish humanism from Protestant scholasticism would have little or no meaning.

in Kristeller's words, "made some attempts to invade the field of logic," but these attempts ought not to be understood as invasions of the field of logic per se. Rather, as Kristeller has noted, they were "chiefly attempts to reduce logic to rhetoric." That is to say, logic was not studied for the sake of logic, but rather the uniquely humanist pattern was maintained—rhetoric was the main interest and so even logic became a sort of rhetorical exercise. This was no doubt true of Ramus. Indeed, it is probable that Ong's discussion of the relation of the Ramean dialectic to Italian humanism would make a great deal more sense if he had recognized this distinction.[8] Ong makes much of Ramus' anti-Italian bias, citing his refusal of the chair offered him at Bologna, his refusal to visit Italy, and other such incidents. He then claims that in the light of Ramus' prowess and reputation as an orator, and of the strong "rhetorically centered culture" of Italian humanism, Ramus' "violent rejection of Italy while he promotes the cause of eloquence thus suggests an uneasiness at his own rhetorical prowess and aims which amounts to something like schizophrenia."[9] This judgment may be less than acceptable if a proper understanding of the Italian Renaissance is maintained. In the first place it is not to be uncritically accepted, as it apparently is by Ong, that the Italian Renaissance presented a uniform picture characterized solely by humanism. As we shall have occasion to illustrate more fully shortly, there were at least three quite distinct branches of the Italian Renaissance: humanism, Platonism, and Aristotelianism or scholasticism. And, moreover, this scholasticism was particularly strong, perhaps especially so at Bologna; recent studies have sufficiently documented a burgeoning Aristotelian scholasticism centered particularly at the universities of Padua and Bologna. Thus Ramus' aversion to the Italian intellectual movements may well evidence not schizophrenia but rather a keen awareness that from this source Aristotelian scholasticism was a very real threat. And if

8. Walter J. Ong, *Ramus: Method, and the Decay of Dialogue* (Cambridge, Mass., 1958), pp. 48–49. An immensely erudite study, but one wonders if Ong's frequent fulminations against Ramus may not be the reaction of a modern-day Aristotelian. I fully agree, however, with his main thesis that Ramism short-circuited *philosophical* discourse and development.

9. *Ibid.*, p. 49.

one accepts Ong's interpretation of Ramus, that much of his anti-Aristotelianism is in fact directed against the corruption of the true Aristotle, his "violent rejection of Italy" may take on even more meaning, since it is certain that to the humanist mind the Averroist, or for that matter the Alexandrian, tradition was far from pure Aristotle.

It is just this humanist orientation, I would maintain, which characterized the Saumur school, and any attempt to understand the theology developed there must necessarily be made with this in mind. Evidences of the humanistic spirit of the Salmurians are manifold, though no single one would by itself substantiate such a claim and one must consider them all. Because this is of such profound importance for the theology of Saumur, it would be well to indicate some of these.

In the first place let us turn again to the historical dimension of Salmurian thought. The Salmurian interest in history was manifest on all fronts, but was unique in the Reformed Protestantism of the time. We have seen already the contribution that the Salmurians made to the sphere of controversy in terms of an historical understanding. Add to this what Polman in his erudite study concerning this historical dimension of the religious controversy of the sixteenth century says: "To consider it in its historical orientation, the religious controversy of the sixteenth century is tied up with humanism."[10] Or again, "This different orientation of the polemic is due to the Protestants themselves, to the humanistic mentality of the French Calvinists which led them to familiarize themselves with the Fathers of the Church . . ."[11]

Secondly, we find manifested in the Salmurian theologians an interest in moral philosophy or ethics almost precisely as described by Kristeller for the humanists. We should note again Amyraut's massive, six-volume study, *La Morale chrestienne*. To my knowledge he is the first theologian within Reformed Protestantism to dedicate a major, separate work to the topic of ethics.[12]

10. Polman, *L'Elément historique dans la controverse religieuse du XVIe Siècle,* p. 239.

11. *Ibid.,* p. 277.

12. The existence of two short treatises, one by Lambert Danaeus, *Ethices chris-*

The method of procedure, the authorities cited (primarily Cicero, and Aristotle's *Nicomachean Ethics*), and the emphasis upon the practical intellect rather than upon the speculative intellect, all reflect almost perfectly the humanist models of the sixteenth century.[13] In any case, this separate treatment of ethics marks a rather radical break with the Calvinist and Lutheran traditions wherein ethics was linked with dogmatics in a single system. There is in this tendency to separate ethics from dogmatics evidence of an interest in natural theology not present in either Luther or Calvin. And perhaps this is even more obvious in Amyraut than in the others for in his *La Morale chrestienne* he mentioned that his resolve was to construct "upon the basis of *la Nature* the teachings which have been given by revelation."

Thirdly, one finds at Saumur critical work on the biblical texts, reflecting the humanist heritage. The outstanding example is of course Louis Cappel's *Arcanum punctationis revelatum,* published anonymously in 1624, and his *Critica sacra* of 1650, in which he pointed out that the vowel points of the Hebrew Bible did not date from Old Testament times but rather were additions of the Jewish grammarians sometime after the completion of the Babylonian Talmud. That this same humanist interest in critical work and truth was not accepted in other Reformed academies is evidenced by the fact that the Buxtorfs, father and son, of Basel, though universally esteemed for their Semitic studies, attacked these writings bitterly. Or, still more significant perhaps, that even some years after Cappel's death the *Formula consensus helvetica* (1675), drafted by John Henry Heidegger and Francis Turrettin to controvert the Salmurian theology, went so far as to assert the essential inspiration of these vowel points. In any case, the point is simply that the impulse behind Cappel's work as the father of modern biblical criticism came from humanism.

Fourthly, it is not without some significance that the logic,

---

tianae libri tres (Geneva, 1574), and an even shorter one by B. Keckermann, *Systema Ethicae, tribus libris adornatum & publicis praelectionibus traditum in gymnasio Dantiscano* (London, 1607), might raise doubts about this claim, but neither of these seriously challenges the some 5,000 pages of Amyraut.

13. See Kristeller in *Renaissance Thought II*, pp. 20–68.

and, it appears, to some extent even the epistemology, of Amyraut is Ramean.[14] Use of Ramus' thought, at least of his logic, in no way assures a non-scholastic orientation in theology, but it is another indication of humanist influence. To be sure, no conclusive proof is readily available to show indubitably that Amyraut is Ramean. That is, he does not seem ever to mention Ramus in his writings. Nevertheless we do know that his master Cameron was a zealous Ramist early in his career, and almost every work Amyraut wrote is replete with those wearisome bifurcations so dear to the Ramists.[15] Everything from God's mercy and will to sin and salvation must be considered, Amyraut tells us, "en deux manières." This cannot be documented here, but will become all too manifest as we proceed to discuss his theology.

There are several somewhat less important manifestations of the humanist inclination of the Salmurians. One could note a certain interest in poetry, for instance, an important element in humanism.[16] The first two, or perhaps three, treatises of Amyraut were attempts at poetry;[17] we know that Cameron also composed

14. This has been recognized by both Moltmann and Sabean. Sabean has shown that Amyraut's epistemology apparently derived from Ramus ("The Theological Rationalism of Moïse Amyraut," pp. 213–15). As I suggest below, I think Cicero may have been a more likely source. N. L. Torrey in his introduction to *Les Philosophes* (Capricorn, 1960), p. 15, notes: "We find in Cicero the idea of the essential equality of men and of the natural rights of man based on his submission to reason; also an exaltation of law as an expression of reasonableness." This is strikingly like the ideas of Amyraut. There is an ever-recurrent rational motif in his writings, an element always closely bound up with his doctrine of natural law. This topic deserves further study, but it may be suggested here as an example that in the opening chapters of his *Brief Traitté*, Amyraut develops his argument according to natural law in order to prove the reasonableness of the concept of a predetermined fate.

15. Most of his works could be charted a la the Ramean chart in Ong, *Ramus*, p. 31, or Perry Miller, *The New England Mind: The Seventeenth Century* (Cambridge, Mass., 1939), p. 126.

16. See Kristeller in *Renaissance Thought II*, pp. 12–24, or esp. J. Huizinga's scintillating address on Grotius as reprinted in *Men & Ideas* (Cleveland: Meridian paperbacks, 1965), p. 330: "Grotius wrote more than ten thousand lines of verse in Latin, and almost as many in Dutch, without being a poet. . . . The writing of Latin verse, as it was practiced by the humanists, was one of the most remarkable occupations of the human spirit known to cultural history. It was a pastime, but what a majestic one."

17. See the first entries in bibliography of Amyraut's works.

verse throughout his life.[18] Biography, also a particular interest of the humanists, was an interest shared by Amyraut, evidenced in his life of François de la Noüe. Again, the cosmopolitanism and urbanity of Amyraut probably derived in large measure from the *uomo universale* motif so prominent in Italian humanism. And finally, Amyraut revealed a great interest in Cicero, a favorite from among the ancients for most humanists. In fact, it seems that if one would understand Amyraut's philosophy and epistemology he must look to Cicero rather than to Plato or Aristotle.

But perhaps the most conclusive proof of the humanism of Saumur theologians is brought out by a comparison of their theology and orientation with that of the other Reformed academies of this period. We have briefly outlined in chapter 1 the origins of the scholasticism which so quickly set in within Reformed Protestantism after the death of Calvin. It remains for us to fill in the story so that we may understand the emphases of Salmurian theology in its reaction against that scholasticism.

CALVINIST SCHOLASTICISM

It should be said at the outset, since there is still so much confusion on the matter, that the old idea which held that the very emergence of the Renaissance and Reformation meant a forsaking of Aristotle and scholasticism needs to be abandoned.[19] Recent research by J. H. Randall, Jr.,[20] P. O. Kristeller,[21] E. Cassirer,[22] and others has conclusively shown that we may quite properly speak of Renaissance Aristotelianism, and that it was a very flourishing tradition. "Simultaneously with humanism," Kristeller notes, "Italian Aristotelianism developed steadily

18. See, for example, his *Opera*, pp. 849 and 789ff.

19. A scholarly account of scholasticism and its relation to Reformed theology remains a major desideratum. The old study by Althaus, which was apparently inspired by Ernst Troeltsch's *Vernunft und Offenbarung*, is the best general study to date, although the treatises by Kickel on Beza and by Gründler on Zanchius are learned and useful contributions.

20. Esp. *The School of Padua and the emergence of Modern Science* (Padua, 1961), which includes an interesting essay on Pomponazzi.

21. *Renaissance Thought*, pp. 24–47, 92–118; *Renaissance Thought II*, pp. 111–18; *Eight Philosophers of the Italian Renaissance* (Stanford, 1964), *passim*.

22. Esp. *The Individual and the Cosmos* (New York, 1963), particularly ch. 3.

through the fourteenth century under the influence of Paris and Oxford, became more independent and more productive through the fifteenth century, and attained its greatest development during the sixteenth and early seventeenth centuries, in such comparatively well known thinkers as Pomponazzi, Zabarella, and Cremonini."[23] And one may go so far as to say that this "Renaissance Aristotelianism continued the medieval scholastic tradition without any visible break."[24] Moreover, there was at this time a vigorous and thriving scholasticism in Spain which centered in the Dominican and Jesuit orders, and mainly at the University of Salamanca, though there were strong movements at Alcalá, Coimbra, and other centers. Indeed, this Spanish scholasticism was so strong that Copleston can say with it in mind that "some of the greatest names in Scholasticism belong to the period of the Renaissance and the beginning of the modern era."[25]

Because strong scholasticism existed in Spain, and even more in Italy, the position taken by Althaus, standard up until now, should be somewhat revised. Althaus understood scholasticism to have been introduced into Reformed theology from two streams—from Melanchthon proceeding through Keckermann, Alsted et al., and from the Italian Aristotelians.[26] He stressed the former; but it is most likely that the Italian scholasticism spoken of so briefly above had a much more direct and pervasive influence upon the introduction of scholasticism into Reformed theology than the Melanchthonian tradition.[27] In fact, we would be unable to explain some of the earlier manifestations of Reformed scholasticism if it were dependent on Melanchthon; Italian Aristotelianism must be accorded a much more important role than has been hitherto recognized. There are many reasons for this conviction, but until more research is done into the Italian Aris-

23. Renaissance Thought, p. 36.

24. Ibid., p. 114.

25. F. Copleston, A History of Philosophy (Garden City: Image Books, 1963), III.ii.153.

26. Althaus, Die Prinzipien der deutschen reformierten Dogmatik, p. 12.

27. The Scot Robert Boyd, when teaching at Montauban in the first years of the seventeenth century, urged his students to consult day and night philosophical writers of note, especially the Italian Zabarella (as related in Reid, Divinity Principals in Glasgow, 1:121). Zabarella was, of course, a strong advocate of the Aristotelian tradition.

totelianism of the period our case must necessarily be somewhat fragmentary.

During his lifetime the non-scholastic theology of Calvin generally dominated the theological dimension of Reformed Protestantism. Yet some years before his death elements of scholasticism were impinging upon Reformed theology in rather significant ways. This is seen most clearly in the work of three men, all in part contemporary with Calvin: Girolamo Zanchi, Peter Martyr Vermigli, and Theodore Beza. Zanchi and Vermigli were, of course, Italians and were directly affected by the Italian Aristotelianism; Beza seems to have turned increasingly to this source for his formulations.

The movement of Beza away from Calvin's basic theological position and towards scholasticism has been dealt with in chapter 1. Here it will suffice to underline what was noted in that context and to make a few brief observations. First, it is not unimportant that the treatise Beza requested in his correspondence was the work of the *Italian* Aristotelian, Pietro Pomponazzi. Martin Pine has shown in a recent article that Pomponazzi probably was more interested in reason than faith, arguing that his position "marks a definite turning point in the history of European rationalism."[28] Further we might well consider the following: (1) Beza's movement in the direction of the scholastic spirit was gradual, and it would be a mistake to regard the cleavage between Calvin's and Beza's theology one that was readily apparent to the contemporary observer. In early life Beza, like Calvin, was deeply influenced by the humanism of the French Renaissance. Beza in fact was particularly renowned in two pastimes of the humanist genre, the writing of verse and philological work. However, as the exigencies of a strong theological program to oppose to Roman Catholicism faced Beza day by day, he resorted more and more to the scholastic type of answer. (2) It was Beza who most directly and powerfully influenced Reformed Protestantism in this direction.

At the same time, the influence of men like Zanchi and Peter Martyr was not inconsiderable and so deserves further mention.

28. "Pomponazzi and 'Double Truth,'" *JHI* (1968), p. 176. An especially clear-sighted article.

The scholasticism of Zanchi, indeed his direct dependence on the scholastic theology of St. Thomas, has been convincingly demonstrated in the work of Otto Gründler.[29] Gründler points out that Zanchi differed radically from Calvin's teaching on the knowledge of God, faith (both as to its object and nature), and providence-predestination.[30] But what is more important, he shows that at each of these points of deviation from Calvin Zanchi had in fact substituted the teaching of St. Thomas. Indeed, Gründler can conclude his study in such unequivocal language as the following:

> In the theology of Zanchi, at the very point of transition from Reformation to Orthodoxy, the spirit of medieval Scholasticism has thus begun to replace that of the Reformers at a point where it counted most. To the extent to which—under the influence of the Thomistic-Aristotelian tradition—the christocentric orientation of Calvin's thinking shifted toward a metaphysics of causality in the thought of his successors, Reformed theology ceased to be a theology of revelation.[31]

Peter Martyr's thought has not yet been analyzed for the scholasticism or non-scholasticism of his formulations. In the most recent scholarly presentation of his theology, Joseph McLelland in fact struggles to rescue him from the charge of scholasticism.[32] Yet McLelland's arguments are not wholly convincing, for he does not appear to address himself to the pertinent questions. He readily admits that during Martyr's student days at Padua Aristotle was his favorite philosopher; he does not, however, go on to entertain the possibility that this might portend a scholastic methodology for Martyr's theology. On the other hand Philip McNair, in his excellent, detailed study of Martyr's early career,

29. "Thomism and Calvinism in the theology of Girolamo Zanchi." Cf. Bizer, *Frühorthodoxie und Rationalismus*, pt. 4, pp. 50–60.

30. I agree heartily with the major emphases of Gründler, though when he says that Calvin is supralapsarian I must dissent. Calvin, as we have noted, never spoke of an order in God's decrees. Further, the bulk of his discussion seems to point toward his belief that God elected man out of a fallen mass. See *Institutio* III.xxiii.3.

31. "Thomism and Calvinism," p. 159; German trans., p. 126.

32. Joseph C. McLelland, *The Visible Words of God; An Exposition of the Sacramental Theology of Peter Martyr Vermigli, A.D. 1500–1562* (Grand Rapids, 1957), p. 3.

would seem to present evidence that the scholastic approach was at the very basis of Martyr's theological program.[33] For example, he quotes with approval the following from Simler's *Life of Martyr:* ". . . when Martyr was at Padua he preferred his theology *in via Thomae,* for he exercised himselfe cheefely in the schools divines, speciallie *Thomas,* and *Ariminensis"*; and he can conclude that "Peter Martyr was a Thomist before he became a patrist."[34]

But did Martyr retain this Thomist bent after he had joined the Protestant Reform? This question is not answered by McNair, since he does not deal with Martyr the Reformer. He thus leaves the problem in abeyance, but is able to conclude that "Whatever Martyr came to think in later years of the Thomism of the theologians of Padua, he retained to the end of his life a warm regard for the Aristotelianism of the Paduan philosophers."[35] It would seem from the foregoing that one ought naturally to expect a scholastic methodology in Martyr's theology, and although a definitive statement must wait for more detailed study there is little doubt in my mind that this existed. It is not to be forgotten that Zanchi himself was a product of the school Vermigli established and dominated at Lucca. It would seem surprising if the methodology of the master were not reflected in his student. Moreover, we know that while at Strasbourg Vermigli lectured regularly on Aristotle and that he produced a lengthy commentary on Aristotle's *Ethics.* Such an affinity with Aristotle does not, of course, automatically prove scholasticism, but points in that direction. Perhaps there is no stronger evidence than the fact that B. B. Warfield, no stranger to scholasticism himself, has stated without qualification that "The scholastic theologian among the early Reformers was Peter Martyr."[36]

The farther one advances toward and into the seventeenth century the more scholastic becomes the theology he encounters, whether he studies theology in Protestant Germany, Scotland,

33. *Peter Martyr in Italy* (Oxford, 1967), esp. pp. 102ff.
34. *Ibid.,* p. 106.
35. *Ibid.,* p. 107.
36. B. B. Warfield, "John Calvin the Theologian," appended to his *Calvin and Augustine* (Philadelphia, 1956), p. 481.

the Netherlands, or France.[37] It is true, generally, that until the end of the sixteenth century this scholasticism did not extend to metaphysical speculation. There were myriad handbooks on Aristotelian logic, a great deal of use of his physics, but little or no interest in his metaphysics. By the middle of the seventeenth century, however, most of the Reformed academies had a chair of metaphysics. Dibon has recorded this in his detailed and scholarly study of the universities of the Netherlands and can even make the surprising statement that the Jesuit Suarez "either directly or through the medium of J. Martini, is the uncontested master of the metaphysical renaissance of the Netherlands."[38] Such an orientation was quite antithetical to that of Saumur, where as late as the mid-1650's Amyraut unequivocally expressed his aversion to "metaphysical speculations which contribute little or nothing to the composition of our happiness and which in themselves are incredibly unreliable" (*merveilleusement defectueuses*).[39]

We have maintained that the French Protestants generally lagged behind in their acceptance of the burgeoning scholasticism of Reformed Protestantism. In his recent extended study on the life of du Moulin, Lucien Rimbault recognizes this when he says the French Church inclined "more toward the conciliating theses of Amyraut than toward the intransigency of du Moulin."[40] This less scholastic mood of the French Church I have suggested as one of the reasons Gomarus left Saumur after two short years. But in spite of this tendency of French Protestantism to retain a humanistic spirit, du Moulin made a valiant effort to introduce

37. See for example all works cited in note 84 of chapter 1. Add to these Max Wundt, *Die Deutsche Schulmetaphysik des 17. Jahrhunderts* (Tübingen, 1939); Paul Dibon, *La Philosophie néerlandaise au siècle d'or: L'Enseignement philosophique dans les universités à l'epoque précartésienne (1575–1650)* (Paris, 1954); Ernst Bizer, "Reformed Orthodoxy and Cartesianism," *Journal for Theology and the Church* 2 (New York, 1965), 20–82; introduction to Gerhard in Walther Zeller, ed., *Der Protestantismus des 17. Jahrhunderts* (Marburg, 1963); introduction to Beardslee, ed., *Reformed Dogmatics*, pp. 3–25.

38. Dibon, *La Philosophie néerlandaise*, p. 257.

39. *La Morale chrestienne* (Saumur, 1652–1660), 1:212.

40. *Pierre du Moulin 1568–1658: Un Pasteur classique à l'age classique* (Paris, 1966), p. 8. See also Labrousse, *Pierre Bayle*, 1:56–57.

the more scholastic orientation of the rest of the Reformed world.

The Arminian crisis of the Netherlands was the immediate occasion for du Moulin's precipitous action. The reaction against scholastic Calvinism which had taken place in England before the end of the sixteenth century had its counterpart in the Low Countries in the work of Arminius (Jacob Hermandszoon, 1560–1609) and his followers.[41] Probably because of the extreme position of the Dutch orthodox like Gomarus, Maccovius, Bogerman, and later Voetius and Maresius, the Arminian reaction took an extreme and heterodox position.[42] In the early stages of this quarrel du Moulin had counselled moderation, and had even undertaken some efforts of his own to bring about concord.[43] However by 1617 he had apparently become convinced that there was real heresy in the Arminian position. He was one of the delegates chosen to represent the French Church at the Dort synod, but at the last moment Louis XIII had withdrawn permission for the French delegates to attend. Before the synod had convened, du Moulin had composed a substantial treatise in which he had exposed the errors of the Arminians and had even congratulated the Dort delegates on their judgment of condemnation. His co-ministers at Charenton, Durant and Mestrezat, however, had succeeded in having a measure passed at the provincial synod which forbade its publication before the close of the Dort

41. It is often forgotten that, as T. M. Parker points out, "the major issues in the Arminian dispute had been fought out in England before the name of Arminius was known and long before the Arminian controversy became acute" ("Arminianism and Laudianism in Seventeenth-Century England," *Studies in Church History*, ed. Dugmore and Duggan [London, 1964], 1:26). See also C. W. Porter, *Reformation and Reaction in Tudor Cambridge* (Cambridge, 1958), *passim*, but esp. pp. 376–418, and A. W. Harrison, *Arminianism* (London, 1937), p. 123. Richard Hooker, Lancelot Andrewes, John Overall, and Peter Baro are only a few of the names which could be advanced as representatives of this reaction. For a study of Arminianism, see esp. Harrison, *Arminianism*, as well as *The Beginnings of Arminianism* (London, 1926); also Carl O. Bangs, "Arminius and Reformed Theology" (Ph.D. diss., University of Chicago, 1958).

42. Even the hyperorthodox Pierre du Moulin was distressed at the hard line taken by the Dutch orthodox, and in a letter of 1616 printed in Rimbault (*Pierre du Moulin*, p. 90) says that these extreme positions "do harm to a good cause." I suspect further that the famous remark of John Hales, that at Dort he "bade John Calvin good night," was the result of his aversion to these intransigent orthodox rather than in fact to the theology of Calvin.

43. Harrison, *The Beginnings of Arminianism*, pp. 211, 256, 332.

synod.[44] Nevertheless du Moulin apparently sent the manuscript to Dort, though it must have arrived too late to play any part in the Dort decision.[45] This work was published in 1619 under the title *Anatome arminianismi*.[46] It is a harsh expose of the Arminian heresy, but hardly as violent as his writings against Amyraut which we have considered in the previous chapter.

Evidently du Moulin, recognizing the non-scholastic nature of the French Church, considered Arminianism a real threat to that church. In any case, he took some rather extreme measures at the national synod of Alais (1620), of which he was elected moderator. This synod, at which, as we have mentioned above, he was accused of usurping an *"autorité papale,"* took action which made the Dort Canons binding on the French Church.[47] And we may assume that he was mainly responsible for the accompanying, deplorable subscription clause.

> I N. N. do Swear and Protest before God, and this Holy Assembly that I do receive, approve and imbrace all the Doctrines taught and decided by the Synod of *Dort,* as perfectly agreeing with the word of God, and the Confession of our Churches. I Swear and Promise to persevere in the Profession of this Doctrine during my whole Life, and to defend it with the utmost of my power, and that I will never, neither by Preaching nor Teaching in the Schools, nor by Writing depart from it. I declare also and I protest that I reject and condemn the Doctrine of the *Arminians,* because it makes Gods Decree of Election depend upon the mutable Will of Man, and for that it doth extenuate and make null and void the Grace of God; it exalteth Man, and the powers of Free Will to his destruction, it reduceth into the Church of God old, ejected Pelagianisme, and is a Mask and Vizard for Popery to creep in among us under that disguise, and subverteth all Assurance of Everlasting Life and Happyness. And so may God help me, and be propitious to me, as I swear all this without any Ambiguity, Equivocation or mental Reservation.[48]

But, for our purposes, even more significant than this action

44. Rimbault, *Pierre du Moulin,* p. 89.

45. Harrison, *The Beginnings of Arminianism,* p. 380.

46. Leyden, 1619. The work was immediately translated into English and published under the title *The Anatomy of Arminianism* (London, 1620; again 1624).

47. Quick, *Synodicon,* 2:37ff.; Aymon, *Tous les synodes,* 2:165ff.

48. Quick, *Synodicon,* 2:38–39.

relating to the Dort Canons was an act passed which dealt with the duties of the theology professors in the Reformed academies. We read in this article that there should be at least two professors of theology, one to expound the Scriptures, the other to expound the commonplaces within the space of three years. And then the methodology these professors of the commonplaces are to follow is spelled out. They are to explain all "solidly, and as succinctly as possible, in a scholastic manner, in order that the students may be profited as much as possible and that they may be enabled to apply themselves most forcefully to disputes and metaphysical distinctions."[49]

This appears to be a most explicit regulation to force a scholastic methodology upon the French Church. And it is most interesting that when ratifying these proceedings for their academy the Saumur council deleted the phrase concerning disputes and metaphysical distinctions.[50] Indeed, Quick's version also omits this phrase and also changes the phrase "in a scholastic manner" to read "as becomes a Scholar."[51] We wonder if Quick was not perhaps using a manuscript which had been altered by an advocate of the Salmurian theology. Or perhaps he had secured a copy of the synodal proceedings which was directly dependent on the text used at Saumur.[52] In any case, our interest is to take note of

---

49. The article in full reads: "Il y aura deux Professeurs en Theologie pour le moins, l'un desquels exposera l'Escriture Sainte, sans s'étendre beaucoup sur les Lieux Communs: L'autre enseignera les Lieux Communs, & s'il est possible d'avoir trois Professeurs, l'un Exposera le vieux Testament, l'autre le Nouveau, & le troisieme les Lieux Communs; lesquels il achevera en trois Ans, pour le plus tard, en expliquant le tout solidement & le plus succintement qu'il sera possible d'une Maniere Scholastique, pour faire d'autant mieux profiter les Etudians, qu'ils seront obligés de s'apliquer plus fortement aux Disputes, & aux Distinctions Metaphisiques: Et les Professeurs en Theologie s'obligeront à dicter quelque Sommaire de leurs Leçons" (Aymon, 2:210).

50. Bourchenin, *Les Académies protestantes*, p. 253ff.

51. *Synodicon*, 2:62.

52. A problem does exist here, for Quick's text is generally superior to Aymon's, but I would question whether it is at this point. It is not simply a matter of a variant reading, but rather of a significant deletion in the text, and in my comparison of the texts of Quick and Aymon I have seldom encountered this problem. But even if we should agree that this was a later addition to the Aymon manuscript, it still points toward the scholastic orientation we are interested in setting forth.

this attempt to bring scholasticism into the French Reformed Church. That it did not wholly succeed we shall see shortly.

But the question remains, What specific effects did this scholasticism have upon Reformed theology? While it produced profound alterations in some of Calvin's doctrinal teachings, perhaps the most significant result was a change in methodology. This manifested itself primarily in the approach to theological issues. No longer was the primary approach the analytic and inductive, but rather the synthetic and deductive. Theology was explained not as experienced by man and from his viewpoint but as determined by God and from the perspective of God. This approach was, then, primarily interested in the logical explication of the source of theology—that is, the counsel of God. It is of course true that even the most scholastic of these divines would, paying lip service to Calvin's principle, caution against excessive speculation concerning the incomprehensible counsel of God. Nevertheless, they would then proceed to discuss theology by taking as their starting point the decrees of God, indeed in terms of a specific order in these decrees, giving the impression that there was nothing incomprehensible about them. The famous infralapsarian-supralapsarian debate, of course, offers an excellent example of this.

It was this methodology which underlay the most celebrated of all the alterations of Calvin's system, the placing of the doctrine of predestination in the doctrine of God. This was accomplished by Beza in its most extreme, supralapsarian form.[53] It was also the approach taken by Zanchi.[54] In fact, though this supralapsarian expression of the doctrine of predestination never found its way into the Reformed confessions, it did become the more common position in Geneva, the academies of the Low Countries, and even in Scotland, while it found adherents in all countries where the Reformed faith found currency.[55] It was be-

53. See for example Beza's chart of theology extracted from his *Summa totius Christianismi* and printed in Heppe-Bizer, *Die Dogmatik,* p. 119.

54. See Gründler, "Thomism and Calvinism," p. 143; German trans., p. 112.

55. See Otto Ritschl, *Dogmengeschichte des Protestantismus* (Göttingen, 1926), 3:293–314.

cause the approach taken was synthetic and deductive that predestination became truly the *Centraldogma* of Reformed theology.[56] Since the starting point in theological formulation was the divine decrees, there was no alternative but to discuss the whole of soteriology in terms of divine predestination or reprobation. The use of this methodological principle also explains the oft-cited debate between supra- and infralapsarians.[57] The whole debate was probably based in the precise relation of the fall of man to God's will—that is, in a desire by some theologians to remove any possible implication that God is the author of sin. However, it soon developed into an abstract, speculative debate concerned solely with the logical ordering of the decrees of God. Most certainly one must agree that the whole debate was hardly based on scriptural teaching; at least there is very little in Scripture which would support the supralapsarian position that the object of predestination was *homo creabilis et labilis*. It seems, in fact, clear that the supralapsarian position was taken precisely in order to satisfy the demands of logic. And it cannot be denied that in terms of logic itself it is the more satisfactory position. But this is just the point. Using God's decrees as a starting point demands that a logical connection be realizable to enable one to construct a theological system. Thus it is the methodology which forced theologians into this impasse, a methodology quite foreign to Calvin himself.

This synthetic methodology of the Reformed scholastics was responsible for another teaching in which Beza and Calvinism went beyond Calvin himself, the doctrine of limited atonement.[58]

---

56. This is the approach popularized by Alexander Schweizer in his 2-volume work *Die Protestantischen Centraldogmen* (Zurich, 1853–56). Though hotly contested by J. H. A. Ebrard, this view has characterized most Calvin studies until very recently; William Hastie, *Theology of the Reformed Church* (London, 1904) p. 224ff., is a good example of an English-speaking advocate.

57. Ritschl in *Dogmengeschichte,* 3:295, maintains that "strictly speaking, this theory known as supralapsarian could more properly be called supracreationism." Though the term might be appropriate to its later stages, it would tend to obscure the original relation of the theory to the Fall, as described above.

58. Many have argued that Calvin himself favored the view that Jesus died only for the elect (see esp. Roger Nicole, "Moyse Amyraut and the Controversy on Universal Grace"). I cannot but feel that this position flies in the face of the evidence in Calvin's writings. There are many passages in which he makes the universal

For even this doctrine, as developed by orthodox Calvinism, is a consequence of the starting point in the divine decrees. If one approaches theology in this way, accepting the idea that the order of decrees has a strict logical sequence, a universal atonement becomes untenable. For the decree of election for both infra- and supralapsarian theologians was thought to be the basis for the decree of sending Christ. That is, Christ is sent to redeem the elect. In this schematization any idea of a universal atonement becomes an affront to the God who does all things decently and in order.

Again, perhaps one of the most overlooked changes in later Reformed theology from the theology of Calvin is the radical change having to do with the doctrine of faith. For Calvin, faith was the key to all theological knowledge, indeed, the locus under which all of theology was to be discussed and understood.[59] Cal-

---

reference of Christ's atoning work quite explicit. In his "De aeterna Dei predestinatione" this topic arises and Calvin responds that the teaching that Christ died for all is beyond controversy: "Controversia etiam caret, Christum expiandis totius mundi peccatis venisse. Sed confestim occurrit illa solutio: Ut quisquis credit in eum non pereat, sed habeat vitam aeternam (Joann. 3,15). Nec vero qualis sit Christi virtus, vel quid per se valeat, nunc quaeritur: sed quibus se fruendum exhibeat" (CO, 8:336). Again, in his sermon on Isaiah 53 he says: "Ainsi donc il nous faut bien noter ces mots du Prophete, quand il dit que la correction de nostre paix a este sur nostre Seigneur Jesus Christ: d'autant que par son moyen Dieu est appointé et appaisé: car il a porté sur soy tous les vices et toutes les iniquitez du monde" (CO, 35:627). In his commentary on John 3: 16–17 he states that God "has ordained His Son to be the salvation of the world" (CO, 47:66). In his commentary on Romans 5:10 he states that Christ's death was "an expiatory sacrifice through which the world was reconciled to God." And in his important sermon on I Timothy II:3–5 he repeats this sentiment often: ". . . Jesus Christ est venu pour estre Sauveur commun de tous en general, . . ." (CO, 53:149). "Pourquoy donc est-ce que maintenant nous sommes domestiques de la foy, enfans de Dieu, et membres de nostre Seigneur Jesus Christ? c'est d'autant qu'il nous a recueillis à soy. Or n'est-il point Sauveur de tout le monde aussi bien? Jesus Christ est-il venu pour estre Moyenneur seulement entre deux ou trois hommes? Nenni: mais il est Moyenneur entre Dieu et les hommes" (CO, 53:159–160). Moreover, he can even lament that "it is no light matter that souls should perish who were bought by the blood of Christ" (Sermon on II Timothy 2:19). When this evidence is compared with what is presented in our chapter 4, notes 73, 81–83, and esp. 87, it would seem that the position is untenable which holds that Calvin teaches Christ died for the elect only.

59. See Dowey, The Knowledge of God in Calvin's Theology, p. 151ff.

vin's approach was basically in terms of the experience of the believer, as directed by the Word of God. But when the synthetic methodology was introduced, faith automatically lost its overarching position in theological formulation and was relegated to the position of one of many topics, or loci, usually one quite far down the line. Not only did faith lose its position as central and introductory to theological formulations, but, treated simply as one of many loci, it quickly lost the existential quality present in Calvin's formulations. Gründler has carefully detailed the very significant reorientation of this doctrine of faith in Zanchi. He has shown that the object of faith for Zanchi is simply an assent to the truth of the Scriptures. "In unequivocal terms faith, or the act of faith, is described as assent to the propositions of the entire body of Scripture as the true Word of God."[60] This far-reaching position was to become the common idea in orthodox Calvinism but is a far cry from Calvin's definition, which makes faith founded not upon the truth of the Scriptures but "upon the truth of the freely given promise in Christ, both revealed to our minds and sealed upon our hearts through the Holy Spirit."[61]

A different object of faith is not the only change Zanchi introduces to this doctrine, however; the nature of faith, as well, becomes something else than it was in Calvin. In the description of faith which Gründler has quoted from Zanchi we find it to be "the living and perpetuous virtue or power freely infused by the Father."[62] As Zanchi goes on to develop this idea he does so in such a way that Gründler can say without hesitation, "there can be no doubt that Zanchi's view represents a conscious and clear return to the Thomistic understanding of faith as an infused habit and virtue, a supernatural quality by which we believe."[63] Again, this conception of the nature of faith found much currency in orthodox explication, although it is not found nearly as frequently as that reorientation which made the truth of God's revelation the object of faith.

Against the scholasticism of seventeenth-century Reformed

60. "Thomism and Calvinism," p. 57; German trans., p. 49.

61. *Institutio*, III.ii.7. *OS*, IV.16.33–35. See also III.ii.29, where Calvin says that "faith properly begins with the promise, rests in it, and ends in it" (*OS*, IV.5–6).

62. "Thomism and Calvinism," p. 57; German trans., p. 48.

63. *Ibid.*, p. 69; German trans., p. 58.

theology, and particularly against the methodology we have described, the Salmurian theology was directed. It is in the light of this reaction that it is to be understood. Orentin Douen has admirably summed up its fundamental orientation:

> It is the glory of the university of Saumur, established in 1598 by du Plessis-Mornay, to have, on the one hand, enlarged the dogmatic formulas so as to give place to the conscience, that is to say, to have subordinated the metaphysical element to the ethical and religious element; and on the other hand, to have founded theology upon the terrain of facts and observation.[64]

The Motif of Amyraut's Theology

"Since the one aid to life and the one impulse for the acquisition of supreme happiness depends on the knowledge of true religion, such as ought to be obtained from divine revelation, and since *all true religion necessarily consists in some covenant which exists between God and men,* then no one can doubt that it is of the highest importance that one diligently apply himself to the explication and understanding of the divine covenants."[65] So wrote Amyraut sometime before 1637. The more one reads the treatises of Amyraut the more he realizes that the peculiar covenant theology he expounds is the key to the whole theological program at Saumur. This has been shown convincingly in Jürgen Moltmann's doctoral dissertation, "Gnadenbund und Gnadenwahl." Though Moltmann uses the original sources rather carelessly, one cannot quarrel with his ultimate position. Because of his work, and because a précis of it is readily available in the *Zeitschrift für Kirchengeschichte,*[66] the following presentation will not go into great detail, but will ask some questions which Moltmann did not ask, principally *why* the covenant theology?

---

64. *La Révocation de l'édit de Nantes à Paris,* 1:273.

65. Emphasis added. The passage reads: "Cum in notitia verae Religionis, qualis ab hominibus ex Divina revelatione haberi debet, situm sit unicum vitae praesidum unicumque momentum ad summam beatitudinem obtinendam, omnem autem veram religionem consistere necesse sit in aliquo foedere quod inter Deum & homines intercedat, quin summa sit adhibenda diligentia in explicanda & intelligenda natura *foederum divinorum,* nemo est qui dubitare possit" (thesis 1, "De tribus foederibus divinis," *Theses Salmurienses,* 1:212).

66. Vol. 65 (1954), 270–303.

Moltmann tells us that Amyraut's covenant theology is an *"absolut treue Kopie"* of Cameron's covenant teaching.[67] With but slight revision this claim can be accepted, and the reader is therefore referred to the section on Cameron's covenant teaching in chapter 1 of this study.

By Amyraut's time the covenant theology had become an integral part of much of Reformed theology. Though Cocceius' classic work on federal theology did not appear until 1648,[68] one finds evidence of a carefully and extensively developed version of the teaching in all of the Reformed countries long before this time. Perry Miller has traced it back to the early part of the century in English Puritanism.[69] We have noticed above that Rollock as early as 1597 had unequivocally proclaimed that "God does not communicate to man except it be through a covenant," and that he taught a double covenant. As is well known, the Westminster Confession also develops a double covenant teaching,[70] an idea which had been clearly presented, among other places, in William Ames' *Medulla sacrae theologiae* (1623), in Johannes Wollebius' *Compendium theologiae christianae* (1626), and in the supralapsarian John Downame's *Body of Divinitie* (1645), often ascribed to Archbishop Ussher.[71] From this we may conclude that covenant theology per se was in no way incompatible with orthodox Calvinism. Indeed, curiously enough, one of the main features of this orthodoxy, the insistence upon a limited atonement, was thought to be made more conclusive by the exposition of the inter-Trinitarian pact.[72]

67. *Ibid.*, p. 285.

68. *Summa doctrinae de foedere et testamento Dei.*

69. See his much-acclaimed article, "The Marrow of Puritan Divinity," *The Publications of the Colonial Society of Massachusetts* 32 (1935), 247–300, or his *The New England Mind: The Seventeenth Century*, app. B, pp. 502–5. The former has been conveniently reprinted in his *Errand into the Wilderness* (New York: Harper Torchbooks, 1964), pp. 48–98.

70. See ch. 7 of the Confession in Philip Schaff, *Creeds of Christendom* (New York, 1931), 3:616–17.

71. This work has been frequently reprinted as Ussher's and is even today attributed to him by learned authors. Elrington, in his life of Ussher prefaced to Ussher's *Works* (17 vols. [Dublin, 1864]), has shown it was not Ussher's. He has published a letter of Ussher's explicitly denying his authorship (see 1:249).

72. In an interesting sermon by David Dickson before the General Assembly of the Church of Scotland held at Glasgow in 1638 Dickson distinguished 3 cove-

However, despite the adaptability of covenant theology to orthodox dogma, one cannot but conclude that, in fact, the Saumur version of covenant theology must be regarded as the device seized upon and employed by the Saumur theologians in order to correct what they considered to be the unhealthy emphases of orthodox Calvinism. This becomes quite clear from the very first. Our concern will not be to judge whether or not it was a successful cure-all, but (1) to give an exposition of the content of their corrective theology and (2) since their claim was that they were recapturing the emphases of Calvin, to give some attention to the alleged dependence of the Saumur theology on the theology of Calvin.

The Saumur theologians envisioned a manifold function for their covenant theology. It became the basis for an attempt to resolve the thorny problem of the relationship of God's mercy and justice, for the attempt to restore faith to its rightful position in the Calvinist theological system, for the attempt to restore the dynamic ministry of the Holy Spirit in that system, for the attempt to correct the legalistic orientation of Calvinist orthodoxy, and for the attempt to restore a more historical perspective to the understanding of God's revelation unto, and dealings with, man. But all of these seem to pale into insignificance in the light of the following consideration: unquestionably the predominant design of this covenant scheme was to restore what these men firmly believed to be the teaching of Scripture, Calvin, and the Dort Canons concerning the matter of predestination. That is, the placing of predestination in the doctrine of God, where it became an a priori principle for the development of theology, was attacked as gross metaphysical speculation and therefore invalid theological procedure, an attempt to comprehend the incomprehensible. Amyraut insisted that predestination must enter theology only at the point where Calvin discussed it—as an ex post

---

nants: the covenant of redemption between God and Christ, the covenant of works, and the covenant of grace. On the basis of the covenant of redemption he held that the agreement was made between God and Christ that only payment for the sins of the elect would be made (sermon in W. K. Tweedie, ed., *Select Biographies* [Edinburgh, 1847], pp. 17–27).

facto explanation of the work of salvation with special reference to the work of the Holy Spirit. (See chapter 4.)

As Amyraut develops his covenant theology he begins, as did Cameron, by distinguishing two types of covenant by which God relates himself to man: (1) the *foedus absolutum,* the type of covenant made by God with Noah and which does not require, or depend on, the fulfillment of any condition or stipulation on man's part;[73] (2) that genus of covenant which is established upon a reciprocal agreement (*reciprocis conventionibus constant*) and is, therefore, more properly designated as "covenant."[74] We have seen that in Cameron this distinction was based on a distinction between the antecedent and consequent love of God. Such a distinction does not reappear in the writings of Amyraut in this precise form. Amyraut, however, does make use of a similar distinction which may have its basis in this bifurcation of Cameron's and which is pivotal in Amyraut's theology *in extenso.* We shall take up this distinction in the following chapter.

It is the latter, or conditional covenant, corresponding to Cameron's *foedus hypotheticum,* which Amyraut regards as the proper object of theological discussion. It is this covenant in which God has accommodated himself in establishing a means for his restored relationship with man. All of the gospel promises are comprehended in this relationship. ". . . it must be singularly observed that all the dispensation of God towards his creature which has to do with punishment and reward, with life and death, all this depends on these covenants which God has transacted with that creature."[75] This type of covenant has two necessary elements, the stipulation of an obligation and a promise of

73. "Notum est *foederis* nomen in Scriptura nonnunquam significare **Dei** *promissiones* eas quae nulla conditione nullaque restipulatione rei ab hominibus praestandae nituntur, & ideò nuncupantur *absolutae*" (thesis 2, "De tribus foederibus divinis," *Theses Salmurienses,* 1:212).

74. *Ibid.*

75. "Or est-il singulierement à remarquer que toute la dispensation de Dieu envers sa creature, en ce qui regarde les peines & les recompenses, la vie & la mort, tout cela depend des alliances que Dieu a traittées avec elle" (from a sermon on Ezekiel 18:23 preached in 1635, *Sermons sur divers textes de la sainte ecriture* [Saumur, 1653], p. 59).

reward upon fulfillment of that obligation.[76] And, Amyraut contends, "there are three such divine covenants mentioned in Scripture: First, that which was contracted in the earthly paradise and ought to be called *natural;* secondly, the one which God transacted in a special way with Israel and is called *legal;* and thirdly, that which is called *gracious* and is set forth in the gospel."[77]

This insistence upon a threefold covenant marks a major point of divergence on the part of Salmurian theology from the covenant theology within orthodoxy. Wollebius could claim on the behalf of orthodoxy that "God's covenant with man is twofold, a covenant of works and one of grace: the first before the fall, and the second after it."[78] Orthodoxy interpreted the covenant made with Moses as did Calvin, as in substance and reality one and the same with the covenant of grace, differing only in *administratio.*[79] At Saumur, however, the theological program revolved around an interpretation which made a strict opposition between the Mosaic covenant and the covenant of grace. And it was Amyraut who worked this interpretation for all it was worth. Cameron had suggested the idea, but had spoken of the Mosaic covenant as *foedus gratiae subserviens.* His terminology implied a basic unity with the covenant of grace, even though he had called it a third covenant. Amyraut, however, by using the terminology *foedus legale,* emphasized the radical opposition of the two covenants in a way which recalls Luther's law-gospel distinction.

76. ". . . omnia Dei federa duabus rebus contineantur, officij stipulatione, & promissione praemij . . ." (*Dissertationes theologicae sex* [Saumur, 1660], p. 10).

77. "Memorantur autem justismodi *divina foedera tria* in Scripturis, *Primum,* quod contractum fuit in Paradiso terrestri, & *Naturale* dici solet, *Secundum,* quod Deus pepigit peculiari ratione cum Israelo, & appellatur *Legale. Tertium* denique quod *Gratiae* dicitur, & patefactum est in Evangelio" (thesis 2, "De tribus foederibus divinis," *Theses Salmurienses,* 1:212).

78. *Compendium theologiae christianae,* ch. 7, as translated by Beardslee in *Reformed Dogmatics,* p. 64. See also Franciscus Turrettini, *Institutio theologiae elencticae* (1688), XII.ii.3: "Tale autem duplex cum hominibus iniit *foedus,* primum *Legale* seu *operum* cum homine integro, Alterum fidei et Evangelicum cum lapso e peccatore" (Edinburgh ed. [1847], 2:155).

79. Calvin, *Institutio,* II.x.2. *OS.* III.404.5ff. Cf. Wollebius, in Beardslee, *Reformed Dogmatics,* pp. 118ff.; and Turrettini, *Institutio theologiae elencticae,* XII.vii.1., who speaks of *unitas substantialis* of the *foedus gratiae* (2:192).

As Amyraut develops his disputation *"De tribus foederibus divinis"* perhaps the first feature one notices is the historical dimension of his thought. The three covenants are viewed as three steps in God's revelatory process, each step representing an advance upon the preceding one. Here we encounter for the first time the rudiments of what Moltmann has properly designated Amyraut's *"Theologie der Heilsgeschichte."*[80] To underline this progressive-revelation understanding of the relationship of God with man in the three covenants, Amyraut employs a method of comparison in his exegesis throughout. This is a most important consideration if one is to understand his theology, yet I know of no one who has pointed it out. It is the favorite exegetical method in all his work, although it shows up most clearly in his paraphrases of the New Testament books. In one of these he applies it to point up the more excellent nature of the resurrection life over the life under the gospel dispensation.[81] In another, not content with the explanation that the word *perfect* in the New Testament means mature, Amyraut says the Apostle is speaking in comparison with the sanctification effected through the legal covenant.[82] Again, the moral laws of the Old Testament are seen to be useless, even damaging, in the light of the New Testament

80. "Prädestination und Heilsgeschichte," p. 285.

81. "Mais c'est que quand nous comparons cette demeure icy avec l'autre, nous trouvons la future si avantageuse, que ne pouvâs en estre jouissans sans dépouiller celle-cy, à quelque prix que ce puisse estre nous desirons d'en estre revestus, afin que cet estre mortel icy, qui ressemble plutost là une mort qu'à une vie, soit englouti dans cette heureuse & seule veritable vie, laquelle est si souverainement desirable, quoy qu'on n'y entre que par la mort" (paraphrase on II Corinthians 5:4, in *Paraphrases sur le seconde epistre de l'apostre saint Paul aux Corinthiens* [Saumur, 1647], p. 59).

82. "Ce que je vous ay dit cy-dessus de la vertu de l'Evangile à produire une parfaite sanctificatiô en nous, se doit entêdre de la fin à laquelle il nous appelle, & de ce la chose deuroit estre selô sa nature, & non pas qu'il y ait quelcun en cette vie effectivemêt parfait. S'il y a quelcun dont je die qu'il est effectivement parfait, c'est pour ce que si vous côparez la sanctification Evangelique avec la Legale, la sincereté, la grandeur, l'excellence de l'une, la fait trouver parfaite en comparaison de l'autre, si imparfaite, si forcée, si foible, & si aisée à vaincre, quand elle vient aux prises avec la tentation. A la considerer hors de cette comparison, il n'y a aucun en la communion de Christ, en qui il ne demeure jusques à la mort quelques restes de cette corruption naturelle" (paraphrase on Romans 8:10 in *Paraphrases sur l'epistre aux Romains* [Saumur, 1644], p. 169).

revelation.[83] In these and many other ways he shows his predilection for this exegetical method.

In his *"De tribus foederibus divinis"* Amyraut applies comparative exegesis to five basic elements of the three covenants, in this way showing the progression in God's revelation. These five elements are (1) the contracting parties; (2) the condition (*restipulatio*) and the nature of that condition; (3) the promise; (4) the mediator; and (5) the efficacy of the covenant. He develops his thought along the following lines, always assuming that the movement is for the better.

(1) The development in terms of the contracting parties is seen in the progressive enlargement of God's design in these covenants. In the covenant of nature the contracting parties were God and one man, Adam. In the covenant of law the contracting parties were God and a nation, Israel. In the covenant of grace the contracting parties are God and all mankind. (2) The progressive enlargement of God's design in the condition is revealed in the decreasing difficulty in its fulfillment. In the covenant of nature the condition was perfect obedience to the law of nature, in the legal covenant perfect obedience to the law of nature clarified by the written law and the ceremonies, and in the covenant of grace simply faith. (3) As for the promise, an enlargement is shown in both the quality of the reward and its comprehensiveness. In the covenant of nature it was a blessed, continuous life in Eden, in the legal covenant the promise of a blessed life in Canaan, and in the covenant of grace, salvation and eternal life. (4) The development, in relation to the mediator, is thought of in terms of the effectiveness of that person. In the covenant of nature there was none, in the legal covenant a mere man, Moses, and in the covenant of grace the perfect God-

---

83. "Car qu'y peut nuire d'estre né du sang d'Abraham, ou d'avoir esté circoncis comme le reste des Juifs, ou de tascher de côformer ses actions aux commandemens que Dieu nous a donnés, notamment en la Loy Morale? Mais c'est que quant à celles qui sont indifferentes d'elles mémes, si vous venés à les comparer avec l'excellence de la connoissance de nostre Seigneur Jesus Christ, elles se trouveront non inutiles seulement, mais mesmes en quelque sorte dommangeables" (paraphrase on Philippians 3:8 in *Paraphrases sur les epistres de l'apostre s. Paul aux Galates, Ephesiens, Philippiens* . . . [Saumur, 1645], p. 265. Cf. on 3:13, pp. 269–70).

man, Jesus Christ. (5) The development, in the idea of efficacy, is seen both in terms of its nature and its certainty. In the covenant of nature there was no efficacious work which did not depend on man's perfect obedience, in the legal covenant the efficacy was simply one of restraining men from evil, though not without compulsion, and in the covenant of grace the efficacy is that of the power and mercy of God which brings full liberty and a spontaneous inclination to the good (that is, piety and holiness).[84]

This is the broad outline of Amyraut's *heilsgeschichtlich* covenant teaching. It is his favorite idea, and to it he returns over and over again in all possible contexts. He develops numerous variations of this theme, always stressing the twin ideas of the progression of God's revelation and the final full and perfect experience of God's redemption in the ages to come, though he is constantly concerned with setting forth the excellency of the period of the covenant of grace.

Of the above-contrasted topics, the one which has the most far-reaching implications has to do with the idea of efficacy,[85] and it will be discussed more fully in the following chapter, but it needs to be recognized here that Amyraut places an unusually

---

84. All of the foregoing has been drawn from his "De tribus foederibus divinis," *Theses Salmurienses*, 1:212ff.

85. In a striking passage in his *Pharaphrases sur l'epistre de l'apostre aux Hebrieux* (Saumur, 1645) Amyraut shows various ways in which the new covenant is superior to the Mosaic, and shows that the idea of efficacy is foremost. He is speaking of the mediatorship of Christ: "Car estant Mediateur de la Nouvelle Alliance, il faut que sa charge soit élevée au dessus de celle du Mediateur de L'Ancienne, à proportion de ce que les alliances mesmes ont entr'elles d'inegalité. Or est il bien vray que la nouvelle à [sic] quantité d'autres grands avantages par dessus l'ancienne. L'une est pour la seule nation Judaïque, l'autre pour tous les peuples de la terre universellement. L'une met la justification dans les oeuvres, & dans la ponctuelle observation de ses commandemens, l'autre la fait dependre de la Foy seulement. L'une est pléne d'observations penibles & laborieuses, & qui sont côme un ioug dessus le col de ceux qui y sont assujettis; l'autre met ses sectateurs en cet égard en une liberté toute entiere. Et s'il y a encore quelque autre chose semblable. *Mais l'excellence paroist notamment en ce point; c'est que le succés & l'efficace de la Nouvelle, depend de Promesses qui sont meilleures infiniment. Car elles promettent d'en accompagner la revelation d'une telle Vertu, que les hommes l'executeront;* au lieu que l'autre en estant destituée, il a esté inevitable qu'elle demeureroit enfrainte" (on Hebrews 8:6, pp. 110–11. Emphasis added).

strong emphasis upon the work of the Holy Spirit. This is because he believes that the Holy Spirit is the member of the Godhead who works efficaciously. The Spirit is, as the Confession testifies, God's virtue.[86] And it is only under the gospel covenant that the Spirit is communicated to men.[87] So Amyraut emphasizes that the spiritual nature of the covenant of grace renders it superior to the other covenants. There is, running throughout his writings, a sort of dualism between spirit and flesh, between the supernatural and the natural, a dualism which sounds almost Neoplatonic.[88] "The kingdom of God," he says, "is of a totally different nature than the kingdoms of the world, and the means of entrance thereto are marvelously different."[89] Not only that,

86. *Confessio gallicana,* art. 6.

87. "Le seule dispensation de l'Evangile est le ministere de l'Esprit . . ." (*Quatre sermons sur le chap. vi de l'epistre aux Hebrieux, v. 4, 5, & 6* [Saumur, 1657], p. 39). See also the paraphrase on Galatians 3:3 in *Paraphrases sur les epistres de l'apostre s. Paul aux Galates, . . .* (Saumur, 1645), ". . . l'Evangile est le ministere qui communique l'Esprit . . ."

88. Cf., for example, his *Paraphrase de l'evangile de Jesus Christ selon s. Jean* (Saumur, 1651), on 4:24, where he seems to imply that matter is in some way evil: "Or est-il que Dieu est esprit: cette benite essence-là n'a du tout rien de corporel ny de meslé avec la matiere" (p. 148). On the previous verse Amyraut had set forth an interpretation of spiritual worship as separated from carnal things. He paraphrases: "L'heure vient, & mesmes elle est desia venuë. & tu t'en peus prevaloir si tu veux, que les vrais adorateurs, & qui seront seuls agreables à Dieu, se separans de toutes ces choses charnelles ausquelles le service de Dieu a esté attaché jusqu'à maintenant, luy rendront un service spirituel, qui consistera principalement dans les mouvemens d'un entendement bien pur, & d'une chaste & sincere conscience. Et ce service-là aura cet avantage, que l'autre est comme l'ombre & la figure, & cetuy-cy au contraire est le corps & la verité. Car celuy là n'a quasi esté institué autrefois, sinon pour faire une obscure delineation du service spirituel auquel desormais s'adonneront les fideles. Et c'est de tels adorateurs que le Pere requiert: sans cette interieure disposition de l'esprit, tout ce Culte ceremoniel & corporel ne luy peut estre agreable" (pp. 147–48). See also his sermon on I John 5:7 in *Sermons sur divers textes,* pp. 389–90: ". . . les choses spirituelles & immaterielles sont sans comparison plus agissantes, que celles qui sont revestues de corps. Et dans les corps, les substances les plus subtiles, & qui approchent le plus de la nature des esprits, sont celles qui ont le plus de vigueur pour le mouvement, & le plus d'efficace & d'activité." Perhaps also his "particuliere inclination" for the gospel of John which he mentions in the "Preface au Lecteur" of his *Paraphases sur la premiere epistre de l'apostre Paul aux Corinthiens* (Saumur, 1646) stems from this dualistic tendency.

89. *Paraphrase de s. Jean* 3:3, p. 95. See also on John 3:5: "Parce que la chair est un principe naturel & corrompu, tout ce qui en naist est naturel & corrompu pareillement, & n'est propre qu'à la jouissance & à la participation des choses

there is a fundamental difference between the outlook of the natural man and of the spiritual. The natural man looks to outward appearances, to pomp and circumstance and show; the spiritual man has a totally different perspective, recognizing that the natural man is at enmity with God. This concept, at times reminiscent of Luther's "hidden and revealed" dialectic,[90] is clearly enunciated in Amyraut's paraphrases on II Corinthians 5:14ff. Here he emphasizes that the Christian minister must identify with the humiliation of the suffering Christ and must fight his natural inclination to cultivate and practice habits which tend to external show.[91] What all of this means for the present discussion is that Amyraut uses the idea of spirituality to stress the excellency of the covenant of grace in comparison with the covenants of nature and law, neither of which was accompanied with the ministry of the Spirit:

> As for the dispensation of nature, it was not accompanied by the grace of the Spirit of God. He has been content to deploy in this dispensation some efficacy of His providence only, a providence which has rendered this dispensation efficacious just to the point of keeping man in some way respectful toward God and of maintaining in him some esteem for moral virtues so that his corruption would not bring the world to total ruin. The revelation of the legal covenant, insofar as it was legal, was not accompanied with the efficacy of the Spirit of consolation and of true sanctification either. God was content to deploy in this covenant some virtue of the Spirit, of servitude which gave to the Jews a greater respect toward God than the Gentiles had, with a more profound terror of His judgment and a more exact knowledge of the nature of piety and holiness, in order to maintain the society of the republic of Israel and to encourage this nation to look for the Messiah. But as for the Gospel, God has

---

naturelles & corrompues. Mais parce que l'Esprit est un principe surnaturel, ce qui en naist est surnaturel & spirituel comme luy, & propre à la jouissance & à la participatiô des choses spirituelles & surnaturelles."

90. See Philip Watson, *Let God be God!* (London, 1947), p. 103.

91. *Paraphrases sur II Corinthiens* 5:15ff., pp. 67–71. Also see *Paraphrase de s. Jean* 7:24, pp. 300–301: "Ceux qui regardent aux apparences exterieures, & qui ont acceptation de personnes, ne peuvent qu'ils ne pervertissent leur jugement. Au lieu que ceux qui mettent à part toutes autres côsiderations, & qui ne regardent à rien qu'aux actions mesmes sur lesquelles il est question de prononcer, en font d'ordinaire un jugement droit & raisonnable."

willed that its proclamation would be accompanied by the grace
of His Spirit, who illumines the understandings and converts
the heart of those who are elect from all eternity and through
faith brings their thoughts under the obedience of the Savior
of the world. This is what the Apostle teaches when He says
that the Gospel is the ministry of the Spirit. And this is said of
the Gospel not only absolutely, considered in itself, but even to
the exclusion of all the other dispensations with which it can
be compared.[92]

Scattered abroad in his various writings are many other topics
upon which Amyraut focuses in order to show the idea of progression in his comparative analyses of the three covenants.[93] Of
these, by far the most frequent is the idea that in the covenant

92. "Et pour ce qui est de la dispensation de la Nature, elle n'a point esté
accompagnée de la grace de l'Esprit de Dieu. Il s'est contenté d'y desployer quelque efficace de sa providence seulement, qui a rendu cette dispensation efficacieuse jusques à ce poinct, que de retenir les hommes en quelque respect de la
divinité, & en quelque telle quelle estime des vertus morales, à ce que leur corruption ne portast le monde en une totale ruine. La revelation de l'Alliance
Legale, entant que Legale, n'a point esté accompagnée de l'efficace de l'Esprit de
consolation & de vraye sanctification non plus. Dieu s'est contenté d'y desployer
quelque vertu de l'Esprit de servitude, qui a donné aux Juifs un plus grand
respect envers la divinité, que n'en avoient les Gentils, avec une plus grande
terreur de son jugement, & une plus exacte connoissance de la nature de la pieté
& de la sainteté, pour maintenir la societé de la Republique d'Israel, & acheminer
cette nation à l'attente du Messie. Mais quant à l'Evangile, Dieu a voulu que sa
predication ait esté accompagnée de la grace de son Esprit, qui illumine les entendemens, & convertit le coeur de ceux qui sont esleus de toute eternité, &
emmene par la foy leurs pensées prisonnieres sous l'obeissance du Sauveur du
monde. Et c'est ce que l'Apostre enseigne quand il dit que l'Evangile est le
mynistere de l'Esprit. Ce qui se dit de l'Evangile, non pas seulement absolument,
& à la considerer en soy, mais encore à l'exclusion de toutes les autres dispensations avec lesquelles on le pourroit comparer" (*Action sur le dimanche XLVII du
catechisme*, printed with *Sermons sur divers textes*, pp. 474–75). See also *Sermons*,
p. 164 and p. 236: ". . . l'efficace de l'Esprit n'accompagne, comme nous avons
dit, aucune autre dispensation que celle de la predication de la parole."

93. E.g., in his *Paraphrases sur Hebrieux* 8:6–7, following a section wherein he
has considered Christ as a more excellent mediator than Moses: "Or est il bien
vray que la nouvelle à [sic] quantité d'autres grands avantages par dessus
l'ancienne. L'une est pour la seule nation Judaique, l'autre pour tous les peuples
de la terre universellement. L'une met la justification dans les oeuvres, & dans
la ponctuelle observation de ses commandemens, l'autre la fait dependre de la
Foy seulement. L'une est pléne d'observations penibles & laborieuses, & qui sont
côme un joug dessus le col de ceux qui y sont assujettis; l'autre met ses sectateurs
en cet égard en une liberté toute entiere. Et s'il y a encore quelque autre chose
semblable" (pp. 110–11).

of grace God has his most perfect revelation, that is, that in this covenant he is revealed as supremely merciful (*souverainement misericordieux*). Indeed, this idea is so frequently encountered and so vehemently stressed that it must be regarded as the heart of Amyraut's *heilsgeschichtlich* program. ". . . among His virtues," Amyraut claims, "it is His mercy which He has desired to be clearer, more vital, more resplendent than the others, and, in a manner of speaking, gloriously to outshine them all by the grandeur of its light."[94] To be sure, there is a strongly apologetic flavor to his argument at this point, for he is combatting the charges of both the Arminians and the Catholics that the followers of Calvin make of God a tyrant, glorying in the exercise of his justice.[95] Nevertheless, the very fact that Amyraut makes such a point of elevating this particular virtue of God is in itself indicative of his own theological predilection. Again and again he returns to this theme, and one finds in his writings numberless occasions in which he uses such phrases as *"infiniment misericordieux"* and *"souverainement misericordieux."*[96] At any rate, to return to the point at hand, Amyraut contends that God's mercy was not revealed either under the covenant of nature or the legal covenant, but has been most clearly displayed in the covenant of grace.[97]

94. ". . . entre ses vertus, . . . celle de sa misericorde . . . il a voulu estre plus claire, plus vive, plus éclattante que les autres, &, par maniere de parler, les éblouïr toutes en quelque façon de la grandeur de sa lumiere" (sermon on Ezekiel 18:23, *Sermons sur divers textes*, p. 54). ". . . la charité de Dieu & son inenarrable misericorde, soit s'il faut ainsi dire, la qualité predominante dans la doctrine de la Grace & de la Redemption" (*Discours chrestien sur les eaux de Bourbon* [Charenton, 1658], p. 27).

95. It is interesting that in his disclaimer Amyraut undertakes only to exonerate Calvin and not the Reformed theology *en bloc*. This seems a most positive indication that he too thought seventeenth-century Reformed theology had erred at this point, that it had incorporated those very speculations about the nature of God against which Calvin had so insistently warned. Amyraut repeatedly expresses his conviction that "if ever a man since the Apostles has preached the mercy of God, that man has been Calvin" (preface to *Six Sermons*, p. viii).

96. E.g., in *Six Sermons*, pp. 23, 84, 105, 122, and *passim*. It will be remembered that Amyraut composed his treatise on predestination in order to render God's mercy as "souverainement recommandable." See also *Defense de la doctrine de Calvin* (1644), p. 609: "Car il n'y a rien de plus vray, rien de plus serieux, que cette proposition, que Dieu est souverainement misericordieux . . ."

97. A typical example of this comparison is found in his sermon on I Corin-

Closely tied up with this stress on God's mercy is the persistently recurring theme, touched on above, of the universal design of the evangelical covenant. This idea of universality forms a large part of Amyraut's conception of the improvement of the covenant of grace over the legal covenant. In the covenant of grace the distinction of peoples into Jews and Gentiles has been abolished on the grounds of the universal design of Christ's death. "The legal covenant had placed a division between the Jews and the Gentiles, . . . had placed a division in the affections and caused animosity between these peoples." But in the covenant of grace "Christ, by making propitiation for the sins of all equally, has changed the economy which had put a distinction between them and has reconciled them and led them into one family." The decisive feature in this whole argument, as Amyraut sees it, is that "these two dispensations cannot exist together" for the very reason that the covenant of grace "put in evidence grace in favor of all people indifferently."[98] Or, in other words, "our

---

thians 1:21: ". . . l'Apostre appelle le ministere de Moyse, ministere de mort: . . . si vous considerez Moyse precisement en ce qui estoit de propre à sa charge, il estoit entremetteur de l'alliance legale: alliance legale qui au reste considerée en elle-mesme, ne fasoit aucune mention de la misericorde de Dieu, & ne tonnoit autre chose que sa justice" (*Sermons sur divers textes*, p. 153).

98. This passage reads in full: "L'alliance de la Loy avoit mis separation entre les Juifs & les Gentils, & la separation en la profession de religion, avoit mis de la division dans les affections, & causé de l'animosité entre ces peuples. Les Juifs rejettoyent les Gentils comme profanes & enemis de Dieu; & les Gentils avoyent les Juifs en mépris & en detestation, comme des fols & des impies. Mais Christ en faisant propitiation les pechés d'eux tous également, a changé l'economie qui mettoit distinction entr'eux, & les a reconcilés & ramenés en un, en abolissant l'Alliance de la Loy, qui estoit comme au Temple de Jerusalem autrefois, la muraille de separation, laquelle estoit entre deux, & qui les éloignoit les uns des autres. Car ces deux dispensations ne pouvans pas subsister ensemble, c'est à sçavoir la Legale, qui estendoit la pedagogie de ses commandemens, & les ombres de ses ceremonies sur la nation Judaïque seulement, & l'Evangelique qui met en evidence la grace en faveur de tous peuples indifferemment, Christ ayant establi la seconde par les souffrances de sa chair, a aboli le premiere & détruit la haine qu'elle fomentoit, en l'abolissant. Afin que tout le genre humain, qui par l'ordre de sa premiere creation, ne devoit composer qu'un corps, comme si c'eust esté un seul homme, estant comme coupé en deux parties par la separation des Juifs & des Gentils, il les recomposast ensemble, pour en faire par une nouvelle creation, comme un seul homme tout nouveau, qui dependist non d'Adam, qui estoit le commun principe de cette unité naturelle, laquelle devoit estre auparavant

Lord Jesus Christ, by the fact that he willed to be man, has shown that he did not wish to exclude from his grace any of those with whom he has this union in his humanity. Also he has given himself as a ransom for the redemption of them all. This was hidden and unknown in times past and is why the Jews have believed that the Redeemer was only for their people."[99]

Though we shall have occasion later to dwell at more length upon Amyraut's teaching of the universality of Christ's atonement, it is worth noting here that the foregoing passage helps us to understand some of the reasons for his insistence upon this doctrine. For, above and beyond the many reasons he may elsewhere adduce for his rejection of the orthodox formulation of the doctrine of limited atonement, it is clear from this discussion that he views such a teaching as a return in some way to, or at least a significant step in the direction of, the legalistic spirit presented in the law covenant. In addition, the idea of a limited atonement would mark a reversal in the developing revelation of God.

It should be pointed out that all of the foregoing comparisons have been made by considering the three covenants, as Amyraut says, *"praecisè atque absolutè in se."*[100] Though the particular covenantal function of each was abrogated by the promulgation of its successor, at least some vestiges of each existed side by side until Christ's ascension. In this sense, then, the neat distinctions discussed above do not hold, though in Amyraut's mind this in no way threatens the validity of those distinctions. Moreover, the existence of these simultaneous covenants only serves to allow for a strengthening of his *heilsgeschichtlich* emphasis, for this emphasis is developed within the covenants themselves, particularly within the covenant of grace.

Like Calvin and all Reformed theologians Amyraut held that

---

entre les humains, mais de luy mesme, en la communion duquel nous sommes faits un entre nous par la paix de laquelle il nous est auteur . . ." (Paraphrase on Ephesians 2:14–15, in *Paraphrases sur les epistres l'apostre s. Paul aux Galates, Ephesiens . . .* , pp. 150–52).

99. Paraphrase on I Timothy 2:5–6, in *Paraphrases sur les epistres a Timothée, a Tite, a Philemon* (Saumur, 1645), p. 15.

100. *Theses Salmurienses,* 1:212.

the covenant of grace was initiated with Adam immediately after the Fall, though very obscurely indeed. Amyraut in fact places so much emphasis upon the obscure nature of the early announcements of the covenant of grace that his position is significantly more sober than the orthodox, and perhaps even more sober than that of Calvin. Probably the strong exegetical interest at Saumur helps account for this, but we cannot overlook the fact that this emphasis upon the abstruse nature of the beginnings of the covenant of grace serves to accentuate the development of this covenant, an idea so integral to Amyraut's theology. It is repeatedly encountered in almost all of his writings, whether he is discussing a text from Hebrews (where he expounds it at length) or delivering a sermon on the healing waters of Bourbon. An interesting example of his sensitivity to historical development within the covenant of grace itself, and of his insistence on the obscurity of the early revelations of this covenant, occurs in a passage in which he discusses the so-called proto-evangelium text, Genesis 3:15:

> . . . what does this oracle, *The seed of the woman, etc.,* contain? To be sure, it contains the Christian religion, the incarnation of the eternal Wisdom, the passion of the Redeemer, his glorious resurrection, his ascension into heaven, and all these other divine matters of which we learn in the Gospel. But all these things are so enveloped in the rudiments of their origins that in the consideration of them no human understanding would be capable of guessing or understanding distinctly whether it would be an animal or plant that would be born—if he did not learn it elsewhere.
> . . . And if the sacrifices have added something to this knowledge, it was only that man had merited death and, as Calvin says, that he had need of some propitiation . . . Then this knowledge was augmented, this light was made clearer, in proportion as it has pleased God to renew his oracles from time to time through the ministry of his prophets until finally the Gospel appeared and filled the whole universe with the glory of its splendor.[101]

101. ". . . que contient cet oracle? *La semence de la femme, &c.* Certes il contient la Religion Chrestienne, l'incarnation de la Sapience eternelle, la passion du Redempteur, sa glorieuse resurrection, son ascension aux Cieux, & toutes ces autres divines matieres que nous apprenons en l'Evangile. Mais c'est comme toutes choses sont enveloppées aux rudimens de leurs origines, de la consideration des-

Though the very rudimentary origins of the covenant of grace were first available to Adam in the promise God made to the serpent (Genesis 3:15), this message was very quickly "almost completely extinguished."[102] Because of the "unbelievable malice of men" God finally destroyed the world by the flood, at which time he renewed this covenant with Noah.[103] However, even this renewal with Noah was "contained in words so obscure" and its net result was so insignificant that, Amyraut says, "when the Apostle argues for the antiquity of the gospel over the law he never goes further back than to the promises made to Abraham; of Noah and the covenants made with him there is in Paul's epistles a profound and perpetual silence."[104] It is, then, only with Abraham that we may properly speak of the promulgation of this covenant. And although "the promise of the Messiah was given very much plainer and clearer to Abraham than it had been to

---

quelles nulle intelligence humaine, si elle n'en estoit informée d'ailleurs, ne seroit capable de deviner & connoistre distinctement quels auroient à estre les animaux ou les plantes qui en naissent: . . . Et si les sacrifices ont ajousté quelque chose à cette connoissance, elle en est revenüe là que l'homme a merité la mort, &, comme dit Calvin, qu'il estoit besoin de quelque propitiation, . . . Puis cela s'est augmenté, cette lumiere s'est esclaircie, à mesure qu'il a pleu à Dieu renouveller ses oracles de temps en temps par le ministere de ses Prophetes: jusques à ce qu'enfin l'Evangile est apparu, & a rempli tout l'Univers de la gloire de sa lumiere" ("Sermon sur l'Epistre de S. Paul aux Romains, chap. 1, vers. 19.20," *Sermons sur divers textes,* pp. 107–8; originally preached in 1635 and included in his *Six Sermons* of 1636). See also *Defense de la doctrine de Calvin,* pp. 346ff., where in speaking of the Noachic renewal of the covenant of grace adumbrated in Genesis 3:15 he says: ". . . ce qui concernoit le Redêpteur en cette alliance dressée comme tout de nouveau avec Noé, y estoit contenu en paroles si obscures, pource que la condition des têps le portoit ainsi, que quand l'Apostre dispute de l'antiquité de l'Evangile par dessus la Loy, il ne monte jamais plus haut que les promesses faites a Abraham; de Noé & des alliances traittées avec luy, il y a dans ses Epistres un profond & perpetuel silence"; also his remarks on the progressive revelation of the wisdom of God, in *Disçours sur les eaux de Bourbon,* p. 30: "Cette divine sapience, qui côme l'Apostre l'enseigne, a esté cachée dans les temps passez, s'est de petits commencemens, & qui ne contenoient sinon les semêces & les premiers rudimens de l'esperance du salut, éclarcie par degrez, & avancée de peu à peu, Dieu adjoustant oracle à oracle, jusques à ce qu'enfin nostre Seigneur a espandu une si grande lumiere au monde par son apparition, qu'il ne faut plus desormais attendre de nouvelle revelation jusqu'à la consommation des siecles."

102. *Defense de la doctrine de Calvin,* p. 345.
103. *Ibid.,* p. 346.
104. *Ibid.;* quoted in note 101.

Noah"[105] still a great amount of obscurity remained and further renewals, clarifications, and additions were from time to time necessitated until the full revelation of the Messiah in the gospel.

Part of this revelation of the covenant of grace in Old Testament times Amyraut saw as types and prefigurements of Christ. In the third of his sermons upon Hebrews 1:3 he lists the death of Abel at the hand of his brother as an image of the death of Christ at the hands of his brethren, the translation of Enoch as emblematic of Christ's ascension, the near-sacrifice of Isaac as foreshadowing the sacrificial death of Christ, etc. All of this is in the best orthodox tradition. But even here Amyraut departs from the traditional orthodox explanation by stressing the necessity for the event typified to be accomplished before it could be understood. In emphasizing the inappropriable nature of these Old Testament types of Christ for the Old Testament saints, Amyraut conjoined two considerations, considerations which have great importance in pointing up his methodology. For, he says, there are two reasons for the lack of understanding in Old Testament times: "that on the one hand these predictions have been so imperfect and these types so enigmatic because of the condition of the times, and that on the other hand the understandings of men were so little clarified by the grace of the Spirit, because then the Church was still in its infancy, so that this had been a secret which was never understood until the accomplishment of the time through the manifestation of the things themselves."[106] Thus we have, combined, Amyraut's *heilsgeschichtlich* emphasis on the imperfect, obscure, and enigmatic nature of these types, and his point of departure: the knowledge man is able to have of any particular revelation.

Finally, we need to make clear that all of these manifestations of the covenant of grace pointed to Christ. From the time of the Fall it is only through Christ that any man ever has been or will be saved.[107] In this regard, of course, there is no progression in

---

105. *Ibid.*, p. 347.

106. *Cinq sermons prononcez a Charenton* (Charenton, 1658), p. 11.

107. "Car c'est de sa plenitude, & non de celle d'aucun autre, que nous avonstous, tant Anciens que Modernes, receu tout le bien que nous possedons . . ." (*Paraphrase de s. Jean* 1:16, p. 30). "Ce Jesus Christ que nous vous annonçons, est toujours le mesme, il a esté sous le Vieil Testament, il est encore maintenant, il

John Cameron

From a copy of a portrait presumably now lost. Done for the University of Glasgow
by John Scougall, portrait painter of Edinburgh, in oil on canvas.
Reproduced by permission of the University of Glasgow.

BRIEF
TRAITTE
DE LA
PREDESTINATION
ET DE SES PRINCIPA-
LES DEPENDANCES

Par MOYSE AMYRAVT
Pasteur & Professeur en Theo-
logie à Saumur.

A SAVMVR,
Par IEAN LESNIER, &
ISAAC DESBORDES.

M. DC. XXXIV.

D. d. Willham,

DEFENSE DE LA
DOCTRINE DE
CALVIN·
SVR LE SVIET DE
LELECTION ET DE
LA REPROBATION.

Par MOYSE *AMYRAVT, Pasteur & Professeur*
en Theologie a Saumur.

A SAVMVR,
Chés ISAAC DESBORDES Imprimeur & Li-
braire, demeurant à l'Enseigne de l'Imprimerie.
M. DC. XLIV

Pierre du Moulin

From a portrait housed in the Library of the Society of French Protestantism
in Paris. Courtesy Pasteur Henri Bosc. Photo by Michel Cabaud.

the covenant of grace per se. However, the point of departure for Amyraut is always the knowledge that man is able to have of the saving revelation of God in Christ. In this respect "our condition is incomparably more advantageous."[108]

---

sera toûjours à perpetuité, la cause du salut des hommes" (*Paraphrases sur Hebrieux* 13:8, p. 201).

108. *Paraphrases sur Hebrieux* 1:2, p. 8.

4

THE DOCTRINE
OF PREDESTINATION

IT IS WITH THE DOCTRINE OF PREDESTINATION that Amyraut's name has traditionally been associated in the history of theology, and there is good cause for this, for his deviation from (and one may even say his attack upon) Calvinist orthodoxy is most acute at this point. We have seen that his *Brief Traitté de la predestination* of 1634 was the object of the most violent attack by orthodox Calvinists and that it was for positions taken in this book that Amyraut was tried for heresy. We have further remarked that the peculiar emphases of Amyraut's covenant theology appear to have been expressly designed to controvert the orthodox discussions of the decrees of God and of predestination itself. Despite the importance of Amyraut's doctrine of predestination, however, it seems that all of his interpreters, from Schweizer to Laplanche, with the sole exception of Moltmann, have missed the significance of the most important element in his discussion of this doctrine—the juxtaposition of God's secret and revealed will.

One of the most arresting features of Amyraut's doctrine of predestination is that his opposition to orthodox teaching was made in the name of Calvin and the early reformers, presenting at the same time a decided bias against Beza, Martyr, and Zanchi. Indeed, du Moulin acrimoniously complained that Amyraut made Calvin *coryphoeum theologorum*.[1] Yet because his own

1. *De Mosis Amyraldi . . . libro judicium,* p. 4. The passage is so interesting in

158

career was constantly in jeopardy Amyraut did not dare wage open war against orthodox doctrine. Nevertheless the unmistakable implication of much of his writing is that he was presenting a most explicit criticism of orthodox teaching. As has been shown in chapter 2 he persisted throughout his career in teaching a universal will of God to save. We have also seen, in chapter 1, that Cameron had the reputation of opposing Beza at every turn, so that du Moulin could call him *Bezae Mastyx*— "Beza's scourge." One can hardly conclude otherwise than that in Cameron's opinion the bad turn in Reformed theology originated with Beza.

Amyraut's dislike of Beza is more concealed but is obvious nonetheless. In his *Defense de la doctrine de Calvin* he is concerned to show his complete orthodoxy, and that concern for the most part precludes any open pronouncements of his opposition to orthodox Reformed theologians. Nevertheless he mildly criticizes Beza for his supralapsarianism and for his harsh doctrine of reprobation. For example, Amyraut interprets Beza to have taught that God condemns man without taking his sin into consideration. Amyraut then states that at this point Beza "has had a peculiar method (*methode particuliere*) which no one is obliged to follow if he does not so desire . . ."[2] In another place, Amyraut refuses to defend Beza and Maccovius in their teaching on God's will to harden the heart of man.[3] All such sentiments are in sharp

---

terms of Amyraut's authorities for theology, and of the asperity of du Moulin, that it follows in full: "Joculare est quod vir doctus se infert Aristarchum ingeniorum & judicem. Pronuntians hunc quidem esse primû Theologorum, illum esse secundum. Calvino primas tribuit, eumque facit coryphoeum Theologorum. Cameroni secundum locum assignat, Praef. [preface of Amyraut's *Specimen animadversionum,* p. 31] eumque facit secundum à Calvino: Vir singularis modestiae, non ausus est pronuntiare, quis sit tertius. An quia timuit ne ipse sibi inferret injuriam? quia putat sibi tertium locum deberi? Nempe haec ait ut aegrè faciat Riveto & Spanhemio, cum quibus tamen Camero nulla ratione potest conferri. Ego verò ausim dicere, Cameronem ab ipso Amyraldo ingenio, & industria & astutia superari. Alibi Musculum & Bucerum vocat Theologos incomparabiles, eos praeferens Cameroni. Petrum Martyrem virum tantum frigidissimè laudat, vocans eum authorem non ineptum" (pp. 4–5).

2. *Defense de la doctrine de Calvin,* p. 206.

3. *Ibid.,* pp. 193–94.

contrast to his passionate defense of Calvin throughout the treatise.

But perhaps the most decided rebuttal to Beza's doctrine of predestination is found in a most unlikely place—in a chapter title of the *Defense de la doctrine de Calvin*. As will become clear from what follows Amyraut claims that Calvin taught a twofold will of God in predestination, one which was universal and conditional, another which was particular and absolutely unconditional. This teaching on the universal, conditional will is definitively ruled out by Beza's supralapsarian interpretation. And the significant fact is that Beza claims that Romans 9 requires a supralapsarian interpretation. This argument is especially prominent in Beza's *De praedestinationis doctrina et vero usu tractatio absolutissima, ex Th. Bezae praelectionibus in nonum epistolae ad Romanos . . .*[4] Amyraut on the other hand, presenting the above-described teaching of Calvin, entitles chapter 15 "That the doctrine of Calvin is based on the ninth chapter of the epistle to the Romans."[5] It is difficult to understand this in any other way than as a frank answer to Beza's interpretation.

PREDESTINATION IN THE STRUCTURE OF THEOLOGY

Before proceeding to the discussion of Amyraut's doctrine of predestination proper it is requisite that a word of caution be inserted. The order chosen to expound his teaching is not Amyraut's. Following Calvin, he taught that predestination ought not to appear in theology before the whole of the doctrine of grace is expounded. Though he is known in theology for his doctrine of predestination, the deviation which has caused this renown was in fact his denial of the propriety of ordering theology around this doctrine which by his time had become the central doctrine of Reformed theology. No, *for Amyraut predestination is only permissible in theology as an ex post facto explanation of why some have believed and others have not.* He often repeats his conviction on this matter:

> For, since we believe in Jesus Christ, and since we give ourselves as much as possible to the works of sanctification, and since ex-

4. Geneva, 1582.
5. *Defense,* pp. 512–68.

perience shows us that many others do not believe and that they are abandoned unto sin, it is necessary either that this difference depends on something in us or that God has vouchsafed to us some grace that He has not given to others. Now it is at this point at which predestination is introduced—when it is a question of knowing the origin of this difference. For we are taught that by nature we are not better than others and consequently, since we believe and so many others do not, this means God has dealt with us disparately.[6]

There are good reasons, I believe, for presenting the material in the order here chosen, especially since the problem itself is perhaps the major one for Amyraut. Yet we must be well aware that this order does violence to his emphatic insistence that predestination is only an implicate of grace, that only after having discussed the faith which unites us to Christ is it legitimate to discuss this doctrine.

A second reason for considering predestination first in a discussion of his religious thought is that Amyraut's claim that he is recapturing the emphases of Calvin is most vehement with regard to this doctrine. He not only believed that he was true to Calvin when he contended that the doctrine of predestination was legitimate in theology only as an ex post facto explanation of grace, but he also used Calvin to justify and support his own position.[7] While Calvin research has only recently proposed this

---

6. "Car puis que nous croyons en Jesus-Christ, & que nous nous adonnons tant que nous pouvons aux oeuvres de sanctification, & que l'experience nous fait voir que beaucoup d'autres n'y croyêt pas, & qu'ils se laissent emporter au peché à l'abandon, il faut necessairement ou que cette difference vienne de nous, ou que Dieu nous ait fait en cela quelque grace, laquelle il n'a pas faite aux autres. *Or est-ce là où on commence à nous parler de la Predestination, lors qu'il est question de sçavoir d'où vient cette difference.* Car on nous enseigne que de nature nous ne sommes pas meilleurs que les autres, & par consequent, puis que nous croyôs, & que tant d'autres ne croyêt pas, il faut que Dieu nous ait traittez inegalement" (*Apologie pour ceux de la religion* [Saumur, 1648], p. 109. Emphasis added). See also *Defense*, pp. 312–13: "Mais apres que nous avons creu en Christ, alors faut-il que la pensée de nos entendemens se replie dessus elle mesme, & qu'elle considere cette vertu divine, & ce conseil eternel de Dieu par lesquels nous avons creu, pour reconnoistre que c'est Dieu qui seul a peu destourner nos esprits du mal auquel ils estoyent si fort attachez pour les convertir & les appliquer a Christ; & que nous tirions de là un indubitable argument de nostre election, puis que Dieu ne fait rien en temps qu'il n'ait resolu de faire devant tout temps & de toute eternité."

7. *Defense*, pp. 274–313.

interpretation of Calvin's doctrine and is still divided on the issue, in my opinion Amyraut has properly interpreted Calvin. In opposition to Otto Ritschl and others[8] I believe that the location of predestination at the end of book III of the *Institutio* is the proper and logical setting for Calvin's doctrine.[9] In the light of his remark in the epistle to the reader that only in the last edition was he satisfied with the order of topics, it appears untenable that Calvin did not carefully consider the final disposition of this doctrine, and most defensible that he probably would have disapproved of the relocation of it in the doctrine of God as was done by the Protestant scholastics.

It is clear that this new approach (in which he believed he was following Calvin), this new methodology, was a basic factor in Amyraut's reformulation of theology. But methodology in itself would not have been such an important issue were it not for the results which that methodology had in the subsequent theology.

One of Amyraut's favorite criticisms of orthodox theologians was of their metaphysical speculations, which he apparently felt resulted from their methodology. He was fond of emphasizing Calvin's principle that God's essence is incomprehensible for ra-

8. Ritschl, *Dogmengeschichte*, 3:156ff.; A. M. Hunter, *The Teaching of Calvin*, 2d ed. (London, 1950), pp. 88ff.; James MacKinnon, *Calvin and the Reformation* (London, 1936), pp. 247–51.

9. Cf. Paul Jacobs, *Prädestination und Verantwortlichkeit bei Calvin* (Oncken, 1937), pp. 41ff.; Wendel, *Calvin*, pp. 269ff.; Niesel, *The Theology of Calvin*, pp. 159ff.; Brian Gerrish, *Reformers in Profile* (Philadelphia, 1967), pp. 157ff.; and esp. J. Pannier's ed. of the 1541 French *Institution*, 3:293 *note a*, 294 *note a*. For a statement from Calvin closely paralleling the passages reproduced above from Amyraut see the *Congregation faite en l'eglise de Geneve, en laquelle a esté traitté la matiere de l'election eternelle de Dieu* of 1551, *CO*, 8:94: "Or voicy par où il nous faut commencer: c'est assavoir, que quand nous croyons en Jesus Christ, cela ne vient pas de nostre propre industrie, ne que nous ayons l'esprit tant haut, ne tant aigu, pour comprendre ceste sagesse celeste, laquelle est contenue en l'Evangile: mais que cela vient d'une grace de Dieu, voire d'une grace laquelle surmonte nostre nature. Il rest maintenant à voir si ceste grace est commune à tous ou non." See also sections 1 and 2 in the *Institutio*, III.xxi, and his *Second Defense of the Faith Concerning the Sacraments in answer to Joachim Westphal:* "If out of my lucubrations he can produce a syllable in which I teach that we ought to begin with predestination in seeking assurance of salvation, I am ready to remain dumb" (*Tracts and Treatises*, 1844 trans. of Henry Beveridge [Grand Rapids, 1958], 2:343).

tional man, that "Men who . . . resolve to seek out what God is are but merely amusing themselves with insipid speculation."[10] In particular, Calvin cautioned that this principle must be applied in any consideration of the doctrine of election; it can be a source of consolation only if man begins with faith rather than the counsel of God. He says:

> The election of God will be a fatal labyrinth for anyone who does not follow the clear road of faith. Thus, so that we may be confident of remission of sins, so that our consciences may rest in full confidence of eternal life, so that we may boldly call God our Father, under no circumstances must we begin by asking what God decreed concerning us before the world began. Rather we must begin by seeking what through His paternal love He has revealed to us in Christ and what Christ himself daily proclaims to us through the Gospel. We must seek nothing more profound than that we become the sons of God.[11]

Amyraut considered the orthodox doctrine of predestination, with all its speculation about the order of God's decrees, an outright denial of this principle, and constantly called on Calvin in his desire to correct this orthodox tendency. Concerning the ordering of the decrees he makes the following incisive judgment:

> . . . I am well aware that Calvin has said many things relating to the "impulsive" causes of the decrees of God, but as to their order I do not see that he has ever said a word. Why God has created man for hope of perpetual blessedness, he states that the only reason for this is His goodness. Why, man having fallen into sin and condemnation, God willed to send His son into the world to redeem men by His death, Calvin states that the only reason for this is an admirable love of God for mankind. Why He has elected some and passed by others in imparting the grace of faith, Calvin states that the only reason for this is the mercy and severity of God. Why God has preferred one individual to another in the distribution of this grace, Calvin does not recognize any other reason than solely the perfectly free will of God. Why He has willed to save believers and to condemn unbelievers unto eternal punishment, Calvin has

10. *Institutio*, I.ii.2. *OS*, III.35.11–12: "Itaque frigidis tantum speculationibus ludunt quibus . . . insistere propositum est, quod sit Deus." See also *Institutio*, I.x.2.

11. "De aeterna dei praedestinatione," *CO*, 8:307.

thought that the reason for the latter must be taken from the justice of God whereas the reason for the former must be taken from His mercy. . . . But what has been the order according to which God has arranged all these things in His eternal wisdom, when it is a question of His having proposed of thinking or willing what comes first or last, Calvin has never explained this nor has he had the least interest in doing so.[12]

Amyraut goes on to say that this order in the decrees is a matter in which the "secrets are so profound, and the abyss so impossible to explore, that whoever will undertake to know them would necessarily be swallowed up by them or will necessarily remain eternally deluded as being in a completely inexplicable labyrinth." Nor, he continues, has the Spirit of God furnished any light on this matter in the Word.[13]

For these reasons Amyraut encourages a careful observance of what he calls Calvin's *"bel advertissement"* to exercise "modesty in the things which concern the incomprehensible counsels of

12. ". . . je voy bien que Calvin a dit beaucoup de choses touchant les causes impulsives des decrets de Dieu, mais quant a leur ordre, je ne voy point qu'il n ait jamais parlé. Pourquoy Dieu a creé l'homme pour l'esperance d'une beatitude perpetuelle, il en allegue pour seule cause sa bonté. Pourquoy l'homme estant tombé en peché & en malediction, Dieu a ordonné d'envoyer son Fils au monde, pour racheter les hommes par sa mort, il en allegue pour seule raison un admirable amour de Dieu envers le genre humain, Pourquoy il a esleu les uns, & laissé les autres en arriere, lors qu'il a esté question de donner la grace de la Foy, il en allegue pour cause la misericorde & la severité de Dieu. Pourquoy Dieu en a preferé l'un a l'autre en la distribution de cette grace, il n'en reconnoist point d'autre cause que la seule tres libre volonté de Dieu. Pourquoy il a voulu sauver les croyans, & condamner les incredules aux pénes eternelles, il a creu qu'il en faloit tirer la raison, icy de la justice de Dieu, & là de sa misericorde. . . . Mais quel a esté l'ordre selô lequel Dieu a arrangé toutes ces choses en son eternelle intelligence, ce que c'est qu'il s'est proposé de penser & de vouloir ou devant ou apres, Calvin ne l'a jamais expliqué, & ne s'en est jamais mis en peine" (*Defense,* pp. 579–80).

13. "Mais quant a la disposition de l'ordre, c'est un oeuvre de sapience, vertu qui est infinie en Dieu, (c'est chose tres-indubitable) mais dont neantmoins les secrets sont si profonds, & les abysmes si impossibles a découvrir, que quiconque entreprendra de les reconnoistre, il faudra qu'il y soit englouti, ou qu'il y demeure eternellement égaré, comme dans un labyrinte entierement inexplicable. . . . Et l'Esprit de Dieu ne nous a dans sa parole fourni d'aucune lumiere, par laquelle nous puissiôs estre addressez a penetrer jusques au fonds les pensées de Dieu, ou parvenir a les agencer cômodément, & a les mettre chacune en son ordre" (*ibid.*).

God."[14] We must, he urges, forget about these vain speculations and instead devote ourselves to what has been revealed:

> . . . we must constantly remind ourselves of this, that God is God—that is to say, that He is an infinite mind whose wisdom is marvelously diverse and inexhaustible, whose will is impossible to examine thoroughly, and whose majesty is to be reverenced with an extreme admiration and submission. So that, as for the things He has revealed unto us, we should receive them, embrace them, and with all our affection, reduce them to the practice of piety and sanctification. And, as for those things of which He has willed that we would be ignorant (and, Lord Almighty! how many and how great are these?), that we would not inquire about them with too much curiosity. In these matters, no matter to what opinion we would attach our spirits and sentiments, there will always remain this great abyss whose breadth and length and depth and height will immeasurably surpass our understanding. It is not necessary that we, wretched little men as we are, be ashamed that we do not know everything.[15]

However, important as this principle is, Amyraut was perhaps even more concerned with what he considered the dishonest exegesis of Scripture to which this methodology of beginning with the decrees of God compelled the orthodox. He was absolutely convinced that Scripture taught both a universalist design in Christ's atonement and a particularist application of its bene-

14. Sermon on Ezekiel 18:23 in *Sermons sur divers textes,* p. 52.

15. *Defense,* pp. 273–74; original passage in n. 74 below. See also *Sermons sur divers textes,* pp. 52–55, 98–99; the latter passage reads: ". . . il veut que nous nous arrestions à considerer ses bontez, & non à sonder les abysmes de sa nature. A admirer ses compassions envers tous les pecheurs, non à epiloguer sur ce qui est de ses decrets. A imiter sa benignité envers tous, non à chercher les raisons pourquoy il en a aimé les uns plus & les autres moins; s'est contenté d'inviter ceux-cy exterieurement, & a laissé leurs coeurs en leur naturelle dureté, dans les autres il a desployé une insurmontable efficace de sa grace. A luy donner la gloire de toute benignité & douceur, mesmes envers les meschans, & à eux la faute toute entiere de ce que ses graces leur ont esté inutiles. Pour luy, s'il en faut parler aux termes des hommes, il en remporte cette satisfaction, qu'il a esté bon à merveilles; & n'ayant eu proprement autre but en ses bienfaits, l'ingratitude de l'homme ne l'a sçeu empescher d'y parvenir." See also *Defense,* pp. 545–46: ". . . il y a en Dieu une certaine majesté, & une certaine hauteur ou profondeur de pensées & de conseils, a laquelle il ne nous est pas permis d'aspirer tant s'en faut que nous y puissions atteindre."

fits.[16] In a striking passage, which carries with it some obvious, searching criticisms of the orthodox, Amyraut shows that Calvin unequivocally affirmed a universal design for the atonement in his commentary on II Peter 3:9.[17] Amyraut remarks concerning this: "The confidence that Calvin had in the goodness of his cause and the candor with which he has proceeded in the interpretation of Scripture have been so great, that he had no qualms about interpreting the words of St. Peter in this manner."[18] This implies that the methodology of orthodoxy destroyed the candor with which one should deal with biblical texts[19] and that orthodoxy manifested an almost neurotic fear that somehow a sacred theological system might crumble if certain interpretations were allowed. In a word, Amyraut and his friends seem to be saying that a faulty a priori methodology had produced in orthodoxy a barrier to honest historico-exegetical research.[20]

16. ". . . Deus jurat apud Ezechielem, se se nolle mortem peccatoris, sed ut convertatur & vivat; Christus apud Joannem testatur, Deum tantopere mundum dilexisse, ut omnibus Filium suum dederit, modò credant; Paulus affirmat Deum velle ut omnes homines serventur; Petrus negat Deum velle ut ullus pereat, & similibus locis, argumentantur Scripturam proponere miserendi voluntatem universalem. Haud malè, si id rectè interpretarentur. Viri docti iique pii & orthodoxi, contendunt Rom. 9.11. Act. 13.48. tradi propositum miserendi particulare. Rectè itidem. Hi idcirco negant ullum esse Dei voluntatem universalem circa salutem hominum, illi verò ullam esse particularem. Utrique haud benè. Nam Scriptura sacra utrumque disertè docet, & propositum particulare, & voluntatem universalem" ("De gratia universali," *Dissertationes theologicae sex*, pp. 125-26).

17. Amyraut not only quotes an extensive passage from Calvin—an accurate quote—but also a long passage from Bullinger's comments on the same text. For the passage from Calvin see n. 97 below.

18. *Defense*, p. 125.

19. See for example the letter in defense of Amyraut by the Parisian pastor Le Faucheur to the Alençon synod of 1637. Le Faucheur states that Amyraut teaches universalism in order to exalt God's mercy and "pour exposer plus commodement divers textes de l'Escriture saincte, qui sembleroient souffrir quelque violence . . ." (*Lettres de Messieurs Le Faucheur et Mestrezat*, p. 26). See also the letter of Mestrezat to the pastors of Bas-Languedoc in the same source, p. 13: "Il faut trop tordre les Escritures, & user de trop de distinctions l'une sur l'autre, pour pouvoir nier que Jesus-Christ soit mort en quelque sorte pour tous & que Dieu vueille en quelque sorte que tous hommes soient sauvez."

20. See *ibid.*, p. 26, where Le Faucheur interprets the stress of the orthodox on limited atonement as frankly defensive—"pour s'opposer plus formellent aux Arminiens . . ." There can be little doubt that the emphasis on honesty and openness in exegetical work goes far to explain Amyraut's hypothetical universalism, de la Place's formulation of the doctrine of the mediate imputation

Again, and at least of equal importance with this desire for an honest handling of the biblical texts, is Amyraut's apparent belief that the orthodox methodology and doctrine had destroyed the effectiveness of Reformed preaching. Again and again Amyraut returns to this theme—that "no one speaks in this manner to invite us to the Faith, 'Believe, for God has ordained from all eternity whether or not you will believe.' "[21] Rather, he says, we must begin by proclaiming "the great mercy of God to the human race."[22] The proclamation of the gospel ought not to be concerned with the determination of events by the will of God. We are simply to preach "Believe in Christ, for He is the redeemer of the world" and to remember that "this is not the time to consider whether or not He has decreed from all eternity if we would believe in this redeemer."[23] In preaching, the minister must faithfully set forth the universality of Christ's work of redemption as revealed in Scripture:

> One must then only fix the eyes of his spirit upon the Lord Jesus, he must concentrate all the strength of his soul upon Him, he must envisage all the aspects of this object and consider how very true He is, how very useful He is, how very necessary He is, how very worthy He is of admiration, and full of contentment, consolation and joy. In a word, how He is divine no matter what the perspective from which He is seen.

of Adam's sin, and Cappel's denial of the originality of the Hebrew vowel points. That Amyraut was right in his judgment concerning the lack of candor and the neurosis of the orthodox is nowhere more evident than in the Cappel affair. The fact that Cappel could only publish his *Arcanum punctationis revelatum* (Leyden, 1624) anonymously, that he could never secure rights to publish his *Vindiciae arcani punctationis revelatorum* (it was not published until 1689 when his son Jacques appended it to the second edition of his father's *Commentarii et notae criticae in Vetus Testamentum*), that he could not secure rights to publish his *Critica sacra* (Paris, 1650) on Protestant presses and had to resort to publishing it on Catholic presses through the royal privilege procured by Father Morin of the Saumur oratory school, that Cappel's *Arcanum* was opposed by the elder Buxtorf of Basel and was bitterly attacked by the younger Buxtorf in 1648, and that as late as 1675 the essential divine inspiration of the Hebrew vowel points was affirmed in the Swiss confessional document, the *Formula consensus helvetica* —all this clearly demonstrates Amyraut's contention.

21. *Defense*, p. 311.
22. *Sermons sur divers textes*, p. 236.
23. *Defense*, pp. 311–12.

> This one must do so that he recognize and embrace in Him
> that infinite mercy which is revealed to us.[24]

And Jesus was sent to reveal this mercy to us, Amyraut tells us,
so that we would not speculate about the election of God.[25] When
speaking of the revealed and secret wills of God, of which we
shall treat later in this chapter, Amyraut advises that "in the
preaching of the Gospel, where it is a question of receiving or
rejecting the faith of Christ, no one bothers to seek out what
is the secret will of God . . ."[26] Many other passages of this sort
could be brought forth, but this is perhaps sufficient to show
how important this practical consideration was for Amyraut.
Laplanche has entitled his treatise on Amyraut *Orthodoxie et
prédication,* and though he himself does not give the reason for
his title, it serves well to point up one of the basic tensions be-

24. "Il faut alors seulement arrester les yeux de son esprit sur le Seigneur
Jesus, il y faut bander toutes les forces de son ame, il faut envisager cét objet de
toutes parts, & considerer combien il est veritable, combien il est utile, combien
il est necessaire, combien il est digne d'admiration & plein de contentement, de
consolation, & de joye, en un mot combien il est divin, de quelque costé qu'on le
regarde: afin d'y reconnoistre & d'y embrasser cette infinie misericorde laquelle
nous y est revelée" (*ibid.,* p. 312).

25. Paraphrasing Jesus' words in John 6:40 Amyraut says: "Mais afin que ce
que je vous di, que telle est la volonté du Pere qui m'a envoyé, touchant ceux
qu'il m'a donnés, ne vous choque pas, & ne vous donne pas l'occasion d'aller
speculer sur l'election de Dieu, pour sçavoir qui sont ceux qu'il a choisis pour
me donner, & vous excuser là dessus de ce que vous ne croyés pas, je vous ex-
pliqueray la volonté de mon Pere encore d'une autre sorte. Je vous di donc que
telle est aussi la volonté de celuy qui m'a envoyé, que quiconque, qui qu'il soit,
sans en excepter aucun, contemplera le Fils de Dieu des yeux de la foy, comme
j'ay dit à quelque autre occasion qu'il le falloit faire, & quiconque croira en luy,
celuy-là jouisse par luy de la vie bien-heureuse & eternelle" (*Paraphrase de s.
Jean,* pp. 244–45).

26. The whole of this very typical passage is: "En effect, ni plus ni moins qu'en
un festin aucun ne se met a penser en soy mesme si dans le secret conseil de
Dieu il a esté ordonné s'il mangeriot ou non; s'il est sage il consulte son estomach,
pour voir s'il a de l'appetit, il regarde les viandes, pour sçavoir si elles luy sont
agreables, il escoute les complimens & les suasions de celuy qui la convié, & advise
s'il est expedient qu'il y obtempere, & puis quand il a bien pensé a tout cela, il
se resoût en fin, a ce qu'il juge estre plus a propos. Ainsi en la predication de
l'Evangile où il s'agit de recevoir la Foy de Christ ou de la rejetter, nul ne se
met en péne de sonder quelle est la secrette volonté de Dieu; chacun se porte du
costé ou il est attiré par la faim & la soif de justice, ou bien destourné par le
degoût & les soulevemens que luy causent, s'il faut ainsi dire, les mauvaises
humeurs dont son ame est imbuë & penetrée" (*Defense,* p. 288).

tween the Salmurian theology and the remainder of Reformed Protestantism. And what is of particular interest at this point in our discussion is that Amyraut's critique of orthodoxy with regard to the lost effectiveness of preaching centers on methodology.

There were other aspects of religion, doctrinal and practical, which in Amyraut's view the methodology of the orthodox had damaged, and these will be discussed in due course. The point to remember now is that Amyraut's arguments return again and again to methodology not because of a simple methodological difference, but rather because of the disastrous results for theology and preaching which he believed had been produced by a wrong approach. He used his covenant theology teaching in an attempt to correct these misplaced emphases.

PREDESTINATION IN AMYRAUT'S THEOLOGY

The usual approach to Amyraut's doctrine of predestination has been to summarize his *Brief Traitté*, singling out the doctrines which are at variance with the teaching of Calvinist orthodoxy.[27] In this way his distinctive teachings relating to this doctrine have been set forth. And the discussions have centered on the problem of the so-called "hypothetical universalism," for no one has missed his insistence that Christ's sacrifice was *également pour tous*, that "the salvation that he has received from his Father in order to communicate it to men in the sanctification of the spirit and in the glorification of the body is destined equally for all . . ."[28] Nor has anyone missed his equal insistence that this universal offer was conditional, that God "has necessarily affixed the condition to it, that of believing in His son," that "these words *God wills the salvation of all men* necessarily meets with this limitation, *provided that they believe*. If they do not believe, He does not will it, this will of making the grace of salvation universal and common to all men being in such a way conditional that without the accomplishment of the condition

27. This for example has been the method of both Schweizer (*Die Protestantischen Centraldogmen,* 2:279–97) and Laplanche (*L'Oeuvre d'Amyraut,* pp. 87–108). Of these two Laplanche best presents Amyraut's teaching.

28. *Brief Traitté,* 1634 ed., p. 77; 1658 ed., p. 66. The 1658 edition drops the word *également*.

it is completely inefficacious."[29] But at the same time it has also been recognized that Amyraut taught a doctrine of absolute predestination. It has been noticed that alongside his teaching that Christ died equally for all men on condition of faith he taught that our participation in salvation "depends absolutely on this—that God employs His mercy with perfect liberty and concerning which we cannot seek out any cause other than His will": that "there is no cause whatever in men for this diversity of the favor of God toward them . . ."[30]

Yet, even though these two teachings have been recognized, there has been a general misunderstanding about how to interpret them, about how two positions, seemingly so contradictory, could exist in the same system. The general assumption has been that they must be reconciled, thereby placing Amyraut in the orthodox mold and missing his precept that it is not necessary for everything in theology to be perfectly reconciled and perfectly coherent, since man is at all times incapable of comprehending God and his actions. Likewise, apart from Moltmann, no one has adequately grasped the fact that Amyraut's attempt to resolve this tension, "at least," he says, "so far as is necessary to satisfy a sober and modest reason,"[31] relates wholly to his formulation of covenant theology and the juxtaposition of the absolute and conditional covenants.

At least part of the reason for this general misunderstanding of Amyraut's doctrine of predestination probably stems from the fact that his interpreters have not taken seriously enough the fact that Amyraut's *Brief Traitté* was composed for a very special purpose. We have seen that this treatise was written in order to relieve the mind of a recent convert from Catholicism to whom the predestinarian teaching was repugnant—especially perhaps the common idea, which had resulted from the orthodox formu-

29. ". . . la condition qu'il y a necessairement apposée, de croire en son Fils. . . . Et partant ces paroles, *Dieu veut le salut de tous les hommes,* reçoivent necessairement cette limitation, *pourveu qu'ils croyent.* S'ils ne croyent point, il ne le veut pas. Cette volonté de rendre la grace du salut universelle & commune à tous les humains, estant tellement conditionelle, que sans l'accomplissement de la condition, elle est entierement inefficacieuse" (*ibid.,* 1634 ed., pp. 89–90; 1658 ed., p. 76).

30. *Ibid.,* 1634 ed., pp. 117–18; 1658 ed., pp. 99–100.

31. *Sermons sur divers textes,* p. 55.

lation of this doctrine, that God created the greater part of mankind expressly in order to have an object for His wrath.[32] Unquestionably this highly specialized design for his book led Amyraut to order his material somewhat less fully than he would have done had he undertaken to write a thorough exposition of the subject. Indeed, he hints that this is true in his preface. Not, of course, that he included material which did not properly express his position, for he was willing to defend without equivocation the substance of the thoughts expressed, though later he did change his terminology at points. But it does seem that the discussion in the *Brief Traitté* is so brief that a simple reading fails to show how Amyraut would relate his various materials. The importance and function of his formulation of covenant doctrine in particular is less than readily apparent. For this reason I shall not give a systematic analysis of the *Brief Traitté*[33] but shall utilize its contents by relating them to the more complete presentation of his thought found in the various answers Amyraut gave to the critics of his *Brief Traitté*.

There may be an even more important reason for the misunderstanding of Amyraut's doctrine of predestination: most of his interpreters appear to have assumed that Amyraut was working within the same categories as the orthodox. There has been no appreciation of the different nature of his theology. The situation is comparable to that of a person immersed in medieval scholasticism who undertakes a study of Luther's theology. He soon has to learn that he is in a different world of thought and that Luther's teaching is somewhat difficult to understand. Once he does grasp the drift of Luther's argumentation, however, one particular insight may well be serviceable for that theology *in extenso* if it is consistently applied. Amyraut's theology, at least in the matters which concern predestination, is of much the same nature.

It appears that there are two insights which are prerequisite to any right understanding of Amyraut's doctrine of predestination.

32. See *Eschantillon de la doctrine de Calvin touchant la predestination*, 1658 ed., pp. 167–68.

33. The discussion in Laplanche, *L'Oeuvre d'Amyraut*, pp. 87–108, is highly recommended.

Without an understanding or appreciation of these (we might call them basic assumptions) Amyraut's doctrine will almost inevitably remain a riddle—as it apparently did for all of his orthodox opponents. One has to do with his doctrine of God, which he develops according to a rather unique emphasis on the distinctive activity, and periods of activity, in the work of salvation of each member of the Trinity—Father, Son, and Holy Spirit. Because it is the language Amyraut himself used we shall call this an "economic" doctrine of the Trinity, though technically he does not hold a purely economic theory, one which destroys the unity of the Godhead. His position here seems to be another indication of his consistent use of an inductive method. That is to say, it is from his understanding of the doctrine of redemption that Amyraut comes to his formulation of the idea of the Trinity. He presents the redemptive process as falling into three historical periods or economies, in each of which one member of the Trinity has a peculiar activity, as we shall elaborate shortly. In particular this means that the historical dimension of the work of redemption is given considerably more recognition than it is generally accorded in the writings of orthodox Calvinists.[34] Now it is to Moltmann's credit that he has been the first to point up the importance of this more or less unique feature of Amyraut's thought. He has shown well the significance of this teaching and how it complements the *heilsgeschichtlich* understanding of the covenants which has been outlined in the previous chapter.[35]

The fullest exposition of Amyraut's economic doctrine of the Trinity is, of course, his *"De oeconomia trium personarum in operibus divinis, dissertatio,"* first published in 1645.[36] Right at

34. Of course neither Amyraut nor Cameron was by any means the first theologian to teach an economic doctrine of the Trinity. Among the medievalists, Rupert of Deutz, Anselm of Havelberg, and even Joachim de Fiore taught a comparable doctrine (see M. D. Chenu's article "Conscience de l'histoire et théologie au XIIe siècle," *Archives d'Histoire doctrinale et litteraire du moyen age* [Paris, 1954], pp. 107–33, esp. pp. 125–26). It is, however, impossible to determine if Cameron or Amyraut developed their teaching from some such source or if it was a result of Cameron's original mind expanding a doctrine contained in germ in Calvin's *Institutio,* I.xiii.18.

35. See especially Moltmann's dissertation, chapter 7, "Die Lehre von der 'heilsgeschichtlichen Trinität.' "

36. In *Dissertationes theologicae quatuor* (Saumur, 1645); *Dissertationes theo-*

the outset of this *dissertatio* he makes clear that he bases his teaching on article VI of the *Confessio Gallicana,* a confession which, incidentally, he considered as deriving from Calvin.[37] Moreover, he stresses from the first that this is simply a convenient way of expressing the *operationes* of God and that it in no way explains the essence of the Trinity, which he always called a mystery.[38] A distinction of the activities of the three persons is predicated of the Trinity simply, to use his favorite phrase, *"secundum modum concipiendi atque considerandi nostrum."*[39] God has, in other words, by this "admirable economy," accommodated himself to our capacity.

Such an idea of accommodation, which we will be discussing at greater length is perhaps the key concept in Amyraut's doctrine of the knowledge of God. Calvin had taught that ". . . every declaration God makes of himself He accommodates (*attemperat*) to our limited capacity."[40] This teaching practically disappeared in orthodox Calvinism; at least, I have not found a single example in seventeenth-century orthodox writers. However, the

---

logicae sex (Saumur, 1660), pp. 1–55. I have used the latter edition. See also his sermon upon I John 5:7 in *Sermons sur divers textes,* esp. pp. 381–98; also a compressed statement of this element of his theology in *Paraphrase de s. Jean* 17:6, pp. 754–55.

37. *Dissertationes theologicae sex,* p. 2, where he quotes the article. See also *Replique a M. de la Milletiere,* in which he speaks of "cette incomprehensible oeconomie des trois Personnes de la bien-heureuse Trinité" and again quotes the article (1658 ed., pp. 224–25. The pagination of this edition is badly mixed up, the 200's numbered twice. The reference above should be 324–25; the first pagination through the 200's skipped from 267 to 98). This expression of the economy of persons in the work of redemption is an exact restatement of Calvin's doctrine of the Trinity as set forth in *Institutio,* I.xiii.18: "Quam tamen Scripturis notatam distinctionem animadvertimus, subticeri non convenit. Ea autem est, quod Patri principium agendi, rerumque omnium fons et scaturigo attribuitur: Filio sapientia, consilium, ipsaque in rebus agendis dispensatio: at Spiritui virtus et efficacia assignatur actionis" (*OS,* III.132.7–11). Nevertheless, this economy of persons did not play as large a role in Calvin's theology as it did in Amyraut's.

38. The Trinity, or "subsistance de trois personnes en une seule essence divine," is one of those doctrines "à la comprehension desquelles la capacité de nos entendemens ne soit nullement proportionnée" (*De l'elevation de la foy et de l'abaissement de la raison,* pp. 65–67). See also the discussion in (even the title of) his treatise of 1661, *De mysterio trinitatis.*

39. *Dissertationes theologicae sex,* p. 8.

40. *Commentary on Romans* 1:19; see the whole context in *CO,* 49:23–24. See also *Institutio* II.vi.4, II.x.6.

Salmurian theology of Cameron, Amyraut, Cappel, and de la Place, in the tradition of Calvin himself, made the concept of accommodation all-important. Amyraut's economic understanding and presentation of the Trinity both underlines this teaching and can be properly understood only in the light of it.

As we have seen, it is in relation to the work of redemption that Amyraut utilizes his economic doctrine of the Trinity. He consistently avoids any extended remarks concerning the Trinity as a metaphysical concept, since the Trinity is a mystery. The doctrine must be understood as part of God's condescending grace. When the doctrine of the atonement is under consideration Amyraut's theory of the Trinity comes into special use. He had accepted, at least in its broad outlines, the orthodox doctrine of a penal, substitutionary atonement. That is, Amyraut taught that the sufferings and death of Jesus were vicarious in that Jesus took the place of sinners, that their guilt and punishment were transferred to him. He was convinced that if this particular doctrine was accepted, then an economic doctrine of the work of the Trinity in redemption could alone accord with the teachings of Scripture.[41]

There are many interesting aspects of Amyraut's theology which derive from this economic understanding of the Trinity,[42] but what is germane to our present discussion can be explained in a relatively brief space. Before we turn to that discussion, however, we should emphasize once more his exegetical method. He applies rigorously his comparative exegesis when discussing the Trinity and so understands each predication made of one of the persons of the Trinity to refer peculiarly to that person.[43]

41. "Doctrinam autem de satisfactione, doctrina de distinctione personarum necessario sequitur" (Dissertationes theologicae sex, p. 13).

42. For example, by means of this he is able to give a rather simple explanation of the much-debated unforgivable sin against the Holy Spirit. As we shall see, since the Spirit is interpreted to be that member of the Godhead who works efficaciously, it follows that whoever sins against him, that is rejects his gift of faith, cannot be forgiven.

43. Thus he can say concerning the Holy Spirit: ". . . il n'est pas appellé Esprit proprement, pource qu'il est d'une nature spirituelle & immaterielle: cela convient aussi & au Pere, & à la Parole, qui sont entierement separez de la nature & de la condition des corps. Mais il luy est donné pource qu'il est la vertu & l'efficace de l'un & de l'autre, par laquelle s'execute effectivement ce dont le Pere

The Father is regarded as the "first source and author of all things."[44] He is the One who wills that such and such an action be accomplished,[45] who, as it were, "forms the first designs" of any action and then turns the work over to the other two members of the Trinity.[46] Or, to put it simply, the Father makes the decisions which are then carried out by the Son and the Holy Spirit. Thus in particular matters it is "properly to his Person as Superintendant of the Common right of the Three in what relates to the unity of their Essence, that satisfaction ha's [sic] been rendered; And the first source of that Mercy whereby he was moved to determine to raise man from the misery into which he was fallen; And the Invention (if I may so speak) of that Expedient in order to it by his incomprehensible Wisdom."[47]

In this economy of the Trinity the Son is spoken of as God's Word (*parole* or *Verbum*) and eternal wisdom (*sapience éternelle* or *sapientia aeterna*). These are simply the predications made of Christ by article VI of the confession, but in Amyraut they are applied exclusively to the Son in the most literal fashion. Any activity of the Godhead which would involve wisdom is im-

---

forme les premiers desseins, & dont le Fils conduit le devis, comme estant la Sapience du Pere. Car les choses spirituelles & immaterielles sont sans comparison plus agissantes, que celles qui sont revestuës de corps. Et dans les corps, les substances les plus subtiles, & qui approchent le plus de la nature des esprits, sont celles qui ont le plus de vigueur pour le mouvement, & le plus d'efficace & d'activité. Et il est appelle Saint, non pas simplement pource qu'il est sans macule, & infiniment esloigné de toute corruption de peché: car cela est commun & au Pere, & à la Parole encore; mais pource que c'est luy qui par ses saintes operations & ses inspirations puissantes, engendre la sainteté en nos ames, & y repare l'image de la sienne, & de celle du Pere, & du Fils" (sermon on I John 5:7, *Sermons sur divers textes,* pp. 389-90).

44. *Paraphrases sur Galates* 1:3, p. 4.

45. "Nam Pater in eo considerari debet tanquam in ex cujus voluntate totius negotii consilium processit" (*Dissertationes theologicae sex,* p. 14). "Pater enim in eo consideratur tanquam is qui rem designat, tum cum Filium in mundum mittere decernit, juxta illud, *Sic Deus dilexit mundum, ut Filium suum dederit,* &c. Joh. 3. Item, *At Deus charitatem suam maximopere commendavit, eo quod cùm impii eramus, Filium suum,* &c. Rom. cap. 5. Tum etiam cùm discrimen inter homines per electionem constituit, juxta illud, *Tui erant Pater, & tu mihi eos dedisti,* &c. Joh. 17. Ista enim ad primam personam referri debere, videtur esse positum extra omnem dubitationem" (*ibid.,* p. 22).

46. See *Sermons sur divers textes,* p. 389.

47. *A Treatise Concerning Religions,* p. 477.

mediately ascribed to Christ. For this reason, since "all order is a work of wisdom," Christ is affirmed to be the member of the Trinity who has "given that beautiful order to this great universe and to all the parts which make it up."[48] As for the Word, it seems in Amyraut simply to be synonymous with wisdom. For, he says, a word is the "production of an intelligent nature" since it is only of rational creatures that we predicate speech.[49] And so also Christ as the Word is spoken of as the instrument of God in creating;[50] and creation is a process which is continuous so that Christ is also spoken of as governor of the world.[51]

This idea of governing introduces us to Amyraut's favorite predication of Christ, and one which even more dramatically points up the economic nature of His activity: His work as mediator. Time and again the only name Amyraut gives Christ is that of *Mediateur*,[52] and frequently speaks of him as *moyenneur*[53] and occasionally *canal*.[54] This mediatorship relates both to creation[55] and, more especially, to the new creation or to the work of redemption. In the second relationship the activity of Christ as mediator consists in two main functions, making satisfaction for sin and governing the Church with an absolute power.[56] Such a pervasive use of the term mediator emphasizes

48. Sermon on I John 5:7 in *Sermons sur divers textes*, p. 387.

49. Sermon 2 on Hebrews 1:3 in *Cinq sermons prononcez a Charenton*, p. 60.

50. See *Paraphrase de s. Jean* 1:1, pp. 1–4, or *Paraphrases sur la premiere espistre de s. Jean* 1:1, pp. 1–7.

51. In this context Amyraut introduces another predication of Christ, calling him the Father's "Lieutenant," especially frequently in the *Paraphrase de s. Jean:* ". . . le Pere . . . l'ayant estably son Lieutenant en toute son autorité" (on 5:23, p. 190). "Mais le Pere, comme j'ay dit, l'establissant son Lieutenant au Gouvernement de l'Univers, luy a donné une puissance absoluë sur toutes choses . . ." (on 5:27, p. 193). See also on 5:36, and esp. on 10:36, p. 467, where Christ is said to act as God's Lieutenant in the exercise of his functions as mediator.

52. E.g., *Paraphrase de s. Jean* 6:56, 10:18, 10:36, 17:8; *Paraphrase sur Colossiens* 1:2, 1:16, 1:19; *Paraphrases sur Ephesiens* 5:20; *In symbolum apostolorum, exercitatio* (Saumur, 1663), pp. 69ff.

53. *Paraphrases sur Philippiens* 1:2; *Paraphrases sur Galates* 1:3.

54. *Paraphrases sur Tite* 3:6. Speaking here of justification and regeneration Amyraut says that they are "par Jesus Christ nostre Sauveur lequel est le canal par lequel tous ces biens decoulent à nous" (p. 110).

55. *Paraphrases sur Colossiens* 1:16, p. 14.

56. "Filius in eo consideratur ut is cui munus demandatum fuit effectum dandi quod consilio paterno jam designatum erat: primùm satisfactionem, quae neces-

the thoroughly economic nature of Amyraut's christology, for the term relates everything naturally back to the Father as the director of the activity.

The Holy Spirit in this economic understanding proceeds from both the Father and the Son and is the "virtue and efficacy of both" and "executes effectively that of which the Father forms the first designs and of which the Son works out that design." In the work of salvation it is the Spirit who creates faith, who unites the believer to Christ, who regenerates and repairs the lost image of God. In short, the Spirit makes effective to the particular believer what Christ had accomplished for the world. This is a very crucial part of Amyraut's theological system and we shall return to it again.

In sum, it seems that Amyraut's teaching of an economic Trinitarian activity in the work of salvation is neither complicated nor difficult to understand. But the relative simplicity of the teaching must not be allowed to obscure its immense importance in the theology of Amyraut. It is particularly important as a major point of difference between Amyraldian theology and orthodox Calvinist belief.

The second consideration which is prerequisite to a proper understanding of Amyraut's doctrine of predestination concerns a distinction which we have mentioned before—his juxtaposition of God's secret and revealed will. None of Amyraut's interpreters until Moltmann had noticed the full implications of this distinction, and even Moltmann did not properly qualify his discussion. The best way to explain this particular distinction is by analyzing Amyraut's doctrine of predestination. To that task we now turn.

Amyraut's Doctrine of Predestination

As one begins a discussion of Amyraut's doctrine of predestination he is immediately confronted with a baffling problem. To begin as Amyraut does in the *Brief Traitté de la predestination*

---

saria fuit, praestando; deinde auctoritatem & potentiam infinitam vice Patris exercendo, ut rem ad exitum perduceret" (*Dissertationes theologicae sex*, pp. 22–23).

would present him opting for an entirely rational explanation of
the fact of, if not the reasoning behind, this doctrine. However,
in all of his discussions of predestination subsequent to that in
the *Brief Traitté* Amyraut denies that it can be comprehended
by reason. The tension involved in the two positions is one
which I have been unable to resolve—unless all Amyraut is saying in the opening chapters of the *Brief Traitté* is simply that
this doctrine ought not to be rejected as an idea unworthy of
rational approbation.[57] While I tend toward this interpretation,
I also feel that it is too simple a resolution of a complex problem.
Perhaps the most persistent and recurring problem, one not easily
solved, is the implication of natural theology in these opening
remarks of the *Brief Traitté*. At this point Amyraut seems to have
moved beyond his beloved Calvin and evidences affinities rather
with the orthodox Calvinist writers in whose doctrine of God
rationalization and natural theology played a large part. Later
he seems largely to abandon this direction of thought, but one
cannot help wonder how far he would have progressed had it not
been for his running battle with the orthodox. In the end though,
whatever the reason may be, Amyraut's presentation of the doctrine of God remains much less influenced by natural theology
and rationalization than is that of orthodox Calvinists.

A prime example of interest in natural theology among the
orthodox is Pierre du Moulin's *De cognitione Dei*.[58] Of the
seventy pages of the French translation, forty-two are devoted to
the knowledge of God from creation and through reasoning.
True, he states that for true, saving knowledge of God man has
need of another teacher than nature and reason (pp. 42–43), but
in the light of the forty-two eloquent preceding pages one wonders how much significance would be attributed to this passage

57. It is more than likely only a very good instance of the constant warfare
between the incipient rationalism (the contagious optimism of the seventeenth
century with regard to reason, to use J. Huizinga's phrase) and the strongly
revelational theology of Amyraut. Sabean and Rex may properly write of
Amyraut's rationalism (see Sabean, "The Theological Rationalism of Moïse
Amyraut," pp. 204–16, and Rex, *Essays on Pierre Bayle*), but it is only one side
of the coin. One could find sufficient material to write as convincing a study on
Amyraut's disparagement of reason in theological matters.

58. Leyden, 1625. I have used the French translation by S. D. S., *Traitté de la
connoissance de Dieu* (Geneva, 1637).

by his contemporaries. In any event, natural theology is certainly much more prominent than it ever is in Amyraut and the ratiocination in these pages differs markedly from Amyraut's. Amyraut's reasoning is inductive, du Moulin's is deductive; Amyraut's is experiential, du Moulin's is metaphysical. Du Moulin has frequent recourse to Aristotle's *Metaphysics* (see pp. 16, 22, 25) and develops all the old scholastic arguments for the existence of God: Aristotle's "prime mover" argument (pp. 10–11), the cause-effect argument (pp. 11–12), the argument from degrees of perfection (pp. 12–13), the argument from numbers (p. 13), etc. These "proofs for the existence of God" are generally studiously avoided by Amyraut. When he does use such arguments his reasoning is not syllogistic as in du Moulin's. For example, when arguing (in a very striking passage) that order presupposes a rational arranger (i.e., God), du Moulin first posits an axiom or principle (*Fortune est mere de confusion: & l'industrie produit l'ordre* [p. 9]) and then argues deductively and syllogistically from there. Amyraut uses the same argument from order (see appendix 1) but does not posit this type of axiom and so climbs the ladder the other way. Deductive logic is the determinative factor of all orthodox formulations; inductive logic is the consistent approach of Amyraut.

Though Amyraut's teaching generally contrasts with the rational approach of orthodoxy, it is a temptation to overemphasize this contrast. Thus, because of the importance of the rational element in the *Brief Traitté* I have felt it necessary to give a brief résumé of the argumentation in the opening chapters; I will then turn to what seems to be his consistent subsequent position, leaving the tension unresolved—as I think it must remain.

In the opening chapter of the *Brief Traitté* Amyraut answers the question, "What is predestination?" The underlying assumption of the chapter seems to be that the universe is governed by law.[59] Following his usual and consistent pattern of argument, Amyraut develops his discussion by analyzing observable phe-

59. The concept of law, both natural law and jurisprudence, appears to have an important role in the whole of Amyraut's theology, and we shall have occasion to mention his direct use of juridical concepts. The question deserves more detailed consideration, especially in the light of Amyraut's reported degree of licentiate in jurisprudence at the University of Poitiers.

nomena, beginning with "natural things" and then ascending the scale to God. The further assumption seems to be that these observable phenomena in some way are a proper reflection of the divine.[60] The argument is the following: Natural causes, such as the heavens and the elements, "act according to a blind and inevitable necessity" (p. 1). The members of the animal world are "induced to their actions by brute instincts and appetites" (p. 1). Intelligent beings, such as angels and men, are "governed (*conduites*) by a more excellent faculty," reason, and so "there is always some end (*but*) chosen by our understanding (*intelligence*), upon which, whatever we do, we have our mind set" (pp. 2–3). Now, even from nature we learn "that God is an intelligent being (*essence*), indeed, even the source from which all that there is of reason in His creatures has proceeded" (p. 3). Since it would be absurd to think that an architect ever drew up plans for a building without some end in sight, "so it would be a conception unworthy of the beauty which appears in the constitution of the world, and of the wisdom of this one who has made it, to think that He brought it into being simply at random, without having specifically designated each thing for a particular purpose" (p. 4). And, since man is "the *chef d'oeuvre* of His hand, and the epitome of the marvels which He has here and there dispensed in all the rest of His works, it is obvious that His care had ought to be directed in a particular way toward that which concerns him in order to lead him to that end which is most suitable to his nature" (p. 5). This particular care directed toward man, "that most precious part (*piece*) in the universe," is commonly called predestination (pp. 5–6).

Predestination is part of providence. Providence is "the care that in his wisdom God, the Creator of the universe, takes in the conservation and conduct of all things both which are and which are done in the world; so that nothing takes place either in that which depends on natural causes—such as the movements (*influences*) of the heavens, the *mélange* of the elements in the composition of things, the procreation of the animals for the

---

60. E.g., he can say that "la Nature" teaches us "que Dieu est une essence intelligente" (p. 3 of both the 1634 and 1658 editions. The page numbers which follow in the text refer to the 1658 edition).

propagation of their species, and similar things—or in that which occurs, as is said, fortuitously (that is to say, of which one does not perceive the causes in the order of nature), or in the actions of men themselves (as that which He has ordained in his counsel)" (p. 6).

Predestination is a less general term and is employed "to denote not only that providence which commonly watches over the actions of men, but particularly that care according to which God has ordained these men to their final disposition (*but*)" (p. 7).

This predestination, which in biblical terms relates to our adoption into Christ, presupposes sin. And sin "seems to have changed not only the whole face of the universe, but even the entire design of the first creation, and, if one may speak this way, seems to have induced God to adopt new counsels" (p. 8). So, Amyraut believes, it is necessary to discuss these matters in chronological order, beginning with a consideration of why God first created the world and proceeding to his purpose in ordaining man's adoption into Christ.

These two last paragraphs call for further comment. First, it has become obvious that Amyraut's definition of predestination here is drawn from the realm of philosophy commonly known as *la morale*. Or in theology we would say he has begun with natural theology. He has, then, applied to the biblical concept of predestination the general concept that everything in nature is governed by certain immutable laws. This is, to my knowledge, the only attempt at a formal definition in his writings.[61] It is significant that he does not mention either election or reprobation in this context. This tends to confirm the suspicion that he is only hoping to show that the doctrine of predestination is not contrary to reason or to the natural order in created things—that he is not trying to explain the doctrine per se. Or, since this treatise was written to dispel the qualms of a recent convert from Catholicism, perhaps one should interpret it as an attempt to win an audience by initiating the discussion in a realm which would admit of mutual understanding and agreement. But in any case, Amyraut's point of departure in the *Brief Traitté* is

61. See, however, his *Apologie pour ceux de la religion*, pp. 104–6, where a similar concept is presented.

novel for a Reformed theologian at this period of the seventeenth century and implies that the subsequent discussion is founded upon a concept drawn from nature. To be sure, William Perkins can preface his treatise on predestination by writing that it is "requisite that this doctrine agree with the grounds of common reason, and of that knowledge of God which may be obtained by the light of nature,"[62] but it is something else again to build the discussion on the basis of nature as Amyraut seems to do.

Secondly, we find in these two paragraphs the idea that sin caused God, as it were, to adopt new counsels. This was a consistent teaching of Amyraut. Of course the orthodox theologians were scandalized by such a position and attacked Amyraut bitterly at this juncture. His refusal to discard anthropomorphic language, as he customarily called it, is a most explicit example of his theological methodology. He always insisted on an analytic method and explanation, refusing to adapt and synthesize his material according to an a priori theological principle. And while he was willing to admit that God does not in fact change his mind, he contended that we cannot think in terms which transcend our experience and so insisted on expressing himself in terms which are agreeable to "our weak manner of understanding."[63]

---

62. Preface to the reader, *A Christian Plaine Treatise of the Manner and Order of Predestination, and of the Largeness of God's Grace,* vol. 2 of his *Works* (London, 1613), p. 605.

63. See for example his letter to Irminger of Zurich of 1647: "At, si, quemadmodum in multis aliis rebus sic etiam in praedestinationis negotio aeternas illas atq; simplicissimas Dei cogitationes ad modum considerandi nostrum accommodemus, et inter decreta Dei, non secundum momenta temporum, sed secundum naturam rerum ipsarum ordinem aliquem instituamus, . . ." (Archives Tronchin, vol. 130, folios 9, 2–10, 1. MS). See also the *Defense,* p. 582: "Mais l'immensité & l'infinité de la nature divine ne souffre pas, que divers objets entrent par la succession de divers temps en son entendement. Il faut que de toute eternité il ait en un mesme moment, veu, connu, decreté, disposé, & mis en ordre toutes choses, par un seul & indivisible acte de son intelligence. Ce donc que nous voulons que les decrets de Dieu succedent les uns aux autres, c'est pour soulager en quelque façon nostre infirmité, & en nous accommodant a la façon de raisonner laquelle nous suivons quant a nous. Car nostre entendement a ses limites trop estroits, & est borné de trop prés, pour pouvoir comprendre en mesme temps diverses choses."

The first chapter sets the tone for the whole of the *Brief Traitté*. He proceeds to discuss briefly the main parts of the history of salvation (why God created the world and man, why he permitted the Fall, what are the effects of sin, etc.), and the whole discussion finds its originating point in the realm of *la morale*. Of course biblical texts are used, but more as a confirmation of the information garnered from the above-named source than as in themselves first establishing the particular teaching at hand. In chapter 7 Amyraut discusses conditional predestination and in chapter 9 absolute predestination. These are the center of his doctrine of predestination and to them we turn, though our point of departure will be the consistent approach in his writings subsequent to the *Brief Traitté*.

We have mentioned that Amyraut was convinced Scripture taught that the sacrifice of Christ was universal in intention and scope[64] and even that God willed the salvation of all men.[65] But of course he also taught that God had willed that only a select few would enjoy participation in this universal salvation procured by Christ. And, uniquely enough, he was of the opinion that it was wrong to subject these two seemingly contradictory wills of God to the judgment of reason,[66] that it was wrong to slight one part of this revelation solely for the sake of a rationally constructed, logically coherent theological system. At this junc-

---

64. "Aiunt ergo Deum sua φιλανθρωπια & generis humani misericordia impulsum, decrevisse ab aeterno Filium suum in mundum mittere, qui praestita pro peccatis satisfactione, remissionem peccatorum & salutem aeternam ea lege omnibus acquireret, si ipsum per fidem amplecterentur, neque dedignarentur tantae salutis esse compotes. Statuunt ergo quidem & Deum aliquo modo voluisse, & homines pariter potuisse servari omnes, modò crederent" ("De gratia universali," *Dissertationes theologicae sex*, p. 123). See also *Brief Traitté* of 1634, pp. 77ff.; from p. 77: "La misere des hommes estant egale & universelle, & le desir que Dieu a eu de les en deliver par le moyen d'un si grand Redempteur, procedant de la compassion qu'il a euë d'eux, comme de ses creatures tombées en une si grande ruïne, puis qu'ils sont ses creatures egalement, la grace de la redemption qu'il leur a offerte & procurée a deu estre egale & universelle . . ." The term *equal* was bitterly assailed by the orthodox and was deleted from the 1658 edition.

65. "Dieu donc a voulu faire misericorde a tous, pourveu que tous recherchassent par Foy cette misericorde" (*Defense*, p. 106).

66. ". . . ce seroit grievement pecher alencontre de luy, que d'abandonner ou de tordre la verité de sa parole, & luy donner quelque espece de gesne, pour luy faire dire ce qu'elle ne veut pas" (*Sermons sur divers textes*, p. 53).

ture he once again emphasized that man's reason is not capable of fathoming the working of God, that reason must bow to the revelation of God. In the first of his *Six Sermons* of 1636, preached in defense of the *Brief Traitté*, he makes this abundantly clear:

> . . . when He has revealed something to us in His word having to do with the dispensation of His will towards men, it is not our business to explore this in order to see whether or not it is agreeable to His nature, or to see whether or not this puts two wills in God which are opposed—as if His nature were something which could be comprehended by our understandings. His nature is an abyss which not only men's spirits, but even the intelligence of angels, cannot thoroughly examine. . . . No, my brethren, when on the one hand the Word of God will teach me that He has reprobated some and consigned them to eternal punishment, and that on the other hand this same Word will teach me that God wills all men to be saved, that He invites them to repent, that He extends his arms to them, that He goes before them and calls them with a lively voice . . . although my reason found there some things which seemed to be in conflict, although whatever effort that I exert I am not able to harmonize nor reconcile them, still I will not fail to hold these two doctrines as true. Nor will I undertake to resolve the opposition of these two wills of God which seem so repugnant. Either God will some day give us a greater illumination of His Spirit, or at least in the appearance of His Son He will manifest all things. However, I will keep what He has revealed to me, and I will not permit that the presumption (*hardiesse*) of my reason do any injury to His unspeakable grace toward men.[67]

---

67. *Sermons sur divers textes*, pp. 52, 54-55. See also *Defense*, pp. 273-74: ". . . cette pensée nous doit perpetuellement revenir en l'esprit, que Dieu est Dieu, c'est a dire, un entendement infini, dont la sagesse est merveilleusement diverse & inépuisable, la volonté impossible a approfondir, & la Majesté a venerer avec une admiration & une submission extreme. Afin que quant aux choses lesquelles il nous a revelées nous les recevions nous les embrassions & les reduisions de toute nostre affection a la pratique de la pieté & de la sanctification: & pour celles qu'il a voulu que nous ignorassions (or quelles, Dieu immortel! & combien grandes sont elles?) que nous ne nous en enquerions pas avec trop de curiosité. En ces matieres, a quelque opinion que nous attachions nos esprits & nos sentiments, il restera tousjours de grands abysmes, dont la largeur & la longueur & la profondeur & la hauteur surpasseront extrémement nostre intelligence: & ne faut pas, chetif petits hommes que nous sommes, que nous ayons honte de ne sçavoir pas tout. Car tels, dit Aristote mesme, que sont les yeux des chauvesouris eu égard a la lumiere du jour, telle est cette puissance de nostre ame qui côsiste en intelli-

Although Amyraut indicated that, if necessary, he was perfectly content to leave these two wills in tension, such an idea was utterly inconceivable to the orthodox.[68] L. Rimbault has well characterized du Moulin's reaction to Amyraut's thought: "It is possible to say that he found in it more transgressions of logic than breaches of the authority of Scripture. The more rationalistic of the two is perhaps not he who is assumed to be."[69] Repeatedly du Moulin returns to this particular criticism of Amyraut, and one may well conclude that in his attack this charge of faulty logic takes second place only to the charge that Amyraut has reversed the order of the decrees. In fact, the charge of inept logic is even a large part of his criticism of the

---

gence, eu égard aux choses de leur nature les plus claires & plus manifestes." See also *ibid.*, pp. 151, 242; *Sermons sur divers textes*, pp. 98–99; sermon 2 of *Quatre sermons sur Hebrieux* 6, pp. 64–65; sermon 2 of *Le Ravissement de s. Paul expliqué en quatre sermons* (Saumur, 1660), pp. 39–41, and 57–58; and *Sermon sur le sujet de la paix* (Saumur, 1660), pp. 16–17. All these passages sound very much as though Amyraut had drawn his inspiration from the principle that Calvin set forth, evidently following St. Augustine, that in these matters there is a certain "learned ignorance" (*Institutio*, III.xxi.2, III.xxiii.8).

68. It is clear that the orthodox were simply unable to understand these apparent breaches of logic. Du Moulin is a good example of their complete inability to comprehend how Amyraut could possibly believe that both a universal design in Christ's atonement and a particular application of its benefits were rationally acceptable. In du Moulin's mind, if one said that God wills the salvation of all men, then all men must in fact be saved. Time and again he states the following argument in many forms: "M. Amyraut, enseignant, que Dieu ne veult pas donner la foy à tous, sans laquelle nul ne peut estre sauvé, monstre assés, qu'il ne les veult pas sauver tous, combien qu'il face semblant d'enseigner le contraire" (*Esclaircissement des controverses Salmuriennes* [Leyden, 1648], p. 111). See also his sarcastic remarks on p. 135: "Par ceste predestination universelle, que maintenant on appelle *premiere misericorde*, Dieu veult sauver Pierre, & Jehan, conditionellement, pourveu qu'ils ayent la foy. Et par la seconde misericorde il les veult sauver non conditionellement, & combien qu'il ne trouve point en eux la foy. Sont-ce pas là des conceptions bien enfilees? Certes si on croit ces Messieurs, on ne les croira pas. Car ils ne se croyent pas eux mesmes." He then goes on to speak of the "pareille absurdité" that "Jesus Christ est mort pour les reprouves quant à l'intention, mais non quant à l'evenement . . ."

69. "Un traité d'Amyraut: Du gouvernement de l'eglise," p. 162. The charge that du Moulin is the more rationalistic can be supported in many ways. For example, in section 5 of his *Esclaircissement,* when discussing the absurdity of a general decree of God to save all men, he spends one chapter showing that such an idea is contrary to Scripture and the Canons of Dort, and one chapter showing it is contrary to reason. The chapter on reason is twice the length of the former!

general order Amyraut propounded for these decrees. Indeed, on this particular matter du Moulin regards Amyraut's teaching as more unacceptable than that of Arminius: "Here then is the difference between Arminius and M. Amyraut. Namely, that the decrees as presented by Arminius are logically connected (*bien liés*) and do not contradict each other."[70]

After having made this enjoinder not to allow our reason to mutilate God's revelation by insisting upon a logically coherent explanation of God's actions, Amyraut proceeds to indicate the direction in which a solution may be sought. Indeed, he believes that there is a solution to the problem—at least, he says, "insofar as such is necessary in order to satisfy a sober and modest reason."[71] And it is at this point that he executes his master stroke. For, he says, *Calvin* has provided this "excellent means" (*excellente ouverture*),[72] and he has followed Calvin in this. He gives a five-page quotation from Calvin's commentary on Ezekiel 18:23 in which he shows that Calvin presents the distinction between the revealed, conditional will of God which desires the salvation of all men and the hidden, absolute will of God which deals with electing a certain few. Amyraut then concludes that Calvin's interpretation shows that "the Word of God . . . presents His mercy to us to be considered in two ways,"[73] and upon this

70. *Esclaircissement*, p. 8. See also pp. 90–91, and esp. 103 where speaking of Amyraut's relations with the Arminians he says: "lesquels il a tort d'appeller ses adversaires, puis qu'il emprunte d'eux ses argumens, & est quasi en toutes choses de mesme opinion qu'eux, *hors mis és choses esquelles il se contredit à soy mesme*" (emphasis added); also p. 132, in which chapter 2 bears the title "Opinion d M. Amyraut & Testard, & comment ils se contredisent à eux mesmes."

71. From the sermon on Ezekiel 18:23, *Sermons sur divers textes*, p. 55.

72. *Ibid.*

73. "La parole de Dieu . . . nous presente sa misericorde à considerer en deux manieres" (*ibid.*). See also *Eschantillon de la doctrine de Calvin*, pp. 203–6 of 1658 edition: "Calvin donc considere la misericorde de Dieu en deux manieres. Car premierement il remarque en la parole de Dieu une soit vertu, soit propriete en luy qui le rend enclin à pardonner universellement à tous ceux qui sont repentans, mais aussi qui exige necessairement la repentance de la creature pecheresse. De façon que si elle ne se repent & ne croit, il est impossible que Dieu luy pardonne. [Amyraut then quotes Calvin's commentaries upon Rom. 11:32, II Peter 3:8, Rom. 5:17, and, at length, Ezekiel 18:21–22.] Puis apres il considere cette misericorde entant qu'elle ne se contente pas d'exiger la repentance, comme une condition necessairemêt prealable à la remission des pechés; mais qu'elle a resolu de creer elle mesme cette condition en la creature, à ce que reellement & de fait

twofold mercy depends a twofold will. With this twofold will as his basis Amyraut has constructed his covenant theology, the distinction between the *foedus absolutum* and the *foedus hypotheticum,* indeed the outline of the whole of his theology. And he appeals to Calvin as the source of that distinctive approach.

Since Amyraut did so consistently appeal to Calvin, insisting that he himself was only teaching what Calvin had taught, it is perhaps appropriate that we investigate that claim at more length. Certainly one of the striking aspects of Amyraut's work is the complete familiarity he shows with Calvin's writings. In his writing he piles quotation upon quotation from Calvin, drawing from a great variety of Calvin's work. There are, for example, more than a dozen quotes from Calvin in the *Six Sermons* of 1636, some thirty-seven often lengthy quotes in the *Eschantillon de la doctrine de Calvin* of 1636,[74] at least 103 extensive passages from Calvin in his *Defense de la doctrine de Calvin* of 1644,[75] and frequent references from Calvin in each of the writings in which Amyraut was defending his own position.[76] There is an almost complete identification with Calvin at times, especially in the *Defense de la doctrine de Calvin* in which he often switches back and forth from the first to the third person.

This thorough familiarity with and use of Calvin by Amyraut is even more remarkable in the light of the fact that there is an almost total lack of reference to Calvin in the orthodox writers

elle obtienne la remission des offences. Et au lieu que la precedente est universelle, celle cy est particuliere: . . ."

74. Ten are from the *Institutio,* 7 from the commentary on Romans, 5 from the commentary on John, 5 from the treatise on predestination, and the remainder from scattered writings.

75. Eighteen from the treatise on predestination, 15 from the *Institutio,* 13 from the commentary on John, 12 from the commentary on Romans, and the remainder from widely scattered sources. Amyraut was especially fond of Calvin's preface to the French Bible, although because of the brevity of this preface the extent of quotation from it was never great in any of his writing. Amyraut was also very partial to Bullinger, Musculus, and Bucer.

76. E.g., some nineteen quotations from, or references to, Calvin in an apologetic letter to T. Tronchin of Geneva (Archives Tronchin, 26:138ff. MS) and as many in "De gratia universali," *Dissertationes theologicae sex.* I have not counted the references in *Specimen animadversionum,* but they are probably more numerous than in any writing except the *Defense.*

of the period. Laplanche is correct in maintaining that for the orthodox "the thought of Calvin does not in any way assume a normative value,"[77] but it hardly seems proper to include Amyraut in such a statement.[78] Moreover, it seems that the orthodox were completely surprised and confused by Amyraut's appeal to Calvin. It does not seem too much to say that these orthodox theologians were not well read in Calvin and so were unprepared to counter the tremendous mass of relevant Calvin material marshalled by Amyraut. Nor does it seem that the reason for this relative ignorance of Calvin is difficult to determine. The answer is most certainly to be sought in the scholasticism which began with Beza, Martyr, and Zanchi and which by the seventeenth century held sway in Reformed theology. The theology of Calvin was simply not attractive to the mind set which accompanied and characterized this scholasticism.[79] The authorities of the orthodox were much more frequently Beza, Martyr, or Zanchi—or even St. Thomas. It is not mere coincidence that du Moulin, for instance, in his various discussions of the topics of providence and predestination, never once so much as alludes to Calvin but does more than once quote St. Thomas.[80] And it is to be observed that this rejection of Calvin was by no means unconsciously done. This is shown by the remarkable passage discussed briefly in chapter 2, in which du Moulin seems to indicate his preference for Beza, Martyr, and Zanchi in a most explicit way.

We have mentioned that Amyraut takes his distinction of the two mercies and the two wills of God from Calvin. In the passage which Amyraut uses, the commentary on Ezekiel 18:23, Calvin clearly indicates this twofold character of God's will; indeed even a twofold character of God Himself:

77. L'Oeuvre d'Amyraut, p. 273.

78. Simply because Calvin was overwhelmingly Amyraut's favorite theologian. The laudatory language he uses when referring to Calvin is not used for any other theologian except, at times, Cameron.

79. In the words of A. M. Schmidt, the Reformed "seem to have found that certain peculiarities of his genius had a cramping effect in their efforts to fulfill their task of teaching" (Calvin and the Calvinistic Tradition, tr. J. K. S. Reid [New York, 1960], p. 175).

80. E.g., his chapter on predestination in Anatome arminianismi, pp. 73–82.

But it is to be noted that God assumes a twofold role, for He desires to be taken at His word. . . . the prophet is not here engaging in a subtle dispute about His incomprehensible counsel but desires to keep our minds, as it were, bound to the word of God. And what in itself comprises the word of God? The law, the prophets, and the gospel. As everybody knows, all men are called to repentance and the hope of salvation is promised to them when they do repent. . . . however, this will of God which He has set forth in His word does not stand in the way of His having decreed from before the creation of the world what He would do with each individual.[81]

In this revealed word God is seen as desirous that all men be saved. In a passage to which Amyraut has frequent recourse Calvin makes this explicit: ". . . God longs for nothing more sincerely than that whoever was perishing and rushing to destruction should have returned to the way of salvation." But, Calvin goes on to say, "the way in which God wills all to be saved must be noted, namely, *when they shall turn themselves from their ways*."[82] Or again, "We hold, therefore, that God does not will the death of the sinner inasmuch as He calls all men indifferently to repentance and promises that He is prepared to receive them, on condition that they earnestly repent."[83] Here, then, is the conditional will of which Amyraut makes so much. It is the formula of his hypothetical universalism, namely, God wills the

---

81. *CO,* 40:446.

82. ". . . Deum scilicet nihil magis cupere, quam ut quicunque peribant, et ruebant in mortem, redeant in viam salutis. . . . Atqui notandus est modus, quo Deus vult omnes salvos fieri, nempe *ubi se converterint a viis suis*" (*CO,* 40:445).

83. *Ibid.*: "Tenemus itaque nunc Deum nolle mortem peccatoris, quia omnes indifferenter ad poenitentiam vocat, et promittit se paratum fore ad eos recipiendos, modo serio resipiscant." For a typical orthodox explanation of this passage clearly revealing their rejection of Calvin at this juncture see du Moulin's "De voluntate Dei," *Thesaurus theologiae Sedanensis* (Geneva, 1641), p. 106: "Dicimus, Deum nolle mortem peccatoris qui convertitur, ut indicant verba sequentia. At Deum nolle mortem peccatoris qui perseverat in incredulitate & impoenitentia nefas est dicere, cum Scriptura sexcenties contrarium affirmet: Esa. cap. 1.24. Deus sic loquitur, *Hem, ego me solabor super hostibus meis, & vindictam sumam de inimicis meis:* Et Ezech. cap. 5. *Requiescere faciam furorem meum, super eis, & inde consolationem accipiam:* . . . Justitia Dei una est de Dei virtutibus: At Deus nullam suam virtutem aegrè aut invitus exercet. Nec approbat aut ipsi placent impossibilia, & quae decreuit non esse, & quae non vult largiri. Denique quotiescunque illud abiiciunt *Nolo mortem peccatoris,* semper respondebimus, supplendum esse *qui convertitur*."

salvation of all men on the condition that they believe. It is, moreover, the basis of the conditional covenant. It shows God as supremely merciful and is the basis on which the gospel may be proclaimed sincerely to all men.[84]

Amyraut was absolutely confident that this distinction of two wills in God was true to Calvin's theology. Nor is this passage from the Ezekiel commentary the only one in Calvin's writings to which he has recourse. He was especially fond of the passage in Calvin's *De aeterna dei praedestinatione* quoted below on pages 198-99.[85] Here Amyraut finds an explicit exposition of these two wills in the following words of Calvin:

> God requires conversion from us; wherever He finds it, a man is not disappointed of the promised reward of life. Hence God is said to will life, as also repentance. But the latter He wills, because He invites all to it by His word. Now this is not contradictory of His secret counsel, by which He determined to convert none but His elect.[86]

84. "Selon cette volonté que l'on appelle communément revelée, Dieu témoigne qu'il y a pardon & remuneration preparée par devers luy a tous ceux qui ne refuseront pas de faire leur devoir; & accômode a cette fin la doctrine par laquelle les hômes y sont invitez. Il plante par maniere de dire la palme au milieu de la carriere & la monstre a tous, pour les convier a courir; il les y incite par ses exhortations, il les alleche par ses promesses, il les aiguillonne & les y picque par les denonciations de ses jugemens; a ce qu'il n'en soit excepté aucun, que tous indifferemment soient eslevez en l'esperance d'emporter le prix, que tous universellement y considerent la vie comme offerte soubs mesmes conditions, & qu'en un mot il ne soit rien laissé en arriere de tout ce qui peut servir a engendrer une certaine confiance qu'il en est ainsi. D'ou viennent ces paroles de Calvin. *Certainement si nous considerons à quel but tend la doctrine celeste, nous trouverons que tous sont appellez indifferemment a salut. Car la Loy a esté la voye a la vie, comme Moyse le témoigne. Cette est la voye, cheminez en icelle. Item, quiconque fera ces choses vivra par elles. Item, c'est icy vostre vie. Puis apres Dieu s'est aussi volôtairement presêté côme misericordieux a son peuple. En fin la doctrine celeste doit estre salutaire a tous, Et l'Evangile, qu'est-ce? C'est la puissance de Dieu en salut a tout croyant, dit S. Paul.* Que si Dieu se manifeste tel aux hommes, certainement il est tel, & ne trompe pas les miserables mortels par les apparences d'un faux masque de misericorde" (*Defense*, pp. 115-16). The quotations from Calvin are from his commentaries on Ezekiel 18:32 and Luke 14:23.

85. Amyraut used this passage in the *Eschantillon*, 1658 ed., pp. 209-10; *Defense*, pp. 595-96; and *Specimen animadversionum*.

86. "Conversionem exigit a nobis Deus: eam ubicunque invenit, promisso vitae praemio non frustratur. Vitam ergo velle dicitur Deus, qualiter et poenitentiam. Hanc autem vult, quia verbo suo omnes ad eam invitat. Caeterum, id cum arcano

Or again, Amyraut frequently refers to Calvin's comments on II Peter 3:9, where the same idea is present:

> Here is His extraordinary love toward man, that He wills all men to be saved, and is prepared to bring even the perishing to salvation. However we must notice this order—God is prepared to bring all men to repentance so that none may perish. For the means of obtaining salvation is indicated by these words. Therefore any one of us who aspires to salvation must learn to apply himself to this way. But here one may ask, if God desires no one to perish, why then do many perish? I answer, here no mention is made of the secret will by which the reprobate are destined to their deserved fate, but only of the will which is revealed to us in the gospel.[87]

Calvin also makes the same distinction in the *Institutio* III.xx.43 when explaining the third petition in the Lord's Prayer—that God's will may be done on earth as in heaven. Calvin explains that "Here, then, it is not a question of His secret will by which He governs all things and destines them to their end. . . . Rather," he says, "here that other will is designated, namely, that to which voluntary obedience corresponds."[88] To these and other passages Amyraut refers when setting forth his own doctrine of a twofold will in God.[89]

---

ipsius consilio non pugnat, quo nonnisi suos electos convertere decrevit" (*CO*, 8:301).

87. "Mirus hic erga humanum genus amor, quod omnes vult esse salvos, et ultro pereuntes in salutem colligere paratus est. Notandus autem hic ordo, quod paratus est Deus omnes ad poenitentiam recipere, ne quis pereat. His enim verbis obtinendae salutis modus indicatur: proinde quisquis nostrum ad salutem adspirat, discat hac via ingredi. Sed hic quaeri potest, si neminem Deus perire velit, cur tam multi pereunt? Respondeo, non de arcano Dei consilio hic fieri mentionem quo destinati sunt reprobi in suum exitium: sed tantum de voluntate quae nobis in evangelio patefit" (*CO*, 55:475-76).

88. "Porro non agitur hic de arcana eius voluntate qua omnia moderatur et in suum finem destinat. . . . Sed his notatur alia Dei voluntas, nempe cui respondet voluntarium obsequim" (*OS*, IV.354.7-8, 12-13).

89. E.g., Calvin's comments on Romans 11:33-34 which he concludes with the following remarks: "*Tenenda vero est quam nuper attuli distinctio inter arcanum Dei consilium et voluntatem in scriptura patefactam. Quamvis enim tota scripturae doctrina hominis ingenium altitudine sua superet, non tamen ad eam praecluditur accessus fidelibus, qui reverenter et sobrie spiritum sequuntur ducem, Sed alia est arcani consilii ratio, cuius profunditas et altitudo percontando attingi nequit*"

It would be difficult to overemphasize the importance of this distinction between the revealed and hidden (or secret) will of God. While the division in itself fits perfectly with his Ramism, it should not be regarded as simply a mechanical observance of the bifurcation scheme of the Ramists. It is in fact the very heart of his attempt to reformulate Reformed theology. As an apprehension of the distinction of law and gospel is the key to understanding the theology of Luther, so an apprehension of this bifurcation of the will of God is the key to understanding the doctrine of predestination in Amyraut. In this bifurcation lies not only his attempt to restore a proper balance to theology, but also his criticism of, and answer to, the overemphasis of Reformed orthodoxy on the doctrine of predestination.

This distinction took various forms in his writings through the years. In the 1634 edition of the *Brief Traitté* he had spoken of two counsels of God as well as two types of predestination. At the beginning of chapter 13, for example, he had emphasized that "we must carefully distinguish between predestination to salvation and predestination to faith . . ."[90] Here predestination to salvation relates to the revealed will of God and predestination to faith relates to his secret will. Because of the great uproar caused by this terminology in later writings he generally dropped it, or severely qualified it when he did use it. Nevertheless the concept remained even though clothed in a different garb. For instance, the passage just quoted reads in the 1658 edition: ". . . we must carefully distinguish between the will of saving men (which some call, contrary to Scriptural usage, predestination to salvation) and election or predestination to faith . . ."[91]

This terminology of a two-fold predestination was so offensive to the orthodox that, according to du Moulin, "being reproved by his friends," he abstained from using those particular forms of expression in his *Six Sermons* of 1636.[92] In these sermons he spoke instead, following the precedent of Calvin in the *Institutio*

(*CO*, 49:231). Amyraut also believed he could find this distinction in *Institutio*, III.xxi.1, *ad fin*. See also I.xvii.2.

90. P. 163.

91. P. 138.

92. *Esclaircissement*, p. 102.

III.xxi.6–7, in his commentary on Romans 9–11, etc., of general and special election.[93] But even this terminology is rare in Amyraut's writings. What was his most common—in fact, almost his exclusive—terminology from 1636 on was that of a two-fold mercy in God[94] upon which was based a two-fold will of God.[95] Apparently these "two degrees of mercy in God" are the direct correlate of Cameron's distinction of antecedent and consequent love.[96] In any case, the use of the idea that one must recognize two parts in the will of God becomes standard in Amyraut. Du Moulin accuses him of using the term "will" for the very reason that it is ambiguous—"In this ambiguity these men hide themselves."[97] More than likely du Moulin is correct in this particular judgment for as he noted, the term "will" was used by Amyraut as a substitute for *décret*, *propos*, or *arrest* of the counsel of God.[98] He might also have added that in fact Amyraut sometimes substituted *volonté* for the term *conseil* itself.[99]

93. Sermon 5 of his *Six Sermons* of 1636, on Rom. 11:33; pp. 212–48 of *Sermons sur divers textes*. It should be noted, however, that Calvin generally used this terminology with reference to the election of Israel, whereas Amyraut applied it to the time of the gospel.

94. "La parole de Dieu, mes Freres, nous presente sa misericorde à considerer en deux manieres" (*Sermons sur divers textes*, p. 55). See also p. 57 where he speaks of "ces deux degrés ou especes de misericorde . . ."

95. See *ibid.*, p. 61.

96. In the *Brief Traitté* Amyraut used the terminology of antecedent and consequent grace (see 1634 ed., pp. 102–19).

97. *Esclaircissement*, p. 53. Du Moulin was no doubt especially distressed by Amyraut's use of "will" to express his ideas, for he himself, and the orthodox, also held that the will of God was two-fold: "Duplex est Dei voluntas; altera est Decretum, altera est Mandatum." "Duplicem diximus esse Dei voluntatem, quarum altera est decretum divinae providentiae, altera vero est Dei mandatum & lex. Per priorem voluntatem Deus constituit quid velit agere. Per alteram pronuntiat quid velit a nobis agi & quae obsequia a nobis exigat" (from "Thesium theologicarum de Dei, Pars prima" and "Pars altera," *Thesaurus theologiae Sedanensis*, (pp. 103, 108). He of course would therefore charge Amyraut with confusing God's commandment for his will: *Esclaircissement*, pp. 20, 36, 59–61, 97, 113, 153, 165. For the same charge see Turrettini, *Institutio theologiae elencticae*, IV.xvii.41–48, pp. 367–71.

98. *Esclaircissement*, p. 52.

99. E.g., in chapter 11 of the *Brief Traitté* of 1634 he spoke of "Les conseils de Dieu qu'on nomme conditionels" (p. 131), which was changed in the 1658 edition to "Les dispositions ou volontés" (p. 111). Two other times in the same chapter *conseils* was changed to *volontés* or *dispositions de la volonté de Dieu*. Compare pages 132 of the 1634 edition and 112 of the 1658 edition.

Although Amyraut places great stress upon the bifurcation of the will of God into revealed and hidden, nevertheless he agrees with the orthodox that "Certainly the will of God is only one and of a supremely simple nature."[100] But he repeatedly emphasizes that we cannot even begin to think in these modes which are God's, and so must have recourse to the order of things as He has revealed them to us. Therefore, Amyraut contends in language which probably comes straight from Calvin, this one, simple will "ought to be considered in two ways—according to our weak manner of conceiving."[101] He describes these two ways of considering God's will in human terms. For, he says, there are two ways of willing something, one which simply makes the desire known, another which determines that the particular desire will be effected and therefore provides the necessary means for the implementation of that desire.[102] According to this description he presents the will of God as having two parts:

100. *Defense,* p. 115.

101. *Ibid.* Calvin sets forth this same teaching in *Institutio,* I.xviii.3. Speaking of God's will he says: "sed quum una et simplex in ipso sit, nobis multiplex apparet: quia pro mentis nostrae imbecillitate, quomodo idem diverso modo nolit fieri et velit non capimus. . . . ubi non capimus quomodo fieri velit Deus quod facere vetat, veniat nobis in memoriam nostra imbecillitas, et simul reputemus, lucem quam inhabitat, non frustra vocari inaccessam, quia caligine obducta est" (*OS,* III.224.26–29, 35–39). See also I.xviii.4. *ad fin.* (*OS,* III.227.22–31). This strong emphasis upon the incapacity of man's mind to comprehend the divine will is a most striking example of Amyraut's affinity with Calvin and of his removal from the orthodox, whose writings one searches almost in vain for this concept. See, for example, du Moulin's two disputations "De voluntate Dei" in *Thesaurus theologiae Sedanensis,* pp. 102–16. He makes no mention of man's weakness to comprehend this subject; on the contrary, one notes an air of real confidence throughout the theses.

102. "Or y a-t'il ou deux degrez ou deux façons de vouloir les choses. Car il y en a une, comme nous avons desja dit, selon laquelle on se content entre ces bornes, que non seulement on n'a point d'aversion contre son objet, mais on y a certaine inclination & certaine pente, tellement que si par quelque moyen que ce soit ce que l'on desire advient, non seulement on ne le trouve pas mauvais & n'en est-on pas marry, mais on l'aggrée & en a-t'on du contentement & de la satisfaction & de la joye. Mais c'est en telle façon pourtant que, quoy qu'il en soit, ce desir ou cette inclination ne porte pas la volonté jusques a ce point, que celuy qui en est touché prenne une ferme resolution en soy mesme d'employer tous ses moyens & toutes ses forces, pour faire reüssir a quelque prix que ce soit, cela a quoy cette siêne inclinatiô & ce mouvement de sa volonté le porte. Quant a l'autre, ce mouvement de la volonté va si avant qu'il porte celuy qui veut agir, &

For either it consists in the description and declaration of the obligation of the creature—which was done as much through the establishment of the law (whether the law as given by nature or as revealed in the Word of God) as through the manifestation of mercy and the call to repentance; for this reason some call it the *will which commands.* Or else it consists in the determination of the occurrences which must come to pass: For this reason some call it the *will which discerns.*[103]

Upon the distinction of these two parts, which previously he had called "the will of agreement" and "the will of good pleasure,"[104] Amyraut builds his theology, placing the emphasis upon the former.

In the preceding chapter we observed that Amyraut indicated two types of covenant mentioned in Scripture, one which required the fulfillment of a certain condition on man's part and one which did not. It can be seen now that this covenant structure is simply the logical correlate of the bifurcation of the will of God. The conditional covenant relates to the revealed will of God, the absolute to his secret will. And early in his *"de tribus foederibus divinis"* Amyraut indicates that he will discuss the type of covenant which is frankly and overtly conditional. "Here

---

a s'efforcer, & a travailler, a ce qu'en quelque maniere que ce puisse estre il execute, & parface, & obtienne ce qu'il veut, & ce qu'il s'est proposé. Ce qui ne consiste plus desormais en un certain agreément & inclination d'esprit seulement, mais en un propos deliberé & en une resolution determinée. Certainement celuy qui veut en cette dernier maniere, veut les moyens comme il veut la fin, & ne laisse en arriere chose quelconque de celles qui semblent absolument necessaires pour y parvenir. Et le charactere de cette sorte de volonté est l'effort, & la contention d'esprit, & l'ardeur, & la mouvement, & l'employ de toutes les choses qui peuvent en quelque sorte contribuer a la perfection ou a l'acquisition de ce que le desir & la volonté se proposent" (*Defense,* pp. 268–69).

103. "Car ou bien elle consiste en la description & declaration du devoir de la creature. Ce qui se fait tant par l'establissement de la Loy, soit que ce soit la nature qui la donne, ou la parole de Dieu qui la revele; que par la manifestation de la misericorde & l'invitation a la repentance; a raison dequoy quelques uns l'appellent la volonté *qui commande.* Ou bien elle consiste en la determination des evenemens qui en doivent arriver; a cause dequoy elle est appellée par quelques uns *decernante*" (*ibid.,* p. 115). Amyraut takes this terminology from William Twisse.

104. *Ibid.,* p. 114. This terminology, incidentally, had been used by Lefaucheur in his letter to the Alençon synod of 1637 (see *Lettres de Messieurs Lefaucheur et Mestrezat,* pp. 25–26).

we discuss that type of covenant which is made up of reciprocal clauses and which for this reason is more properly called covenant."[105] With our understanding of his equation of the *foedus absolutum* with the secret will of God the reason for this almost exclusive interest in the conditional type of covenant is not difficult to divine. For, if the *foedus absolutum* is rooted in the incomprehensible counsel of God, it follows that there is no point of contact upon which a rational analysis may be made concerning it.

As he develops the argument concerning the covenant of grace in his theses on the covenant, Amyraut discloses the maneuver he hoped would correct the excessive interest in predestination which Reformed Protestantism displayed. Because, as he says, predestination, and even election, is a part of God's secret will, it follows that election falls "outside the compass of the evangelical covenant."[106] It is, then, not a proper topic for extended theological discourse. The inclusion of this doctrine within theology is justifiable with the understanding that it is simply an affirmation of faith that what has happened in grace has been according to the will of God, but a rational discussion of the reason for the doctrine itself, of the ordering of the decrees of God, is nothing but fruitless speculation.

This removal of election from the confines of the covenant of grace proper has been noticed by Moltmann, who sees the far-reaching implications of the move.[107] But Moltmann has missed the intricacy of Amyraut's argument at this juncture. If Amyraut had completely removed election from the covenant of grace

---

105. "Nos hîc id genus foederum consideramus *quae reciprocis conventionibus constant,* atque ideò magis propriè foedera vocantur" (thesis 2, "De tribus foederibus Divinis," *Theses Salmurienses,* 1:212).

106. Thesis 46, *ibid.,* p. 223. See also his sermon on Ezekiel 18:23 in *Sermons sur divers textes,* p. 60: "& estoit impossible que l'alliance de la grace eust son rapport à cette misericorde de Dieu, qui ne presuppose point la condition de la foy en l'homme, mais l'y crée"; also *Defense,* p. 562, where he speaks of ". . . le mystere de l'election & de la reprobation, qui n'a du tout rien de commun avec la doctrine des alliances."

107. "Prädestination und Heilsgeschichte," pp. 296, 302. He speaks forcefully of the "Eliminierung der Prädestinationslehre aus der Lehre vom Gnadenbund . . ." The very title of his dissertation is based on this maneuver—"Gnadenbund und Gnadenwahl"—for he develops these two themes as in dialectic.

there would be good basis upon which to found the thesis that he is a thoroughgoing rationalist, for this would mean that he had removed a large part of the mysterious element of the Christian faith from consideration as a theological topic. But this he has not done—at least not in theory. It is true that he comes dangerously close to such a position, but he is unwilling to take such a radical step. He has made an attempt to have it both ways, recognizing that predestination is an integral part of the covenant of grace, yet emphasizing that one ought not to build a theological system around this doctrine. He had pointed out two theses earlier, and this Moltmann apparently missed, that he was about to discuss "two things which are not included within the compass of the evangelical covenant *when it is considered strictly in itself.*"[108] In a later work Amyraut remarks concerning this: "You see that I distinguish between the evangelical covenant strictly considered and this covenant considered generally. And I say that it is in this first regard that election and the grace of the Spirit which depend on it are outside of its compass."[109]

From the above we may conclude, then, that both types of covenant, the *foedus absolutum* as well as the *foedus hypotheticum*, are included within the *foedus gratiae*—when it is considered in a general way. Once again we have an example of the ever-present Ramean bifurcation which allows Amyraut to speak of the covenant of grace *"en deux manieres."*[110] So the comparison between the covenant and God's will is complete. For as "the will of God is only one . . . yet, which, according to our weak manner of apprehending, ought to be considered in two ways"[111] so likewise the one covenant of grace is to be considered in two parts.

108. "At duo sunt quae tametsi *foederis Evangelici strictè in se considerati* complexu non contineantur . . ." (thesis 44, *Theses Salmurienses*, 2:223. Emphasis added).

109. *Replique a M. de la Milletiere*, 1658 ed., p. 343.

110. "Je considere la dispensation de l'alliance Evangelique en deux manieres; ou plus estroittement, ou plus largement" (*ibid.*, p. 346). See also "de gratia universali" in *Dissertationes theologicae sex*, pp. 151–52: "Fedus Evangelicum considerari debet, vel ut absolutum est, hoc est praestita conditione: vel ut conditionatum, hoc est, ut spectat ad eos à quibus conditio exigitur nondum praestita."

111. *Defense*, p. 115.

The justification for considering the one covenant of grace as made up of these two types of covenant is once again found in Calvin.

> Calvin in his book on predestination gives, as it were, two heads to the evangelical covenant. To the one relate those promises by which salvation is promised to all who believe and repent, and which for this reason he called conditional. To the second head apply those promises which are absolute and by which God promised that He himself would give the faith which is required of men . . .[112]

Amyraut then quotes at length a remarkably apropos passage from Calvin which, because it is generally overlooked by Calvin scholars and so constantly resorted to by Amyraut, we shall give here. Calvin has just explained that though Christ's sacrifice was for all, the gift of faith was not:

> All this Pighius contradicts, adducing the opinion of Paul (I Tim 2.4): God wills all to be saved. That He does not will the death of a sinner is to be believed on His own oath where He says by the prophet: As I live, I do not will the death of a sinner, but rather that he may be converted and live (Ezek 18.23, 33.11). But I contend that, as the prophet is exhorting to penitence, it is no wonder that he pronounces God willing that all be saved. But the mutual relation between threats and promises shows such forms of speech to be conditional. To the Ninevites, as also to the kings of Gerar and Egypt, God declared that He would do what He was not going to do. Since by repentance they averted the punishment promised to them, it is evident that it was not firmly decreed unless they remained obstinate. Yet the denunciation had been precise, as if it were an irrevocable decree. But after terrifying and humbling them with the sense of His wrath, though not to the point of despair, He cheers them with the hope of pardon, that they might feel there was room for remedy. So again with the promises which invite all men to salvation. They do not simply and positively declare what God has decreed in His secret counsel but what

---

112. "Calvinus in libro de Praedestinatione, duo facit veluti capita foederis Evangelici. Ad unum refert eas promissiones quibus salus promittitur omnibus credentibus atque resipiscentibus, & quas ideo conditionales appellat. Ad alterum revocat eas promissiones quae sunt absolutae, & quibus spondet Deus se se daturum fidem quibusdam ex hominibus . . ." ("De gratia speciali," *Specimen animadversionum,* p. 273). Amyraut had used this passage from Calvin as early as 1636 in his *Eschantillon,* 1658 ed., pp. 209–10.

He is prepared to do for all who are brought to faith and re-pentance. But, it is alleged, we thereby ascribe a double will to God, whereas He is not variable and not the least shadow of turning falls upon Him. What is this, says Pighius, but to mock men, if God professes to will what He does not will? But if in fairness the two are read together: I will that the sinner turn and live, the calumny is dissolved without bother. God requires conversion from us; wherever He finds it, a man is not disap-pointed of the promised reward of life. Hence God is said to will life, as also repentance. But the latter He wills, because He invites all to it by His word. Now this is not contradictory of His secret counsel, by which He determined to convert none but His elect. He cannot rightly on this account be thought vari-able, because as lawgiver He illuminates all with the external doctrine of life, in this first sense calling all men to life. But in the other sense, He brings to life whom He will, as Father regenerating by the Spirit only His sons.

It is indeed certain that men are not converted to the Lord of their own accord; nor is the gift of conversion common to all. For this is one of the two heads of the covenant, which God promises to make with none but with His children and His elect people: He will write His laws on their hearts. For it is madness for anyone to say that this is promised to all in general: I will make a covenant with them, not like that I made with their fathers; but I will write my laws on their hearts (Jer 31. 33).[113]

This passage from Calvin contains another element which is important in Amyraut's thought, the distinction between the two roles of God—between God acting as lawgiver and God acting as father. God's role as father relates to the absolute covenant. His role as lawgiver relates to the conditional covenant. And throughout Amyraut's discussions of the conditional covenant one encounters both the terminology and the concepts which suggest that this covenant is understood in jurisprudential terms. The whole concept of covenant as a mutual pact or contract

113. "De aeterna dei praedestinatione," CO, 8:300–301. The translation, with slight emendation, is that of J. K. S. Reid, Concerning the Eternal Predestination of God (London, 1961), pp. 105–6. Beza's edition of this work, as well as the Amsterdam edition, inserted an if clause in the sentence which speaks of the conditional promises and threats. In this way the conditional meaning of Calvin's original work was rendered ambiguous. The reason for this is not hard to deter-mine, for the tension of a conditional will within the structure of Reformed theology was not acceptable to Beza and the orthodox.

suggests jurisprudential influence. In fact, Amyraut, when explaining that a covenant (one that is properly speaking a covenant) must contain reciprocal clauses (*conventions reciproques*), practically makes such explicit by adding, "For such is the nature of the agreements (*alliances*) which men make with one another whence this name has been borrowed."[114] Secondly, he consistently defines the meaning of the word "condition" in lawyers' terminology.[115] And thirdly, he draws frequent analogy between laws which "are promulgated not in secret, but publicly so that no one can be ignorant of them" and the gospel message which is to be universally proclaimed.[116]

But although Amyraut has resort to Calvin as the source of his parcelling the *foedus gratiae* into two heads, the use that he makes of this bifurcation is quite peculiar to Amyraldian theology. For while using it to emphasize the hidden and revealed nature of God's will, the absolute, incomprehensible and the conditional, accommodated work of God in grace, he shifts his emphasis decidedly to the latter as the proper object of religious contemplation. That is, while there can be but little doubt that Amyraut regarded this bifurcation as native to early Reformed theology—to Calvin in particular—his own use of it tends to sound a great deal like Luther.[117] Indeed, Luther had propounded the same bifurcation of God's will in his *de servo arbitrio*[118] in a passage in which he forcefully urges that one restrict

114. *Replique a M. de la Milletiere,* 1658 ed., p. 346.

115. "Conditio enim, aiunt Jurisconsulti, est lex addita negotio, quae eius eventum suspendit, ut si lex illa praestetur, succedat, si minus, pro planè nullo existimetur" ("De gratia universali," *Dissertationes theologicae sex,* p. 166. Cf. the preface to *Du merite des oeuvres* [pp. vii–viii], and *Defense,* pp. 251–54, where he quotes Cuias, Paulus, and Grotius in this connection.

116. *Defense,* pp. 234ff.

117. There is, however, no hint of Luther's idea that where God is most revealed there He is the most hidden. Although Amyraut employs concepts of hidden and revealed to express in a most explicit way the limitation of reason vis-à-vis God, reason is not disparaged but rather the opposite, when matters in the category of what has been revealed are under consideration. Amyraut's position reminds one more of Calvin's dictum that both excessive curiosity concerning God's hidden counsel and excessive neglect of what He has revealed are improper (*Institutio,* III.xxi.4. *OS,* IV.373. 18–21).

118. *W.A.,* XVIII.68off., but esp. XVIII.685.1–686.3. Luther here is also considering Ezekiel 18:23, so it appears that Calvin may have taken the interpretation

himself to a contemplation of the word of God where His mercy is portrayed, while eschewing any rumination about His inscrutable will.[119] This is the basic import of Amyraut's use of this distinction. He taught that both God's absolute will and his conditional will are operative in the evangelical covenant, but since the absolute will relates to his incomprehensible counsel it cannot be the object of investigation, nor is it possible to build a rational discussion which takes this absolute will as the starting point.

This does not mean, of course, that Amyraut does not affirm absolute predestination. Like Luther, he does this in the most unequivocal language. In exercising his absolute mercy God is "purely, and simply, and absolutely free."[120] By this arbitrary operation of his will God takes no account of man's condition or response but creates faith in him and imputes to him Christ's righteousness. But while only through this will of God is one able to fulfill the condition of the evangelical covenant, one cannot construct a theological system on it, due to the great gulf between the infinite God and finite man.

It is, then, the conditional will, and therefore the conditional covenant, which is the primary object of consideration in Amyraut's theology. Though he firmly believes, and presents evidence, that Calvin sometimes taught that grace is conditional,[121]

---

from Luther. But though the idea has its likely source in Luther, there are at least two concepts common to the Calvin-Amyraut exposition which are not present in Luther: the covenant terminology and the express mention that the first part of God's will is conditional. This tends to indicate that Amyraut did in fact learn the distinction from Calvin and not from Luther.

119. See esp. *W.A.*, XVIII.685.13–17; 25–686.3.

120. Sermon on Ezekiel 18:23 in *Sermons sur divers textes*, p. 57.

121. Beyond the overt conditional teaching of the passage in Calvin's *Commentary on Ezekiel* 18:23—that "God wills all men to be saved *when they shall be converted from their ways*," that God promises salvation to all "modo serio resipiscant"—there are several other passages in Calvin to which he refers: frequently to the closing sentence of Calvin's comments upon Romans 11:32, "Certam quidem est, omnibus indifferenter expositam esse hanc misericordiam, sed qui eam fide quaesierint" (*CO*, 49:229–30); or to the passage in *Institutio*, III.ii.1, where Calvin affirms that God willed to be merciful to us *if* we embrace that mercy through faith: "Hoc tertio explicatum fuit unam esse liberationis rationem quae nos a tam misera calamitate eruat: ubi apparet Christus redemptor, per cuius manum caelestis Pater, pro sua immensa bonitate et clementia nostri misertus,

he frankly acknowledges that his own emphasis at this point is different from Calvin's, that "Calvin has respect to that second way of considering God's mercy according to which it does not require any condition of man but rather creates it [i.e., faith] in man."[122] But Amyraut apparently believed that the predestination doctrine of the orthodox, which was concerned exclusively with the absolute decree of God and which categorically denied His conditional will, both destroyed the balanced presentation of Calvin and justified his own heavy emphasis on the conditional will.[123]

Therefore Amyraut determined that God's conditional will should be most in view. And, although he maintained that God is a simple essence, he declared that because of the limitations of man's mind in seeking to conceive of God and His will we must speak of it "according to our mode of understanding."[124] Our understanding must derive from an observation of the order

---

succurrere nobis voluit: siquidem et solida fide misericordiam hanc amplectimur, et in ipsa constanti spe acquiescimus" (OS, IV.7.4–9). Perhaps his favorite passage and the one he most frequently quotes is Calvin's Commentary on John 3:14–17, used seven times in the Defense alone. He understands Calvin to be teaching conditional salvation throughout this section, but especially presses the comment of Calvin on 3:17 that no one is excluded from salvation provided that he holds to the way of salvation: "Repetitur iterum mundi nomen, ne quis omnio arceri se putet, si modo fidei viam tenet" (CO, 47:66).

122. Eschantillon, 1658 ed., pp. 216–17. At this point Laplanche is surely correct when he judges that Amyraut's predestination teaching is a "présentation 'orientée'" of Calvin's doctrine (L'Oeuvre d'Amyraut, p. 288).

123. It is difficult to definitively answer why Amyraut laid so much stress on the conditional will in his doctrine of predestination. We know he felt it corrected the emphasis of the orthodox, but it may also be true that his humanistic spirit, which inclined toward a moralistic explanation of the doctrine, goes far to explain his emphasis. It is certain that he was very much interested in presenting God as souverainement misericordieux and free from all responsibility in the matter of man's sin. He apparently thought these interests were best served by accentuating God's conditional will.

124. See "De gratia specialis," Specimen animadversionum, pp. 463–64: "Deinde si voluntatem divinam in se spectemus, quia est ipsissima Dei essentia, essentia autem Dei prorsus immutabilis est, utique ejus voluntatem pariter immutabilem esse oportet. At si voluntatem Dei spectemus quatenus à nobis consideratur, secundum modum concipiendi nostrum, tanquam facultas aliqua, non modò varios producit actus, secundum varietatem objectorum, sed etiam negari non potest quin circa idem objectum à non volendo ad volendum, à volendo ad non volendum aliquo pacto transeat."

of God's economy in redemption. From Scripture and "the nature of things" we understand that this conditional will, which relates to the work of Christ, is first; and that the absolute will, which relates to the work of the Spirit, is second. And, Amyraut adds, there is no reason to think that it is impossible that the conditional will and the absolute will are mutually exclusive.[125] Here he introduces two further important elements of his doctrine of predestination: (1) That the conditional will and covenant reveals God as drastically accommodated to man's capacity, and (2) that the economic understanding of the work of the Trinity is closely tied up with the sequential presentation of the two parts of God's will. We shall briefly discuss both, in the order mentioned.

In the revelation of His conditional will, which is the basis of the conditional covenant, "God has especially accommodated himself to the capacity of our spirits, and has voluntarily borrowed the manner of speaking which is used among men."[126]

---

125. "Esto igitur priore loco actus ille divinae voluntatis, quo misereri voluit omnium hominum modo credant; juxta illud, *Sic Deus dilexit mundum, ut Filium suum dederit* . . . Esto posteriore actus ille, quo decrevit quibusdam ex aliorum numero selectis indulgere fidem ut credant, & sic ad salutem perducantur; juxta illud. *Miserebor cujus miserebor* &c. Sic Scripturam sequemur, & rei naturam. Et rei naturam primùm. Nam in iis quae conditionata sunt, cogitatur primùm de re constituenda, quae sub conditione offertur: deinde, si id ita necesse est, proceditur ad conditionis executionem. Scripturam etiam. Nam cùm sic loquitur, *Dedit Filium, ut quicunque credet;* Filii donationem tanquam ratam & jam executioni mandatam proponit, conditionem hactenus reliquit in suspenso, quasi nihil esset de eâ determinatum. Determinatio illa scilicet, ad alterum quoddam decretum spectat, quod non est ista Dei voluntate atque φιλανθρωπια quae filium dedit, inclusum. Sic etiam corruet tota vis illius argumenti. Non enim sequitur posito illo priore actu universali voluntatis divinae, posteriorem particularem poni non posse. Quid prohibet quominus Deus omnium misereri velit, modò credant, deinde nonnullorum ita absolutè velit misereri, ut illis statuat vim eam indulgere, per quam credant? Non etiam praevisio eventus cujusquam decretum ex quo dependet, antecedet. Neque enim sic Deus praeviderit, Christum in mundum venturum ut salutem omnibus offerret, modò crederent, nisi quia eum mittere decreverat: neque praeviderit fore ut Petrus potius quàm Judas credat, nisi quia statuit Petro dare fidem, Judae minimè. Non denique Petri salus suspensa erit ex incerta conditione, quandoquidem id quod Deus sese effecturum esse constituit, certissimè & infallibiliter futurum est" ("De gratia universali," *Dissertationes theologicae sex,* pp. 155–57).

126. ". . . Dieu s'est encore accommodé a la capacité de nos esprits, & a volontiers emprunté la façon de parler laquelle est en usage entre les hômes" (*Defense,*

In this sense one must think of all knowledge of God which is rationally appropriable as having a radically accommodated character. As we have seen, Amyraut is very much aware of the inaccessibility of God by way of reason, that God as an object of cognition does not fall within the range of human understanding. In order to bridge this gulf it was necessary for God, as it were, to descend to man's level and to reveal himself as acting, feeling, and thinking in ways which are analogous to man's experience. To portray this condescendence of God Scripture uses anthropomorphic language.

As an example of this use of anthropomorphic concepts we turn to his description of the revelation God gives of himself in the conditional covenant. Discussing Calvin's teaching in a passage in which he obviously identifies himself with Calvin, Amyraut maintains that God "with a most eminent affection has willed the salvation of all men . . . "[127] We must understand, Amyraut tells us, that "these vehement compassions, desires, commiserations, and other similar things which witness an affection joined with some grief, are anthropopathies used in Scripture . . ." And the important thing is that these anthropopathies are means "by which God accommodates himself to our capacity and, in a manner of speaking, descends to us by an admirable

---

p. 606). See also *Le Ravissement de s. Paul*, p. 42: ". . . quant à ce que nostre Seigneur dit qu'au royaume des Cieux nous *serons assis à table avec Abraham, Isaac, & Jacob*, & qu'à celuy qui *vaincra, il donnera à manger de la manne cachée*, & du fruit *de l'arbre de vie qui est au milieu de Paradis de son Dieu*, ce sont des façons de parler symboliques, qu'il emprunte des choses qui se font en la terre, pour nous representer celles du ciel, qui sont d'une nature toute differente, & qu'à cause de nostre foiblesse, il seroit absolument impossible que nous peussions comprendre entierement." Here again Amyraut claims to be following Calvin. There is good basis for this claim, for Calvin uses the same concept in much the same language, e.g., his twelfth sermon on Deuteronomy 5: "Retenons donc que nostre Seigneur n'a point parlé selon sa nature. Car s'il vouloit parler son langage, seroit-il entendu des creatures mortelles? Helas non. Mais comment est-ce qu'il a parlé à nous en l'Escriture saincte? Il a begayé. . . . Notons bien donc que Dieu s'est fait quasi semblable à une nourrice, qui ne parlera point à un petit enfant selon qu'elle feroit à un homme: mais qu'elle regarde à sa partée. Ainsi donc Dieu s'est comme demis: d'autant que nous ne comprendrions pas ce qu'il diroit, sinon qu'il condescendist à nous" (*CO*, 26:387). See also *CO*, 29:168, 356; 43:161, 176.

127. *Defense*, p. 262.

condescendence."[128] Amyraut then goes on to indicate that each anthropopathy "represents something in God which has some analogy and some correspondence with the faculties and emotions of our spirits—nevertheless without affecting in any way the disposition of the infinite excellence of his nature."[129]

This accommodated character of all of our knowledge of God had been taught by Calvin,[130] but in Amyraut the use and content of this concept are much more far-reaching.[131] In fact, Amyraut's primary emphasis relating to the doctrine of God within the conditional covenant is that God has so accommodated himself that he acts according to the qualities of his nature. He argues that every sovereign has a two-fold right—to act freely, not being answerable to or governed by any law, or, if he chooses, to act in a way determined by the laws of his nature.[132] And,

128. ". . . ces vehementes plaintes, souhaits, commiseratiôs & autres choses semblables, qui témoignent une affection conjointe avec quelque douleur, sont des anthropopathies usitées en l'Ecriture, par lesquelles Dieu s'accommode a nostre capacité, & par manier de dire descend a nous par une admirable condescendance" (*ibid.*).

129. *Ibid.*

130. See E. A. Dowey, Jr., *The Knowledge of God in Calvin's Theology*, pp. 3–17.

131. For instance, Amyraut repeatedly refers to accommodation as used by Jesus in teaching his disciples, an idea not frequently employed by Calvin (see *Paraphrase de s. Jean* 3.12, pp. 103–4, where Amyraut explains Jesus' use of "earthly things" to mean things accommodated to the capacity of His hearers; *ibid.*, on 5.33–34, pp. 198–99; and the paraphrase on Acts 1:7 in *Paraphrases sur les actes des saintes apostres* [Saumur, 1653], pp. 10–12).

132. See, for example, *Defense*, pp. 210–11. He has just mentioned that God *could* condemn an innocent creature: "Mais encore que Calvin eust enseigné que Dieu le peut faire selon son droit absolu & indefini, il ne s'ensuivroit pas pourtant qu'il eust enseigné que Dieu l'ait jamais fait effectivement. L'infinie Majesté de Dieu nous oblige a reconnoistre & a dire que quand il le feroit, il ne seroit pas tenu d'en rendre conte: mais sa justice & son equité incomparable nous oblige encore davantage croire fermement, que ce que son souverain droit luy permet de faire, il ne le fait jamais pourtant. Car comme parle Calvin, il ne se peut renier soy mesme. Et ce que ne se fait jamais a sans doute quelque cause certaine & definie pourquoy jamais il ne se fait. Or n'y peut-il avoir aucune autre cause qui empesche que Dieu n'use jamais de ce sien droit absolu, sinon sa justice & ses autres proprietez, lesquelles selon nostre maniere de concevoir, tiennêt lieu comme de vertus morales en sa nature." Here again Amyraut draws an argument from the realm of jurisprudence, building his latter argument upon the authority of Grotius. For the same type of reference to law when discussing God's absolute power see Calvin's *Institutio,* I.xvii.2.

while Amyraut maintains that God could, if he so desired, act according to his absolute, indefinite right, his purpose is to emphasize the idea that God has willingly accommodated himself so that his actions are determined by the moral qualities of his nature, a feature which makes his mercy even more commendable.[133]

He does not mean by this that God is determined by some law which transcends him. Rather He is his own law.[134] In language which has a strong Thomistic tinge Amyraut maintains that God is limited by the moral qualities or virtues of his nature and that "the more powerful these virtues are in Him, the less able he would be to do things which are contrary to them."[135] And he illustrates this concept in the following manner:

> For example, then, if the creature is good and holy, God cannot help but love him—not because He owes anything to his creature, but because He is infinitely good. Similarly, if the creature is corrupt, He cannot help but hate him because of his sin— not because He has to give an account of His actions to anyone other than himself, but because He is infinitely just. And similarly also, if the sinful creature has recourse to His mercy, He cannot help but have compassion on him—not because He is obliged to do it, but because He is infinitely merciful.[136]

133. ". . . actus ille conditionalis & universalis est actus virtutis cujus exercitium Deo non est absolutè liberum, sed necessariò determinatum ad certam qualitatem, quae vel est vel esse debet in creatura. . . . Actus verò misercordiae absolutus atque particularis, est natura sua longè liberrimus, ut qui non est ad ullam certam qualitatem determinatus. Quapropter actus universalis magis, ut ita dicam, cum natura Dei convenit, quàm particularis. Magis enim cum natura Dei conveniunt ea a quibus ipsi non est liberum abstinere citra labem aliquam perfectionis naturae suae, quàm ea quae talia sunt ut ab eo usurpari vel omitti queunt pro liberrimo arbitrio" ("De gratia speciali," *Specimen animadversionum,* p. 417). Cf. *Sermons sur divers textes,* pp. 59ff.

134. ". . . n'est pas que Dieu ait quelque loy au dessus de luy qui l'oblige à rien faire: mais c'est qu'il est sa propre loy à soy-mesme" *Sermons sur divers textes,* pp. 58–59.

135. ". . . plus grandes sont ses vertus en luy, moins sçauroit-il faire les choses qui leur sont contraires" *(ibid.,* p. 59).

136. "Comme donc si la creature est bonne & sainte, Dieu ne peut qu'il ne l'aime; non pource qu'il doive rien à sa creature, mais pource qu'il est infiniment bon: ainsi si la creature est corrompuë, il ne peut qu'il ne le haïsse à cause de son peché: non pource qu'il ait à rendre raison de ses actions à autre qu'à soy; mais pource qu'il est infiniment juste. Et ainsi encore, si la creature pecheresse à

This quotation points up another peculiarity of Amyraut's doctrine of God. Like Calvin, he consistently speaks not of the attributes of God but rather of his virtues or qualities. And of these qualities or virtues the three here mentioned predominate in all of Amyraut's discussions—that is, goodness, mercy, and justice. What is more, Amyraut relates them quite strictly to the three covenants in a sort of historical sequence. Viz., under the covenant of nature the quality of God which for the most part governed his actions with man was his goodness. Likewise during the law covenant God dealt with man in justice. Now under the evangelical covenant he deals with man preeminently according to his mercy. Mercy is, in this program, understood as God's good favor in the light of sin. Goodness does not comprehend God's benevolence towards sinners. Therefore goodness and mercy are understood as two quite distinct and different concepts.

This differentiation between goodness and mercy may at first seem to be a mere scholastic distinction, but as formulated by Amyraut it attains great importance. First, as may be seen in the foregoing paragraph, it serves to underline the historically oriented character of his thought, since it implies a progression in the way God deals with man. Secondly, and perhaps more importantly, this distinction serves to provide an added reason for his rejection of the supralapsarian teaching of many of the orthodox Calvinists. For Amyraut thinks the idea of a merciful God without a sinner toward whom to exercise that mercy is utter nonsense. Mercy is neither necessary nor comprehensible except in the light of sin. Thus he suggests that God's relationship toward man assumes a new dimension after the Fall, changing from an expression of goodness to an expression of grace when sin comes into the picture.

Now, not only does Amyraut believe that God's actions are bound up by his nature in his covenantal accommodation, but he also says that God's purpose in creating the world must have something to do with the manifestations of his virtues. In chap-

---

recours à sa misericorde, il ne se peut qu'il n'en ait compassion: non pource qu'il y soit obligé, mais pource qu'il est infiniment misericordieux" (*ibid.*).

ter 2 of the *Brief Traitté* Amyraut discusses "Why God has created the world." There are, he believes, two answers to this proposition, depending on one's perspective. For, he says, we must distinguish between the purpose of the worker and the purpose of his product,[137] that is, between God and the world. He answers quickly to the purpose of the world in true Calvinist fashion: "To be sure, the natural end of the world can be nothing else but the glory of the One who has made it."[138] But he maintains that there is something unworthy in the idea that God created solely for his own glory. Thus he thinks a precise consideration of the matter reveals that God's purpose in creating the world is that He might have a place to exercise His virtues[139] (a concept that clearly points up the strong moralism of Amyraut's thought).

An understanding of Amyraut's teaching on the accommodation of God is crucial if one is to comprehend properly the implications of the role given the two wills of God and the two covenants in the totality of his doctrine of predestination. But even more important and enlightening is his teaching, included also under God's accommodation, that there is an admirable economy of the persons of the Trinity in the execution of the work of salvation.[140] Because of the close correlation of this teaching with his *heilsgeschichtlich* understanding of the covenants we shall call this, following Moltmann, a *heilsgeschichtlich* trinitarian teaching.

As he develops his *heilsgeschichtlich* theology it becomes clear that each member of the Trinity has his period or time of activity not only in relation to the three covenant periods, but also within the covenant of grace itself.[141] It is the latter which inter-

137. *Brief Traitté*, 1634 ed., p. 11; 1658 ed., p. 9.
138. *Ibid.*, 1634 ed., p. 11; 1658 ed., p. 10.
139. See *ibid.*, 1634 ed., pp. 18ff.; 1658 ed., pp. 16ff.
140. ". . . quemadmodum tres istae personae beatae Trinitatis, habent operationes distinctas secundum admirabilem illam oeconomiam, . . ." ("De oeconomia trium personarum," *Dissertationes theologicae sex*, p. 25).
141. "Posterius illud est, quòd tres istae personae, perinde ut respectu operationum inter se distinguuntur, habent quaeque suam σχέσιν ad tres varios status in quibus homo considerari potest. Etenim spectari homo potest ut creatura quaedam rationalis, legem divinarum & pietatis capax, at nondum peccato con-

ests us here and to which the earlier remarks in the chapter pertain, those which have shown that in the matter of redemption the Father conceived the plan of redemption, the Son executed the work of redemption, and the Spirit applies the benefits of this redemption. According to this argument, in the work of redemption the Father is not properly active—He simply drew up the plan. The Son and the Spirit, however, have each his proper period or time of activity. And what is most important, their periods of activity coincide with the two heads of the covenant of grace we have previously discussed. The work of the Son is the fulfillment of God's conditional will and the basis of the *foedus hypotheticum,* while the work of the Spirit is in response to God's absolute will and illustrates the *foedus absolutum.*

Christ was sent by the Father acting in the role of lawgiver. According to jurisprudential concepts Amyraut explains therefore that one ought not to think that the work accomplished by Christ carries with it the means by which it is appropriated. A lawgiver in his relationship to his people does not necessarily provide the ability to fulfill the law to which he commands obedience. So God in this role "remains within the terms of this relationship. For it is not the task of a lawgiver as such to furnish the means which are necessary for the execution and ac-

---

taminata. Deinde ut creatura rationalis quidem, & peccato contaminata, at in qua Deus nondum vim ullam sui spiritus exeruit, ut eam liberet à peccato. Ac denique ut est creatura non modo rationalis atque peccatrix, sed etiam cujus Deus virtute sui spiritus mentem illuminavit, ut rationem suae liberationis agnoscat & aliquatenus amplectatur. In primo illo statu, homo & persona Patris ad se se mutua σχέσει referuntur. Ita ut id peccatum quod homo tum admittit, praecipuè adversus Patrem admittere putetur, quia, ut jam diximus, Persona Patris se se tum ei praecipuâ quadam ratione cognoscendam atque venerandam obijcit. In secundo, homo & Persona Filij se se invicem pariter respiciunt, adeò ut peccatum quod homo perpetrat dum gratiam rejicit, praecipuè adversus Filium perpetratum esse existimetur, quia tum Filius se se homini singulariter offert, tâquam Redemptorem amplectendum. In tertio homo & Persona Spiritus mutuum respectum ad se habent invicem, adeò ut peccatum cujus homo se reum constituit, cùm gratiam illam respuit quam Spiritus offert efficaciter, aut cum eam jam istius efficaciae interventu aliquatenus admissam, abijcit atq; contemnit, censetur esse commissum adversus Spiritum sanctum, quia lucem ab eo indultam praefocat & exstinguit" (*ibid.,* pp. 27–28).

complishment of that which he ordains. In order to command a certain response sincerely and without fraud it suffices that one require those things which he has the right to require."[142]

So then the redemption accomplished by Christ must be viewed in this way. By Christ's satisfaction salvation has been obtained for us, but with this stipulation attached—provided that we believe.[143] That is, the work of Christ is explained in terms of God's conditional will and the conditional covenant in which man is required to fulfill his part of the contract before it will become effective. And, Amyraut claims, there is no necessary cause and effect relationship between salvation as procured by Christ and its application. In fact, salvation can be considered in one of two ways: either absolutely, including both its procuration and application, or conditionally, including solely its procuration by the work of Christ. Amyraut believes that the proper theological approach can only work with the second of these two ways.[144] Thus one of his favorite ways of explaining is by saying that Christ's acquisition of salvation remains *in suspenso* until the condition is fulfilled.[145] Strictly speaking, while he maintains repeatedly that no salvation would have been possible without Christ's death and resurrection,[146] in this economic understand-

142. *Defense,* p. 236.

143. "Satisfactio Christi salutem integram nobis impetravit, . . . sub eadem fidei conditione" (*Dissertationes theologicae sex,* p. 290).

144. "Redemptionem à Christo factam, duobus modis considerari debere: nimirum ut est absoluta, quatenus eam quidam revera amplectuntur. Deinde, ut est affecta conditione, quatenus offertur cum ea lege, ut siquis eam amplectatur, ejus compos fiat. Priore modo particularis est, posteriore universalis. . . . Ad priorem igitur modum pertinet locus ex Joan. 10.26.29. In altero miror praestantis Theologi securitatem. Gratiae universalis defensores doctrinae suae fundamentum in eo loco collocant, *Sic Deus dilexit mundum,* &c." (*ibid.,* pp. 157–58). "Il y a donc . . . en la Redemption que nous avons par nostre Seigneur, deux choses à considerer distinctement: la satisfaction mesme, & la connoissance qu'ô en a" (*Sermons sur divers textes,* p. 107). See also *Defense,* pp. 134–36.

145. ". . . Filii donationem tanquam ratam & jam executioni mandatum proponit, conditionem hactenus relinquit *in suspenso,* quasi nihil esset de eâ determinatum" (*Dissertationes theologicae sex,* p. 156. Emphasis added). Cf. *Eschantillon,* 1658 ed., p. 268. Here Amyraut is discussing God's conditional will and states that bringing it to fruition "depend d'une condition, & que par consequent l'evenement est en cet égard en suspens, . . ."

146. It is an interesting feature of Amyraut's theology that in the matter of salvation Christ's death cannot be spoken of without mentioning His resurrection:

ing of Christ's work of satisfaction no one can be saved simply through this work.

Of course the major emphasis of this economy in which Christ purchased redemption is upon the mercy of God, inasmuch as the work of Christ has been for all men.[147] He writes in the *Brief Traitté*:

> The sacrifice that He has offered for the propitiation of their offenses has been equally for all. And the salvation that He has received from His Father in order to communicate it to men in the sanctification of the spirit and the glorification of the body is destined equally to all, provided, I say, that the disposition necessary in order to receive it is also equally present.[148]

Here we see not only that the sacrifice of Christ is a sufficient price for the sins of the whole world, a statement which most of the orthodox would have endorsed, but also that He *intended* to die for all men, a position wholly untenable for the orthodox. But perhaps even more scandalous in the eyes of the orthodox was Amyraut's constant insistence that this universal offer in the atonement was in fact the expression of the eternal will of God, even for those to whom the gospel message never comes:

> And although there are many nations toward which perhaps the clear preaching of the Gospel has never yet come, neither by the Apostles nor by their successors, and which have no distinct knowledge of the Savior of the world, yet one need not think that there are any people, nor even any individual, excluded by the will of God from the salvation that He has acquired for mankind—provided that he profit from the testimonies of mercy that God gives him.[149]

"... la passion de la croix de Christ, & son glorieux retour de tombeau, sont absolument inseparables en la redemption des hommes" (Sermon on I Corinthians 11:24, *Sermon sur ces paroles* ... [Saumur, 1663], p. 2).

147. "Il a offert cette sienne misericorde pesle mesle & sans distinction a tous, pourveu qu'ils croyent. ... la misericorde qui exige la foy, ... est offerte indifferement a tous, soubs la condition de la foy" (*Defense*, p. 544). See also *ibid.*, p. 106: "Dieu donc a voulu faire misericorde a tous, pourveu que tous recherchassent par Foy cette misericorde."

148. 1634 ed., p. 78; 1658 ed., p. 66. In each case the word "equally" was dropped from the 1658 edition.

149. "Et bien qu'il y ait plusieurs nations vers lesquelles peut estre la claire predication de l'Evangile n'est point encore parvenuë par la bouche des Apostres,

It is to be noted, of course, that each mention of the universality of the design of Christ's atonement is qualified by a "provided that."[150] Amyraut is very much concerned that it be understood that the will of God which desires universal salvation is made on the condition that the stipulation be fulfilled, and that if that stipulation is not fulfilled He does not will it.[151] This is perhaps the most adequate definition of "hypothetical universalism" which can be given. Fulfilling God's will for universal salvation, Christ procured it for all. Here is Amyraut's universalism. It is hypothetical, for salvation is only effectual *when and if* such and such a condition is fulfilled. Amyraut may also explain this hypothetical universalism from a viewpoint closer to moral theology, for he often utilizes his idea that God acts within the confines of this conditional will according to the qualities or virtues of his nature, and if he does not find the corresponding quality in man this will is not effectuated:

> . . . between these divine virtues and properties which are exercised upon objects already composed in such and such a way, according as their nature and constitution requires, and the qualities themselves, there is so strict a liaison that if you remove from the objects these qualities, these virtues and properties will necessarily remain without exercise and without use. And it is from here that these hypothetical propositions come: if Adam had not forsaken his holiness he would have remained eternally blessed. If man had not sinned he would not have fallen into condemnation and death. If you believe, you will not come into judgment, for the Lord Jesus has satisfied God's justice in your place. If you do not believe, the wrath of God will remain upon you forever.[152]

ni de leurs descendans, & qui n'ont aucune distincte connoissance du Sauveur du monde, il ne faut pas penser pourtant qu'il y ait ni aucun peuple, ni mesmes aucun homme exclus par la volonté de Dieu, du salut qu'il a acquis au genre humain, pourveu qu'il face son profit des tesmoignages de misericorde que Dieu luy donne" (*ibid.*, 1634 ed., pp. 80–81; 1658 ed., p. 68).

150. To be sure, in Amyraut's system, whether the design of Christ's work were universal or not, this qualification would still stand.

151. *Brief Traitté*, 1634 ed., p. 90; 1658 ed., p. 76.

152. *Defense*, pp. 606–7. From this passage we can gather that Amyraut taught a substitutionary theory of the atonement which stressed the legalistic aspect of this theory. His doctrine agrees with the orthodox at this point, but he did not believe with them that logic therefore requires the conclusion that if Christ took

This *heilsgeschichtlich* understanding of the work of Christ in procuring salvation as distinct from the application of that salvation is but part of the dualism which runs throughout Amyraut's theology.[153] Throughout there is a juxtaposition of these two ways that grace may be considered. Amyraut repeats this bifurcation of grace under various terms. Sometimes the dialectic is in terms of external-internal.[154] When this terminology is used Amyraut frequently refers to Calvin's distinction between the general call and the special call.[155] But by far his most common distinction is between objective and subjective grace, which distinction he presses, in du Moulin's words, *ad nauseam*.[156] And he relates to this terminology his favorite image, the analogy of light and seeing: "Objective grace is as the sun, subjective grace as the faculty of seeing with our eyes."[157] And as the sun was designed to give light to all men, so the objective grace procured by Christ is designed for all men. However this sufficient objective grace must be desired, must be willingly received. If a man does not open his eyes the light of the sun is of no avail to him. The analogy holds in relation to grace as well, for although Jesus is the light of the world, he is of no avail to the one the eyes of

---

upon himself the punishment due all men therefore all men must be saved. Their logic demanded that if the doctrine of the substitutionary atonement were true then there was no escaping the doctrine of the limited atonement. This was unnecessary for Amyraut because (1) he would deny that logic of this sort was valid in theology and (2) his placing of Christ's atoning work within the conditional will of God did not require such a conclusion.

153. It is worthwhile to compare this dualism with that which characterized much of the writing of Lefèvre. I have not been able to establish any direct reliance of Amyraut on Lefèvre, but there are striking similarities in their teachings.

154. See *Defense*, pp. 23–25, 510–11.

155. *Institutio*, III.iii.21, III.xxi.7, III.xxi.10, and esp. III.xxiv.8.

156. In a work in which he is considering Amyraut's *Specimen animadversionum:* "Distinctionem verò causae objectivae, & subjectivae, quam sexcenties & ad nauseam ingerit, non invenio in aliis ejus scriptis" (*De Mosis Amyraldi adversus Fridericum Spanhemium libro judicium*, p. 62).

157. "Gratia *objectiva* est ut sol, subjectiva, ut facultas videndi in oculo" (*Dissertationes theologicae sex*, p. 274). This language was also common in the orthodox writings of the period but with nothing of the frequency or importance with which it is used by Amyraut. It is the very center of Amyraut's explanation of universal and particular grace, and how both can be retained within one system.

whose understanding have not been illumined, who does not participate in this light through faith.[158] Faith is in fact the condition of the evangelical covenant,[159] and unless we are united to Christ by faith his procuring of salvation remains useless for us.[160] Amyraut's emphasis here is, as he claims, precisely that of Calvin as set forth in *Institutio*, III.i.1.[161] In fact, a thorough study of the concept of the mystical union with Christ in Calvin's writings cannot fail to show that Calvin too regards the benefits which accrue from the work of Christ as, to use Wendel's words, "no more than a kind of potential grace." Wendel is also correct when he adds that for Calvin "Communion with Christ, the *insitio in Christum*, is the indispensable condition for receiving the grace that the Redemption has gained for us."[162]

158. See esp. *Trois sermons sur l'epistre aux Ephesiens, ch. I., v. 16.17.18. 19. & 20.* (Charenton, 1639), *passim;* also *Defense*, p. 510: "La grace de Christ donc, laquelle est offerte exterieurement, est suffisante de la façon, que la lumiere du Soleil est suffisante pour produire l'action de la veuë, si vous avez de bon yeux."

159. *La Morale chrestienne*, 3:53; *Brief Traitté*, 1634 ed., pp. 85–90 and *passim*. See also *In symbolum apostolorum, exercitatio*, p. 235: ". . . fides est conditio annexa foederi Evangelico, ex cujus praestantione promissionum divinarum executio pendet."

160. "Il faloit donc necessairemêt, avant que ce Redempteur à qui a esté commise la charge d'accomplir nostre salut en nous, desployast la puissance de son esprit en nostre regeneration & en nostre glorification, & nous fist sentir l'effect de sa cômunion en ces choses, que les hommes le receussent & vinssent à luy pour s'y conjoindre. Et c'est ce qu'il appelle luy mesme, *venir à luy*, & *le contempler*, & *croire en luy*. C'est à dire estre entierement persuadé de cette verité qu'il est le Sauveur du monde, afin de chercher en luy le remede à nos maux: ce que ses Apostres appellent en tant de lieux *la foy*, qui si elle est veritable & syncere, nous ente au corps de nostre Seigneur Jesus, comme gresses sauvages en un olivier franc, pour tirer de luy le suc & la seue de vie spirituelle: si elle ne se trouve pas en nous, nous demeurons en nostre corruption & misere naturelle" (*Brief Traitté*, 1634 ed., pp. 86–87; 1658 ed., pp. 73–74). See also *Sermons sur divers textes*, p. 236: "Les esleus donc ne se receillent ou ne s'entent au corps de nostre Seigneur Jesus que par la foy: . . ."; *Paraphrase de s. Jean* 6:56,57, pp. 260–62; Cameron, *Opera*, p. 535,1: ". . . est enim fides quae mortem Christi reddit efficacem, non ullâ quae ei insit dignitate aut meritò, sed quia Deus voluit nos inseri per eam Christo capiti."

161. See also Calvin's *Commentary on Romans* 5:17: "At vero, ut in participationem gratiae Christi veniamus, in eum inseri nos per fidem oportet: . . . Ut Christi justitia fruaris, fidelem esse necessarium est: quia fide acquiritur eius consortium" (*CO*, 49:100).

162. *Calvin*, pp. 234, 235. See also Niesel, *The Theology of Calvin*, pp. 120–23, and esp. R. S. Wallace, *Calvin's Doctrine of the Christian Life* (Grand Rapids, 1959), pp. 17–27, and Gerrish, *Profile of the Reformers*, pp. 157ff.

How does one fulfill this condition of faith and so become united to Christ? With this question we enter into the realm of God's absolute will and election. For the answer is, "His Spirit . . . is the bond of your communion with Christ . . ."[163] And in the *heilsgeschichtlich* understanding of the Trinity it is the work of the Spirit which has to do with the absolute will of God.[164] But before we turn to this we shall say a word about the subject of the chapter (ch. 8) which in the *Brief Traitté* appears between his exposition of the conditional will and the absolute will.

In this intervening chapter Amyraut considers "What, since the Fall, is the inability of man for the accomplishment of this condition" of faith. He proceeds to emphasize in the strongest terms the Calvinist anthropology—that by his own strength man is absolutely unable to come to faith: ". . . we contribute nothing to the efficacy by which our understandings are induced to receive the doctrine of salvation and our wills are induced to follow it."[165] However, as he proceeds in this explanation he propounds a distinction which was very important to him and which reappears in all of his later writings, a distinction between natural and moral ability.[166] Doubtless this reflects his humanistic orientation, for the distinction is framed partly to emphasize that man remains man in the work of grace. Amyraut felt that the orthodox explanation of grace made of man a mere block of wood, so like Cameron he stressed that man has the faculties necessary to respond to grace. There is also a strong moralistic interest evidenced by this distinction, for he believed that since man has the faculties necessary to respond to grace he can be justly con-

163. *Paraphrases sur Romains* 8:11, p. 171. Cf. Calvin, *Institutio*, III.i.1.

164. "Pour le regard de l'efficace de l'esprit, elle depend de cette second sorte de misericorde: c'est à dire, de cette volonté de creer la foy dans les hommes, que nous appellons l'eslection" (sermon on Ezek. 18:23, *Sermons sur divers textes*, p. 63).

165. ". . . nous ne contribuons rien à l'efficace par laquelle nos entendemens sont induits à recevoir la doctrine de salut, & nos volontez à la suivre" (*Brief Traitté*, 1634 ed., pp. 95–96; 1658 ed., p. 81).

166. A distinction which appeared in Cameron (see ch. 1). It is interesting that it became very important in later Edwardian theology in America; in fact, there is a striking similarity between the whole of Amyraldian theology and that of New School Presbyterians and some 19th-century American Congregationalism.

demned for not responding, but that he could not be condemned for not responding if he had no faculties for doing so.[167] The distinction itself is a very simple one, namely that man *can* respond to grace because he has been endowed with understanding and will, but that he *will not* respond because he is sinful. So, he explains, we have been endowed with the faculties of understanding and will "from the beginning, and God has preserved them in us in spite of our sin, otherwise we would not be men." But, he continues, our "inability comes from the fact that we are corrupt, that is to say, that the vice which is in us has cast its roots so deeply, has so strongly confirmed its habits in us, has acquired an empire so absolute, possesses so strongly all the faculties of our souls, that we not only cannot free ourselves when we would like . . . , but even that it is impossible that we will to do so."[168]

Having declared the complete moral inability of man to believe in the gospel, to attain to the condition of the conditional covenant, Amyraut goes on to speak of the operation of God's absolute will. This will is expressed in absolute promises such as Jeremiah 31:33 or Romans 9:15. It "does not presuppose the condition of faith in man but creates it in him."[169] In a passage

167. "Impotentia illa quaecunq; est, ut jam vidimus, non consistit in privatione facultatis, sed in ejus perversa constitutione. . . . Prioris enim generis impotentia culpâ vacat, posterioris sclerosa est. Prioris generis impotentiae Deus auctor est; omnia enim ista mala, quae vel *miseriae,* vel poenae vocanbur, ad Deum auctorem referuntur. Posterioris causa est in uno homine. Prioris generis impotentia excusationem praebat hominibus, si minùs ea faciunt, quibus eorum facultates sunt à natura destinata. Posterioris generis impotentia est ejusmodi ut qui eâ laborat, omni excusatione privetur" (from his letter to Irminger of Zurich, Archives Tronchin, 130:28,1–28,2. MS). See also *Eschantillon,* 1658 ed., pp. 176ff., and for an extended defense and explanation of this distinction *Fidei Mosis Amyraldi, circa errores arminianorum, declaratio,* pp. 42–64.

168. *Brief Traitté,* 1634 ed., pp. 99, 100; 1658 ed., pp. 84, 85. See also *Eschantillon,* p. 198, where Amyraut says that man's refusal to embrace the gospel "consiste en ce que les hommes ont naturellement les affections du coeur si attachées aux choses de la terre, qu'il ne se peut faire qu'ils s'en déprennent."

169. Sermon on Ezekiel 18:23, *Sermons sur divers textes,* p. 60. See also *Brief Traitté,* 1634 ed., p. 105; 1658 ed., pp. 89–90: ". . . en cecy tant s'en faut que l'amour de Dieu puisse presupposer cette côdition en l'homme, qu'il faut necessairement presupposer qu'elle n'y est pas, & mesmes qu'elle n'y peut estre, sinon que luy-mesme l'y crée par sa puissance."

in which he has built his argument upon a lengthy quote from Calvin he makes this abundantly clear:

> And this great man teaches, according to the Word of God, that this election is precise, absolute, that it does not depend upon any condition but creates that condition in man; that it is not founded upon anything foreseen, but upon the good pleasure of God; that it cannot be hindered by anything fortuitous, but overcomes all types of hindrances, anticipates all types of fortuitous happenings and accomplishes its purpose notwithstanding all resistance.[170]

So when it is a question of this absolute will, which fulfills the conditional will, then God's actions are in no way determined by a consideration of man's response, but rather he operates solely according to the will of his good pleasure.[171]

But having noted that God elects men in this way Amyraut immediately adds: "Thus the mercy in this point exceeds all measure and all understanding."[172] ". . . if you consider the marvel of these mysteries and of our hope in itself, it so far exceeds the understanding of man that even the angels themselves do not understand them perfectly."[173] It follows, then, that there is not much that Amyraut can say directly about the electing act of God.[174] He generally refers to both election and

---

170. *Sermons sur divers textes*, p. 224.

171. ". . . en la dispensation de la grace qui engendre la foy, & en la comparaison de ceux a qui elle estoit donnée ou refusée, Dieu n'a regardé ni les oeuvres, ni les merites, ni chose quelconque de cette nature, mais seulement a suivi la pure liberté de sa volonté, . . ." (*Defense*, p. 523).

172. "Ainsi la misericorde en ce point excede toute mesure & toute intelligence" (*Brief Traitté*, 1634 ed., pp. 105–6; 1658 ed., p. 90).

173. *Paraphrases sur I Pierre* 1:12, p. 10.

174. E.g., he says that when considering election "On ne peut donc avoir recours qu'à la seule volonté de Dieu, dont il n'y a moyen de sonder la cause" (*Eschantillon*, p. 186); also *Sermons sur divers textes*, pp. 229–30: "Or voyez-vous, comme je croy, quel sujet, il y a de s'escrier, ô profondeur des richesses, & de la sapience de Dieu! que ses jugemens sont incomprehensibles, & ses voyes impossibles à trouver! Car est-il question de l'election particuliere? Qui est-ce, comme nous vous disions il n'y a pas long-temps, qui puisse faire rendre raison à Dieu de ce qu'il a plutost esleu celuy-cy que celui-là? Qu'il ait decreté de donner la foy aux uns, & de laisser les autres en leur misere naturelle? Certes il ne s'en peut rendre aucune raison que celle de son bon plaisir. Il en a plus aimé les uns; en comparaison de l'amour qu'il leur a porté, il peut estre dit avoir eu les autres en

reprobation as a mystery.[175] He steadfastly refuses to speculate about election, believing that it is in such speculation that the orthodox have erred. Yet although "one cannot give any reason for it," still we do know that election exists, "partly by experience and partly by the express words of the Apostle Paul."[176] At all times he is very much concerned to show that only *a posteriori*, only *per eventum* can we know really about election.[177]

Therefore he directs the attention to faith as the effect of election: ". . . it is revealed to us that all those who believe, believe by virtue of the election through which God has separated them from the others. So then if we are obliged to persuade ourselves that we are elect, we must reflect upon the faith which we already feel within ourselves, and then from the effect we reason to the cause."[178] To be sure, election is "the cause of faith," but we can only know election "by the consideration of the effect itself."[179]

Thus it is faith which assures our election by uniting us to

---

haine: Selon qu'il est escrit, j'ay aimé Jacob, & j'ay haï Esaü; Mais d'où vient la différence de cet amour, c'est ce qui est aux hommes impossible à entendre."

175. *Brief Traitté*, 1634 ed., p. 104; 1658 ed., p. 88. Also *Sermon sur la premiere epistre de s. Pierre* 3:20–21, p. 5.

176. *Defense*, p. 399.

177. "Decretum illud divinum *arcanum* . . . est alterum caput Evangelii, ut Calvinus loquitur, quod initio hujus disputationis diximus non innotescere cuiquam, ac ne electis quidem, nisi per eventum; eventum autem situm esse in ipsa fide, ex qua homines à posteriori cognoscunt se esse ex numero electorum" ("De gratia specialis," *Specimen animadversionum*, p. 310. Cf. *Defense*, p. 284: ". . . la secrette volonté de Dieu, qui met différence entre les hommes, ne se manifeste point autrement que par l'evenement, . . ." The same remark is found on p. 287.

178. ". . . nous est-il revelé que tous ceux qui croyent, croyent en vertu de l'election par laquelle Dieu les a separez des autres. Ce donc que nous sommes obligez de nous persuader que nous sommes esleus, est que nous faisons reflexion sur la Foy que nous sentons desja en nous, & que sur l'effect nous raisonnons de la cause" (*Defense*, p. 242). Amyraut then immediately quotes a long passage from Bucer's commentary on Romans 8 in defense of this position.

179. *Ibid.*, p. 243. By centering so dramatically upon faith Amyraut is trying to remove himself as far as possible from speculation about the will of God. In this he certainly recaptures one of the most salient features of Calvin's theology. Calvin, too, emphasized faith and warned against speculation. Cf. *CO*, 51:299: "Voilà donc l'election de Dieu qui est en soy cachee: mais il nous en rend tesmoignage par les graces qu'il nous eslargit, comme la foy est un don du S. Esprit."

Christ. ". . . as one cannot be joined to Him except by this true faith, so one cannot have this true faith except in virtue of this election which is precise, absolute, and particular."[180] But faith only comes through the work of the Spirit who in turn can work only through the Word.[181] Therefore it is evident that, as Calvin had done by placing his discussion of predestination at the end of the third book of the *Institutio,* Amyraut very definitely places election in the work of the Spirit.[182] Here again we have an instance of his teaching the economy of the persons of the Trinity in the work of redemption, for the election of certain individuals to share in the salvation procured for all men by Christ is possible only because of the activity of the Spirit who makes grace effective. It is "the efficacious strength of the Spirit of God which disposes our hearts to comprehend the revelation of His mercy."[183] And He "acts where He pleases, and as the free will of God dispenses Him."[184]

180. *Sermons sur divers textes,* p. 227.

181. "Les esleus donc ne se recueillent ou ne s'entent au corps de nostre Seigneur Jesus que par la foy: & la foy ne s'engendre que par l'efficace de l'Esprit; & l'efficace de l'Esprit n'accompagne, comme nous avons dit, aucune autre dispensation que celle de la predication de la parole" (*Sermons sur divers textes,* p. 236). Cf. Calvin, *CO,* 51:297: "Il est vray que pour estre enfans et heritiers de Dieu, il nous faut estre du corps de nostre Seigneur Jesus Christ, ce qui se fait par foy: mais cependant nous ne pouvons pas croire à l'Evangile sinon que Dieu nous attire par son S. Esprit."

182. See *Sermons sur divers textes,* p. 226, where he says that particular election "est une election à sentir la vocation de l'Esprit"; also pp. 259–60: "Afin donc que cette divine doctrine de la Croix de Christ entre dans nos entendemens, il faut que l'Esprit de Dieu y agisse, voire y agisse de telle façon, y desploye une telle puissance, qu'il n'en arrive pas comme aux mauvais escoliers, à qui on dit cent fois une chose, & si ne la comprennent-ils pas; ou s'ils la comprennent superficiellemêt aujourd'huy, demain ils l'auront oubliée; mais que ces celestes enseignemens s'engravent tres-profondement, & que les traits en demeurent tout à fait ineffaçables." This is again true to Calvin's emphasis. See his two sermons on Eph. 1:13–14 and 1:15–18 in *CO,* 51:295–324.

183. *Sermons surs divers textes,* p. 149.

184. *Paraphrase de s. Jean* 3:8, p. 101. Placing election in the work of the Spirit is of major importance for Amyraut's position, not only because it underlines the consideration of election only as an *ex post facto* explanation of the work of grace but also because it points up the incomprehensibility of the doctrine of election, since it is axiomatic that the work of the Holy Spirit is incomprehensible. See Amyraut's *In symbolum apostolorum,* p. 246: "Et ut venti motus adeò liberi sunt, ut unde procedat, & quò feratur, aut cur potiùs in hanc quàm in illam partem

The Holy Spirit alone works subjectively in man, illumining the mind and disposing the will so that faith may be born.[185] But the work of the Spirit is in turn both tied up with and dependent on the revelation of the work of Christ through the Word. There are two elements necessary for an efficacious call, for engendering faith—"the preaching of the Word and the virtue of the Spirit who works in the inner man (*interieurement*)."[186] Or as he explains it in terms of objective-subjective grace, both graces are necessary to produce faith and bring one into the Church, but the objective grace remains *in suspenso* until the Spirit unites the believer to Christ. Or, in terminology found frequently in Calvin, there is an inseparable bond between Word and Spirit in engendering faith. Faith can never arise unless these two are together.[187]

---

incumbat, hominibus prorsus incognitum sit, sic Spiritus sancti dispensationem adeò ex mera Dei voluntate proficisci Scriptura docet, ut illius, praeter eandem voluntatem, ratio nulla, vel reddi ab hominibus, vel comprehendi possit."

185. ". . . nul homme n'a la foy que par l'efficace de l'Esprit de Dieu . . ." (*Sermons sur divers textes*, p. 107). See also *Defense*, pp. 353–54, where he maintains that it is "cette vertu de l'Esprit qui seule peut destourner les hommes du peché, & les appeller efficacément a l'esperance de la vie."

186. *Defense*, p. 373. See also *Sermons sur divers textes*, p. 63: "Pour engendrer cette foy dans les hommes; il faut necessairement deux choses: l'efficace interieure de l'esprit, & la predication exterieure de la Parole"; also p. 138: "Or pour engendrer la foy aux coeurs des hommes, deux choses sont absolument necessaires: la revelation externe de la doctrine de la religion; & la puissance efficacieuse de l'Esprit de Dieu qui dispose interieurement nos coeurs à la comprendre."

187. "Dieu a tellement attaché la grace de son esprit, par laquelle il convertit les hommes à la foy, mes Freres, à la declaration de sa parole & de sa verité telle que nous l'avons par la revelation de ses Prophetes & de ses Apostres, qu'à cause de cela elle est appellée non seulement la Parole de la foy, mais le ministere de l'Esprit: Voire mesmes l'Apostre S. Paul faisant opposition de sa predication, qu'il dit avoir esté avec demonstration d'esprit & de puissance, avec le ministere de Moyse, prononce que le ministere de Moyse a esté le ministere de la lettre, & le ministere de la condamnation, & que la lettre tuë: mais que le sien & de ses compagnons estant le ministere de l'esprit, est le ministere de vie, & ministere de Justice, & que l'Esprit vivifie. De sorte que le mesme peuple qu'il appelle l'Israel selon l'Esprit, il l'appelle aussi l'Israel selon la Promesse: pour monstrer que ces deux choses, la Promesse qui vient d'une revelation extraordinaire, & l'Esprit qui luy donne entrée en l'entendement de l'homme, s'accompagnent en telle maniere, que si bien la Promesse est exterieurement annoncée à plusieurs en qui pourtant Dieu ne desploye pas l'efficace de son Esprit, (car il y en a beaucoup d'appellez, mais peu d'esleus) il ne desploye pourtant cette sienne efficace de son Esprit que

So in the final analysis we see that the absolute will of God fulfills the conditional will, that while strictly speaking the election of God is outside of the covenantal relationship, which is framed in terms accommodated to our understanding, in the end only this election can bring the conditional will to fruition.

From the foregoing we can see that Amyraut wished to place election in the work of the Spirit, where it is found in Calvin. By emphasizing an economy in the work of the persons of the Trinity, Amyraut is able to break through the orthodox teaching of a limited atonement. By emphasizing the incomprehensibility of God's electing decree, he radically shifts the ground of discussion from speculation regarding God's pretemporal counsel to contemplation of the order of events as they have occurred in history. By emphasizing the sole validity of the *a posteriori* methodology in theological matters, he focuses the attention upon faith as the confirmation of election. By juxtaposing the conditional and absolute wills of God and emphasizing the conditional will, he likewise focuses the attention upon the mercy of God as revealed in Christ, in Christ as the cause of our election. In all of this he thinks he has faithfully represented Scripture and restored the true emphasis of Calvin. He frankly recognizes that in some particulars his own emphasis is not that of Calvin but firmly maintains that Calvin taught a conditional will of God, and he seems to be saying that the orthodox have erred in overlooking it.

---

là où il fait exterieurement annoncer la promesse" (*Sermons sur divers textes,* pp. 149–50).

5

JUSTIFICATION BY FAITH

We HAVE OBSERVED THE HISTORICAL DIMENSION that the three-fold covenant teaching gave to Amyraut's theology and we have seen that this covenant teaching was the determinant in his exposition of the doctrine of predestination. Furthermore, we have observed in our discussion of Cameron's theology that the deviation from orthodox teaching of the covenants came with the distinction between the covenants of grace and law. But we have not asked nor answered the fundamental question for the Salmurian theology—why this distinction of three covenants? Why would Amyraut risk his very career by this evident deviation not only from orthodoxy but even from the greatly admired Calvin, who most certainly did not see the covenants of law and grace as distinct but rather as one, differing only *in administratio?* Why, when the decision of the Alençon synod for his acquittal was so unsure, did Amyraut insist on having removed from interdiction the phrase concerning "the nature of the blessedness proposed by the legal covenant considered precisely"?[1]

These questions have not been entertained by any of the writers on Amyraldianism of whom I have knowledge. Nevertheless I would maintain that the answer to them takes us to the very heart of Amyraut's theology, to his central doctrine. And this can be nothing else than the doctrine of justification by faith.

Justification by faith was beyond question the doctrine at the

1. "Journal sommaire . . ." *Bulletin* 13 (1868), 60. Amyraut taught, as we have shown, that the law covenant promised only a blessed life in Canaan.

heart of the Reformation. It was the genius of Luther which brought it to the fore for the first time since the days of the Apostles and which saw that "if we lose the doctrine of justification, we lose simply everything."[2] Calvin appropriated this emphasis and, though he discussed regeneration-sanctification first in the *Institutio,* regarded justification as the cardinal doctrine of Christianity, "the main hinge on which religion turns."[3] He maintained that "Wherever the knowledge of it is taken away the glory of Christ is extinguished, religion abolished, the Church destroyed, and the hope of salvation utterly overthrown."[4] Moreover, the christocentrism of both Luther's and Calvin's theology is closely allied to the idea that Christian righteousness is in fact Christ's righteousness and not man's own.[5] So a good case can be made that not only for Luther was the doctrine of justification the premiere doctrine of Christianity but also for Calvin—if indeed one is able to call any one doctrine central for Calvin.

By Amyraut's time, at least in Reformed orthodoxy, the doctrinal picture had been significantly altered. Justification was most certainly a secondary consideration, ranking far behind the doctrines of predestination and Scripture in importance.[6] And in the continuing debate with Roman Catholicism all kinds of topics—transubstantiation, auricular confession, the marks of the

2. Luther, *Lectures on Galatians,* trans. Jaroslav Pelikan, vol. 26 of *Luther's Works* (St. Louis, 1963), p. 26. See also p. 106 where he calls it "the principal doctrine of Christianity" and asks the question, "What is all creation in comparison with the doctrine of justification?"

3. *Institutio,* III.xi.1.

4. "Reply to Sadolet," *Tracts and Treatises,* 1:41.

5. Compare Luther's "Argument" to the *Lectures on Galatians* and Calvin's *Institutio,* III.xi.4, 23.

6. One may indeed press the objection that the same issue which was at stake in the Reformation era—*sola gratia*—was in the seventeenth century still being discussed, but that it had evolved into the doctrine of the decrees and predestination. While this is probably true, it does not in any way detract from the thesis that justification was no longer of crucial importance. Amyraut would no doubt complain that this was just the problem—that the focus of attention had shifted from a concrete, existential doctrine to an abstract, speculative formulation. Apparently justification remained of greater importance to Reformed theology on the British Isles. At least in the early part of the century a lively debate was waged over justification and, if C. F. Allison is right, specifically over the formal cause of justification. See his *The Rise of Moralism* (New York, 1966), *passim.*

Church, the authority of the Church, Scripture, etc.—were debated without end, but almost never justification. One finds literally hundreds of accounts of conferences between leading Protestant and Catholic churchmen, but we have yet to find one in the seventeenth century which had for its topic the doctrine of justification. This almost total silence led Rébelliau to conclude that by then "upon this famous principle of justification by faith, for which Luther initiated the Reformation, it is certain that it had been discovered that the disagreement here was merely a matter of words (*purement verbal*)."[7] As we shall see, this certainly was not true of Amyraut, nor do I believe that it fairly represents the substance of the orthodox doctrine of justification. Nevertheless, Rébelliau reflects fairly the practical consequence of the lack of interest in this doctrine.

But again, Rébelliau was not wholly mistaken, even about the substance of orthodox teaching on justification, for there was an almost imperceptible move towards legalism in orthodox theology. Calvin's emphasis upon the unity of the Old and New Testaments apparently tended to blur the sharp antithesis between works-righteousness and faith-righteousness in his thought, and in Reformed orthodoxy the law-gospel distinction was often either minimized or lost altogether.[8] At the same time Arminianism, by emphasizing that faith, as the obedience of the Christian, can be regarded as righteousness, added to the legalistic orientation.[9] Amyraut's bold formulation of a theology which makes justification so central and strongly reaffirms the distinction between works-righteousness and faith-righteousness must be seen, at least in part, as an answer to these two trends.

The centrality of the doctrine of justification in Amyraut's theology can be seen in at least four ways: (1) he expressly declares it to be the central doctrine of Christianity; (2) he justifies

7. Rébelliau, *Bossuet, historien du protestantisme*, p. 24.

8. E.g., the Westminster Confession is silent on the law-gospel distinction, and even emphasizes the unity of justification in the Old and New Testaments with no mention of the two kinds of righteousness: "The justification of believers under the Old Testament was, in all these respects, one and the same with the justification of believers under the New Testament" (ch. 11, par. 6, in Schaff, *Creeds of Christendom*, 3:628). It is also interesting that the Westminster divines discussed justification with reference to God's decree to justify.

9. See Weber, *Reformation, Orthodoxie und Rationalismus*, 1:97.

the continuing separation of the Reformed and Catholic communions on the basis of this doctrine; (3) the formulation of his covenant theology is made on the basis of this doctrine; and (4) it is this doctrine which he uses to illustrate the inviolable relationships of all the basic doctrines of the Christian faith. The four points are by no means mutually exclusive, but in the ensuing discussion, for convenience, they will be dealt with as much as possible individually and in the order given.

Amyraut defines justification in the same terms as did Calvin. That is, justification consists of two parts: ". . . the remission of sins and the imputation of the righteousness of Christ."[10] It is forensic in nature, for we are accounted righteous for the sake of Christ: "We maintain that when God will give us life and the Kingdom, He will not consider any other merit nor any other obedience than that of His Son whom we embrace by faith."[11] Moreover, this manner of justification is in opposition to our natural inclination, for all men believe that they will be justified by their own merit, by their own works.[12] For this reason in this matter man must, according to one of Amyraut's favorite passages, bring into captivity every thought to the obedience of Christ and recognize that "justification by faith is by a totally supernatural revelation and institution, for there is nothing less in accord with the institutions of nature than to justify a guilty man by imputing to him the sufferings of another who has been punished for him."[13]

10. *Sermon sur I Pierre* 3:20–21, p. 28.

11. *De la justification*, p. 32. Again, p. 50: ". . . il est nostre justice pource qu'il a esté obeissant à son Pere jusques à faire pour nous propitiation de nos offenses." Or again, he says it is justification by faith "par laquelle estans revestus de cette justice que nostre Seigneur nous a acquise en obeissant à son Pere jusqu'à la mort de la croix, nous pouvons comparoistre comme justes & irreprehensibles devant Dieu" (*Cinq sermons prononcez a Charenton*, p. 11 of the sermon on I Cor. 2:9).

12. "Les Juifs, & les Grecs, & generalement toutes nations & tous peuples, s'imaginent qu'ils seront justifiés par le merite de leurs actions, & font côsister la pieté & la sainteté ou en l'observation de quelque ceremonies de peu de poids, ou en quelque retenuë dans les actions du corps, sans se soucier du fonds de l'ame" (*Paraphrase de s. Jean* 16:8, pp. 713–14). See also *Sermon sur . . . Jean* 16:8,9,10,11 in *Cinq sermons prononcez a Charenton*, p. 16: ". . . naturellement les hommes sont portez à chercher d'estre justifiez devant Dieu par cette Justice-là." His reference here is to that righteousness which man produces for himself.

13. *Quatre sermons sur Hebrieux 6*, p. 20 of sermon 1. See also the sermon on John 16:8ff. in *Cinq sermons*, pp. 18–19, where he says that the idea of a righteous-

Though in a formal definition Amyraut includes both the imputation of Christ's righteousness and the remission of sins, and though, as we shall see, he contends strongly for the idea of imputation in his rejection of the Roman Catholic doctrine, still one could say that for Amyraut as well as for Calvin "the remission of sins constitutes the very basis of justification."[14] Frequently Amyraut's discussions of justification include only the idea of remission.[15]

But whatever aspect of the doctrine he chooses to emphasize, Amyraut makes it clear that justification is the principal doctrine of Christianity:

> . . . the first care which comes into man's spirit when he thinks about his salvation concerns the means by which he will appear before God and the righteousness with which he must be clothed in order to be acceptable, and to receive from His hand life and remuneration.[16]

Now, it is justification alone which is able to bring consolation to that man.[17] Therefore "it is the foundation of all the other graces which are communicated to us by our Lord Jesus when we are entered into his communion."[18] Therefore "Primarily the gospel teaches us that we are justified by faith alone in our Lord Jesus, and by the remission of our sins in Christ."[19]

---

ness from without "est naturellement inconnuë à l'homme; elle est incroyable à nos entendemens s'ils ne sont éclairez d'ailleurs; elle est directement contraire aux inclinations de la Nature corrompuë de l'homme qui aime a se confier en soy-mesme."

14. See Wendel, *Calvin*, p. 258.

15. E.g. his sermon on justification in *Deux sermons sur la matiere de la justification et de la sanctification* (Saumur, 1658), p. 5: ". . . nostre Apostre enseignoit que le seul moyen d'estre justifié est celuy que l'Evangile nous presente en nostre Seigneur, c'est que nous soyons justifiés par la seule misericorde de Dieu qui nous pardonne nos offenses en consideration de la souffrance de son Fils, & que toute la condition qu'il requiert de nous, c'est que nous croyïons en luy." Cf. *De la justification*, p. 8: ". . . les Evangeliques croyent que nostre justification consiste en la remission de nos offenses, lesquelles Dieu nous remet liberalement en consideration de la seule satisfaction de Christ, . . ."; also *Exposition du chapitre VI . . . de l'epistre aux Romains*, pp. 11 and 42.

16. *Paraphrases sur Romains* 1:17, p. 16.

17. "Quant à la consolation, . . . elle naist de la doctrine de la Justification par la foy . . ." *Sermons sur divers textes*, p. 196.

18. *Quatre sermons sur Hebrieux 6*, p. 18 of sermon 1.

19. *Sermons sur divers textes*, pp. 193–94. See also *Deux sermons*, p. 5: "Au

The extraordinary emphasis Amyraut places on justification may also be clearly seen in his *Paraphrases sur Romains*. He interprets the first five chapters as an extended proof by Paul that neither Gentile nor Jew was justified by works (chs. 1–3) and that the justification which is gratuitous—i.e. by faith—is juxtaposed to legal righteousness. It is especially the latter idea that he emphasizes again and again. The example of Abraham in chapter 4 is precisely to show that the Jews have completely missed the point by seeking justification through works. Justification by faith is here diametrically opposed to thoughts of legal or works justification. Even for Abraham justification was by faith—*before* he received circumcision. He interprets Paul's design in chapter 5 to be to contrast the benefits of faith righteousness with works righteousness. His emphasis may be illustrated in the following ways: (1) verses 20 and 21 (which receive the most extended paraphrase), at the end of chapter 3, state that no flesh will be justified by works and that now justification is manifested *sans Loy;* (2) the "falling short" of chapter 3, verse 23, is interpreted to mean that "all . . . if they wish to be justified by works remain short in this *pretention*"; and especially (3) the antithetical "much more then, being justified by his blood" of chapter 5, verse 9, is interpreted to be an antithesis between legal justification and faith (or gospel) justification. Calvin had interpreted the antithesis to rest in the latter part of the sentence ("we shall be saved from wrath through him") with this opposed to the "sinners" of verse 8 (and so he interpreted "sinners" as those who are condemned). He says the sum of this is: "If Christ has acquired righteousness for sinners by his death, he will now much more protect them when justified from ruin and destruction."[20]

---

commencement de la predication de l'Evangile, mes freres, les Apostres de nostre Seigneur, & particulierement S. Paul, avoyent diverses questions à demesler avec les Juifs, les premiers ennemis du Christianisme. Mais la premiere & la principale estoit touchant le moyen de la justification de l'homme devant Dieu"; also *Cinq sermons,* pp. 10–11, where he has discussed the principal elements in the gospel story and then says: "Et quant à celles qui consistent en doctrines, c'est premierement la justification par la foy, par laquelle estans revestus de cette justice que nostre Seigneur nous a acquise en obeissant à son Pere; jusqu'à la mort de la croix, nous pouvons comparoistre comme justes & irreprehensibles devant Dieu."

20. *Commentary on Romans* 5:8. *CO,* 49:93.

I believe a comparison at this point shows that Amyraut gave more importance to the doctrine of justification that even Calvin.

Amyraut illustrates his teaching on the centrality of the doctrine of justification in a second way, as we have said, by his relationship to the Roman Church. In 1638 he wrote works on justification and the merit of works in answer to a treatise proposing union of the Reformed and Catholic communions. In the light of Amyraut's irenic spirit, in the light of the fact that he was responding to the writing of an old friend and co-disciple of Cameron, in the light of the trend within Calvinist orthodoxy to maintain silence on the matter of justification in their continuing disputes with the Roman Churchmen, and in the light of the fact that Amyraut was the only respondent to this treatise who selected the topic of justification for his point of rebuttal, these two writings are most significant. Certainly they suggest that Amyraut did not regard the difference between Catholics and Protestants on the doctrine of justification as merely a matter of words.

In the treatise on justification Amyraut quickly establishes the issue at stake to be "whether justification consists in inherent righteousness, or in the remission of sins and in imputed righteousness."[21] And although even de la Milletière holds that the formulation of this doctrine at Trent is "a leaven capable of spoiling the whole of the doctrine of justification,"[22] Amyraut cannot accept his continued espousal of inherent righteousness as the formal cause of justification even though de la Milletière affirms that this inherent righteousness is a gift of grace.

---

21. *De la justification*, p. 20. See also pp. 31–32: ". . . le poinct de nostre différêt consiste a sçavoir en quoy gist le droit en vertu duquel nous esperons la vie & la gloire du royaume des cieux: Si c'est l'obeissance que Christ a renduë à son Pere pour nous jusques à la mort de la Croix; ou bien la Justice laquelle est inherente en nous par la grace de l'Esprit de Christ. Nous soustenons que quand Dieu nous donnera la vie & le royaume, il n'aura égard a autre merite ni a autre obeissance que celle de son Fils que nous embrassons par foy. Monsieur de la Mill. avec l'Eglise Romaine maintient qu'il n'aura égard qu'aux merites de la justice qui nous est inherente par sa grace . . ." This passage Amyraut also quoted in the preface of *Du merite des oeuvres* as the basic disagreement between him and de la Milletière. For an even more explicit elaboration of this difference between imputed righteousness and imparted righteousness see pp. 61ff.

22. *De la justification*, p. 25.

In this treatise Amyraut is concerned to show that the whole controversy between the Catholics and Protestants, and therefore between himself and de la Milletière, reduces to one point, and that this point is precisely the one Paul had contested with the Jews; namely, that justification does not have to do with deliverance from the bondage of sin but with "deliverance from its condemnation by the imputation of an alien righteousness (*justice estrangere*)."[23] Or in other words, he believes de la Milletière has confused sanctification and justification and so continues to propound a form of works-righteousness.

What this all means in our exposition of Amyraut's doctrine of justification is that this dispute with de la Milletière clearly illustrates his radical distinction between the dispensation of the law and the dispensation of the gospel. The Roman Church, he believes, is in essence teaching Jewish legalism by its insistence upon inherent righteousness and therefore a form of merit. In this way it introduces confusion into religion and constructs almost insurmountable barriers to the doctrine of justification by faith alone. It has not recognized that it is combining "two types of justification which are completely incompatible."[24]

> In fact, has this not been the reason for the stumbling of the Jews, and the opinion that the Apostle Paul has tried so hard to wrest from their minds by these divine disputes on justification that we have in the Epistles to the Romans, to the Ephesians, and to the Galatians? And is it not this which even now loses those of the Roman Church, that when it is a question of the doctrine of justification instead of sticking to the doctrine of the gospel as we have it in the New Testament they go and gather from here and there in the Old Testament all those promises that God made concerning the keeping of His com-

23. *Ibid.*, p. 194.
24. *Ibid.*, p. 198: ". . . ces deux sortes de justification estans entierement incompatibles. Pource que si j'ay observé la loy, je n'ay point afaire de Christ. Si j'ay afaire de Christ, l'observation d'une partie de la loy ne me sert à rien pour me justifier: car elle ne justifie personne si elle n'est entierement parfaite." See also his sermon on justification in *Deux sermons*, p. 6: ". . . l'Apostre represente ces deux moyens d'obtenir la justification comme absolument incompatibles. Tellement que selon sa doctrine constante & universelle, qui veut estre justifié par les oeuvres & par la Loy, renonce absolument au salut que nous avons en Jesus Christ; & au contraire, qui veut estre sauvé par nostre Seigneur Jesus Christ, renonce à la justification par la Loy & par les oeuvres."

mandments, and they resurrect this formula, *Do these things and you will live,* that the gospel had buried? Then in order to argue against us, that is to say, against the doctrine of the Apostle, from the books of the Law they move to the Prophets and from there gather all those ways of speaking which come from this legal dispensation, things which have to do with those former times but which are completely out of place in evangelical preaching. I say, brethren, that it is as a kind of miracle that a man, brought up in the doctrine of the law, can taste the doctrine of justification by faith alone. And with great regret we see every day the experiences of those of the Roman communion, to whom God has given some taste of the truth of our profession, who only with incredible difficulty are able to surmount the hindrance which the preaching of the ministry of Moses restored among them brings to their minds. And we also see the perpetual conflict between this preaching and the words, disputes, and arguments of the Apostle Paul in the gospel.[25]

So in his considerations of this doctrine vis-à-vis the Roman Catholic doctrine Amyraut was concerned to lay stress on the radical difference between works-righteousness and faith-righteousness, and to accentuate the concept of imputation through which we do not actually become righteous but rather receive an alien righteousness which is accounted as ours. By this latter concept Amyraut hoped to turn the attention to Christ and the absolutely gratuitous nature of justification. Elsewhere he makes this most explicit. He contends that all in the gospel is a gift, but then remarks how this seems to be particularly true of justification.

> . . . I judge that there is one among all the other graces with which the Apostle has here principally to do, and to which also the name of celestial gift pertains in a special way, namely the remission of sins, or justification. For it is the foundation of all the other graces which are communicated to us through our Lord Jesus since we have entered in His communion. . . . It is it also that the Apostle, in Chapter 5 of the Epistle to the Romans, in that beautiful contrast that he makes of our Lord Jesus Christ with Adam, calls two or three times by this name of *gift,* in contrasting it with the condemnation which the sin of the first man had subjected the world. In fact, if you compare justification by the law with this that you obtain through the gospel

25. *Sermons sur divers textes,* pp. 194–95.

in the remission of sins you will find the latter is truly a *gift* which proceeds from the sheer mercy of God . . ."[26]

Thirdly, the unique importance of justification for Amyraut is nowhere more dramatically portrayed than by the role given it within the structure of his theology. Here we approach the answer to the questions posed at the outset of this chapter. For it becomes quite apparent that the insistence on distinguishing the covenants of law and grace, the Old Testament and the New Testament, as separate and different covenants is made on the basis of the belief in justification, the belief that this is how one receives eternal life.[27] And since the covenant structure is determinative for all of Amyraut's theology, it is not difficult to ascertain the importance of justification.

Amyraut does not appear to have explicitly declared that it was his approach via justification which led him to make two separate covenants of the periods of law and grace, but that such is the case there can be no doubt. We have remarked in the section on Cameron's theology that his understanding of the covenants of law and grace paralleled the distinction made by Luther and Calvin between law and gospel. This is likewise true of Amyraut. The whole force of his formulation of the covenant of grace is as "opposed to that of works only, and it is not considered except insofar as it has to do with the manner of justification."[28] Again, this can be seen in sermon 4 of his *Six Sermons* of 1636. Here he develops his thought on the distinction between the covenants of law and grace, taking as his text II Corinthians

---

26. *Quatre sermons sur Hebrieux 6*, pp. 18–19 of sermon 1.

27. In this distinction and the resultant teachings one sees a great deal of affinity of Amyraut with Luther. Or was it Melanchthon? In any event, because justification is so central in Amyraut's theology he must constantly oppose law to gospel as did Luther. Thus also we see Amyraut teaching that the law promised the Jews simply a blessed life in Canaan, a teaching Luther also espoused. Cf. Luther's *The Babylonian Captivity of the Church*, trans. A. T. W. Steinhäuser, in *Three Treatises* (Philadelphia, 1959), p. 157: "For the old testament given through Moses was not a promise of forgiveness of sins or of eternal things, but of temporal things, namely, of the land of Canaan, by which no man was renewed in spirit to lay hold on the heavenly inheritance."

28. ". . . l'alliance de grace est opposée à celle des oeuvres seulement, & n'est considerée sinon entant qu'elle regarde la maniere de la justification" (*Replique a M. de la Milletiere*, 1658 ed., p. 355).

3:6ff. where Paul contrasts the ministries of the law and gospel, calling the law the minister of death, of condemnation, and of the letter which kills. Paul speaks in this derogatory manner of the law because "he teaches constantly that the law has justified no one, that it was not given in order to bring life . . ."[29]

As Amyraut develops his argument in this sermon he claims to be following the interpretation of the passage made by Calvin, "who distinguishes in the over-all economy of the Old Testament, between the things which were properly of the ministry of Moses and those which were not. And as for those which were properly of the ministry of Moses, he calls them law; of the others, he says that they pertain to the gospel." So Amyraut concludes, "The ministry of Moses, then, ought to be considered in two ways, either insofar as he was a great prophet chosen by God to renew among the people of Israel the promises, and even to add some others, which from the very beginning had been made concerning the Messiah, or insofar as he was the mediator of a covenant which God made in a special way with this people."[30] Or as he elsewhere speaks in more common terminology:

> The word law, brethren, has two meanings in Scripture: namely, all the legal dispensation, insofar as it comprehends the promises and the invitations of the gospel, and the covenant of Law considered precisely in itself, excluding those things which concern the Messiah and in which the beginnings of the covenant of grace consist. David ordinarily takes this word in its first meaning in the Psalms, and St. Paul takes it in the second sense in the disputes in which he compares and contrasts the gospel and the law.[31]

29. *Sermons sur divers textes*, 1653 ed., p. 169.

30. *Ibid.*, pp. 170–71, 173. Calvin does use the exact language attributed to him by Amyraut: ". . . Paulum hic considerare quid fuerit proprium legis: nam quamvis Deus tunc per spiritum operaretur, illud tamen non erat ex ministerio Mosis, sed ex Christi gratia. . . . Certe gratia Dei toto illo tempore otiosa non fuit: sed sufficit, quod non fuerit proprium legis beneficium" (*CO*, 50:40).

31. "Ce mot de Loy, mes freres, signifie nommément deux choses en l'Escriture: sçavoir toute la Dispensation legale, entant qu'elle comprenoit les promesses & les semonces de l'Evangile, & l'alliance de la Loy precisément considerée en elle mesme, mises à part les choses qui concernoyent le Messie & esquelles les commencemens de l'alliance de la Grace consistoyent. David prend ordinairement ce mot en cette premiere signification dans ses Pseaumes, & S. Paul en la seconde dans les disputes dans lesquelles il fait comparison & opposition de l'Evangile à la Loy" (Sermon on justification in *Deux sermons*, pp. 13–14).

Calvin uses this same terminology but more commonly refers to law as comprehending the whole of the Old Testament period. In this way he places the emphasis on the unity of the covenant of grace.[32] Amyraut, however, most commonly uses law in the more restrictive sense, as part of the covenantal relationship established through Moses. In this way he emphasizes the opposition of law and gospel. And it is his stress on justification which brings about this emphasis.

In his exposition of the opposition of these two ways for coming to life Amyraut frequently quotes what he calls the "formula" of the two covenants. It is from this perspective that one sees that "these two covenants are of a nature so different that it is impossible that the matters of them be mixed or combined together."[33] The law considered in itself is, then, "a covenant in which on the one hand man promises to God that he will obey all His commandments and, conversely, if he does not fulfill them he will submit himself to the condemnation that the Law pronounces. On the other hand, God promises life to those who fulfill them and to those who transgress them He threatens eternal condemnation." The formula is *"Do these things and you will live* and *Cursed is he who does not continue in all the things of the law to do them."*[34] To this Amyraut opposes the covenant of grace and its formula: *"Believe and you will be saved."*[35] His constant recourse to these two "formulas" keeps clearly in the

---

32. See his comments on Rom. 10:5: "Lex bifariam accipitur: nunc enim significat universam doctrinam a Mose proditam, nunc partem illam, quae ministerii eius propria erat: quae scilicet praeceptis, praemiis, et poenis continetur" (*CO,* 49:198). See also *Institutio,* II.xi.7. Nevertheless, though Calvin speaks of the law in these two ways, by far his most common use refers to the whole Old Testament religion, including the promises of mercy and grace. The parent discussion of his understanding of law in the *Institutio,* II.vii, bears the title "Legem fuisse datam, non quae populum veterem in se retineret, sed quae foveret spem salutis in Christo usque ad ejus adventum" (*OS,* III.326.19–21). In the text itself he adds: "Legis nomine non solum decem praecepta, quae pie justeque vivendi regulam praescribunt, intelligo, sed formam religionis per manum Mosis a Deo traditam. Neque enim datus est Moses legislator qui benedictionem generi Abrahae promissam aboleret: imo videmus ut passim revocet in memoriam Judaeis gratuitum illud foedus cum patribus eorum percussum, cujus haeredes erant" (*OS,* III.326.27–33).

33. *Sermons sur divers textes,* p. 176.

34. *Ibid.*

35. See esp. the last chapter of *Replique a M. de la Milletiere, passim.*

forefront Amyraut's desire to oppose works-righteousness and faith-righteousness.[36]

The sharp distinction between these two covenants also serves to augment Amyraut's *heilsgeschichtlich* methodology. In the closing pages of chapter 3 we saw that he regards the covenant of grace as having been initiated with Adam immediately after the Fall, but in a very obscure manner. The abstruse nature of the covenant of grace in the Old Testament is accentuated by a consideration of the doctrine of justification. For it is the doctrine of justification which is most difficult to attain under the period of the law. It is in this context that he remarks that "it is as a sort of miracle that a man brought up in the doctrine of the law could taste the doctrine of justification by faith alone."[37]

One of the results of justification is a consolation and tranquility of spirit which is "marvelously altered and disquieted by the *mélange* of the doctrine of justification by works."[38] In fact even David, who is held up as an example of godliness, was unable to attain the tranquility of spirit available to those under the covenant of grace:

> . . . because he lived under the economy of the law (which in-

36. See esp. pp. 15–16 of the sermon on John 16:8–11 in *Cinq sermons*: ". . . il y a de deux manieres de Justice qui viennent en consideration sur ce sujet-là: L'une est interieure à l'homme, & consiste en ses vertus & en ses bonnes actions: L'autre luy est externe, & consiste en l'obeissance que Christ à [sic] renduë à son Pere jusques à la mort de la Croix. L'une est naturelle & l'homme eust esté justifié par elle s'il eust persisté en son integrité, l'autre est surnaturelle & absolument necessaire à l'homme quand une fois il est tombé en peché. L'une est contenuë en cette formule de l'alliance legale, *Fai ces choses & tu vivras:* l'autre, en cette formule de l'alliance Evangelique, *Croy & tu seras sauvé.* L'une peut-estre appellée la Justice des hommes, parce que ce seroient les hommes qui la presenteroient à Dieu si effectivement ils l'avoient; l'autre est par l'Apostre S. Paul appellée la *Justice de Dieu,* parce que c'est Dieu qui la donne. Par l'une, les hommes seroient justes en eux-mesmes, & la cause de leur justification seroit inherente en leurs personnes: Selon l'autre, ils sont reputez Justes par la Justice d'autruy." See also his sermon on Mark 11:22, pp. 3ff.

37. *Sermons sur divers textes*, p. 195. See also p. 201: when speaking of the elect of the Old Testament he says, "Ils ont veu la justice qui est par la foy, mais ce n'a pas esté sans avoir souvent à luitter contre la pensée de la Justification par les oeuvres. Ils ont veu la consolation par l'asseurance de la remission: mais ce n'a pas esté sans sentir souvent de merveilleuses alarmes en leurs consciences."

38. *Ibid.*, p. 196.

sists perpetually upon commandments and prohibitions, upon promises and threats, in consequence of obedience or transgression), sometimes by the sentiment of his sins he experienced extreme distress, and in Psalm 32 he says they have given him unimaginable inquietude.[39]

Like Luther, Amyraut holds that this same anxiety and inquietude which was the constant lot of the saints in the Old Testament period is also a threat to believers under the covenant of grace. For man naturally falls back into the trap of thinking that his own works are meritorious, and when this happens God deprives that one of the Spirit of consolation, so that uncertainty and anxiety arise:

> Thence come these terrors, these distresses, these agonies, these continual trepidations, these cruel doubtings that those have who question whether or not they will be saved, whether or not they are in a state of grace, whether or not they ought to have the boldness to raise their eyes to heaven or to resolve themselves, if one can so resolve himself, to eternal pains. This comes, I say, from the fact that one perpetually drums into their ears the ministry of the law, that one pronounces to them the condemnation of God upon those who fail to fulfill it, that one proposes to them the kingdom in the heavens as the reward for their good works and their holiness, and that one takes away from them the hope of attaining it except upon the ladder of their own merits.[40]

But even though Amyraut sees lapsing back into reliance upon works-righteousness as a constant danger even under the covenant of grace, he still speaks very unequivocally of the advantage given to those who live in this period that the Old Testament saints did not have. Much of his sermon on justification is taken up with just this theme. He does not regard it as an advantage derived from any natural capacity of man to fulfill the requirement of the gospel, for "naturally we are not better disposed to believe in the gospel of Christ than to execute the commandments of the law . . ."[41] But in terms of the facility of actually fulfilling the requirement, those under the covenant of grace are much better off:

39. *Ibid.*, p. 197.
40. *Ibid.*, pp. 198–99.
41. Sermon on justification in *Deux sermons*, p. 14.

For there is no power either of the body or of the spirit of man to which one of the commandments of the law does not correspond. Again, it requires of each faculty such a great quantity of acts and operations that these extend almost to infinity. For the moral, ceremonial, and political commandments are of an overwhelming number in their requirements, and the necessity of executing them is extended to people of all ages and to all parts of life. Whereas the justification which is by the gospel, not requiring anything but faith, it corresponds to only one of our faculties, namely the understanding, and only requires one operation of this faculty, which is truly and firmly to believe.[42]

So he can say that the latter is a "means of being justified and of being saved that the Apostle claims to be incomparably easier than the other."[43]

Finally, the centrality of the doctrine of justification in Amyraut's theology is illustrated by the way in which he relates all of the other doctrines of salvation to it. This he does not attempt with any of his other doctrines.

Primarily he maintains, like Calvin, that there is an inseparable bond between justification and sanctification. This was a conspicuous feature of Calvin's discussion: that only through our union with Christ is his righteousness imputed to us. Therefore "as Christ cannot be dissected into parts, so these two, righteousness and sanctification, which we perceive to be in Him together and conjoined (simul et conjunctim), are inseparable."[44] This inseparable bond between the two doctrines was, however, at least partially lost in Calvinist orthodox theology. Perhaps this was due to the custom of discussing theology under various loci. In any case, by the time of Wollebius there is hardly a mention of their inviolable connection.[45] In the Westminster Confession even the meagre mention we find in Wollebius has completely disappeared.[46] In Amyraut, however, one encounters a teaching

42. Ibid., pp. 19–20.
43. Ibid., p. 14. See also pp. 7–8, and Paraphrases sur Romains 10:8, pp. 232–34.
44. Institutio, III.xi.6. OS, IV.187.20–22. See also III.xi.11.
45. See the discussion in his Compendium, chs. 30, 31, pp. 164–74 of Beardslee's translation. Wollebius does begin his discussion of sanctification with the sentence "Sanctification is related to justification as light is related to the sun" (p. 171) but this is the only statement of its kind in the entire discussion.
46. See chs. 11 and 12 (Schaff, Creeds of Christendom, 3:626–28, 629–30).

on their absolutely inseparable nature which restores the emphasis of Calvin. Like Calvin, Amyraut speaks of justification as somehow first, meaning not so much a chronological order as a logical order. In Amyraut the concept of the inseparability of justification and sanctification is tied up on the one hand with his teaching on sin and on the other hand with his teaching on our union with Christ, and also concerning the inseparability of Christ's death and resurrection.

Amyraut teaches that sin must be understood in two ways. According to one, "it consists in the corruption of our nature and in the vice of the actions which it produces; according to the other it subjects us to condemnation and requires that we be punished."[47] Yet these are but two facets of one reality: "Now these two regards are joined by an indissoluble line. For the first necessarily produces the second, there not being any vice or bad action which does not merit punishment."[48] This idea is normative in Amyraut when discussing sin.

Now to these two aspects of sin the two aspects of grace, i.e. justification and sanctification, relate in a very integral way:

> As sin has two aspects, so grace ought to be considered in two ways. According to one, it is a remedy to condemnation; according to the other, it delivers us from the corruption of sin and sanctifies us. And these two things are in such a way dependent upon one another that they cannot be divided.[49]

Or in another place:

> Sin is but one and the same thing, though it is so described that it may be considered as having two aspects. For it is a corruption of our nature, and is the cause of our condemnation. But this only makes one whole . . . composed of two parts absolutely inseparable. . . . and the evil, so composed, is only one whole, so the remedy which is opposed to it is also only one whole which is likewise made up of two parts, which although they are distinct are nevertheless joined by an absolutely inviolable line. To condemnation is opposed justification, which consists in the remission of sins; to corruption is opposed sanctification. But there is no sanctification where sins have not first

47. *Paraphrases sur Romains* 6:2, p. 116.
48. *Ibid.*
49. *Exposition du chapitre VI . . . de l'epistre aux Romains*, p. 42.

been pardoned, and no one's sins are pardoned but that this remission necessarily draws sanctification in consequence of it.[50]

The inviolable line between sanctification and justification exists primarily, however, not because of the unity of the sin which it is designed to remedy but because both of these benefits come to us in virtue of our union with Christ. This union with Christ cannot be with just one part of Christ, so that all the graces which he acquired for us are therefore necessarily ours as we enter into communion with him. ". . . whoever has entered into the communion of Christ is a participant of the whole Christ, and as Christ communicates to him the fruit of His satisfaction in his justification, He also necessarily communicates to him the Spirit of sanctification who regenerates him."[51]

Indeed perhaps the most impressive aspect of Amyraut's doctrine of justification is its christocentrism, and especially the emphasis on the incarnate Christ. We have seen that he firmly believes that the righteousness we receive in justification is Christ's righteousness imputed to us, an alien righteousness. But this righteousness can be ours only in virtue of his death, resurrection, and ascension.[52] And these are acts which only man can experience, since God is incapable of death and coming to life again.[53] Now it is by his death that he has made satisfaction for our sins, and it is by his resurrection and ascension that the Father attests his acceptance of this payment.[54]

50. *Ibid.*, pp. 10–11. Cf. *De la justification*, pp. 19–20 where he says there is ". . . entre la justification & la sanctification une connexité necessaire & inseparable, & la justification, comme j'ay dit, ne venant qu'en consequence de la resurrection de Christ, la sanctification en depeud aussi necessairement par l'entremise de l'autre."

51. ". . . qui est entré en la cômunion de Christ, est participant de luy tout-entier, & comme Christ luy communique la fruit de sa satisfaction en sa Justification, il luy communique aussi necessairement l'Esprit de sanctification qui le régenere" (*Exposition sur Romains* 8:1–2, pp. 8–9).

52. ". . . nostre justification est fondée sur la mort & sur la resurrection de Jesus Christ, & sur son ascension dans les cieux" (Sermon on justification in *Deux Sermons*, p. 23).

53. See esp. *Sermon sur ces paroles*, p. 9ff.

54. "Comme c'a esté dans la mort que nostre Seigneur Jesus-Christ a payé pour nous, ç'a esté dans sa resurrection qu'il nous a apporté la quittance de nostre payment, de sorte que nous devons estre pleinement asseurés que nous sommes quittes. Et c'est ce qui fait dire à saint Paul au quatriéme chapitre de l'Epistre

By thus focusing the attention upon Christ and his saving work Amyraut effectively guards against man's looking upon himself as capable of producing works which justify. No, it is necessary that one guard against the preaching of the merit of man.

> Of ourselves we can merit nothing but death; all our merit is in Jesus Christ who died for our sins and was resurrected for our justification. Whoever puts his confidence in his own actions is leaning on a broken reed which will pierce through his hand. But he who is assured in his redeemer will never be confused and can never forfeit his right to the enjoyment of life.[55]

It is the doctrine of justification which, above all, teaches us to have recourse to Christ.

> Without Him the knowledge of sin, the continual fear of death, the declaration of the wrath of God, the curse of the law would have our souls in irremediable terror, would engulf them in the melancholy state of the world, would cast them into inconsolable despair. . . . Christ is the One who has delivered us from all of this. Christ is the One the knowledge of whom assures us of this deliverance. Christ is the ladder by which our hearts mount up from the present into the heavens and by which the holy angels descend from the heavens for the protection of the elect in the world. In sum, Christ is the image of God in whom we dare to contemplate this One of whom it was once said, we will die, for we have seen the Eternal.[56]

It is clear, therefore, that justification is the central doctrine of Amyraut's theology, and that only in the light of his heavy emphasis upon it does his threefold covenant teaching make sense. Moreover, justification serves as the doctrine in his theological formulations to which all others can be related. His teaching in this is another of his attempts to restore Calvin's emphasis to Reformed theology. His strong christological focus is revealed, especially his teaching concerning our union with Christ as the

---

aux Romains, que *Christ a esté livré pour nos offenses, mais qu'il est ressuscité pour nostre justification*" (*Sermon sur I Pierre* 3:20,21, p. 47).

55. Sermon on justification in *Deux sermons*, p. 35.

56. *Sermons sur divers textes*, p. 207.

basis upon which Christ's benefits are transmitted to the believer. He follows Calvin faithfully in the idea that "Christ was given in vain for our righteousness if we are not joined to Him by faith."[57] We turn, then, to consider his teaching on faith.

57. Calvin, *Comm. on Romans* 3:26. *CO,* 49:63.

6

THE DOCTRINE OF FAITH

WHILE AMYRAUT DISCUSSES JUSTIFICATION AS A BENEFIT which flows from Christ and which consists of remission of sins and the imputation of Christ's righteousness, he repeatedly and emphatically teaches that it is only by faith that we are justified. It is faith which unites us to Christ from whom this blessing, as indeed every spiritual blessing, flows. Beyond question Amyraut's teaching was designed to give faith a new place of prominence in Reformed theology. We have spoken above of the gradual demise of the importance of faith in Reformed theology after Calvin. By emphasizing faith as the condition of the covenant of grace Amyraut, following Cameron's lead, made a bold attempt to recapture the place this doctrine had had in the theology of Calvin. This is evident in every context. When he stresses that in order to know God's absolute election we must contemplate the *événement*, that only *per eventum* do we know about election, he is directing the attention to faith: *"eventum autem situm esse in ipsa fide."*[1] When he insists that Christ has procured (*impetrauit*) salvation for all men, that Christ has, however, left the outcome *in suspenso*, the object is to accentuate the role of faith, for it is through faith that this salvation becomes effectual in the elect. This whole program, which as we have seen was initiated by Cameron, was designed to return Reformed theology to the precedent set by Calvin, who regarded faith as the locus under which all of theology must be ordered, and from the perspective of which alone all theology can be understood.

1. "De gratia specialis," *Specimen animadversionum*, p. 310.

But though Amyraut, by making faith the condition of the covenant of grace, the bond which unites us to Christ so that we may actually participate in the spiritual benefits He has won for us, clearly pointed up the importance of the doctrine, he has been sharply attacked for divesting faith of its existential character, for completely rationalizing the act of faith. Though he could speak of justification as "in a particular way a heavenly gift" he has been accused of reducing faith to a simple operation of man's natural faculties.

There can be no question but that this criticism is, at least in part, well founded. Max Geiger and H. E. Weber have both scored Amyraut for having seriously departed from orthodox doctrine by defining faith as "simply to be persuaded of the truth of anything."[2] Geiger especially presses this point, interpreting Amyraut's explanation to mean that there is no difference between the persuasion of the truth of the gospel and the truth of a mathematical proposition. We believe that this criticism is both justified and misrepresentative. Amyraut frequently defined faith in the language ascribed to him by Geiger, yet when giving a full discussion of the doctrine of faith showed that he did not regard this as an adequate definition.

Following Cameron, Amyraut tried to revise the orthodox definition of faith, as well as to relate it to a new understanding of faculty psychology. The result was at the same time a dynamic new formulation of the doctrine and a new step toward complete rationalization of the doctrine. In short, perhaps nowhere in Amyraut's theology is the ever-present dialectic between reason and grace more dramatically evident than in his teaching on faith.

To understand Amyraut's doctrine of faith one must have an understanding of both his doctrine of man and his epistemology, both inextricably involved in his explanation of the nature of faith. We have mentioned in chapter 1 that Cameron introduced a slightly different explanation of faculty psychology than that generally held among the Reformed theologians of his time. Amyraut followed Cameron in this attempt at a more existential, a more unified concept of man. For Amyraut taught that there

2. See the discussion in appendix 2.

is such a perfect correspondence between the two rational faculties of man, the understanding and the will, that no possibility
of a warfare between these two faculties exists.[3] Rather, the understanding is the absolute governor of the faculties of the soul.[4]
The understanding is, as it were, "the eye of the soul."[5] It is the
office of the understanding, then, to make a judgment concerning
the worthiness or unworthiness of an object.[6] The power of
choice resides in the understanding, and whatever choice it
makes the will must follow.[7] The will, therefore, is seen as an
inclined faculty which Amyraut regards as free, since coaction
is not involved. But this freedom consists solely in a freedom of
spontaneity, for its function is to follow the judgments of the
understanding.

By stressing that all choice is an act of the understanding Amyraut regards the act of faith as properly an operation of the
understanding, not of the will.[8] He defines faith, as had Cameron, as a certain *persuasio*. But since persuasion comes not by
force, but by apprehending the beneficial qualities of the object
under consideration, by recognizing a good reason for accepting
an object, the rationality of the act of faith is underlined.[9] In

3. ". . . l'entendement & la volonté conservent toujours entr'eux une parfaite
correspondance. Car si l'entendement est en son entier, les mouvemens de la
volonté sont reguliers & bien composés: si l'entendement est corrompu, la volonté
l'est pareillement; & de quelque costé que la Raison s'encline à bien ou à mal,
c'est aussi de ce costé là que l'appetit raisonnable [i.e., the will] se determine" (*La
Morale chrestienne*, 1:46).
4. ". . . il est appellé par les Grecs, le gouverneur, entre les facultez de l'ame"
(*Sermons sur divers textes*, p. 269).
5. "Et qu'est-ce l'oeil au corps, sinon ce qu'est l'intelligence en l'ame?" (*ibid.*,
p. 262).
6. "L'entendement void, & entend, & raisonne, & nie, & affirme, & rejette, &
acquiesce, selon qu'il est touché des qualites qu'il apperçoit dans les choses qui
luy sont offertes à contempler" (*La Morale chrestienne*, 1:55).
7. ". . . au moment que l'entendement se resout, il n'y a personne qui ne sente
que sa volonté se determine de ce costé là, & qu'il n'est pas possible qu'elle se
porte à l'opposite de ce qu'en fin l'Entendement a prononcé estre expedient ou
raisonnable" (*ibid.*, 1:49–50).
8. ". . . le croire a son siege en l'entendement. . . . La volonté donc à proprement parler ne peut pas croire. Le croire . . . agit bien necessairement sur la
volonté. Mais de soy ce ne peut estre la volonté qui croye" (*Sermons sur divers
textes*, p. 266).
9. "La croyance est une persuasion. Et on ne persuade personne par la force.

fact, Amyraut is very clear about his interest in teaching that faith is an act of man and therefore a rational act. He apparently believes that the orthodox explanation of the work of God in causing faith so violates the nature of man that he loses his identity as man. To be a human act, Amyraut seems to be saying, an act must be rational,[10] and so when discussing faith we must "carefully distinguish between the action itself of believing and the virtue by which we believe . . ."[11]

> For the action itself of believing is an action of our understandings. These are men who believe, it is not God who believes in them just as these are men who repent, who are conscious of their sins, who feel regret, who weep and moan through the knowledge of their misery, who also taste consolation and rejoice through the assurance of mercy. None of these things can pertain to God. But, to Him alone pertains the giving of the virtue which produces these sentiments in men.[12]

It is clear, then, that though he believes God must work in man before faith is born Amyraut opts strongly for understanding faith as the act of a rational creature.

When we ask how this persuasion in which faith consists comes

---

Ce sont les raisons qui induisent les hommes à recevoir quelque verité, non la contrainte & la violence" (*Brief Traitté*, 1634 ed., p. 156; 1658 ed., p. 132).

10. "Or est'ce une chose merveilleuse, que l'homme que Dieu a doüé de raison & d'entendement expressement afin de comprendre les motifs de ses actions, & en cela l'a tiré du pair des creatures brutes & destituées d'intelligence, fasse quelque chose sans en avoir aucune raison. . . . ce soit la nature de l'homme d'agir par la conduite de la raison & par son ordonnance . . ." (*Sermons sur divers textes,* pp. 270–71). See also p. 273.

11. *Ibid.,* p. 280.

12. *Ibid.* Cf. the remarkable passage, pp. 318–19: ". . . il faut bien distinguer les operations de nos ames en ce qui regarde l'oeuvre de nostre salut, d'avec la vertu qui fait que nous les produisons. Pour le regard des operations, à les considerer en elles-mesmes, elles sont de nous. Ce n'est Dieu qui croit en nous: ce n'est pas Dieu qui se repent: ce n'est pas Dieu qui pleure, ni qui gemit, ni qui lamente par le sentiment de ses pechez, ni qui recourt à sa propre misericorde. C'est le fidele qui fait tout cela: qui embrasse la croix de Christ, qui en tire sa consolation, qui y fonde son esperance avec asseurance. Mais pour ce qui est de la vertu qui nous donne de le faire, elle est de Dieu. C'est luy qui illumine nos entendemens pour nous faire connoistre & la grandeur de nostre misere, & la grandeur de sa misericorde tout ensemble. C'est luy qui touche nos coeurs de sentiment de leurs pechez, & les meut à repentance. C'est luy qui nous remplist de la connoissance de son Fils; d'où naist la consolation & la joye."

to man to be rationally apprehended, we are brought face to face with his general theory of knowledge. His answer is given in terms of a far-reaching ethical determinism. He has not, as far as we know, worked out a detailed theory of knowledge, but he does present the broad outlines of his position. The mind, he believes, does not come into the world with innate ideas but as Aristotle noted is to be viewed as a *tabula rasa;* however, by a contemplation of "clear and evident" objects certain propositions are learned.[13] This knowledge is acquired through the senses.[14] And he particularly stresses the sense of seeing.[15] There is, he claims, a certain natural proportion or agreement between objects and a properly constituted understanding, so that knowledge is not only natural but inevitable.[16] Man is so constituted that when the understanding perceives the true quality of an object knowledge necessarily follows.

Building upon this general theory he teaches that man is so constituted that he naturally and inevitably seeks the highest good.[17] Or perhaps better, man seeks what he perceives to be the

13. "Je consens volontiers a l'opinion d'Aristote, qui a pensé que nous apportons du ventre nostre esprit comme une table rase, & dans laquelle il n'y a du tout rien d'écrit; mais que depuis qu'il s'est développé les liens de l'enfance, & qu'il commence a s'adôner a la contemplation des choses, il recueille des objets qui sont clairs & evidens d'eux mesmes, certaines propositions, qui s'appellent communes, pource qu'en tous les hommes elles sont d'une mesme façon, & naturelles & immuables encore, pource qu'elles n'ont peu estre conceuës autrement. De sorte que je ne pense pas mesme que les hommes ayent autrement appris de la Nature, que deux & deux font quatre, sinon que l'entendement ayent diverses fois supputé le nombre de diverses choses singulieres, il a perpetuellement remarqué que deux unitez font le nombre binaire, & que le nombre binaire repeté ne manque jamais d'arriver a quatre. Ce qu'ayant ainsi observé, & l'ayant consideré attentivement, non seulement il a remarqué qu'il estoit ainsi, mais il a tres-certainement apperceu & reconnu qu'il ne pouvoit pas autrement estre" (*Defense de la doctrine de Calvin,* p. 438).

14. "Les sens que Dieu & la nature nous ont donnés, sont les premieres principes de nos connoissances . . ." (*Sermon sur ces paroles,* p. 13).

15. ". . . on ne connoist point ceux qu'on ne peut voir de ses yeux . . ." (*Paraphrases sur Romains* 10.10, p. 238). See also *Paraphrase de s. Jean* 14:16, pp. 641ff.

16. E.g., in *Defense,* p. 399, he says, "entre l'entendement & la verité il y a une certaine naturelle proportion ou convenance, d'ou non seulement la science naist, mais mesmes qui engendre je ne sçay quel sentiment de soy, qui ne permet pas que celuy qui est veritablement sçavant, doute de sa propre science."

17. "Tout le monde accorde que c'est naturellement & necessairement que les

highest good, for the corruption caused by sin destroys the ability to know the truly good. But with this ethical concept, that man naturally inclines to the perceived good, Amyraut joins a strong rational emphasis: "We are naturally so composed that we value things, or else think nothing of them, according to the knowledge that we have of their excellence."[18] Real knowledge is a product of reasoning concerning an object so that the true nature of the object is perceived, and this whole process is governed by the laws of nature:

> The virtue then of the operation of the understanding in this regard is of considering its object, and of reasoning upon it in such and such a way; and the virtue of the knowledge and cognition which results from this operation is its conformity with the nature of the object itself. And, on the contrary, the natural vice of these operations consists in that they depart from the rules that nature prescribes, and the resulting vice is that the opinion which the understanding conceives of its object does not accord with its nature. Now as the perfection of knowledge when it conforms to its object is determined by nature, so also the operations of the understanding by which it arrives at this knowledge ought to depend on certain rules determined by nature.[19]

Not only is the knowing process determined by natural laws but also the act of embracing an object. For, he teaches, the movement of the will is infallibly determined by certain motives. These motives he usually explains as including the honest, the useful, and the delightful as these are mediated to the will through the understanding.[20] To be sure, in his various writings

---

hommes aiment leur souverain bien, & qu'il est impossible qu'ils ne l'aiment" (*Sermons sur divers textes*, p. 274).

18. *Action sur le dimanche XLVII du catechisme,* appended to *Sermons sur divers textes,* p. 462.

19. *Considerations sur les droits par lesquels la nature a reiglé les mariages,* p. 47.

20. "Toutes les natures de bien dont elle [the will] peut estre touchée se rapportent à *l'honneste,* à *l'utile,* & au *delectable,* & n'y a rien au monde capable de nous émouvoir que sous l'une ou plusieurs de ces qualites" (*La Morale chrestienne,* 1:55). Cf. *Sermons sur divers textes,* pp. 354–55: "Chacun sçait par experience que les causes qui nous induisent, ou à embrasser, ou à rejetter les objets, se rapportent à l'un de ces quatre chefs. C'est que nous croyons les choses, ou nous ne les

there is some variation in the number and description of these motives which determine the will—"the agreeable," for instance, is frequently substituted for "the delightful." But in any case, in order for the soul to be persuaded to embrace an object it must see in that object one or more of these factors. And where they are present the soul necessarily and inevitably embraces them.

Man in *statu integritatis* was able to live the good life by following the dictates of his uncorrupted reason, whose judgments concerning these factors were infallible. However sin intervened. And its primary effect has been to cause "so thick a darkness in the understanding that now it cannot be made clear except by a supernatural light."[21] Due to this corruption caused by sin the judgments of the understanding cannot be trusted in matters of morals and religion. Amyraut explains that this corruption may be likened to a bandage[22] or film over the eyes which causes the eyes of the understanding to be darkened: "Our understandings, then, having been darkened by sin, and their darkness thickened daily by the habit of sinning, so that their blindness is comparable to a growth which grows on the pupil of the eye and entirely takes away the faculty of seeing, they are no longer able to receive this spiritual light which consists in the truth . . ."[23]

Therefore by this corruption caused by sin the understanding is blinded, and rendered incapable of properly receiving any moral or religious object which is presented to it. The natural proportion or agreement between the object and the understanding has been lost. Now Amyraut maintains that "faith is engendered in us by the grace of God almost in the same way that a blind man is made to see."[24] And he explains that for there

---

croyons pas, selon ce qu'elles nous apparoissent ou veritables ou fausses. Nous les honorons, ou les detestons, selon ce qu'elles nous paroissent honnestes, ou deshonnestes. Nous les prisons, ou les dedaignons, selon ce qu'elles nous paroissent utiles, ou dommageables. Nous les recherchons, ou les rejettons, selon ce qu'elles sont, ou qu'au moins nous les jugeons capables de nous donner du contentement, ou de la fascherie. Et n'y a chose quelconque au monde qui puisse esmouvoir nos esprits d'une façon tant soit peu considerable, sinon par quelques-unes de ces qualitez ou par toutes ensemble."

21. *Brief Traitté,* 1634 ed., p. 48; 1658 ed., p. 41.
22. *Six Sermons,* pp. 148–49.
23. *Brief Traitté,* 1634 ed., pp. 98–99; 1658 ed., p. 82.
24. *Sermons sur divers textes,* p. 357. See also *Sermon sur le xii verset du chap.*

to be sight there must be an external light which gives light to the object in question, and there must also be an internal light which consists in the faculty of seeing. So for the understanding, which is the eye of the soul, to be able to see, there must be both an external presentation of a proper object and an internal illumination which renders this faculty capable of seeing. And in keeping with his ethical determinism, he contends that in order for persuasion, which is faith, to arise, the external presentation must show the object to be true, honest, useful, and delightful.

We have spent some time in chapter 5 detailing the necessity of Word and Spirit in the production of faith. Here we should add that the object of faith is not, properly speaking, the whole of the Word of God. For not all of the Scripture would be useful or delightful even if it did happen to be true and honest. Certainly there was nothing delightful about the law. So then, like Calvin, Amyraut teaches that the proper object of faith is Christ or the gospel.[25] Or frequently he will call the promises the object of faith.[26] In any case, like Calvin, he is concerned to show that the external object of faith has to do with God's revelation of mercy and grace in Jesus Christ. It is the task of the preacher to present this external gospel before the mind for contemplation. And it is to be presented as possessing one or all of the motives which infallibly determine the movement of the will.

---

1 de la 2. Epistre a Timothée (Charenton, 1645), pp. 19–20: "Vous n'ignorez pas, Freres bien aymés, que comme la veuë se fait par la rencontre des choses visibles, qui se presentent à nos yeux, & de la faculté de voir laquelle est dedâs les yeux mesmes, ainsi la foy se forme de la rencontre des promesses & des choses qui nous sont presentées exterieurement par la predication, & de nos entendemens, illuminés & constitués d'une certaine façon par quelque efficace de l'Esprit de Dieu, pour les pouvoir comprendre. Et comme telle qu'est la nature de ces objets exterieurs que nous voyôs, & la constitution de la faculté de voir par laquelle nous les appercevons, telle est aussi la nature de nostre veuë; Ainsi quelle est la nature de ces choses, que la predication de l'Evangile nous propose, & la façon de laquelle nous les embrassons, telle est aussi la nature de nostre foy."

25. "Il y a donc . . . deux actes en la foy. L'un est celuy par lequel l'entendement se porte directement sur Christ, comme sur celuy en qui Dieu témoigne qu'il sera misericordieux & propice universellement a tous" (*Defense*, p. 334). For Calvin's definition of faith see E. A. Dowey, *The Knowledge of God in Calvin's Theology*, pp. 153ff. and 191ff.

26. "At praecipuum tamen & maximè proprium objectum fidei, situm est in promissionibus" (thesis 7, "De natura fidei," *Theses Salmurienses*, 2:86).

This presentation of the external light, the gospel, is however not sufficient to engender faith. For although, as we have seen in chapter 5, Amyraut insists that both with regard to sufficiency and clarity the gospel offer ought to produce faith, it does not, because of the blindness caused by sin. "Not only is external instruction necessary in religion, but there must be something else which internally disposes the faculties of our souls."[27] This internal disposition must come from the member of the Godhead who works efficaciously, the Holy Spirit:

> Therefore so that this divine doctrine of the cross of Christ enters our understandings, the Spirit of God must act within, that is, act within in such a way, deploy within such a power . . . that these celestial teachings are very profoundly engraved in the soul and that their marks will remain completely ineffaceable.[28]

Thus Word, or rather gospel, and Spirit are both indispensable. The gospel is the external light, the Spirit disposes the faculties of the soul to receive the gospel. And so from "the encounter of our understandings so disposed by the Spirit with the gospel of Christ faith arises."[29]

To explain this work of the Spirit Amyraut used almost exclusively the concept of *illuminatio*. Because of his emphasis on the understanding, because the understanding was responsible for judging the desirability or undesirability of any object, and because the effect of sin on the soul had primarily to do with the blinding of the understanding, it was only logical that the concept of illumination would be predominant in Amyraut's conversion vocabulary. By the illumination of the understanding man could perceive the qualities of the external offer, the gospel, and if they were recognized as honest, useful and delightful the will necessarily would embrace them.

27. *Sermons sur divers textes*, p. 258.
28. *Ibid.*, pp. 259–60.
29. *Ibid.*, p. 357. The formula "Word and Spirit" so common in Luther and Calvin has become in Amyraut "gospel and Spirit." This does not mean he has changed the substance of Calvin's teaching, for by "Word" Calvin most certainly meant what Amyraut does when he says "gospel." However, the orthodox equation of "Word" with the whole scriptural record, with the book rather than the message of the book, has apparently been the cause for Amyraut to employ the more precise formula "gospel and Spirit."

It is obvious, then, that the concept of illumination was the central concept in Amyraut's understanding of how faith is engendered. Yet it would not be fair to conclude that all of this had nothing to do with the will, for in Amyraut's mind whatever work the Spirit of God accomplishes in the understanding automatically includes the will. This point was not fully appreciated by the orthodox and was the basis for much of their attack on Amyraut's doctrine of faith. They regarded this intellectualistic explanation of persuasion as nothing more than the old Pelagian doctrine of "a simple moral suasion."[30] They did not see in Amyraut's explanation any real change of heart, any immediate renewal of the will: "More is necessary to make a new creature and bring new life than suasions and deliberations."[31]

However, what du Moulin and the orthodox missed (or thought unimportant) was that this persuasion of which Amyraut and Cameron spoke was a *persuasio moralis,* a determination *of the will.* True enough, Amyraut taught that it is the office of the intellect, the understanding, to make the decision to reject or accept an object of contemplation. He could even say that "if you have regard to the ways of speaking which Holy Scripture uses to represent the manner in which God works conversion in men, you will see that almost all of them have their rapport with what we call the understanding (intelligence), whether these ways of speaking are to be taken literally or figuratively."[32] Yet one must remember that it is the will which moves the soul to embrace the honest, the useful and the delectable. That is to say, while Amyraut unquestionably put the emphasis on the noetic aspect of faith, knowledge in itself in no way exhausts his meaning of faith. This he had made clear even before he defensively reasserted it after being attacked. For in the *Brief Traitté,* immediately after defining faith as "nothing except to be persuaded of the truth of something" (*rien sinon estre persuadé de la verité de quelque chose*) he adds,

We must not content ourselves with the simple and bare knowl-

30. See du Moulin, *Esclaircissement,* pp. 225–31.

31. "Il faut plus, que des suasions, & conseils, pour faire une nouvelle creature, & donner une nouvelle vie" (*ibid.,* p. 225).

32. *Sermons sur divers textes,* p. 261.

edge of that which is true, but we must be moved by the love of that which is honest and beautiful, and touched with the desire of the enjoyment of that which is useful, in agreement and in proportion with its excellence.[33]

Now, one who reads Amyraut carefully will recognize that the will must be involved here, for one does not "love" or "desire" with the understanding but with the will. Nevertheless one must also agree that he has not made the involvement of the will very clear, so that the interpretation of du Moulin and the orthodox was almost inevitable.

Max Geiger has also not seen the full implications of Amyraut's explanation and has concluded that he marked a radical departure from Calvin and orthodoxy at this point, indeed that he had overturned "a central pillar of reformed doctrine."[34] Geiger has especially fastened on Amyraut's use of a geometric demonstration for illustrating his meaning of persuasion, and the criticism here is well taken, for Amyraut certainly comes very close to reducing faith to a simple rational apprehension. In his *Six Sermons* of 1636 Amyraut, most likely in response to criticism, though he already had the precedent of Cameron, explained how such an illustration could serve his exposition of the nature of faith. First he qualified somewhat his previous definition of faith—though he evidently assumed that this qualification would be understood in his former definition. The qualified definition says: ". . . there is no one who does not know that to believe is to be persuaded of the truth of a thing which is proposed to us to understand; *but, I say, to be persuaded of the truth according to the nature of the thing itself.*"[35] By this qualifying sentence Amyraut drew a distinction between truth which might be called scientific truth and truth which is moral-religious.[36] He explained:

33. ". . . il ne nous faut pas contenter de la simple & nuë intelligence de ce qui est vray, mais il nous faut estre esmeus de l'amour de ce qui est honneste & beau, & touchés du desire de la jouyssance de ce qui est utile, convenablement & proportionnément à son excellence" (*Brief Traitté*, 1634 ed., p. 140; 1658 ed., p. 119).

34. *Die Basler Kirche und Theologie*, p. 118.

35. *Sermons sur divers textes*, p. 253. Emphasis added.

36. This distinction is consistent with his whole system. He had never taught that the understanding was blinded with respect to the mundane affairs of life.

For of one sort is the persuasion that we have that the eclipse of the sun comes from the interposition of the moon between it and the earth; but of another sort is that persuasion which we have that God is supremely worthy of being loved (*souverainement aimable*) and that to Him the creature owes the grateful recognition of all this that he is. This first sort of persuasion stops right there and does not draw after it any consequent action. The understanding having found this truth, rests upon it and is contented with it. The other sort of persuasion, if it is as it ought to be, necessarily draws after it the love of God and the deference that the creature ought to render Him in and through all things. Now, our Lord Jesus, dead for the expiation of our offences and resurrected for the assurance of our justification, is an object of this nature, so that the faith by which one embraces Him does not consist solely in some vague thought of His truth, but is a lively, profound persuasion which goes down so deeply into the soul that it completely penetrates it and draws after it all the affections and leads prisoner all the thoughts of man.[37]

Here is the real substance of Amyraut's doctrine of faith. One can readily see that it is more than a "simple moral suasion" and more than simply a *"stark intellektualistischen Verständnis des Glaubens."*[38]

This definition is characteristic of all of his later discussions of faith. Nor can it be doubted that he intended this concept of faith as an answer to what he must have regarded as a weakness in the orthodox doctrine. There seems to be no other answer

---

Like Calvin (*Institutio*, II.ii.12–16), he is very much aware of the discoveries unregenerate men have made in medicine, science, mathematics, etc., but in matters of religion "l'homme est naturellement si corrompu & si meschant, que quoy que ce soit qu'on luy presente exterieuremêt pour le ramener au bien, il ne le touche pourtant non plus qu'une roche, si Dieu l'abandonne entierement à l'aveuglement & à l'opiniastreté invincible de son esprit, . . ." (*Paraphrase sur Romains* 7.14, p. 151). Cf. Calvin's statement in *Institutio*, II.ii.18, that in spiritual matters "qui sunt hominum ingeniosissimi, talpis sunt caeciores" (*OS*, III.260.32–33). Nevertheless one does see here in Amyraut the tendency to regard these two types of knowledge as the same in kind, differing only insofar as religious knowledge is on a higher plane. On the other hand, Calvin seems to regard them as different in kind: ". . . esse aliam quidem rerum terrenarum intelligentiam, aliam vero caelestium" (*Institutio*, II.ii.13. *OS*, III.256.22–23).

37. *Sermons sur divers textes*, pp. 253–54.
38. *Die Basler Kirche und Theologie*, p. 114.

to the fact that the orthodox, whether Lutheran or Calvinist, almost invariably discussed faith as composed of three elements, *notitia, fiducia,* and *assensus,*[39] whereas Amyraut almost never employs more than two elements, *notitia* and *persuasio.* Unquestionably *persuasio* was meant to underline the absolute submission of man to the gospel. As *persuasio* is explained by Amyraut one is impressed especially by the totality of the conquest of the soul of man. "To believe in our theology is to be so vigorously and so profoundly persuaded of the truths of the gospel of Jesus Christ that this persuasion masters all the others and that it makes such an impression within the wills and the affections that it diverts them from their evil inclinations and regenerates them."[40]

But, Amyraut says, one must have a knowledge of that in which this persuasion consists. In a remarkable sermon on Mark 11:22, "Have the faith of God,"[41] Amyraut appears to be directing his remarks against the predominant idea of the orthodox that faith is a belief in the truth of the biblical witness. For he says, "there are some people who regard the death and resurrection of our Lord, and the promises which are founded on it, as we regard the history of the wars of Alexander and of Caesar . . ."[42] He proceeds to show that faith is much more existential than such

39. See for example J. W. Jäger of Stuttgart: "PARTES INTEGRALES FIDEI sunt Notitia, Assensus & Fiducia. . . . NOTITIA est prima pars & est *cognitio eorum, quae ad salutem nobis necessaria.* . . . ASSENSUS est *actus alter, quo credimus promissionibus* Evangelicis in VERBO *oblatis.* . . . Tertius Actus est FIDUCIA, quae est *acceptio & applicatio promissionum Evangelicarum* AD SE *in individuo,* cum acquiescentia voluntatis in Christi merito conjuncta" (*Compendium theologicae* [Stuttgart, 1740], pp. 425–28). See also Heppe-Bizer, *Die Dogmatik,* pp. 408ff.

40. "Croire en nostre Theologie, est estre si vivement & si profondement persuadé des veritez de l'Evangile de Jesus Christ, que cette persuation maistrise toutes les autres, & qu'elle fasse telle impression dedans les volontez & les affections, qu'elle les détourne de leurs mauvaises inclinations, & qu'elle les regenere" (*Apologie pour ceux de la religion,* p. 104). See also his *Sermon sur le xii verset . . . Timothée,* pp. 18–19: ". . . je dis que croire à Dieu . . . est demeurer vivement persuadé de la verité de cette promesse que Dieu nous fait en l'Evangile, que si nous recevons le Seigneur JESUS pour tel qu'il nous est donné du Pere, c'est à dire, pour Sauveur, & pour Redempteur, il nous pardonnera tous nos pechez liberalemêt, il sanctifiera nos ames . . ."

41. Saumur, 1659. Bound with *Le Ravissement de s. Paul.*

42. *Sermon sur Marc* 11:22, p. 19.

rational persuasion. He does agree that Jesus apparently describes this as faith in the parable of the sower, but he feels it is hardly worthy of the name faith,[43] for in order that faith be the faith of which the gospel speaks the promises of the gospel must be embraced under three relations:

> I say then that these objects have principally three ideas or three relations under which our understanding can consider them. One is that they are true: that which naturally relates to our intellect for the understanding (*intelligence*) is the faculty which is destined to the knowledge of the true. Another is that they are useful and advantageous (*utiles & avantageux*), for these are those things which show the way by which we come to happiness; and this relates to our appetites, and to the love that we have of ourselves. Finally, the third is that they lead us to piety and to virtue, to the love of God and the love of neighbor; in which regard their splendor and beauty ought to fill all the parts of our souls.[44]

For there to be true faith the gospel must be embraced in all three of these relations. Amyraut is willing to concede that "According to these various relations the Scripture speaks to us of different types of faith . . ."[45] And Amyraut goes on to speak of faith which may be understood under the first relation—that is, as merely intellectual persuasion of the true. He concludes that "because these people have not even conceived of the gospel under the idea that it can be supremely useful and advantageous, either now or in the future, when the least temptation arises . . . they say: 'Let this truth fare for itself; as for me, I will take thought of my own life and my affairs.' "[46] In like manner he believes that faith which embraces the gospel only under the first two relations—that is, as true and useful—is not lasting faith.[47]

---

43. See *Sermon sur le xii verset . . . Timothée*, pp. 15ff.

44. *Ibid.*, pp. 21–22.

45. *Ibid.*, p. 22.

46. ". . . pource que ces gens n'ont pas mesmes conceu l'Evangile sous cette idée, qu'il leur peut estre souverainement utile & avantageux, soit pour le present ou pour l'advenir, à la moindre tentation qui survient, . . . ils disent, Il sera de cette verité ce qu'il pourra; Quant à moy, je penseray à la seureté de ma vie, & de mes affaires" (*ibid.*, p. 24).

47. *Ibid.*, pp. 25–29.

Having discussed these two preliminary types of faith Amyraut elaborates his concept of true, evangelical faith:

Finally, there are those in whom faith is formed by the concurrence of all these things. It is that the gospel appears to them as true and as a clear, evident, and indubitable truth, the understanding illumined by the Spirit of God apprehends it (*le saisit*) and, in a manner of speaking, incorporates it to itself as something supremely suitable to its nature. It is that the gospel appears to them useful and advantageous, in a way which cannot be explained nor understood all their appetites and all their affections are drawn to it with a marvelous ardor as to their supreme happiness. And as is mentioned in the gospel parable, this pearl that they have found seems to them of such great value that they sell all that they have in order to purchase it. . . . Finally, it is that this beautiful, majestic, and adorable image of piety and of virtue which shines forth in the gospel and to which its promises lead us penetrates our understandings in such a way, and from there so strongly irradiates all the affections of their souls that it becomes the master of them and leads them prisoner under the obedience of Christ, triumphing gloriously and magnificently over everything which is capable of offering resistance. And, true faith does not exclude from its confines either the first consideration—namely, that the gospel is true—or the second—that it is marvelously advantageous and useful. In fact, on the contrary, it includes and necessarily presupposes them. Yet, however, that which gives the proper nature and essence to faith is the impression of the admirable beauty which appears in the gospel of Christ and of the motifs by which it draws us to love God and be charitable towards men.[48]

48. "Enfin il y en a en qui la foy se forme par le concours de toutes ces choses. C'est que l'Evangile leur apparoissant côme vray, & d'une verité claire, evidente, & indubitable, l'entendement illuminé de l'Esprit de Dieu le saisit, & par maniere de dire se l'incorpore côme une chose souverainement convenable à sa nature. C'est que l'Evangile leur apparoissant utile & avantageux, d'une façon qui ne se peut ny exprimer ny comprendre, tous leurs appetits & toutes leurs affections s'y portent avec une merveilleuse ardeur, comme à leur felicité souveraine. Et comme il est dit en la Parabole de l'Evangile, cette perle qu'ils ont trouvée leur semble de si grand pris, qu'ils vêdent tout ce qu'ils ont pour l'acheter. . . . C'est finalement que cette belle, & majesteuse, & adorable image de la pieté, & de la vertu, qui éclatte dans l'Evâgile, & à quoy ses promesses nous induisent, rayonnent tellement dedans leurs entendemens, & de là irradie si puissamment toutes les affections de leurs ames, qu'elle s'en rend la maistresse, & les emmeine prisonnieres sous l'obeissance de Christ, triomphant glorieusement & magnifiquement de tout ce qui est capable de luy faire de la resistance. Et bien que la vraye foy n'exclue pas hors de son enceinte, ny cette premiere consideration, c'est que l'Evangile est vray,

Or in a passage from his sermon on Mark 11:22 he again sets forth the same teaching in a somewhat more positive vein. Again he reveals the close relationship between his understanding of how faith arises and his general epistemology:

> The gospel of our Lord Jesus Christ is true. The faith by which we embrace it, if it is such as it ought to be, is an imprint (*emprainte*) of its truth that our understandings receive so distinctly and so deeply that they are not so vigorously touched by even the most evident demonstrations. It is beautiful (*beau*), because it is made up of many noble truths which relate to each other in an admirable proportion. True faith, recognizing the marvel of its beauty, fills our souls with an inexpressible contentment in embracing it. The gospel is supremely useful and advantageous, because it is the sole means of arriving at the highest good. Faith, if it is such as we ought to have, when we receive it, produces in our consciences a peace which surpasses all understanding, and a glorious hope. The gospel is holy, and alone contains in itself the true and admirable motifs which lead to holiness. Faith, if it embraces it as it must, is so enraptured (*ravie*) that it deploys and diffuses its light and its efficacy into all our affections, sanctifies and regenerates our passions, crucifies us with Christ, resurrects us with Him, and leads all our thoughts prisoners under His obedience.[49]

In these two definitions at least two things stand out most clearly. First, it is obvious that his understanding of faith is based on a unique and innovative epistemology. This is rather refreshing to encounter after a struggle through the tedious sameness of the interminable discussions of the orthodox. At the

---

ny la seconde non plus, c'est qu'il est avantageux & utile à merveilles, & qu'au contraire elle les enferme, & les presuppose necessairement; si est'ce pourtant que ce qui donne proprement la nature & l'essence à la foy, est l'impression de la beauté admirable qui paroist dans l'Evangile de Christ, & des motifs par lesquels il nous porte à l'amour de Dieu, & à la charité envers les hommes" (*ibid.*, pp. 29–32).

49. *Sermon sur Marc* 11:22, pp. 20–21. See also *Action sur le dimanche XLVII du catechisme* in which he says one who has a properly disposed understanding "reconnoistra en l'Evantile toutes ces belles qualitez qui le rendent si recommendables, & le croira entant qu'il est vray, l'admirera entant qu'il est beau, le recevra & l'embrassera entant qu'il est plein de contentement, & d'une utilité absolument inestimable. Or est-ce en cela que consiste la foy" (bound with *Sermons sur divers textes*, p. 467).

same time, however, it runs the same danger as did the orthodox explanation inasmuch as Amyraut, too, seems to have sanctified one particular epistemological approach.

Secondly, the basic idea in these explanations is that man is simply overwhelmed, overcome and mastered by the gospel. The action is so dynamic that it is certainly less than fair to call it a simple moral suasion, and it is certainly much more than a rational persuasion. Indeed, Amyraut is fond of contrasting true faith with simple rational perception:

> The other persuasion, in which consists true faith, is that by which we receive so profound an impression in our souls from considering exactly the gospel in all its qualities that it becomes absolutely the master of all our affections and disposes us in such a way that in comparison with its possession all other things become contemptible.[50]

The conception expressed in these passages can leave no doubt about Amyraut's dynamic, existential understanding of faith, and yet even with these concepts one does not yet have the whole of his doctrine of faith, for to him the gospel is only the external offer which remains inefficacious without the work of the Spirit. Left to ourselves we are blind and cannot recognize the qualities of the gospel. Therefore faith cannot arise without the internal disposing of our faculties by the Holy Spirit:

> It is, then, the efficacy of the Spirit of God in our understandings on which depends that good disposition of our souls by which we are capable of recognizing the excellence of the gospel when we apply ourselves to it. And then afterwards it is from the application of our understandings so disposed upon an object so true, so holy, so beautiful, so agreeable, and so advantageous that the faith of which we speak results.[51]

Once again we see the necessary conjunction of gospel and

---

50. "L'autre persuasion, en qui consiste la vraye foy, est celle par laquelle en considerât exactement l'Evangile en toutes ses qualités, nous en recevons dans l'ame une si profonde impression, qu'elle se rend absolument la maistresse de toutes nos affections, & nous dispose de telle façon, qu'en comparaison de sa possession, toutes autres choses nous deviennent mesprisables" (*Sermon sur Marc* 11:22, p. 20).

51. *Action sur le dimanche XLVII du catechisme,* app. *Sermons sur divers textes,* pp. 467–68.

Spirit. And this work of the Spirit is also described in terms of "overcoming," though because it relates to the secret, absolute decree of God in election the operation itself remains inexplicable.

> Now this action of the Spirit upon the understanding of man is such that it completely overcomes (*surmonte*) without doubt all the effects of nature. For God neither employs in it natural causes nor does the understanding of man comprehend how this supernatural operation delivers the understanding from the natural darkness with which it is possessed. We surely feel the effect of this operation by the great grace of God, but we do not know what is the nature of the operation itself.[52]

As Amyraut goes on to explain the necessary work of the Spirit in engendering faith he leaves no doubt about the source of this faith. It is a gift of God's sheer grace.

> How, then, speaks the Scripture? Whether it uses literal or figurative forms of speech, it always attributes not the power of believing if we have the desire but the effect itself of believing to divine grace as to the cause by which alone faith is produced.[53]

Or, elsewhere he says it is Christ who gives us the grace of his Spirit, who in turn "clears our understandings and determines our wills, and acts so forcefully and so efficaciously in our hearts that in spite of all resistance He brings us into the communion of Christ . . ."[54] It is *"God Who with efficacy works in you both the will and the doing, according to His good pleasure."*[55]

> So that, whether you consider the causes of our salvation, or the effects which proceed from it; whether in these effects you consider the first efforts and the first movements, or you have

---

52. *Defense*, pp. 451–52.

53. *Sermons sur divers textes*, p. 280. The mention of the power of believing if we have the desire (le pouvoir si nous voulons) is another reference to his distinction between moral and natural ability or inability. Even in the doctrine of faith this distinction plays a very important role for him, for he rejects any explanation which destroys the idea that it is a man who believes. He is willing to take the risk which accompanies this position rather than completely dehumanize the individual in the act of faith.

54. *Sermons sur Marc* 11:22, p. 23.

55. *Sermons sur divers textes*, p. 302. This is an obvious paraphrase of Philippians 2:13, upon which this sermon is based.

regard to the degrees by which our salvation advances; or, finally, if you look upon its end and coronation, the glory is entirely due to this One who is its source and author . . .[56]

Thus, whether you regard Amyraut's doctrine of faith from its nature, its results, or its source, it becomes evident that it is far removed from and is a much more dynamic concept than the moral suasion doctrine of which he is accused by the orthodox. His profound concept of *persuasio* stands out in sharp contrast to the orthodox teaching of *assensus* and *fiducia. Persuasio,* in fact, is almost never encountered in the writings of the orthodox.[57] Again at this point of doctrine the orthodox have lost some of the dynamic of Calvin's teaching, for Calvin, as Augustine before him, also had made *persuasio* a basic ingredient in his doctrine of faith. Frequently one encounters this terminology in Calvin's writings. Although the word *persuasio* does not appear in the famous definition of faith in *Institutio* III.ii.7, yet when Calvin goes on to explain his definition the importance of the idea becomes clear. In fact, in III.ii.12, even before he begins this explanation we read that "faith is the knowledge of the divine benevolence toward us and the certain persuasion (*certa persuasio*) of its truth . . ."[58]

As Calvin proceeds in his explanation of the various parts of his definition of III.ii.7 it becomes obvious that Amyraut's favorite term "persuasion" is at the very heart of that definition. When Calvin examines the concept of knowledge as the first ingredient in the definition he identifies it with persuasion or assurance. Knowledge of this sort, he says, is above rational comprehension, believers "are rather confirmed by the persuasion (*persuasione*) of divine truth than taught by rational demonstration."[59] Or again, when Calvin enlarges upon the adjectives *"cer-*

56. *Ibid.*

57. This admits of some qualification when referring to F. Turrettini, for at times he does use this terminology, though his basic discussion is still in terms of the three elements of faith as generally held by the orthodox—*notitia, assensus,* and *fiducia.* See his *Institutio theologiae elencticae,* XV.vii–viii, pp. 492ff. of vol. 2.

58. *OS,* IV.21.36–22.1.

59. *Institutio,* III.ii.14. *OS,* IV.25.16–17. This is remarkably similar to Amyraut's explanation that "l'Evangile de nostre Seigneur Jesus Christ est vray. La foy, par

tam et firman" with which he had described the knowledge of faith, he explains that it was the addition of these adjectives "by which a more solid constancy of persuasion was expressed" (*quo solidior persuasionis constantia exprimatur*).[60]

In fact, it is perhaps not too much to say that along with *notitia, persuasio* is one of the basic elements in Calvin's doctrine of faith. This appears quite manifest in his commentary on Ephesians 1:13:

> I answer, the effect of the Spirit in faith is twofold even as faith is made up of two principal parts. For He both illumines the intellect (*mentes*) and confirms the mind (*animos*). The beginning of faith is knowledge (*notitia*); the consummation of faith is a fixed and steady persuasion (*fixa et stabilis persuasio*) which admits of no opposing doubtings.[61]

Elsewhere he can say most unreservedly that "our faith is nothing unless we are persuaded (*persuadeamus*) for certain that Christ is ours and that the Father is propitious to us."[62] Or again, in the Geneva catechism of 1542 we read that "the Holy Spirit by his illumination makes us capable of understanding those things which otherwise greatly exceed our ability, and forms us to a steadfast persuasion (*certam persuasionem*) by sealing the promises of salvation in our hearts."[63]

One could say much more regarding this element in Calvin,

---

laquelle nous l'embrassons, si elle est telle qu'elle doit, est une empreinte de sa verité, que nos entendemens recoivent si distinctement & si avant, qu'ils ne sont pas si vivement touchés des demonstrations les plus evidentes" (*Sermon sur Marc* 11:22, p. 20).

60. *Institutio*, III.ii.15. *OS*, IV.25.24–25.

61. *CO*, 51:153.

62. *Commentary on Romans* 8:34. *CO*, 49:165. Cf. *CO*, 9:726: "Confiteor nos fieri participes Jesu Christi et omnium bonorum ipsius per fidem quam habemus evangelio, quum videlicet vere ac certo persuasi sumus promissiones in eo comprehensas ad nos pertinere."

63. *OS*, II.92.22–25. See also *OS*, II.88.12–19: "Intelligo spiritum Dei, dum in cordibus nostris habitat, efficere ut Christi virtutem, sentiamus. Nam ut Christi beneficia mente concipiamus, hoc fit spiritus sancti illuminatione: ejus persuasione fit, ut cordibus nostris obsignentur. Denique solus ipse dat illis in nobis locum. Regenerat nos, facitque ut simus novae creaturae. Proinde, quaecunque nobis offeruntur in Christo dona, ea spiritus virtute recipimus."

but perhaps this is sufficient to show that Amyraut's use of persuasion has good precedent in the writings of Calvin. It is my belief that here once again is illustrated a basic difference between the theologies of Calvin and Amyraut on the one hand and the theology of most of the orthodox on the other. Specifically, Calvin and Amyraut are willing to run the risk of having terminology and concepts which are rather delicately balanced and therefore could easily be misappropriated play a large part in their theology; whereas the orthodox are chiefly concerned in building a theological system which has no weak links, which in its expression carefully guards against the appearance of unorthodox opinion. *Persuasio* was much too close to the Arminian doctrine of *suasio moralis* for the orthodox. Amyraut, however, was willing to risk possible misunderstanding because it best expressed his understanding of faith. Most likely at the same time he hoped to appeal to the Arminians themselves with this explanation which did not reject out of hand their total position.

There is another way in which one may see that Amyraut and Calvin were alike in maintaining a balance or tension in their doctrines of faith. After Calvin had defined faith as a *firmam certamque cognitionem* of the divine benevolence toward man, and after he had gone on to maintain that faith does not exist without this perfect assurance, he immediately turned his attention to the fact that "we cannot imagine any certainty which is not affected by some doubt, nor any assurance that is not assaulted by some anxiety."[64] This idea of struggle rarely appears in orthodox teaching.[65] For Amyraut, however, in spite of faith being a total persuasion the life of faith is a constant struggle. The very basis of Amyraut's assurance is the doctrine of justification, and especially the words that "Christ was crucified for our sins and raised for our justification."[66] Yet these two ideas

---

64. *Institutio*, III.ii.17. *OS*, IV.27.28–29.

65. A prime example of this is F. Turrettini, who concludes his locus on calling and faith with a resounding "quaestio" entitled "De certitudine fidei" (*Institutio theologiae elencticae* XV.xvii, pp. 541–54). Even after Descartes, or perhaps because of Descartes, there is no reference to doubt!

66. Romans 4:25. We know of no other verse as frequently found in Amyraut's discussions. It is, of course, related to his interest in justification.

are "two things of which it is difficult really to persuade the flesh."[67] For it is "beyond (*au dessus*) the comprehension of our understanding and the ability (*puissance*) of our reason" to believe "that God is manifested in the flesh, that is to say that He has joined the divine nature to the human in the same person."[68] Such a belief is indispensable for a full persuasion of God's mercy toward us but is, Amyraut believes, an incredibly difficult persuasion to maintain because of our constant warfare with the flesh.

In summary we must conclude that in his doctrine of faith Amyraut again restored some of the dynamic and balance of Calvin's theology. True enough, Amyraut introduced some elements which reveal an incipient rationalism, but a sympathetic understanding of his entire doctrine uncovers a very profound recognition of God's complete mastery of every aspect of the soul in the act of faith.

67. *Sermon sur ces paroles,* p. 62.
68. *Ibid.*

7

SUMMARY AND CONCLUSION

IN THE SEVENTEENTH CENTURY a lively opposition to Reformed scholastic theology developed within French Protestantism, receiving its intellectual impulse from the famed academy at Saumur and its practical expression in the great Charenton church. A careful examination of the nature and program of this opposition has brought us to the conclusion that the scholasticism which won out over humanism in Continental Reformed theology soon after Calvin's death failed to choke off the humanism within France itself. Although the first French Reformed national synod produced a confessional document somewhat more scholastic in content than the theology of Calvin, for some reason (was it the involvement of the French Huguenots in the wars of religion, or was it the more deeply rooted humanist tradition of France?) this scholasticism failed to gain the upper hand in the French Reformed academies. Even though the majority of Huguenot ministers were trained under Beza at Geneva, and even though these ministers developed a theory of resistance which more closely resembled Beza's teaching than Calvin's, the spirit of French Reformed theology remained closer to Calvin than to Beza and the other more scholastic divines. To be sure, one could find here and there in France a Reformed theologian who revealed strong scholastic tendencies, Daniel Chamier for instance, and preeminently Pierre du Moulin, yet these are but occasional examples and cannot be regarded as normative.

The opposition to Reformed scholasticism which because of the strength of the humanist tradition in France was latent in the French Church was brought into the open by the appearance of

John Cameron at Saumur in 1618. There are many signs that by
1620 the scholasticism which by then characterized Continental
Reformed theology (especially Berne, Zurich, Geneva, and the
Dutch academies) was beginning to overcome the influence of
humanism in France, and that the French Church was slowly
succumbing to it. So if one happens to judge negatively of
scholasticism he must regard Cameron's arrival at Saumur as
having come at a most propitious moment.

John Cameron's was one of the few original minds in seventeenth-century Reformed theology. In his view this theology had
taken many bad turns, and he put his originality to work in an
attempt to reshape it. As a result of his teaching the warfare
between scholasticism and humanism erupted in earnest. Outside
of France Cameron would almost certainly have been condemned
for heresy. But Cameron was a convinced humanist, and because
of the influence of humanism in France his teaching was generally well received, so well received, in fact, that he soon had a
large following of loyal and dedicated disciples. Cameron apparently openly criticized Beza at every turn, hence du Moulin's
complaint that he might well be called Beza's scourge. His attack
upon Beza and Reformed orthodoxy centered on the doctrines of
predestination, justification, faith, and conversion.

Cameron's attempted reformulations in these areas have been
but briefly set forth. We have seen that his whole theological
program must be understood in terms of his historically oriented
development of a rather unique threefold covenant teaching.
He made distinct covenants of the Mosaic covenant and the new
covenant. By this distinction, rather one might say opposition,
he radically shifted the center of attention away from the orthodox formulations on predestination and back to the Reformation
emphasis on justification by faith. He taught that the evangelical
covenant is conditional, thereby giving faith, which is the condition of the covenant of grace, a new prominence. He reformu-
lated the orthodox definition and understanding of the nature
of faith by giving primary attention to the concept of *persuasio*
as the major component of faith. And he emphasized the conditional aspect of the covenant in such a way that the object of
attention in predestination was not the doctrine of the decrees
but rather the experiential aspect, the work of the Spirit in en-

gendering faith. There is a great deal more to be learned of Cameron's life and work. He is certainly one of the more exciting theologians of the century.

Moïse Amyraut was Cameron's most illustrious pupil. His was the task of amplifying and systematizing the elements of Cameron's original contribution to seventeenth-century Reformed thought. Practically every insight which Amyraut revealed he owed, as he acknowledged, to Cameron. Yet the interesting fact is that Amyraut claimed to be expounding the theology of Calvin, claimed that in fact the orthodox had seriously departed from Calvin's emphasis and that he, Amyraut, was simply teaching what Calvin had taught. This alleged reliance upon Calvin is, to say the least, fascinating. Certainly no other seventeenth-century theologian had such a thorough working knowledge of Calvin's writings. At least there can be no question but that he meant to make Calvin the "prince of the theologians" and that he contrasted Calvin's theology with orthodox theology. I have resisted the temptation to make this study simply an investigation of that claim, though perhaps not wholly successfully. Because Amyraut's theology has not until now, I believe, been properly understood, I have thought it expedient to make an exposition of that theology the main interest of this book. I believe that once this theology is properly interpreted a study devoted to a comparison between the theologies of Amyraut and Calvin on the one hand, and of the orthodox on the other, could be a fascinating and fruitful undertaking. I have indicated at various junctures where I believe that Amyraut recaptured some of the genius of Calvin's teaching which had been lost by the logically constructed theologies of the orthodox.

Like Cameron, Amyraut developed his whole program on the foundation of a threefold covenant teaching. He taught that there is a manifest progression, a manifest development in the revelation of God. He saw a very real history of God's redemptive work —a clear indication of his humanist heritage. And so as we have followed the development of his covenant teaching we have seen that there is a radical difference in the *nature* of his theology from that of the orthodox. Amyraut worked with a quite different set of presuppositions. Rather than attempting to set forth his theology according to the logic of how God must have determined the course of events in his eternal counsel, Amyraut began with experience and revelation and expounded his theology from this perspective. Therefore we have concluded that methodology is a major element in differentiating Amyraldianism from Reformed orthodoxy.

Amyraut's doctrine of predestination was the primary point at issue between him and the orthodox. For positions espoused in his *Brief Traitté de la predestination* of 1634 he was tried for heresy at the national synod of Alençon in 1637. Yet it was at the point of this particular doctrine that Amyraut argued most strenuously that he was simply following the precedent of Calvin. I believe we have enough evidence to substantiate this claim.

Above all Amyraut claimed that predestination had been given a place of prominence in the structure of theology which it should not have had. Therefore, following Calvin, he argued strongly and emphatically for a removal of predestination from the doctrine of God. He insisted that this doctrine is only legitimate in theology as an *ex post facto* explanation of the work of God in salvation, that to discuss theology in the light of this doctrine is to do violence to Scripture, the theology of Calvin, and even the Canons of Dort. Both from the standpoint of preaching and of honest biblical exegesis Amyraut felt that the orthodox formulation of the doctrine of predestination was particularly damaging.

Amyraut's humanist heritage must be regarded as very important in his exegetical work. He refused to allow an *a priori* theological principle to govern that work. And on the basis of his understanding of such texts as John 3:16, II Peter 3:9, and Ezekiel 18:23, Amyraut taught a universal design in God's will to save. At the same time he found in texts such as Romans 9:12ff. the teaching that God was merciful only to a select few. He therefore, not willing as he says to "twist" Scripture, maintained that both were true, that God willed to save all men in Christ but that he willed that Christ's benefits would be efficaciously applied only to the elect. And he produced an impressive collection of texts from Calvin to show that "this incomparable man" had also taught the same.

Amyraut maintained that even if there were no way to reconcile these two wills of God (or two parts of one will) it would be the height of audacity to deny one just for the sake of logical consistency. Again calling upon Calvin for support, he emphatically cautioned against trying to penetrate the mysteries of God's secret counsel. It is obvious that he believed that this is what the orthodox had done. Yet he did believe in a means by which these two wills might be reconciled, at least enough to satisfy a modest reason, and that this means had been provided by Calvin. One needed to look to a distinction between the hidden and revealed wills of God. According to his revealed will God has shown himself merciful to all men. And upon this revealed will we must base our theologizing, for there is no point of contact between man and God's hidden will except the effect of that will which is faith. This is an immensely important distinction for all of Amyraut's theology. These two wills are to be thought of, according to our mode of understanding, as sequential. The universal will was first and was made conditionally, the particular will was second and was designed to supply the condition, thus making the blessings of the prior will effective.

These two wills relate very integrally to his covenant teaching. For he taught that there are two types of covenant, a conditional covenant and an absolute covenant. Or, in terminology borrowed from Calvin, he maintained that there are two heads to the covenant of grace, one which requires the fulfillment of the condition of faith and one which effectuates that condition. To dramatize his aversion to discussing grace in the light of predestination Amyraut discussed the conditional covenant (or will) almost exclusively, claiming that predestination does not fall within the compass of this conditional covenant. Rather, predestination relates to the absolute, hidden will of God and we have no capacity to discourse concerning this.

To bolster and give added coherence to this teaching Amyraut taught a very strict economy of the persons of the Trinity. This concept was intimately related to the distinction between the revealed-conditional will and the secret-absolute will. For Christ is the expression of the former. In his redeeming work on the cross Christ procured salvation for all men. However, these benefits remain *in suspenso,* are not applied, until our union with Christ, accomplished when the condition (faith) is fulfilled. It is the work of the Spirit which makes this condition possible.

It is the Spirit who engenders faith in the elect, who is the line of our communion with Christ. The ministry of the Spirit relates to the absolute, hidden will. We can speak of this work only by contemplating the faith which is its result. It is folly to speculate about the cause of that faith, for it is hidden in the secret counsel of God. At all times, Amyraut enjoined, we are to focus our attention upon Christ and contemplate God's merciful nature as revealed to us in Christ.

While predestination, and specifically the universal will of God, was the doctrine most bitterly assailed by his orthodox opponents, Amyraut extended his critique of orthodox theology to other doctrines. The practical result of his removal of predestination from the position of central importance in theology was that he had to replace it with another doctrine—for Amyraut's critique of orthodox theology was made not so much by means of an outright attack as by proposing alternative positions. He replaced predestination by making the doctrine of justification his central teaching. Here perhaps his affinity with Calvin and the early reformers is the most obvious. His explanation of the doctrine itself is an almost exact restatement of the Reformation position. He was especially concerned that the emphasis of the Protestants should be placed upon the teaching of the imputation of Christ's righteousness in justifying man, that man is justified by an alien righteousness which is accounted his.

Amyraut differed from Reformed orthodoxy on the doctrine of justification in two important ways. The first was the obvious result of making justification central in his theology; he defended the Reformation principle of *sola gratia* on the basis of this doctrine and not on the basis of a doctrine of election. This in turn served to direct his attention to the law-gospel antithesis, which had almost completely disappeared from orthodox theology. Amyraut also strongly emphasized the inviolable connection of justification and sanctification, a theme so prominent in Calvin's discussions. This again contrasted sharply with the tendency of the orthodox to discuss the two doctrines as separate, autonomous units.

Finally, all have recognized that Amyraut gave special prominence to faith; yet he has been charged by both orthodox and modern interpreters with rationalizing the act of faith. We have seen that his definition of faith did indeed differ from that of the orthodox theologians, but it has also become clear that his doctrine of faith was by no means devoid of an existential element, as has been charged. Moreover, his explanation of faith was made in terms of *notitia* and *persuasio*, the two elements most prominent in Calvin's various discussions. I believe that a proper understanding of this doctrine as taught by Amyraut shows it to have been an effective corrective to the mechanical theory of the orthodox, recapturing much of the dynamic of Calvin's explanation.

In conclusion, I would offer a judgment on the persistent claim by Amyraut that his teaching was consistent with the emphases of Calvin. On the basis of all that I have learned I would maintain that his claim is substantially correct. He frankly admitted that his almost exclusive emphasis on the conditional will of God is different from that of Calvin, but insisted that Calvin, too, taught this conditional will. He documented his argumentation well enough to prove his claim. Furthermore, the various positions that he defended by means of this teaching on the conditional will are surely positions Calvin himself had propounded. Calvin, too, taught that Christ died for all men. Calvin, too, taught that the benefits of Christ's death are only potential until our *insitio in Christum* through faith. Calvin, too, taught that predestination must be properly discussed under the work of the Spirit. And Calvin, too, taught that predestination is only a legitimate topic in theology as an *ex post facto* explanation of the work of grace. On the doctrines of justification and faith Amyraut made less of a point of his affinity with Calvin's teachings, but the affinities remain just the same. While there is room for a more detailed comparison of these two theologies, at the points which we have studied it is clear that Amyraut showed a knowledge of and insight into Calvin's theology that was unique in his century.

REFERENCE MATTER

APPENDIX 1
A Note on Amyraut's Rationalism

THE PROBLEM OF AMYRAUT'S RATIONALISM is both complicated and baffling (at least to this writer). In chapter 4 we have shown that he is very acutely aware of the limitations of man's reason in relation to God. Yet in that same chapter, pp. 179ff., we have indicated that his *Brief Traitté de la predestination* contains a strong rationalistic element. Rex and Sabean have shown that his *De l'élévation de la foy et de l'abaissement de la raison en la créance des mystères de la religion* of 1640 is an attack on the fideism of the Roman Catholic theologians by means of an assertion of the reliability of reason. Rex has noted that in this work Amyraut "divides all the main Christian doctrines into separate categories according to the degree to which they are discernable to reason" (*Essays on Pierre Bayle and religious controversy*, p. 103). Sabean surveys a larger corpus of Amyraut material and concludes in the same vein. And indeed, I would contend that the case is even stronger than Rex and Sabean have made it. For example, neither of these men has seen that Amyraut makes a very forthright use of the watch illustration usually associated with William Paley's name and the eighteenth century. Amyraut may very well be the first theologian to employ this argument. In his *Sermon sur le verset 1. du Pseaume XIV* (Saumur, 1645), pp. 24–27, he gives the following remarkable passage in order to show the folly of the atheist position:

> Presentez-leur une montre, & leur demandés s'ils croyent qu'elle s'est faite d'elle mesme, & si c'est d'elle mesme qu'elle se monte, qu'elle se demonte, que ses ressorts jouënt, & que ses rouës se remuent avec tant d'ordre & d'agilité; ils vous diront sans doute que non, et vous en allegueront incontinent la raison, c'est que

chose quelconque ne peut estre la cause de son propre estre. Car
ce qui se fait n'est point encore, & ce qui fait, est déjà. Si donc
une chose se faisoit elle mesme, il faudroit qu'elle fust, & que
neantmoins elle ne fust pas en mesme temps. Ce qui s'enveloppe
en une contradiction toute manifeste. Demandés leur si à leur
advis ceste montre s'est ainsi composée par hasard, si toutes les
pieces s'en sont ainsi trouveés toutes taillées fortuitement, puis
apres si fortuitement elles se sont agencées de la sorte, & finalement si c'est fortuitement encore qu'elles se sont ainsi liées
ensemble par certaines cordes & par certains ressorts, qui leur
donnent leurs mouvemens, de sorte que toute la machine se
remuë en mesme temps pour monstrer la distinction des heures?
& ils vous diront encore que non, & auroyent peur qu'on les
tint pour des incensés s'ils respondoyent autrement. Car tout le
monde sçait que ce sont les hommes qui les font, & qu'estant
impossible que le hasard ait joint ensemble tant de parties avec
tant d'art, il faut necessairement que l'operation de quelque
cause doüée d'intelligence y soit intervenuë. De là venés à leur
demander s'ils croyent qu'il y ait moins d'art en la constitution
de monde qu'en celle d'une montre; Si le mouvement d'eguille
qui marque la distinction des heures, est plus reglé que celuy
du soleil qui les fait; si les roües dont le mouvement depend
sont plus artificielles que les spheres celestes: si le ressort qui
les fait tourner est mieux & plus reglement tendu, pour les faire
mouvoir vingt-quatre ou trente heures seulement, que la puissance qui meut si constamment depuis tant de siecles? toute
cette machine celeste? en un mot si la distribution des jours, des
mois, & des années, découvre moins de sapience, que ne fait
la distinction des parties ausquelles une montre a partagé son
mouvement, & ils seront contraints de vous confesser que le
monde est sans comparaison mieux composé que toutes les plus
belles machines de la terre. Venés vous puis apres à leur demander si donc ils croyent que c'est une intelligence qui l'a fait
ou non, ou ils hesitent en respondant, ou tout à fait ils le nient.
Je vous prie, Freres bien-aimés, ceux qui courent les ruës peu-
vent-ils avoir de plus extravagantes imaginations, ni des senti-
mens plus contradictoires? Ou qu'ils nient qu'il soit besoin
d'une intelligence pour former ces belles machines dont je viens
de vous parler; & alors on leur marquera une chambre dans les
hospitaux des insensés; ou qu'ils reconnoissent que c'est une
intelligence souverainne qui a construit cet Univers, s'ils ne
veulent passer pour des gens tout a fait indignes qu'on s'arreste
à eux, ni qu'on s'y arraisonne. Ouy mais, disent-ils, il est bien
certain que la montre n'a peu se faire ni d'elle mesme ni par
hasard, & quainsi il faut que ce soit un homme qui l'ait faite,
pource que ce n'est pas un ouvrage de la Nature. . . .

It will be recognized here that Amyraut used the watch illustration not only to prove the creation of the world, but also its continual governance by some intelligent being. We believe this passage compares well with any such statement in Paley.

Finally, another aspect both Rex and Sabean have left untouched, and which ties in closely with this rationalistic element in Amyraut, is his teaching on natural law. A great admirer of Cicero, it may be that Amyraut learned his natural-law teaching from the Stoics. In any event, natural law is the basis of much of what he has to say about politics, family, and ethics. His writings on these topics are full of such terminology as "la Nature," "le droit de la Nature," "jus naturae," "leges naturae," "jus Gentium," "la loi de la Nature," etc. For example, he states that he purposed to build his discussion in the elaborate *La Morale chrestienne* by applying the teachings given by revelation upon "les fondemens de la Nature" (1:5ff.). He has entitled a treatise on marriage *Consideration sur les droicts par laquelle la nature a reiglé les mariages*. In his *Discours de la souveraineté des roys* he argues that even as "la nature donne au pere sur ses enfans une autorite Royale" so nature has given the king the same right over his people (p. 23ff.). We are not sure of all of the ramifications of these elements in his thought, but it should be recognized that they exist.

APPENDIX 2
A Note on Amyraut Research

THE SEVENTEENTH-CENTURY INTELLECTUAL TRADITION of the Calvinist Churches has received very little scholarly notice. In the light of this, and comparatively speaking, the life and work of Amyraut have received considerable attention. Most of this research has not been widely disseminated, however, and the bulk of the work exists as unpublished theses and dissertations. The following remarks are meant to indicate some of the more important research and to give a brief indication of its strengths and weaknesses.

Before proceeding to this task perhaps a few general comments are necessary. With few exceptions, the studies before 1900 are polemic in nature. Amyraut's teaching was regarded by international Calvinism as a dangerous leaven and so was frequently combatted (e.g., see the section in the bibliography entitled "Opponents of Amyraldianism" and the treatises by W. Cunningham, A. Gibb, A. A. Hodge, C. Hodge, M. Leydecker, H. M. B. Reid and G. S. Smeaton). These opponents of Salmurian theology have influenced most thinking about Amyraut and their legacy is apparent in most of the present-day references to Amyraldian theology in encyclopedias, histories of doctrine, etc. This misrepresentative view of Amyraut has also affected some of the major studies.

In 1856 the Zurich theologian Alexander Schweizer published volume 2 of his *Die Protestantischen Centraldogmen in ihrer entwicklung innerhalb der reformierten Kirche*. On pages 225–438 he discussed Salmurian theology. This is the first really major explication of the thought of Amyraut. Schweizer had at his disposal in the Zurich archives one of the finest collections of Amyraut and related materials available anywhere. Furthermore his training under the great Schleiermacher provided him with the theological approach necessary to understand the historically oriented theology of Amyraut. Consequently his work has remained the classic presentation of Amyraldianism. The combination of historical research and theological insight make this a very important presentation even today.

The bulk of Schweizer's discussion is a very judicious analysis of representative treatises by both Cameron and Amyraut. These analyses retain their value. They are the main strength of his study. There are, however, several weaknesses in Schweizer's study. The most serious of these is his failure to see that all of the Salmurian theology must be understood in terms of the covenant teaching. Though he has noticed that Cameron in 1608 maintained at Heidelberg his theses *De triplici Dei cum homine foedere,* he makes nothing more of this than to note that Reformed theology customarily taught only a twofold covenant. His interpretation of Amyraldianism is limited on two other counts. First, his article in Baur's *Jahrbücher* has the self-explanatory title, "Moses Amyraldus: Versuch einer Synthese des Universalismus und des Partikularismus" (*Theologische Jahrbücher* [Tübingen, 1852], pp. 41–101, 155–207). If it is true that Amyraut envisioned his theology as a wedding of universalism and particularism, such a consideration was only secondary. At bottom, his theology is both more original and more radical than a mere attempt to synthesize two opposing views on the extent of the atonement.

Secondly, Schweizer's insistence that Amyraut developed his universalist teaching "only in order to be able better to maintain a strict particularism" is too forced to demand serious consideration. Beyond these two criticisms of his interpretation, it also appears that Schweizer's discussion is too strongly conditioned by his equation of Amyraut with the orthodox position. So, for example, he apparently misses emphases of Amyraut, such as that we should not assume an *ipso facto* relationship between the extent of Christ's sacrifice and its application. Finally, for our purposes Schweizer has not given serious enough consideration to Amyraut's claim that his own emphases are true to Calvin's, and that the orthodox teaching is not a proper representation of Calvin himself. Excellent descriptively, Schweizer's study is not of real value in interpreting Amyraut's theology and showing its place in the history of Protestant thought.

After Schweizer's study it was almost a century before another substantial attempt was made to investigate and interpret Amyraut. This came in a 1951 doctoral dissertation at the University of Göttingen by Jürgen Moltmann, under the supervision of O. Weber ("Gnadenbund und Gnadenwahl: Die Prädestinationslehre des Moyse

Amyraut, dargestellt im Zusammenhang der heilsgeschichtlich-foederal theologischen Tradition der Akademie von Saumur"). A beneficiary of the *heilsgeschichtlich* trend and thinking in modern theology, Moltmann was thereby well equipped to interpret this vital element in Amyraut's theology. Consequently he has given us the theologically most important study of Amyraut to date. Indeed, knowledge of his study is certainly necessary for anyone doing further Amyraut research.

Moltmann's main contribution comes in showing that Amyraut's theology cannot be understood without an educated awareness of the dynamic role of the covenant idea, that the basic misunderstanding of Amyraut through all previous research has stemmed from an ignorance of the radically historico-empirical orientation of his theology and the corollary concept that there is a discernible progression in God's revelation of his plan of salvation (see especially chapter 6, part 4, "Der Offenbarungsempirismus an Stelle der aristotelischen Logik in Formalprinzip seiner Theologie," and part 5, "Der heilsgeschichtliche Aufriss seiner Theologie, verdeutlicht an der Historisierung des Gesetzbundes"). But perhaps the major emphasis in Moltmann's dissertation is revealed in the title "Gnadenbund und Gnadenwahl." That is, he has seen well the teaching of Amyraut on the twofold will of God and argues that these two parts are to be understood as standing in dialectic, that Amyraut does not include predestination within the covenant of grace. Though he is not entirely accurate in this analysis (see our discussion in chapter 4), he has been the first to follow, in the main, Amyraut's argumentation. This insight of Moltmann's is most important in trying to understand Amyraut's doctrine of predestination. He has also recognized the important part Amyraut's doctrine of the economic Trinity plays in his theology.

Despite these indispensable insights, Moltmann's study has some shortcomings. Beyond the fact that the format of the dissertation is garbled, often differing from the table of contents, both his statements of fact and his original-source quotations are sometimes inaccurate. Certainly one can never quote Amyraut through Moltmann. Yet even though he deals with texts in this cavalier fashion, it is my judgment that his study is consummately accurate. I know of no interpreter of Amyraut who has so well comprehended the heart of Amyraut's theological formulations, even though he must be used with extreme caution on any particular point.

The year after Moltmann completed his study at Göttingen, Lawrence Proctor presented his doctoral dissertation at the University of Leeds, England, on Amyraldian theology ("The Theology of Moise Amyraut Considered as a Reaction Against Seventeenth Century Calvinism"). This is the first substantial study in English devoted to the thought and work of Amyraut, and is a worthy effort. Dr. Proctor shows a working familiarity with the great bulk of the writings of Amyraut. He has given a thorough delineation of the topics of sin, predestination, and atonement as contained in these writings. He has also presented a valuable and thorough description of the three main opponents of Amyraut, Pierre du Moulin, André Rivet, and Friedrich Spanheim. In fact, his is the most thorough treatment of these three opponents that has yet been given, much more comprehensive than my own. For these reasons Proctor's study has to be ranked as one of the better overall descriptions of Amyraut's thought, superior to those of Laplanche and Schweizer in theological insight, and more comprehensive and better organized than Moltmann's.

Dr. Proctor's dissertation has much in common with my own study. I did not discover it until my original draft had been completed, and for this reason it may well be regarded as a good complement to what I have done. Because of the similarity of our judgments, I should like to give a more extended analysis of Proctor's study than I would otherwise have given.

I would judge that there are at least two rather serious short-comings in Proctor's study. The first of these is that it is little more than a simple description of the teachings of Amyraut and the ortho-dox answers to them. It is true that, as the title of his work indicates, Proctor recognizes the necessity of understanding the thought of Amyraut as it developed in reaction to seventeenth-century Calvinist doctrine. Indeed, he even makes the claim that "in this thesis we shall be concerned to a great extent with the strong link between the teaching of Amyraut and original Calvinism" (p. 35). In spite of these promising indications, however, there is very little actual ma-terial which makes the necessary three-way comparison. In fact, the material comparing the thought of Amyraut and Calvin is very scanty, with references to Calvin's writings almost entirely absent. The references that are present are based primarily on two of the weaker secondary writers on Calvin: A. M. Hunter and R. N. Carew-Hunt (Hunter, *The Teaching of Calvin,* 2nd ed. [London, 1950] and Hunt, *Calvin* [London, 1933]). The way in which he uses material from writers representing seventeenth-century Calvinism makes it clear that Proctor has best stated his purpose when he declares that ". . . our aim in this study is to reach a judgement concerning the extent to which Amyraut departed from the Calvinism of his day, . . ." (p. 115). But his methodology leads one to conclude that his criterion of judgment would be, not a development of orthodox Calvinist doctrine and then an evaluation of Amyraut in the light of such a development, but rather an explication of those areas in which the opponents of Amyraut took issue with him. Thus, in reality, his study is a description of Amyraldian teaching with reference to orthodox Calvinist criticisms. He has not attempted to interpret Amyraldian thought against the broader background of orthodox Calvinist thought. It must be said that as a whole the work is disappointing, if one is looking for an interpretive analysis of the thought of Amyraut as a reaction to seventeenth-century Calvinism.

The second major shortcoming of Proctor's study is his failure to recognize the determinative role that covenant teaching had for the whole of Amyraut's thought. He does discuss covenant teaching in chapter 7 under the rubric of the possibility of salvation outside of the Christian religion, but this discussion is quite weak. He was apparently ignorant of Moltmann's work at Göttingen, from which he could have received some direction. He was also evidently not aware of Amyraut's 1634 theses on the covenant in the *Theses Salmurienses* and consequently unable to present this facet of Amyraut's thought coherently. And, most surprisingly, he played down the separation Amyraut made between the Mosaic covenant and the evangelical covenant, claiming that "There were no important objections expressed against this part of Amyraut's doctrine by his chief contemporary critics" (p. 270). This remark overlooks the importance of Amyraut's formulation of this point, and again serves to point up Proctor's unsatisfactory method—his dependence upon contemporary criticisms as the chief measuring stick of the significance of Amyraut's thought. Obviously this approach fails to take into account the possibility that Amyraut was misunderstood by his contemporary critics, a possibility which I believe I have shown to be a most distressing reality.

As he indicates, Dr. Proctor has dealt with three main topics in his work: "They are (A) the doctrine of Predestination, to which Calvinists all over Europe in the seventeenth century were devoting much attention. (B) The doctrine of Atonement, with special reference to the extent of the Work of Christ. (C) The possibility of salvation outside the Christian religion" (p. 41). His description of these three topics gives a good picture of Amyraut's teaching on these points.

In chapters 2, 3, and 4 Dr. Proctor discusses Aryraut's teaching on predestination. He maintains that the divergences from Calvinism on this topic were minor, the major problem arising because Amyraut discussed the act of faith in current psychological terms. He has apparently not seen the revolutionary implications of Amyraut's refusal to regard predestination as discussible as a part of the doctrine of God. His exposition of the various elements of Amyraut's doctrine of predestination is unusually reliable and accurate, but he has no appreciation for the critique of orthodox Calvinism that Amyraut was attempting in his unique formulation of this doctrine. So Proctor concludes that it was not on the matter of predestination that Amyraut seriously departed from Calvinist theology, but rather on the doctrine of atonement (p. 200).

As he develops his discussion of Amyraut's doctrine of the atonement in chapters 5 and 6, Proctor presents what I would judge to be the most substantial contribution of his entire study. There is an especially fine discussion of the two parts, or in Proctor's terminology "moments," of God's will. He points out that Amyraut's design was to exalt the mercy of God and that in this practice "the thought of Amyraut should probably be regarded as nearer to the views of Calvin than to that of his contemporaries in Calvinism" (p. 240). Also, that Amyraut "was seeking to recover for Reformed Scholasticism the doctrines of Calvin who, as Amyraut recognised, greatly emphasized the mercy, grace and love of God" (p. 241). Proctor further rightly sees that the real opposition of the orthodox Calvinists to Amyraut's teaching on the universality of Christ's atonement arose when Amyraut insisted that God willed that Christ would die for all, that His death was *intended* for all. In a striking passage, which can well be used to strengthen my argument that there was a fundamental difference in approach between Amyraut and the orthodox, Proctor documents du Moulin's rejection of the idea of God's universal desire or will: that it was "in conflict with the eternal decree of reprobation" (p. 255). However, Proctor's discussion suffers from missing the dynamic of Amyraut's equation of the two moments of God's will to the work of the Son and the work of the Holy Spirit, respectively.

Chapter 7 is the least valuable of Proctor's analysis. Here he discusses the offer of salvation to all men, apart from the gospel proclamation. He correctly concludes that "we need to recognize that Amyraut did not teach that some may be saved apart from Christ and his work for men" (p. 285). Yet he does not discuss in depth or with perception Amyraut's idea that the revelation of God in nature is sufficient to save if man would avail himself of it, but that sin has precluded this possibility.

In chapter 8 Proctor presents his "historical conclusion." He properly maintains that Amyraldianism "was a theological reaction largely independent of, but akin to, that of the Arminian movement" (p. 295). His overall conclusion, which is rather good, but not fully supported by his previous discussion, is the following:

> The correct assessment of Amyraut's theology seems to be that it occupied a middle position between seventeenth-century Calvinism on the one hand and Arminianism on the other. That is the conclusion to which this investigation has brought us. . . . It appears that Amyraut found the Calvinism of his period an unacceptable version of the theology of John Calvin. At the same time, he was not satisfied with the Arminian alternative. He felt the need both to retain certain elements of Calvinist theology which the Arminians had abandoned and to do justice to ethical considerations such as the Arminians had emphasized. The result can scarcely be termed a compromise between the two theological systems. It is rather to be regarded as an attempt to deal with the problems, which Arminius had faced, by resorting to theories other than those which had been found inadequate at the Synod of Dort. Indeed, we ought probably to conclude that the details of Amyraut's theology owed less to Arminianism than to original Calvinism. It is also probable that Amyraut was influenced by certain ideas of Zwingli, and the doctrines of Lutheranism (mediated perhaps through the theologians of Western Germany and John Cameron), as well as by pre-Reformation theology (p. 311).

In summary, Proctor's study is a useful manual of the teaching of Amyraut on the crucial topics of predestination and the atonement. It is weak in theological insight and perspective, true, but quite sound in the interpretive judgments expressed. Moreover, it is particularly valuable as a presentation of how Amyraut was understood by contemporary orthodox Calvinists. Proctor's basic interpretation is complementary to my own; thus there is quite a good deal of material in his study which may be profitably consulted in substantiation of the interpretation here.

Two other published volumes appeared in 1951 and 1952 which deserve mention. The first was volume 2 of Hans Emil Weber's *Reformation, Orthodoxie und Rationalismus* (Gütersloh, 1951. Pages 128–46 are of particular interest.) Weber, in his characteristically thorough and informed manner, deals with most of Amyraut's teachings. He notes the historical dimension of Amyraut's thought, pointing out the orthodox lack of appreciation for this element in theology (p. 135). He also argues that at "Saumur there was a humanistic heritage" and that "universalism became its symbol (*Doku-ment*)" (p. 135). But the special interest of Weber is what he calls the "intellectualistic psychologism" and the "psychologico-moralistic" inclination of this theology. He develops Amyraut's teaching that the intellect is absolute master in man, that the will always follows the intellect, and that the intellect inevitably chooses what it perceives to be true, useful, agreeable, and honest. This he maintains leads to a "*Gnadendeterminismus.*" He sees this as a departure from Calvinist teaching.

In 1952 Max Geiger's *Die Basler Kirche und Theologie im Zeitalter der Hochorthodoxie* appeared in Zurich, in which account is taken of Amyraldian teaching (pp. 99–118). Geiger is especially useful, for he compares Amyraut's theology at all times with the Canons of Dort and with Turrettini's *Institutio theologiae elencticae*. As a result of this comparison he judges that there is no significant difference between Amyraut and the orthodox on "hypothetical universalism." But where Geiger does see Amyraut "overturning a central pillar" of the Reformed theology is in what he calls the "*stark intellektu-alistischen Verständnis des Glaubens*" (p. 114). He believes that Amyraut has lost the dynamic of Cameron's corrective doctrine of *persuasio,* arguing that Amyraut defined faith as simply "to be persuaded of the truth of anything." If this were true, there would be good cause to say that Amyraut had reduced faith to a purely rational act, to the acceptance of rationally demonstrable truth alone. Geiger is correct in saying that Amyraut at times speaks of faith in these terms. I have shown in chapter 6 that this is not his full teaching on the nature of faith, however. Nevertheless it is certain that his ambiguity at this point is a serious theological blunder—a point at which he comes very close to Zanchi's doctrine as described in chapter 1.

In 1961 David Sabean presented his Master's thesis at the University of Wisconsin under the title "Moise Amyraut and Rationalism" (see bibliography for a published condensation of this). In this study Sabean very clearly sets forth the rational tendencies in Amyraut's thought. It is a valuable work, though in the final analysis only introductory to, and descriptive of, this aspect of Amyraut's thought. In appendix 1 I have presented a passage which is in some ways even more remarkable as an evidence of rationalism than what Sabean presents. Sabean's basic contribution is in distinguishing the "fideist" (indeed even sceptical) position of the Roman Catholic polemicists and Amyraut's boldly asserted principle of the basic rationality of the Christian religion and of the ability of man to comprehend God's revelation. He shows that Amyraut stresses the intellect as man's sole guide in matters of religion, that even the acceptance of the gospel message is an activity of the intellect. This all needs to be compared with the findings of the present study.

Also in 1961 Richard Stauffer's "Moïse Amyraut: Un Précurseur français de l'oecuménisme" appeared in *Eglise et Théologie* (Dec., 1961), pp. 13–49 (also published separately; see bibliography). This is a remarkably well-informed study, setting Amyraut's church-union efforts in the larger context of his basic theological position. Stauffer also gives an unusually fine critical analysis and evaluation of Amyraut's treatises on, and work for, church union. This aspect of Amyraut's thought has been thought by some to be the key to his whole theological program. I agree with this in part, and so consider Stauffer's article to be of prime significance.

In 1965 Walter Rex published at The Hague a somewhat shortened version of his 1956 Harvard dissertation on the forces that shaped the thought of Pierre Bayle (*Essays on Pierre Bayle and religious controversy*). This study may be regarded as an attempt to revise the classic interpretation of Bayle as a "sceptic," inasmuch as Rex traces Bayle's "liberal" ideas to their probable source in Salmurian theology. Or, seen from the other side, it may be regarded as an attempt to show that there were forces at work within Calvinism itself which directly contributed to the rise of the Enlightenment. In any event Rex's study deserves mention here, since he has devoted many pages to the rationalism of Cameron and Amyraut (pp. 19–40 and 136–64). Rex has an especially valuable discussion of the important term *persuasio* in Cameron, correctly showing that Cameron distinguished carefully between *suasio* and *persuasio*. Beyond his rather unique treatment of this idea of *persuasio,* Rex's overall judgments are characteristically sound, though he shows himself somewhat of a stranger to the sophisticated theology of the seventeenth century. He, like Sabean in the article cited above, failed to use the article by Moltmann and also missed the importance of the covenant idea in Amyraldianism. The covenant principle could perhaps have added another dimension to his claim that the Salmurian theology is strongly rationalistic, for it can be regarded as an attempt to limit God to working within a closely defined system, somewhat in the manner of the *potentia ordinata* of late medieval nominalism.

In 1965 there also appeared the exhaustive study by Father François Laplanche entitled *Orthodoxie et prédication: L'Oeuvre d'Amyraut et la querelle de la grâce universelle,* published in Paris, a revised version of his 1954 doctoral dissertation at Angers. This volume is by far the most ambitious study of Amyraut to date. Its comprehensiveness establishes it as the standard work on Amyraut's career, supplanting Schweizer's studies. Father Laplanche has divided his book into three parts: the historical and doctrinal background, an historical account of the whole controversy which arose in the Reformed world because of the Salmurian theology, and a section on Amyraut's theology and its place in Reformed thought. The first two parts are nothing short of remarkable. Especially valuable is a seventeen-page biography of Amyraut, the best available. Until this study by Laplanche all biographical sections on Amyraut were based on the article in Bayle's *Dictionnaire* (see bibliography). Laplanche, refusing to accept the Bayle account unless it could be substantiated elsewhere, constructed his biography from materials gleaned from the correspondence in various scattered manuscript collections, from the often-informative prefaces of Amyraut's works, and from occasional references in the works themselves. Beyond this, Laplanche's great contribution is a blow by blow account of the "Protestant civil war" occasioned by the publication of Amyraut's treatise on predestination. This discussion is an astonishingly complete survey and analysis of a plethora of manuscript sources and of the mass of often-rare, often-prolix published sources. Hardly enough can be said about the industry of Laplanche in this, or about the historical value of this section of his work, and I have used it extensively. Yet this second part remains almost entirely descriptive. Rarely does he make interpretive comments, and then only to point out that a certain teaching—for example, the distinction between natural and moral ability—is especially important for Amyraldian theology. In the third part of his book we find Laplanche the least helpful, indeed quite disappointing. In the first place, by casting Amyraut's theology into the traditional format under the headings "God," "man," "redemption," etc., Laplanche's discussion runs the risk of serious misrepresentation and tends to destroy what is essentially the experientially based and historically oriented character of Amyraut's theology. Secondly, this discussion introduces no new material, and so suffers from a lack of documentation from other than polemic treatises, whereas Amyraut, in a late publication on the Creed, seems to regard his paraphrases of the New Testament as the most important sources for his theology. Thirdly, this whole section seems inordinately dependent on Schweizer, and so Laplanche's interpretation of Amyraldian theology is in essence Schweizer's idea that it was framed as "an attempt at a synthesis of universalism and particularism." As pointed out, this is to miss the radicality and originality of Amyraut's

theology for the seventeenth century. Finally, the most serious weakness of this third part is that Laplanche has not used Moltmann's
study nor has he seen the importance of the covenant theology for
Amyraut. Because an apprehension of the determinative role of the
covenant idea in this theology is an absolute prerequisite for properly
understanding it, this whole section of Laplanche's work fails to
provide us with a useful evaluation. This is not to say, however, that
there is not helpful material here. Certainly it needed to be shown
that, in spite of certain verbal resemblances, Amyraut's theology is
not Arminian. Again, we needed to be reminded that this theology
can only be understood within the framework of the Protestant
scholasticism of the seventeenth century. But one could hope for a
more theologically perceptive interpretation. Despite this it is a
most important book.

Finally, special note must be made of the doctoral dissertation
completed in 1966 at Harvard by Roger Nicole, entitled "Moyse
Amyraut (1596–1664) and the Controversy on Universal Grace. First
Phase (1634–1637)." This was the product of more than a dozen years
of research and is especially noteworthy for its superb bibliography.
The critical, exhaustive, and definitive *bibliographia Amyraldiana* is
really Dr. Nicole's dissertation, comprising more than 200 of the 342
total pages. The bibliography is presented in three sections: chronological, topical, and alphabetical, all carefully cross-referenced. In
addition, he has listed every known location of Amyraut's writings.
This is an immensely useful compilation for students of Amyraldianism.

The text of the study is extremely brief, and Dr. Nicole has placed
himself in a most disadvantageous position by limiting his discussion
to the first three years of the controversy—the years 1634–37. He has
further limited himself to just three of Amyraut's writings in this
time span, his *Brief Traitté de la predestination,* his *Eschantillon de
la doctrine de Calvin,* and his *Six Sermons,* and he has given only a
very truncated synopsis of the most fully developed of these writings,
the *Six Sermons* of 1636. Finally, Professor Nicole is unfortunately an
avowed opponent of Amyraldian teaching, regarding it as "a cor-
rosive factor in the French Reformed Church" which "slowly under-
mined respect for the confessional standards and disrupted internal
unity and cohesion" (from his article in Palmer's *Encyclopedia of
Christianity* [Wilmington, Del., 1964], 1:192).

In the light of the foregoing considerations, it is not surprising
that this study does not contribute significantly to our comprehension
or understanding of Amyraldian thought. In fact, Professor Nicole

has stated that his intention was "to focus the attention particularly on the question of the extent of the atoning work of Christ" (p. 11). While it is clear that this one point of doctrine is his principal interest, nevertheless there is a large share of the material which seems to have little direct relationship to the purported focus. But what is most disappointing in all this is the failure to use this particular point of doctrine as an interpretive principle around which the discussion could have been built. Like Schweizer, Proctor, Laplanche before him, Dr. Nicole has been content to give a summary of what Amyraut said. The significance and import of his teaching is not spelled out.

Dr. Nicole, too, has failed to take into account Amyraut's covenant teaching. Though he was not unaware of Amyraut's 1634 theses on the covenants (since he carefully details them in his bibliography), he has mysteriously chosen to omit them from his discussion. He has also failed to follow up the very excellent leads supplied by Moltmann's work. This oversight means that much of the subtlety and significance of Amyraut's formulations are missed.

What has been said does not of course mean that there is no useful material in Dr. Nicole's study. In particular, on pages 21–28, there is a careful and excellent section on the stand of the Synod of Dort. In general, though, the methodology is quite commonplace and the interpretation characterized far too much by the presuppositions and positions of Amyraut's orthodox Calvinist opponents. Dr. Nicole is able to see the fixation of Pierre du Moulin, who apparently saw Arminians attacking even in his sleep, yet he is content to repeat charges originating with du Moulin which seem to have no basis in fact. (E.g., on p. 65 he repeats du Moulin's charge that Amyraut teaches a doctrine of regeneration via "moral suasion.") The text of Dr. Nicole's study is disappointing, especially in the light of his many years of research. His bibliographic work will remain a permanent and significant contribution to Amyraut research.

BIBLIOGRAPHY

I HAVE NOT ATTEMPTED an exhaustive listing of works relating to the topics discussed in this book, but have included only those works consulted and found useful. On the other hand, I have attempted a reasonably thorough *bibliographia Amyraldiana*. I have listed every work I knew by Amyraut, basing my list on Haag-Bordier. Roger Nicole's recent work is, however, much more complete and will I hope be made available to the scholarly public.

Amyraut's works here have been divided into three sections: Major Treatises, Sermons, and Paraphrases. The entries under each category are listed chronologically. The volumes I have not been able to consult or locate are marked with an asterisk: for example, **Cent Cinquante Sonnets chrestiennes*. Because Amyraut volumes are quite rare, I have added locations for those whose location is known. In addition to symbols used in the National Union Catalog, Library of Congress system, the following have been used:

Bl.	Öffentlich-wissen-schaftliche Bibliothek, Berlin.
BM.	British Museum.
BN.	Bibliothèque Nationale, Paris.
Dr. W.	Dr. Williams Library, London.
Edin.	New College Library, Edinburgh.
Gt.	Niedersächsische Staats- und Universitätsbibliothek, Göttingen.
Leeds	Brotherton Library, Leeds, England.
Ox.	Bodleian Library, Oxford.
Vaud	Library of the free faculty of theology, Lausanne, Switzerland.
Strass.	Bibliothèque Nationale et Universitaire, Strasbourg.
Sion Coll.	Sion College Library, London.
Zr.	Zentralbibliothek, Zurich.

PRIMARY SOURCES

CALVIN

Calvin, John. *Calvini opera selecta.* Edited by P. Barth and G. Niesel. 5 vols. Munich: Kaiser, 1926–36. The best critical edition of Calvin's 1559 *Institutio* and other selected works. All references to the *Institutio* in this book are to this edition.

———. *Calvin's New Testament Commentaries.* Edited by D. W. and T. T. Torrance. 12 vols. Grand Rapids: Eerdmans, 1959–68.

———. *Concerning the Eternal Predestination of God.* Translated by J. K. S. Reid. London: James Clarke & Co., 1961.

———. *Institutes of the Christian Religion.* Edited by J. T. McNeill, translated and indexed by F. L. Battles. 2 vols. The Library of Christian Classics, vols. 20, 21. Philadelphia: The Westminster Press, 1960. Excellent critical edition, exceptionally well annotated, the translation sometimes clumsy.

———. *Institution de la religion chrestienne.* Edited by Jean-Daniel Benoit. 5 vols. Paris: J. Vrin, 1957–63. Modern critical French edition of the 1560 French translation.

———. *Institution de la religion chrestienne.* Edited by J. Pannier. 4 vols. Paris: Société des belles lettres, 1936–39. A critical edition of the 1541 French translation by Calvin, helpfully annotated. Especially apropos for this study, for Amyraut quotes this edition of Calvin almost exclusively.

———. *Instruction in Faith.* 1537. Edited and translated by P. T. Fuhrmann. Philadelphia: Westminster Press, 1949.

———. *Joannis Calvini opera quae supersunt omnia.* Edited by G. Baum; E. Cunitz; and E. Reuss. 59 vols. Corpus Reformatorum, vols. 29ff. Brunswick: Schwetschke, 1863–1900.

———. *On Secret Providence.* Translated by James Lillie. New York, 1840.

BEZA

Beza, Theodore. *Correspondance.* Collected by H. Aubert. Edited by F. Aubert; H. Meylan; A. Dufour; and A. Tripet. 5 vols. to date. Geneva: Droz, 1960–.

———. *De praedestinationis doctrina et vero usu tractatio absolutissima. Excerpta Th. Bezae praelectionibus in nonum epistolae ad Romanos caput.* Geneva, 1582.

———. *Opera.* 3 vols. Geneva, 1583.

CAMERON

Cameron, John. *An examination of those plausible Appearances which seeme most to commend the Romish Church, and to prejudice the Reformed.* Oxford, 1626.

——. *A tract of the soveraigne judge.* Oxford, 1628.

——. "Deux lettres de Jean Cameron à Duplessis-Mornay." *Bulletin de la société de l'histoire du protestantisme français* 23 (1874), 503–6.

——. *Joannis Cameronis Scoto Britanni Theologi Eximij* TA ΣΩZOMENA *siue Opera partim ab auctore ipso edita, partim post eius obitum vulgata, partim nusquam hactenus publicata, vel è Gallico Idiomate nunc primùm in Latinam linguam translata.* Edited by F. Spanheim. Geneva: In Officina Jacobi Chouet, 1642.

——. "Trois lettres inédites de J. Cameron." *Bulletin de la société de l'histoire du protestantisme français* 50 (1901), 158–64.

AMYRAUT

Major Treatises on Various Topics

Amyraut, Moïse. **Cent Cinquante Sonnets chrestiens.* Paris, 1625.

——. **Hymne de la puissance divine.* Paris, 1625.

——. *Traitté des religions contre ceux qui les estiment toutes indifferentes.* Divisé en trois partes. Saumur: Girard & de Lerpiniere, 1631. Zr. Bl. NjPT. BM. Dr.W. OCU. Strass. Leeds. Enl. ed. Saumur: J. Lesnier, 1652. Vaud. NNUT. DLC. CtY. NjNbs. NjPT. MH. English trans. *A Treatise Concerning Religions, In Refutation of the Opinion which accounts all Indifferent.* London: M. Simons, 1660. NNUT-Mc. PHC. ICU.

——. **Lettre du synode national des églises réformées de France, présentée au roi. Ensemble la harangue faite à sa majesté à Compiègne, le 16 septembre 1631, par les sieurs A. et de Vilars, députez dudit synode.* n.p., 1631.

——. *Theses theologicae de sacerdotio Christi.* Saumur: J. Lesnier & I. Desbordes, 1633. NjPT. NjNbs.

——. *Brief Traitté de la predestination et de ses principales dependances.* Saumur: J. Lesnier, 1634. Dr.W. NjPT. Vaud. Zr. Bl. New rev. and corr. ed. *Brief Traité de la predestination. Avec l'eschantillon de la doctrine de Calvin sur le mesme suiet. Et la response a M. de l. M. sur la matiere de la grace et autres questions de theologie.* Saumur: Chés Isaac Desbordes, 1658. NjPT. MH. The pagination in this volume is very inaccurate.

——. *Eschantillon de la doctrine de Calvin, touchant la predestina-*

tion. Prefaced to *Six Sermons*. Saumur: C. Girard & D. de Lerpiniere, 1636. NjPT. BM. Vaud. Zr. Gt. Bl.

————. *Lettre de Monsieur Amyraut, a Monsieur de la Milletière.
Sur son escrit contre Monsieur du-Moulin*. Saumur: Isaac Desbordes, 1637. Ox.

————. *De la justification contre les opinions de Monsieur de la
Milletiere. Où sont examinées les raisons de l'eglise romaine sur
cette maniere, & la doctrine des evangeliques defenduë contre elles.*
Saumur: Lesnier & Desbordes, 1638. Vaud. Dr.W. MWA. WU. Zr.

————. *Du merite des oeuvres contre les opinions de Monsieur de la
Milletiere. Où les raisons des evangeliques sur ce suiet, sont main-
tenuës contre ses exceptions, & celles de l'église romaine refutées.*
Saumur: Lesnier & Desbordes, 1638. Vaud. Dr.W. Zr. WU.

————. *Replique a M. de la Milletiere sur son offre d'une conference
amiable pour l'examen de ses moyens de reunion, où sont traittées
diverses questions theologiques.* Charenton: I. Dedieu, 1638. Vaud.
Dr.W. See also Amyraut, *Brief Traitté*, 1634.

————. *Theses theologicae de providentia Dei in malo*. Saumur: J.
Lesnier, 1638. Zr. Strass.

————. *De l'elevation de la foy et de l'abaissement de la raison, en la
creance des mysteres de la religion*. Saumur: J. Lesnier, 1640. Zr.
Reprint. Saumur, 1641. 2d ed. Charenton, 1644. A Marie . . .
duchesse de la Tremoille. IWU. Strass. 2d ed. reprint. Charenton,
1645.

————. *Defensio doctrinae J. Calvini de absoluto reprobationis decreto*. Saumur: D. Lesnier, 1641. Zr. Gt. Dr.W. BN. Strass. French
trans. *Defense de la doctrine de Calvin. Sur le sujet de l'election
et de la reprobation*. Saumur: Isaac Desbordes, 1644. A messieurs
de l'Eglise en laquelle je sers au ministere de l'evangile a Saumur.
NjPT. Strass. Gt.

————. *Syntagma thesium theologicarum in academia Salmuriensi
variis temporibus disputatorum*. Saumur, 1641, in 2 vols. Saumur,
1653, in 3 vols. Saumur, 1664, in 4 vols. Saumur, 1665, in 4 vols.
Geneva, 1665, in 4 vols. MWA. PPPM. NNUT. NjPT. This collection contains theses by Amyraut, Cappel, and de la Place. There
are sixty theses sustained by Amyraut at various times. Most are
polemic treatises against some point of Roman Catholic doctrine,
though there are important theses on the covenant, faith, and the
Church. The collection is referred to in this book by the short title
used in the 1641 printing, *Theses Salmurienses*.

————. *Mosis Amyraldi dissertationes theologicae quatuor*. Saumur:

I. Desbordes, 1645. BM. Dr.W. Zr. 2d ed., with two additional dissertations. *Dissertationes theologicae sex,* 1660.

————. *Fidei Mosis Amyraldi, circa errores arminianorum declaratio.* Saumur: J. Lesnier, 1646. NjPT. NNUT. Bl. French trans. of first 17pp. *La creance de Moyse Amyraut sur les erreurs des Arminiens.* n.p., n.d. BN. BM. Apparently there is an English translation in manuscript of the latter in Quick's *Icones.* Dr.W.

————. *Discours de l'estat des fideles apres la mort.* Saumur: Jean Lesnier, 1646. NjPT. NNUT. NjP. NjNbs. BM. [2d ed.] Saumur: J. Lesnier, 1657. Dr.W. Strass. Zr. English trans. *The Evidence of things not seen, or Diverse Scriptural, and Philosophical Discourses; Concerning the State of Good and Holy men after Death.* London: Tho. Cockerill, n.d. NjPT. BM. MH. CtY. German trans. *Betrachtungen uber den Zustand der Gläubigen nach dem Tode.* Leipzig, 1696. NjPT.

————. **Exercitatio de gratia Dei universali.* Saumur, 1647.

————. *Apologie pour ceux de la religion sur les sujets d'aversion que plusieurs pensent avoir contre leur personne et leur religion.* Saumur: I. Desbordes, 1647. NNUT. Dr.W. CtY. Strass. [2d ed.] Charenton: Samuel Petit, 1648. A Monsieur Monsieur Sarrau, conseiller du Roy en son Parlement. NjPT. NNUT.

————. *Disputatio de libero hominis arbitrio.* Saumur: J. Lesnier, 1667 [in reality 1647]. NjPT. Dr.W. NNUT. IU. Gt. Zr.

————. *Moses Amyraldi de secessione ab ecclesia romana deque ratione pacis inter evangelicos in religionis negotio constituendae, disputatio.* Saumur: I. Desbordes, 1647. Ad Illustrissimum & Potentissimum Principem Guilielmum VI. Hessiae Landgravium. BM. MH. Dr.W. Gt. [2d ed.] N.p., n.d. Strass. NNUT. Apparently there was also a German translation published at Cassel in 1649.

————. *Mosis Amyraldi considerationes in caput vii epistolae Pauli apostoli ad Romanos.* Saumur: J. Lesnier, 1648. Ad clarissimum et reverendum virum, D. G. Rivetum Chamvernonium, Taleburgensis ecclesiae pastorem. BN. NNUT. Dr.W. Bl.

————. *Specimen animadversionum in exercitationes de gratia universali.* Saumur: J. Lesnier, 1648. BN. BM. CtY. Edin.(2). Vaud. Dr.W. Gt. The first 113 pp. are the "Ad reverendos viros, Ecclesiarum in Gallia Reformatarum Pastores, Mosis Amyraldi Apologetica Praefatio."

————. *Considerations sur les droits par lesquels la nature a reiglé les mariages.* Saumur: Isaac Desbordes, 1648. A Monseigneur le Goux, Seigneur de la Berchere, &c. Premier President au Parlement de Grenoble. Gt. BM. Vaud. NNUT. Dr.W. NjPT. Strass. Latin trans. by Reinhold. *Moysis Amyraldi theol. et philosophi claris-simi de jure naturae quod connubia dirigit dispositiones sex ex gallica versae a Bern. Stade: H. Brammerum, 1712. 2d printing. 1717.

——. Six livres de la vocation des pasteurs. Saumur: J. Lesnier, 1649. Au Tres-Haut et Tres-illustre Prince, Monseigneur Henry-Charles de la Trimoville, Prince de Tarente, de Talmone, &c. Bl. BM. Vaud. NNUT. Dr.W. MH-AH. Strass.

——. Adversus epistolae historicae criminationes, Mosis Amyraldi defensio. Ad reverendum virum, D. Chabrolium, Thoarsensis ec-clesiae pastorem. Saumur: J. Lesnier, 1649. Bl. NjPT. Dr.W. NNUT.

——. Ad reverendi viri, G. Riveti, ecclesiae Talleburgensis pastoris, responsoriam epistolam, Mosis Amyraldi replicatio. Saumur: I. Desbordes, 1649. NjPT. Edin. Dr.W. NNUT.

——. Discours sur la souveraineté des rois. Paris, 1650. NjPT. Vaud. NN Strass. [2d ed.] Charenton: L. Vendosme, 1650.

——. La Morale chrestienne. 6 vols. Saumur: I. Desbordes, 1652–60. A Monsieur de Villarnoul. Zr. NjPT. MH. BM. NNUT. MWA. Vaud. Dr.W. Strass. Gt.

——. Du gouvernement de l'eglise contre ceux qui veulent abolir l'usage & l'autorité des synodes. Saumur: I. Desbordes, 1653. Zr. NNUT. BM. Dr.W. Strass. Gt. *2d ed. Saumur, 1658. Avec un ap-pendice au livre du gouvernement de l'eglise où il est traité de la puissance des consistoires. Strass.

——. Du regne de mille ans, ou de la prosperité de l'eglise. Saumur: I. Desbordes, 1654. BM. NjPT. Vaud. NNUT. Strass. Gt. [2d ed.] *Leyden: Elsevier, 1655. Sion Coll. Gt. [3d ed.] Geneva, 1670. Leeds.

——. Replique au livre de Monsieur de Launay sur le regne de mille ans. Saumur: Antoine Rousselet, 1656. A Mademoiselle, Mademoiselle de la Suze. NjPT.

——. Apologie de Moyse Amyraut contre les invectives de Mr de Launay. Saumur: J. Lesnier, 1657. A Mademoiselle Mademoiselle de la Suze. Dr.W. BN.

——. Exposition du chapitre VI et VIII de l'epistre aux Romains. Charenton: Louis Vendosme, 1659. A Mademoiselle Mademoiselle de la Suze. NNUT. CtY. Zr.

——. L'Exposition du chapitre XV de la premiere epistre aux Corinthiens. Charenton: L. Vendosme, 1659. A Monsieur Monsieur Conrart, Conseiller, & Secretaire du Roy. CtY. NNUT.

——. Discours sur les songes divins dont il est parlé dans l'escriture. Saumur: I. Desbordes, 1659. A Monsieur Monsieur Gaches. NjPT.

Gt. Zr. BM. Dr.W. English trans. by J. Lowde. *A Discourse Concerning the Divine Dreams Mention'd in Scripture.* London: W. Kettilby, 1676. NjPT. BM. Dr.W. DFo. CtY. MH. CLU-C. NNUT-Mc. ICU.

————. *Dissertationes theologicae sex. Quarum quatuor De oeconomia trium personarum, De jure Dei in creaturas, De gratia Universali, De gratia particulari, antehac editae, nunc revisae prodeunt; DUAE, De serpente tentatore, Et de peccato originis, ad superiores additae sunt.* Saumur: I. Desbordes, 1660. Gt. NjPT. BM. Sion Coll.

————. *Lettre de M. Amyraut sur le sujet de quelques endroits de l'apologie de s. Etienne à ses juges.* Saumur, 1660. BM.

————. *Vie de François de la Nouë, depuis le commencement des troubles religieux en 1560 jusqu'a sa mort.* Leyden: J. Elsevier, 1661. BM.(2). NjPT. NjP. Dr.W. PU. ICN. NN CtY. Gt. WU.

————. *De mysterio trinitatis, deque vocibus ac phrasibus quibus tam in Scriptura quam apud patres explicatur, dissertatio, septem partibus absoluta.* Saumur: I. Desbordes, 1661. NjPT. BM. Edin. Dr.W. Zr. Part 4, pp. 163–241, reprinted in J. C. Wagensilius' *Telagnea Satanae.* Nuremburg: Johann Hofmenn, 1681. Frankfurt am Main: J. D. Zunner, 1681. Pp. 140–78.

————. Εἰρηνικον *sive, de ratione pacis in religionis negotio inter Evangelicos constituendae, consilium.* Saumur: I. Desbordes, 1662. Gt. Zr. NNUT. Edin.(2). MBAt. Strass. [2d ed.] *Hesse-Nassau, 1664. Part of this work was also reprinted in Jean Melet, *Syndromus irenicus de pace inter Protestantes.* Hanover, 1664. Pp. 119–69.

————. *In orationem dominicam exercitatio.* Saumur: D. de Lerpiniere, 1662. NjPT. BM. Edin. Dr.W. Zr.

————. *In symbolum apostolorum, exercitatio.* Saumur: I. Desbordes, 1663. BM. Edin. NjPT. Dr.W. Zr. Published with the preceding work as *Exercitationes duae: altera, in orationem Dominicam, in symbolum apostolorum altera.* Utrecht: Abrahamum a Paddenburg, 1767. NjPT. NNUT. NjNbs. WU.

Sermons

Amyraut, Moïse. *Six Sermons de la nature, estendue, necessité, dispensation, et efficace de l'evangile.* Saumur: C. Girard & D. de Lerpiniere, 1636. NjPT. BM. Vaud. Zr. Gt. Bl. In *Sermons sur divers textes,* 1653.

————. *Sermon sur ces mots de l'apocalypse, chap. 2. v. 17. A celuy qui vaincra, je luy donneray un caillou blanc, & en iceluy un nouveau nom escrit, lequel nul ne cognoist, sinon celuy qui le reçoit.* Charenton: Melchoir Mondiere, 1636. NjPT. Dr.W.

———. *Trois sermons sur l'epistre aux Ephesiens, ch. I. v. 16.17.18.19. & 20.* Charenton: M. Mondiere, 1639. Vaud. NjPT.

———. **Sermon sur ces mots "C'est Dieu . . ."* Saumur, 1640. In *Sermons sur divers textes,* 1653.

———. *Sermon sur le verset 55. du Chap. xv. de la premiere epistre de s. Paul aux Corinthiens.* Saumur: J. Lesnier, 1644. BM. Vaud.

———. *Sermon sur le xii verset de chap. i. de la 2. epistre a Timothée.* Charenton: N. Bourdin, 1645. BM. Strass.

———. **Sermon sur ces mots de l'apocalypse, I, 4 et 5.* Saumur, 1645. WU.

———. *Sermon sur le verset 1. du Pseaume XIV.* Saumur: J. Lesnier, 1645. NjPT. Vaud.

———. **Deux sermons sur les versets 7 et 8 du cinquiesme chaptire de la première épistre de sainct Jean, prononcés à Charenton au mois d'octobre 1645.* Saumur, 1646. In *Sermons sur divers textes,* 1653.

———. **Deux sermons, l'un sur ces mots de la Gen. (III.19), l'autre sur ces mots de Christ "En verité je vous dis" (Jean VIII.51).* Saumur, 1646.

———. *Sermons sur quelques sentences de l'ecriture.* Saumur: I. Desbordes, 1647. A Tres-haut et Tres-illustre prince, Monseigneur François-Charles de la Tremoille, Prince de Talmond, &c. NjPT. 2d printing. Saumur: I. Desbordes, 1648. Vaud. Dr.W.

———. *Sermon du voile de Moyse, sur I [sic] Cor. 3.13.14.15.16. Avec deux autres sermons sur les textes suivans.* Saumur: J. Lesnier, 1651. A Madame Madame la Baronne de Villarnoul. NjPT. BM. Strass. Dr.W.

———. *Le mystere de pieté expliqué en quatre sermons, Sur ces mots de la I. à Timothée, chap. 3. vs. 16.* Saumur: J. Lesnier, 1651. A madame madame la Marquise de Vieillavigne. NjPT. Dr.W.

———. **Sermon sur la XLIVe section du catechisme prononcé à Saumur le 3 de mars 1652.* Saumur, 1652. A mademoiselle de la Muce. 2d printing. *Saumur, 1653. Vaud.

———. *Sermons sur divers textes de la sainte ecriture.* 2d ed. Saumur: I. Desbordes, 1653. NjPT. BM. Dr.W. NjP. Zr.

———. **Un sermon sur ces paroles du prophète Jeremie, X, v.2. "Ainsi a dit l'Eternel, n'apprenez point le train des nations."* Saumur, 1654. Strass. [2d ed.] Charenton, 1654.

———. *Sermon sur ces paroles du chapitre douzieme de l'epistre aux Hebrieux, vers. 29. "Car aussi nostre Dieu est un feu consumant*

. . ." 2d ed. Saumur: I. Desbordes, 1656. A Monsieur Monsieur de Superville Docteur en medicine a Nyort. Vaud.

―――. *Melchisedec representé en quatre sermons sur le chap. vii. de l'epistre aux Hebrieux, v. 1.2. & 3.* Saumur: I. Desbordes, 1657. A madame, madame La Marquise Douairiere de la Muce. BM. Vaud. Dr.W.

―――. *Quatre sermons sur le chap. vi de l'epistre aux Hebrieux, v. 4.5. & 6.* Saumur: I. Desbordes, 1657. A madame, madame de Soucelles. BM. Vaud. Dr.W. This group of sermons was bound together with those of the preceding entry and published at Saumur in 1657 with a new title page. Gt. Dr.W.

―――. *Sermon sur ces paroles de Jesus-Christ. "Ayés la foy de Dieu . . ."* Saumur, 1657. Strass.

―――. *Cinq sermons prononcez a Charenton; ensemble un discours chrestien prononcé a Bourbon.* 3 parts. Charenton: A. Cellier, 1658. First section, A madame, madame la controlleuse generale Hervart. Third collection, A son altesse mademoiselle de Buillon. NjPT.(2). BM.

―――. *Trois sermons sur ces paroles de l'epistre aux Hebrieux, chap. 1. vers. 3. Lequelle fils estant la resplendeur de la gloire.* Charenton: A. Cellier, 1658. A son altesse mademoiselle de Buillon. BM. NjPT. These were part of the preceding entry.

―――. *Deux sermons, l'un sur ces paroles de s. Paul, I. Cor. 2.9, l'autre sur ces paroles de Christ, Jean XVI, 8-11.* Charenton: A. Cellier, 1658. A madame, madame la controlleuse generale Hervart. NjPT. In *Cinq sermons prononcez a Charenton,* 1658.

―――. *Discours chrestien sur les eaux de Bourbon.* Charenton: A Cellier, 1658. A monsieur, monsieur Amyot docteur en medecine a Gyen. NjPT. BM. Bound with *Cinq sermons prononcez a Charenton,* 1658.

―――. *Deux sermons sur la matiere de la justification et de la sanctification.* 2 parts. Saumur: I. Desbordes, 1658. A madame, madame de la Beuvriere. NjPT. Vaud. Dr.W.

―――. *Sermon sur la convalescence du Roy.* Saumur: I. Desbordes, 1658. Vaud. Dr.W. Zr.

―――. **Le Tabernacle expliquée en cinq sermons sur Hebr. 9, 2–5, avec un discours sur les habits sacrés d'Aaron.* Saumur: J. Lesnier, 1658. Vaud.

―――. **Sermon sur ces paroles de s. Paul, I Corinth. xv. 28.* Charenton: A. Cellier, 1659. BN.

―――. *Sermon sur le sujet de la paix* (Psa. 75.1–3). Saumur: I.

Desbordes, 1660. A monsieur monsieur de Vivier F.M.D.S.E. Vaud. Dr.W. [2d ed.] Charenton: O. de Varennes, 1660. Dr.W.

———. *Sermon sur la premiere epistre de s. Pierre (III.20.21.)*. Saumur: I. Desbordes, 1660. A monsieur, monsieur de la Boutetiere. Vaud. Dr.W. Also bound in *Deux sermons sur divers textes de l'escriture, Prononcés en presence du synode national assemblez a Loudun par permission du Roy le 24 Novembre mil six cens cinquante neuf*. Saumur: Desbordes, 1660. Dr.W.

———. *Le Ravissement de s. Paul (2 Cor. XII. 1–5) expliqué en quatre sermons*. Saumur: A. Rousselet, 1660. A madame, madame La Marquise de Gouvernet. NjPT. Vaud. Dr.W. Strass.

———. *Sermon sur les paroles de l'epistre de saint Paul aux Hebrieux, chap. ii. vs. 7*. Charenton: R. Rousseau, 1660. A madame, madame la Controlleuse Generale Hervart. Dr.W.

———. *Sermon sur ces Paroles de Christ, Pere, mon desir est touchant ceux lesquels tu m'as donnés, que là où je suis ils soyent aussi avec moy, afin qu'ils contemplent ma gloire. Jean XVII.24. Prononcé à Loudun, le synode y tenant, le Dimanche 11. Juin 1662*. Saumur: I. Ribotteau, 1662. A monsieur monsieur Acere. Conseiller et Secretaire du Roy, Maison et Couronne de France. Dr.W.

———. *Sermon sur la naissance de Christ. Prononcé a Saumur le jour de Noel, 1662*. Saumur: R. Pean, 1663. A monsieur, mons^r Chardon, le jeune, a Tours. NjPT.

———. *Sermon sur ces paroles, Prenés, mangés, cecy est mon corps, qui est rompu pour vous. Prononcé a Thouars le jour de Pasques, 1663*. Saumur: D. de Lerpiniere, 1663. A son Altesse Mademoiselle de la Tremoille. Dr.W.

Paraphrases

Amyraut, Moïse. *Paraphrases sur l'epistre aux Romains*. Saumur, 1644. Vaud. MH. Dr.W.

———. *Paraphrases sur l'epistre de l'apostre aux Hebrieux*. Saumur: J. Lesnier, 1645. NjPT. Vaud. Dr.W.

———. *Paraphrases sur les epistres de l'apostre s. Paul au Galates, Ephesiens, Philippiens, Colossiens, I Thessaloniciens, II Thessaloniciens*. Saumur: J. Lesnier, 1645. Vaud. Dr.W.

———. *Paraphrases sur les epistres a Timothée, a Tite, a Philemon*. Saumur: J. Lesnier, 1645. NjPT. 2d printing. Saumur, 1646. Vaud. Dr.W.

———. *Paraphrases sur les epistres catholiques de s. Jacques, s. Pierre, s. Jean, & s. Jude*. Saumur: J. Lesnier, 1646. NjPT. Dr.W. Strass.

————. *Paraphrases sur la premiere epistre de l'apostre Paul aux Corinthiens.* Saumur: J. Lesnier, 1646. NjPT. Vaud. Dr.W. Strass.

————. *Paraphrases sur le seconde epistre de l'apostre saint Paul aux Corinthiens.* Saumur: J. Lesnier, 1647. Vaud. Dr.W.

————. **Paraphrases sur les epistres aux Corinthiens.* Saumur, 1649.

————. *Paraphrase de l'evangile de Jesus Christ selon s. Jean.* Saumur: C. Girard & l'Erpiniere, 1651. NjPT. Vaud. BM. Dr.W.

————. *Paraphrases sur les actes des saintes apostres.* 2 parts. Saumur: J. Lesnier, 1653. NjPT. Dr.W.

————. *Paraphrasis in Psalmos Davidis una cum annotationibus et argumentis.* Saumur: I. Desbordes, 1662. BM. Edin. Vaud. Dr.W. Gt. Strass. ICU. NjPT. 2d ed. Utrecht, 1769. BM. NNUT. MH. NjNbs.

SUPPORTERS OF AMYRAUT

Blondel, David. *Actes authentiques des églises reformées de France, Germanie, Grande-Bretaigne, Pologne, Hongrie, Pais-Bas, etc. touchant la paix et charité fraternelle que tous les serviteurs de Dieu douient sainctement entretenir avec les protestants qui ont quelque diversité, soit d'espression, soit de méthode, soit mesme de sentiment* . . . Amsterdam, 1655. NNC. NNUT.

————. "Lettre inédite da David Blondel à Philippe Vincent, de la Rochelle, 1646," *Bulletin de la société de l'histoire du protestantisme français* 10 (1861) 385–87.

Daillé, Jean. *Joannis Dallaei Apologia pro duabus ecclesiarum in Gallia protestantium synodis nationalibus, altera Alensone, anno 1637, altera vero Carentone, anno 1645 habitis; adversus Friderici Spanhemii exercitationes de gratia universali.* Amsterdam, 1655.

————. *Joannis Dallaei vindiciae apologiae pro duabus ecclesiarum in Gallia protestantium synodis nationalibus . . . adversus Epicritam gratiam Dei universalem oppugnantem.* Amsterdam, 1657.

Le Faucheur, Michel, and Jean Mestrezat. *Lettres de Messieurs Le Faucheur et Mestrezat, escrites sur les diverses methodes qu'employent les orthodoxes pour expliquer le mystere de la predestination & la dispensation de la grace: Avec les actes dressez sur ce sujet dans les synodes nationaux d'Alençon, tenu l'an 1637. & de Charenton, l'an 1644.* n.p., n.d.

OPPONENTS OF AMYRALDIANISM

Du Moulin, Pierre. *Anatome arminianisme, seu enucleatio controversiarum quae in Belgio agitantur, super doctrinâ de providentiâ, de praedestinatione, de morte Christi, de naturâ et gratiâ, et de conversione.* Leyden, 1619. English trans. London, 1620.

———. "Autobiographie de Pierre du Moulin." *Bulletin de la société de l'histoire du protestantisme français* 7 (1858), 170–82; 333–44; 465–77.

———. *De Mosis Amyraldi adversus Fridericum Spanhemium libro judicium.* Rotterdam, 1649.

———. *Elementa logices.* Leyden. 1596. Many succeeding printings and editions.

———. *Esclaircissement des controverses Salmuriennes.* Leyden, 1648.

———. *Examen de la doctrine de MM. Amyrault & Testard.* Amsterdam, 1638.

———. *Thesaurus theologicae Sedanensis.* 2 vols. Geneva, 1661.

Jurieu, Pierre. *Traitté de la nature et de la grace.* Rotterdam, 1688.

Reveau, Georges. *Gregorii Vellei ad Pamphilium Centinium de Specimene animadversionum Mosis Amyraldi adversus Exercitationes Friderici Spanhemii de gratia universali judicium.* Leyden, 1669. NNUT. BM. Dr.W.

Rivet, André. *Andreae Riveti et Gulielmi fratrum epistolae apologeticae ad criminationes . . . Mosis Amyraldi, in praefatione . . . ad . . . pastores, praefixa Animadversionibus de gratia universali.* Breda, 1648. Dr.W.

———. *Andreae Riveti . . . synopsis doctrinae de natura et gratia. Excerpta ex Mosis Amyraldi . . . tractatu de praedestinatione et sex concionibus Gallicae editis, et Pauli Testardi . . . Eirenico . . .* Amsterdam, 1649.

———. *Operum theologicorum quae Latine edidit . . .* 3 vols. Rotterdam, 1660. Vol. 3.

Spanheim, Frederick. *Disputatio de gratia universali.* Leyden, 1644.

———. *Exercitationes de gratia universali . . .* 3 vols. Leyden, 1646.

———. *Frederici Spanhemii epistolae ad virum clarissimum Matthaeum Cottierium super conciliatione controversiae de gratia universali.* Leyden, 1648.

———. *Vindiciarum pro exercitationibus suis de gratia universali . . . adversus Amyraldi.* Amsterdam, 1649.

Turrettini, Francisco. *Institutio theologiae elencticae.* 1688. Reprinted in his *Opera.* 4 vols. Edinburgh, 1847.

GENERAL PRIMARY WORKS RELATING TO CALVINISM AND AMYRALDIANISM

Aymon, Jean. *Tous les synodes nationaux des églises réformées de France.* 2 vols. The Hague, 1710. A very important source, giving in French text the proceedings of the French Reformed synods. Needs to be compared with Quick's English translation, which is usually more reliable.

Bayle, Pierre. *Critique générale de l'histoire du Calvinisme.* Rotterdam, 1684.

———. *Dictionnaire historique et critique.* 11th ed. 20 vols. Paris, 1820. An under-valued and under-used source containing much that is still important and not readily accessible elsewhere. Bayle's judgments are characteristically reliable.

Corbière, Paul, ed. "Journal de ce qui se passa dans la ville de Alençon lors de l'affaire de MM. Testard et Amyraut." *Bulletin de la société de l'histoire du protestantisme français* 13 (1864), 39–63. An interesting, detailed account of the proceedings of the national synod of Alençon in 1637 at which Amyraut and Testard were tried for heresy. Much more detailed than Aymon or Quick, but also pro-Amyraut in tone.

De Gaultier, François. *Histoire apologétique ou défense des libertés des eglises réformées de France.* 2 vols. Amsterdam, 1688.

"Le Dernier Synode National des églises réformées avant la revocation de l'édit de Nantes. Rapport officiel du Commissaire du Roi au xxixe et dernier synode national tenu a Loudun. 1659–1660." *Bulletin de la société de l'histoire du protestantisme français* 8 (1859), 145–219.

Histoire ecclésiastique des églises réformées au royaume de France. 1580. Edition nouvelle avec commentaire, notice bibliographique et table des faits et des noms propres par feu G. Baum et par Ed. Cunitz. 3 vols. Paris: Librairie Fischbacher, 1883–89. Very fine critical edition of the most detailed of the early French Reformers' histories. Often ascribed to Theodore Beza, but his authorship is generally discounted today.

Kingdon, Robert M., and J-F Bergier, eds. *Registres de la Compagnie des Pasteurs de Genève au temps de Calvin.* 2 vols. Geneva: Librairie Droz, 1962, 1964. Important records very judiciously annotated. Annotation, unfortunately, was severely abridged in Philip Edgcumbe Hughes' English translation (Grand Rapids: Eerdmans, 1966). These records are of great importance in revising the old picture of Calvin as a heavy-handed autocrat.

Le Gendre, Philippe. *La Vie de Pierre du Bosc.* Rotterdam, 1694. An important biography of one of the outstanding proponents of Amyraldianism. Contains many valuable documents.

Quick, John. *Synodicon in Gallia reformata.* 2 vols. London, 1692. English edition of the proceedings of the French Reformed synods.

Based on better manuscripts than Aymon's edition, apparently with some semicritical collation of documents. It could profitably be critically edited, revised, and republished.

MANUSCRIPT SOURCES

Archives Tronchin. Geneva. Folios 8, 9, 26, 27, 28, 29, 38, 39, 50, 130. Important series of letters and treatises relating to the struggles in seventeenth-century Calvinism. There is much to be done in mining this collection for historical research of the relations between Geneva and French Protestantism. There are, especially, many documents yet unused relating to Louis Tronchin, a later proponent of Amyraldianism.

SECONDARY SOURCES

STUDIES OF AND REFERRING TO AMYRAUT, CAMERON, AND THE SAUMUR ACADEMY

Auzière, Louis. *Essai historique sur les facultés de théologie de Saumur et de Sedan.* Strasbourg, 1836. A very light study, but a topic with great possibilities and one which needs developing.

Bodin, Jean-François. *Recherches historiques sur la ville de Saumur.* 2 vols. Saumur, 1812, 1845. Helpful but of only secondary value for this study.

Bonet-Maury, Gaston. "Jean Cameron, pasteur de l'église de Bordeaux et professeur de théologie à Saumur et à Montauban 1579–1625." *Etudes de théologie et d'histoire publiées par MM. les professeurs de la faculté de théologie protestante de Paris* en hommage à la faculté de théologie de Montauban à l'occasion du tricentenaire de sa fondation. Paris: Librairie Fischbacher, 1901. Pp. 77–117. Contains much important detail for a life of Cameron.

———. "John Cameron: A Scottish Protestant Theologian in France." *The Scottish Historical Review* 7 (1910), pp. 325–45. An abridgement and English translation of the preceding.

Bost, Charles. "Pierre du Moulin et Amyraut." *Bulletin de la société de l'histoire du protestantisme français* 77 (1928), pp. 279–80.

Brette, Ernst. *Du système de Moyse Amirault, désigné sous le nom d'universalisme hypothétique.* Montauban, 1855.

Chevallier, Charles. *Moïse Amyraut.* Lausanne, 1864.

Cunningham, William. *Historical Theology.* 2 vols. Edinburgh, 1863. 2:323–70. Cunningham (1805–61) was a member of the Free Church in Scotland, professor of systematic theology and later principal at New College, Edinburgh. A strictly orthodox theologian whose

views are characteristic of Scottish Calvinist repudiation of the
theology of Amyraut. In the pages referred to Cunningham criticizes
Amyraldian thought on one topic, the intended extent of Christ's
atoning work on the cross. He admits that Calvin and the Westminster Confession do not explicitly teach that Jesus died only for
the elect, but regards such a teaching as the only logical position.
He has not read Amyraut but depends on Turrettini.

De Chevigny, D. *L'Eglise et l'académie protestantes de Saumur*. Saumur: P. Godot, 1914.

Drost, A. *Specimen ethico-theologicum de Moyse Amyraldo*. Amsterdam: Apud Fratres Koster, 1859. A useful manual spelling out the
moralism of Amyraut. Superior to either Marthaler or Fraissinet,
though Fraissinet's study is very useful in providing a reliable summary of Amyraut's massive *La Morale chrestienne*.

Dumont, Josephe. *Histoire de l'Académie de Saumur depuis sa fondation en 1600 par Duplessis-Mornay jusqu'à sa suppression en 1685*
. . . Angers: Cosnier and Lachèse, 1862.

————. *L'Oratoire et le cartésianisme en Anjou*. Angers, 1864.

Ebrard, J. H. A. *Handbuch der christlichen Kirchen- und Dogmengeschichte*. 3 vols. Erlangen, 1866. 3:538–52.

Erle, M. Manfred. "Le mariage dans le droit naturel au XVIIe
siècle." Ph.D. dissertation, Göttingen, 1952.

Ferry, Paul. "Resultat d'un synode provincial de l'Ile-de-France tenu
à Charenton touchant le différend de MM. du Moulin et Amyraut,
etc. 1637." *Bulletin de la société de l'histoire du protestantisme
français* 7 (1858), 408–11. Helpful background for the 1637 Alençon
synod. Shows that Amyraut had the full support of the Ile-de-France
and thus of the great Charenton Church.

Fraissinet, Marc. *Essai sur la Morale d'Amyraut*. Toulouse, 1889. Reliable summary of Amyraut's *La Morale chrestienne*.

Galland, A. "Les Pasteurs français Amyraut, Bochart, etc., et la
royauté de droit divin, de l'édit d'Alais à la révocation (1629–85)."
Bulletin de la société de l'histoire du protestantisme français 77
(1928), 14–20, 105–34, 225–41, 413–23. Develops the political
thought of leading seventeenth-century French Protestants, showing the divine rightist belief of most of them, including Amyraut.

Geiger, Max. *Die Basler Kirche und Theologie im Zeitalter der Hochorthodoxie*. Zurich, 1952. Esp. pp. 99–118. Excellent study.

Gibb, Adam. *The Present Truth: A Display of the Secession Testimony*. 2 vols. Edinburgh, 1774. 2:148–91, 273–302. First of the
orthodox Scottish Calvinist writings on Amyraut which have

colored most English-language writing on his thought. Strongly anti-Amyraut and the more "liberal" Calvinist movements.

Haag, E. and E. *La France protestante.* 9 vols. Paris, 1847–59.

Haag, E. and E., and Bordier, Henri. *La France protestante.* New ed. rev. and compl. under the direction of Henri Bordier. 6 vols. (to the letter G). Paris, 1877–92. 1:185–206. Along with the preceding entry, this contains a wealth of important information on all the major and many of the minor figures of French Protestantism. The article on Amyraut referred to here is valuable particularly for its *bibliographia Amyraldiana.*

Henderson, T. F. "John Cameron." *Dictionary of National Biography.* New York, 1886. 8:295–96.

Hodge, A. A. *The Atonement.* London, 1868.

———. *Outlines of Theology.* Rev. ed. Chicago, 1878. Pp. 341ff. In this treatise Hodge treats of Amyraut's distinction between moral inability and natural ability. He agrees with the idea, rejects the terminology.

Hodge, Charles. *Systematic Theology.* 3 vols. New York, 1874. Esp. 2:321–24, but also 265–67. Antagonistic review of Amyraut's "hypothetical redemption" teaching. Follows Turrettini and sees Amyraut's teaching as logical nonsense and as an inversion of the proper order of God's decrees.

Irving, David. *Lives of Scottish Writers.* 2 vols. Edinburgh, 1839. 1:333–46. Brief, reliable biographical notice on Cameron.

Jäger, J. W. *Historia ecclesiastica cum parallelismo profanae . . . ab anno MDC usque ad annum MDCCX.* 2 vols. Hamburg: S. Heylii & J. G. Liebezeitii, 1709–17. First really historical notice on Amyraldianism—by a Lutheran with no particular axe to grind who hoped to find in Amyraut a key to union with the Reformed, but was misled, since he based his account on one of Amyraut's contemporary orthodox opponents, A. Rivet.

Laplanche, François. "L'Enseignement de Moyse Amyraut, professeur à l'Académie de Saumur (1626–1664), sur la grâce et la prédestination: Son Retentissement dans les églises réformées." Ph.D. dissertation, Angers, 1954.

———. *Orthodoxie et prédication: L'Oeuvre d'Amyraut et la querelle de la grâce universelle.* Paris: Presses Universitaires de France, 1965. A slight revision of the preceding entry. It is an excellent study.

Leydecker, Melchior. *De veritate religionis reformatae et evangelicae.* Utrecht, 1688. Bk. 3, ch. 6, sec. 82. Short, antagonistic section on Amyraut's doctrine of man.

Lindsay, Thomas M. "Amyraut." *Encyclopedia of Religion and*

Ethics, edited by James Hastings. 7 vols. Edinburgh, 1908–24. 1:404–6. Very suggestive but undocumented article on the significance of Amyraut's thought in Reformed theology.

Marchegay, Paul. *Chroniques d'Anjou.* 2 vols. Paris, 1856–71.

————. *Chroniques des églises d'Anjou.* Paris, 1869.

————. "Les Anciennes académies protestantes: Saumur." *Bulletin de la société de l'histoire du protestantisme français* 1 (1852–53), 301–16.

Marthaler, Harald. "Amyraut als Ethiker." *Berner Beiträge zur Geschichte der Schweizerischen Reformationskirchen.* Bern, 1884. Pp. 329–49.

Merzeau, E. *L'Académie protestante de Saumur* (1604–1685). Alençon, 1908.

Métayer, L.-J. *L'Académie protestante de Saumur.* Carrières-sous-Poissy and Paris, 1933. Perhaps the best of the various short notices on the Saumur Academy. There is still a great need for a scholarly study of this leading French Reformed Academy.

Moltmann, Jürgen. "Gnadenbund und Gnadenwahl: Die Prädestinationslehre des Moyse Amyraut, dargestellt im Zusammenhang der heilsgeschichtlich-foederaltheologie Tradition der Akademie von Saumur." Ph.D. dissertation, Göttingen, 1951. Best theological analysis of Amyraut to date.

————. "Prädestination und Heilsgeschichte bei Moyse Amyraut," *Zeitschrift für Kirchengeschichte* 65 (1954), pp. 270–303.

Mousseaux, Maurice. "Pierre du Moulin." *Bulletin de la société de l'histoire du protestantisme français* 109 (1963), 160–79.

Nicolas, Michel. "Les anciennes académies protestantes." *Bulletin de la société de l'histoire du protestantisme français* 2 (1853), 43–49, 155–67, 320–32.

Nicole, Roger. "Amyraut, Amyraldus, Amyraldianism, etc." *Encyclopedia of Christianity,* edited by Edwin Palmer. Wilmington, Del., 1964. 1:184–93.

————. "Moyse Amyraut (1596–1664) and the Controversy on Universal Grace." Ph.D. dissertation, Harvard University, 1966. An important work.

Pannier, J. and J. Plattard. "Actualités." *Bulletin de la société de l'histoire du protestantisme français* 74 (1925), 494–501.

Pfaff, Christopher M. *Schediasma theologicum de formula consensus helvetica.* Tübingen, 1723. Early Lutheran study based on Jäger and Calvinist opponents of Amyraut. Uncomprehending, but generally favorable to Amyraut because of a dislike of scholasticism. I have used the edition entitled *De formula consensus helvetica, dissertatio historico-theologica.* Tübingen: Franckianis & Segmundianis, n.d.

Proctor, Leonard. "The Theology of Moise Amyraut considered as a reaction against seventeenth-century Calvinism." Ph.D. dissertation, The University of Leeds, 1952. Fine work.

Prost, Josephe. *La Philosophie à l'académie protestante de Saumur.* Paris, 1907. Mediocre work, but the best to date on the philosophical position at Saumur. Needs revision to explain why the first Cartesian to teach in a Reformed school taught at Saumur.

Read, Charles. "Cameron." *Encyclopédie des sciences religieuses,* edited by Frederick Lichtenberger. Paris, 1877. 2:561–63.

Reid, H. M. B. *The Divinity Principals in the University of Glasgow, 1545–1654.* Glasgow: James Maclehose, 1917. Useful but antagonistic notice on Cameron's life and thought. Based almost entirely on Wodrow.

Rex, Walter E., III. *Essays on Pierre Bayle and Religious Controversy.* International Archives of the History of Ideas, no. 8. The Hague: Nijhoff, 1965. A revision of the following entry and an important work.

———. "Pierre Bayle: The Influence of Protestant Religious Controversies on his Early Work." Ph.D. dissertation, Harvard University, 1956.

Rimbault, Lucien. "Un Traité d'Amyraut: Du gouvernement de l'église." *Etudes théologiques et religieuses de la faculté de théologie protestante de Montpellier* 28 (1953), 157ff. A useful summary of Amyraut's teaching on Church government, and of the seventeenth-century milieu.

Ritschl, Otto. *Dogmengeschichte des Protestantismus.* 4 vols. Göttingen: Vandenhoeck und Ruprecht, 1926. 3:403–8. A very disappointing analysis of Amyraut, based entirely on Schweizer.

Roehrich, Theodore E. *La doctrine de la prédestination et l'ecole de Saumur.* Strasbourg, 1867.

Roth, Jean. "Une apologie protestante au XVIIe siècle: Le 'Traité des religions' de Moïse Amyraut." Bachelor's thesis, Strasbourg, 1953. A worthwhile picture of Amyraut as an apologist.

Sabatier, André. *Etude historique sur l'universalisme hypothétique de Moïse Amyraut.* Toulouse, 1867.

Sabean, David W. "Moise Amyraut and Rationalism." Master's thesis, University of Wisconsin, 1961.

———. "The Theological Rationalism of Moïse Amyraut." *Archiv für Reformationsgeschichte* 55 (1964), 204–16. A précis of the preceding entry. Good, perceptive study on the rational element of Amyraut's thought. Poorly documented.

Saché, Marc. *Inventaire sommaire des archives departmentales d'Anjou.* Angers, 1938.

Saigey, Charles E. "Moïse Amyraut." *Revue de théologie et de philosophie chrétienne* 5 (1852), 178–86.

―――. *Moyse Amyraut: Sa Vie et ses ecrits.* Strasbourg, 1849.

Schaff, Philip. *Creeds of Christendom.* 6th ed. 3 vols. New York, 1931. 1:477–85. Good, dependable short introduction to Amyraut and his colleagues at Saumur.

Schweizer, Alexander. *Die Protestantischen Centraldogmen in ihrer Entwicklung innerhalb der reformierten Kirche.* 2 vols. Zurich, 1854–56. An important work.

Seeberg, Rheinhold. *Lehrbuch der Dogmengeschichte.* 5th ed. Basel and Stuttgart, 1960. pt. 4, sect. 2, pp. 700–706. Surprisingly good understanding of Amyraut, based primarily on Schweizer but perhaps more theologically perceptive than Schweizer.

Smeaton, George S. *The Doctrine of the Atonement as Taught by Christ Himself.* 2d ed. Edinburgh, 1871.

―――. *The Doctrine of the Holy Spirit.* 2d ed. Edinburgh, 1889. This and the preceding entry are strongly anti-Amyraut in the train of Cunningham and Gibb. Smeaton deals with the doctrines of atonement and man, and judges, like Cunningham, that the revocation of the Edict of Nantes was God's judgment on the French Church for tolerating Amyraut!

Stauffer, Richard. *Moïse Amyraut: Un Précurseur français de l'oecuménisme.* Les Bergers et les Mages, no. 22. Paris: Librairie Protestante, 1962. Originally published in *Eglise et théologie* (Dec., 1961), pp. 13–49. A very well-informed essay on an intriguing aspect of Amyraut's thought.

Turrettini, Franciscus. *Institutio theologiae elencticae.* 1688. 3 vols. Edinburgh, 1847. Turrettini studied briefly at Saumur under Amyraut (1645), rejected Amyraldianism, and combatted it throughout his life. In this, his magnum opus, he refutes Amyraldian teaching throughout, especially in loci IV, XII and XIV. This has influenced many works on Amyraut.

Viguié, Ariste. *Histoire de l'apologétique dans l'église réformée français.* Geneva, 1858. Contains a short, useful evaluation of Amyraut as an apologist. Now superseded by Roth.

―――. "Moïse Amyraut." *Encyclopédie des sciences religieuses,* edited by F. Lichtenberger. 13 vols. Paris, 1877–82. 1:273–85. Perhaps the most comprehending of all the short notices on Amyraut; an especially good analysis of the doctrine of predestination.

Vinet, Alexandre. *Histoire de la prédication parmi les réformées de France au dix-septième siècle.* Paris, 1860. Contains an informative introduction on Amyraut as a preacher, and a representative sample of his sermons.

Walch, J. G. *Bibliotheca theologica selecta.* 4 vols. Jena, 1741–58. 2:1028–33. An extremely helpful bibliography of the writings of Amyraut and his friends and opponents.

———. *Historische und theologische Einleitung in die Religionsstreitigkeiten, Welche sonderlich ausser der Evangelisch-Lutherischen Kirche enstanden.* 5 vols. Jena, 1724–36. In this Walch discusses Amyraut, following the studies of Jäger and Pfaff. His main contribution is in recognizing the determinative role covenant theology played in Amyraut's thought, an insight lost in Amyraut research until Moltmann.

Warfield, Benjamin B. *The Plan of Salvation.* Rev. ed. Grand Rapids: Eerdmans, 1942. Antagonistic survey of Amyraut's doctrine of the atonement. Its main burden is to show that Amyraldianism is a logically inconsistent form of Calvinism.

Wodrow, Robert. *Collections upon the Lives of the Reformers and Most Eminent Ministers of the Church of Scotland.* 2 vols. Glasgow, 1848. Vol. 2, pt. 2, pp. 81–223, is a life of Cameron: A full, well informed treatment of his life and thought, but very antagonistic.

GENERAL STUDIES OF CALVIN, CALVINISM, AND
SEVENTEENTH-CENTURY FRANCE

Allison, C. F. *The Rise of Moralism.* New York, 1966. Interesting, well informed study showing that legalism and rationalism were prominent in seventeenth-century Anglicanism and English Calvinism.

Althaus, Paul. *Die Prinzipien der deutschen reformierten Dogmatik im Zeitalter der aristotelischen Scholastik.* Leipzig, 1914. Best general study of early Protestant scholasticism. Needs revision and expansion.

Armand, Emile. *Essai sur la vie de du Moulin.* Strasbourg, 1846. Light and somewhat unreliable.

Baird, Henry M. *The Huguenots and the Revocation of the Edict of Nantes.* Vol. 1. New York: Charles Scribner's Sons, 1895. Old but still-useful study.

Bangs, Carl O. "Arminius and Reformed Theology." Ph.D. dissertation, The University of Chicago, 1958. Intriguing but not wholly acceptable attempt to relate Arminius' teaching to Calvin's.

Beardslee, John W. III, ed. and trans. *Reformed Dogmatics.* A Library for Protestant Thought. New York: Oxford University Press, 1965.

Benoit, Elie. *Histoire de l'édit de Nantes.* 5 vols. Delft, 1693–95. Valuable, detailed contemporary history, though strongly biased.

Bizer, Ernst. *Frühorothodoxie und Rationalismus.* Theologische Studien, vol. 71. Edited by Karl Barth and Max Geiger. Zurich, 1963. Solid study showing the rationalizing tendency of Theodore Beza.

———. "Reformed Orthodoxy and Cartesianism." Translated by C. MacCormick. *Journal for Theology and the Church* 2 (1965), 20–82. Valuable picture of the rigidity of the Protestant scholastics, centering on Voetius.

Borgeaud, Charles. *Histoire de l'Université de Genève: L'Académie de Calvin, 1559–1798.* Geneva, 1900. Fine, reliable work, making good use of manuscript sources.

Bourchenin, P-Daniel. *Etude sur les académies protestantes en France au XVIᵉ et au XVIIᵉ siècle.* Paris: Grassart, 1882.

Breen, Quirinus. *John Calvin: A Study in French Humanism.* Grand Rapids: W. B. Eerdmans, 1931. This remains the best study in English of Calvin's humanism, but needs revision in the light of recent research.

Browning, W. S. *A History of the Huguenots.* New ed. Philadelphia: Lea & Blanchard, 1845.

Brush, C. B. *Montaigne and Bayle.* The Hague: Nijhoff, 1966. Fine study, full of important and suggestive insights.

Budé, Eugène de. *Vie de François Turretini, théologien genevois (1623–1687).* Lausanne: G. Bridel, 1871.

———. *Vie de Jean Diodati.* Lausanne: G. Bridel, 1869.

———. *Vie de Jean-Robert Chouet, professeur et magistrat genevois (1642–1731).* Geneva, 1899.

Busson, Henri. *La Pensée religieuse de Charron à Pascal.* Paris, 1933.

———. *Les sources et le développement du rationalisme dans la littérature française de la renaissance (1533–1601).* Paris: Librairie Letouzey & Ane, 1922.

Comité Farel, eds. *Guillaume Farel, 1489–1565.* Neuchâtel, 1930. The standard reference for Farel's life. Very solid.

De Félice, Guill. *Histoire des synodes nationaux des églises réformées de France.* Paris, 1864. Only a fair history, badly needing augmentation and revision.

———. *Les Protestantes d'autrefois.* 4 vols. Paris, 1902.

Dibon, Paul. *La Philosophie néerlandaise au siècle d'or.* Paris: Elsevier Publishing Co., 1954. Superb analysis and development of philosophical trends in the Netherlands in our period.

Dodge, Guy Howard. *The Political Theory of the Huguenots of the Dispersion, with special Reference to the Thought and Influence of Pierre Jurieu.* New York: Columbia University Press, 1947.

Douen, Orentin. *La Révocation de l'édit de Nantes à Paris d'après des documents inédits.* 3 vols. Paris: Librairie Fischbacher, 1894. Judicious, reliable, and well-informed volumes, full of suggestive ideas.

Doumergue, Emile. *Jean Calvin, les hommes et les choses de son temps.* Vols. 4, 5. Paris: Librairie Fischbacher, 1910 and 1917. Doumergue's study remains the best over-all analysis of Calvin's life and work, extremely nearsighted and hagiographic at times, yet indispensable.

Dowey, Edward A., Jr. *The Knowledge of God in Calvin's Theology.* 2d printing. New York: Columbia University Press, 1965. Dowey's study is still the best introduction to Calvin's *Institutio,* clear-sighted and exceptionally well documented.

Drion, C. *Histoire chronologique de l'église protestante de France jusqu'à la révocation.* 2 vols. Paris, 1855.

Febvre, Lucien. *Au Coeur religieux du XVIᵉ siècle.* Paris: Sevpen, 1957.

Féret, Pierre. *Le cardinal du Perron, orateur, controversiste et écrivain. Etude historique et critique.* Paris, 1877 and 1879.

Gaberel, J. *Histoire de l'église de Genève depuis le commencement de la réformation jusqu'à nos jours.* 3 vols. Geneva, 1855–62. Inaccurate and unreliable.

Ganoczy, Alexandre. *Le jeune Calvin: Genèse et évolution de sa vocation réformatrice.* Wiesbaden, 1966. Much-discussed recent study from the pen of a Roman Catholic. Perhaps too much emphasis is placed on Calvin's alleged training at Paris under the nominalist John Major, a yet-unproved theory.

Geisendorf, Paul-F. *Théodore de Bèze.* Geneva and Paris, 1949. Now the standard account of Beza's life, dealing hardly at all with his thought.

Gory, Gédéon. *Pierre du Moulin: Essai sur sa vie, sa controverse, et sa polémique.* Paris: Librarie Fischbacher, 1888. Light, uncritical monograph.

Gründler, Otto. *Die Gotteslehre Giralmo Zanchis.* Beiträge zur Geschichte und Lehre der Reformierten Kirche, vol. 20. Neukirchen, 1965. A translation of his 1963 dissertation submitted at Princeton Theological Seminary under the title "Thomism and Calvinism in the Theology of Girolami Zanchi." He clearly establishes the Thomistic affinities of Zanchi's thought.

Haag, E. and E., eds. *La France protestante*. 9 vols. Paris, 1847–59.

——. *La France protestante*. New ed. rev. and compl. under the direction of Henry Bordier. 6 vols. (to the letter G). Paris, 1877–92. Full of indispensable information, and would be invaluable if completed.

Harrison, Archibald W. *Arminianism*. London, 1937.

——. *The Beginnings of Arminianism*. London, 1926. The standard work in English on the Arminian reaction to Reformed scholasticism. Needs revision.

Heppe, Heinrich. *Die Dogmatik der evangelisch-reformierten Kirche*. Newly revised and edited by Ernst Bizer. Neukirchen, 1958. The standard introduction to 17th-century Calvinism, a trifle one-sided on the role of covenant theology. Bizer's new introduction enhances its usefulness.

Herzog, Johan Jakob, ed. *Real-Encyclopädie für protestantische Theologie und Kirche*. 22 vols. Leipzig, 1877–88. Full of excellent, reliable articles on the major figures and events of both the sixteenth and seventeenth centuries.

Jacobs, Paul. *Prädestination und Verantwortlichkeit bei Calvin*. Kassel: Oncken, 1937. The best study of Calvin's teaching on predestination, though overemphasizing its christological focus. Calvin is not that Barthian!

Keizer, Gerrit. *François Turretini: Sa Vie et ses écrits et le Consensus*. Lausanne, 1900.

Kerviler, R. and E. de Barthélemy. *Valentin Conrart: Sa Vie et sa correspondance*. Paris: Librairie Académique, 1881. Contains much useful correspondence relating to the seventeenth-century struggle over universal grace.

Kickel, Walter. *Vernunft und Offenbarung bei Theodor Beza*. Beiträge zur Geschichte und Lehre der reformierten Kirche, vol. 25. Neukirchen, 1967. The only major treatise on Beza's thought, and very important. Shows beyond doubt Beza's divergence from Calvin's theology.

Kingdon, Robert M. *Geneva and the Coming of the Wars of Religion in France, 1555–1563*. Geneva: Librairie Droz, 1956.

——. *Geneva and the Consolidation of the French Protestant Movement, 1564–1572*. Geneva and Madison, Wis., 1967. Both treatises by Kingdon are first-class scholarship, judicious in judgment, impeccable in documentation, often from manuscript sources difficult of access and decipherment.

Kristeller, Paul O. *Renaissance Thought: The Classic, Scholastic and Humanist Strains.* New York: Harper Torchbooks, 1961.

————. *Renaissance Thought II: Papers on Humanism and the Arts.* New York: Harper Torchbooks, 1965. Both of these works are excellent contributions to an understanding of the intellectual strains in the Renaissance.

Krusche, Werner. *Das Wirken des heiligen Geistes nach Calvin.* Göttingen: Vandenhoeck and Ruprecht, 1957. An excellent work which deserves an English translation.

Labrousse, Elisabeth. *Pierre Bayle.* 2 vols. The Hague: Nijhoff, 1963–65. A magisterial study containing much useful background material which may well prove that Bayle's intellectual orientation owes much to the Saumur tradition.

Laforgue, G. *Pierre du Bosc. Etude historique, 1623–1692.* Montauban, 1883.

Laval, E. A. *Compendious History of the Reformation in France . . . to the Repealing of the Edict of Nantes.* 7 vols. London, 1737–41.

Le Gendre, Philippe. *La vie de Pierre du Bosc.* Rotterdam, 1694.

Léonard, E. G. *Histoire générale du protestantisme.* vols. 1, 2. Paris: Presses Universitaires de France, 1961–63. Probably the best general study, particularly of French Protestantism. Surprisingly, it is on the whole more accurate on the sixteenth-century theological situation than on the seventeenth-century, his area of specialization. He did not understand Amyraut.

Lichtenberger, Frederick, ed. *Encyclopédie des sciences religieuses.* 13 vols. Paris, 1877–82.

Linder, Robert. *The Political Ideas of Pierre Viret.* Geneva: Droz, 1964.

McCrie, Thomas. *A Life of Andrew Melville.* 2 vols. Edinburgh, 1819. A good study of an important figure in the development of Scotland's (and therefore Cameron's) educational program. It does, however, need revision in the light of recent research.

————, ed. for Wodrow Society. *The Life of Mr. Robert Blair, minister of St. Andrews, containing his Autobiography, from 1593 to 1636 . . .* Edinburgh: Wodrow Society, 1848.

McLelland, Joseph C. *The Visible Words of God: An exposition of the sacramental theology of Peter Martyr Vermigli, A.D. 1500–1562.* Grand Rapids: Eerdmans, 1957. The only recent major treatise on Martyr's thought, but severely limited to discussion of but one main topic—his doctrine of the Eucharist.

McNair, Philip. *Peter Martyr in Italy: An Anatomy of Apostacy.* Oxford: Clarendon Press, 1967. Excellent, superbly documented work presenting much important material on the Italian reformation.

Mc Neill, J. T. *The History and Character of Calvinism.* New York: Oxford University Press, 1954. The best general historical account of Calvinism.

Mailhet, E. André. *La Théologie protestante au XVIIᵉ siècle. Claude Pajon, sa vie, son systeme religieux, ses controverses, d'après des documents entièrement inédits.* Paris: Fischbacher, 1883. Inconsequential study. A good study of Pajon is badly needed.

Marsip, Julien. *Un Vieux Prédicateur Huguenot: Essai sur les sermons de Pierre du Moulin.* Montauban, 1888. Light but interesting presentation. Du Moulin was a powerful preacher.

Mettey, Emile. *Etude sur Jean Daillé, pasteur de l'église réformée de France au dix-septième siècle.* Strasbourg, 1863. This, unbelievably, is the only study devoted to Daillé, although he ranks among the most learned men of his communion in this century. The study in no way does him justice.

Montandon, Albert. *L'Evolution théologique de Genève au dix-septième siècle.* Le Cateau, 1894. A suggestive but rather light analysis.

Monter, William. *Calvin's Geneva.* New York: Wiley, 1967. A fine piece of work, very helpful in setting Calvin in proper historical perspective.

Mours, Samuel. *Les Eglises réformées en France.* Paris and Strasbourg, 1958. Fine, detailed listing of the establishment of French Protestant Churches.

Naef, Henri. *La Conjuration d'Amboise et Genève.* Geneva and Paris, 1922. An exhaustive, solidly documented work, but the servant of many unwarranted presuppositions.

Niesel, Wilhelm. *The Theology of Calvin.* Translated by Harold Knight. Philadelphia: The Westminster Press, 1956.

Nobbs, Douglas. *Theocracy and Toleration: A Study of the Disputes in Dutch Calvinism from 1600–1650.* Cambridge, 1938.

Ong, Walter J., S.J. *Ramus: Method, and the Decay of Dialogue.* Cambridge, Mass.: Harvard University Press, 1958.

Orcibal, Jean. *Louis XIV et les protestantes.* Paris, 1951.

Pannier, Jacques. *De la préréforme à la réforme.* Paris: Librairie Félix Alcan, n.d.

———. *L'Eglise réformée de Paris sous Henri IV.* Paris: Librairie Ancienne Honoré Champion, 1911.

————. *L'Eglise réformée de Paris sous Louis XIII, 1610–1621.* Paris, 1922.

————. *L'Eglise réformée de Paris sous Louis XIII.* Paris, 1931.

————. *Les Origines de la confession de foi et la discipline des églises réformées de France.* Paris: Librairie Félix Alcan, 1936.

————. *Le Témoignage du Saint-Esprit.* Paris: Librairie Fischbacher, 1893.

Petersen, Peter. *Geschichte der aristotelischen Philosophie im protestantischen Deutschland.* Leipzig: Felix Meiner, 1921.

Picot, Michel-Joseph-Pierre. *Essai historique sur l'influence de la religion en France pendant le XVIIe siècle.* 2 vols. Paris, 1824.

Pintard, René. *Le libertinage érudit dans la première moitié du XVIIe siècle.* 2 vols. Paris, 1943.

Polman, Pontien. *L'Elément historique dans la controverse religieuse du XVIe siècle.* Universitas Catholica Lovaniensis, series 2, vol. 23. Gembloux, 1932. A superbly developed essay, especially well documented.

Popkin, Richard H. *The History of Scepticism from Erasmus to Descartes.* Assen, 1960. An important book, setting in bold relief for the first time this major element of the intellectual tradition in the sixteenth and seventeenth centuries.

Port, Célestin. *Dictionnaire historique, géographique et biographique de Maine-et-Loire.* 3 vols. Angers, 1874–76.

Puaux, Frank. *Les Précurseurs français de la tolérance au XVIIe siècle.* Dole, 1880; Paris, 1881.

Rabaut, Pierre-Antoine (the younger). *Details historiques et recueils de pièces sur les divers projets de réunion de toutes les communions chrétiennes, qui ont été conçus depuis la réformation jusqu'à ce jour.* Paris, 1806.

Rébelliau, Alfred. *Bossuet, historien du protestantisme: Etude sur l'"Histoire des Variations" et sur la controverse au dix-septième siècle.* 3d ed. Paris: Hachette and Cie, 1909. Remains perhaps the best general analysis and presentation of the Catholic-Protestant relationship in seventeenth-century France.

Regards contemporaines sur Jean Calvin. Actes du Colloque Calvin à Strasbourg, 1964. Paris: Presses Universitaires de France, 1965. Contains many useful articles, including a particularly interesting presentation by Jean-Daniel Benoît on the relationship of Alexander Vinet and Calvin showing that Vinet is closer to Calvin (or his opponents further from Calvin) than is generally thought.

Renaudet, Augustin. *Humanisme et renaissance.* Travaux d'humanisme et renaissance, vol. 30. Geneva: Librairie E. Droz, 1958.

————. *Préreforme et humanisme à Paris pendant les premières guerres d'Italie, 1494–1517.* 2d ed., rev. and corr. Paris: Librairie D'Argences, 1953. Both works by Renaudet are first-class scholarship, full of reliable and sober judgment.

Reuter, Karl. *Das Grundverstandnis der Theologie Calvins, unter Einbeziehung ihrer geschichtlichen Abhängigkeiten.* Beiträge zur Geschichte und Lehre der reformierten Kirche, vol. 15. Neukirchen-Vluyn, 1963. An uneven and difficult book built entirely upon the questionable assumption that Calvin studied under John Major at Paris.

Rimbault, Lucien. *Pierre du Moulin, 1568–1658: Un Pasteur classique à l'age classique.* Paris: Librairie Philosophique J. Vrin, 1966. A good biographical sketch but not overly perceptive regarding du Moulin's thought.

Ritschl, Otto. *Dogmengeschichte des Protestantismus.* Vol. 3. Göttingen: Vandenhoeck and Ruprecht, 1926. The near-standard work on the Reformed intellectual tradition, but in my mind good only on the teachings of orthodoxy.

Rogers, Jack B. *Scripture in the Westminster Confession.* Grand Rapids, Eerdmans, 1967. An uneven book, much of it simply a skillful compilation of a plethora of secondary sources. At the same time it presents much of value, including (for the first time!) knowledge of the main authors of important parts of the Confession, etc. It also shows that the Westminster divines held Calvin in high esteem—at least professed to. Whether they really followed Calvin is open to question.

Romier, Lucien. *Origines politiques des guerres de religion.* 2 vols. Perrin, 1914. In my mind the soberest presentation of this knotty problem, perhaps a little suspect of French nationalist bias.

Sayous, André. *Histoire de la littérature française à l'étranger depuis le commencement du dix-septième siècle.* Paris, 1853.

Snoeks, Remi. *L'argument de tradition dans la controverse eucharistique entre catholiques et réformés français au XVIIᵉ siècle.* Universitas Catholica Lovaniensis. Dissertationes ad gradum magistri in facultate theologica, ser. 2, no. 44. Louvain: Publications Universitaires de Louvain, 1951. Excellent, well-documented study.

Stankiewicz, W. *Politics and Religion in Seventeenth-Century France.* Los Angeles: University of California Press, 1960.

Stauffer, Richard. *L'Humanité de Calvin.* Neuchâtel. 1964. A fine study, perhaps too uncritical of Calvin, but a picture of Calvin needed to redress long-held misconceptions.

Stéphan, Raoul. *Histoire du protestantisme français*. Paris, 1961. A general, well-informed but popular history.

Tabaraud, M. *Histoire critique des projets formés depuis trois cents ans pour la réunion des communions chrétiennes*. Paris, 1824.

Thils, Gustave. *Les Notes de l'eglise dans l'apologétique catholique depuis la réforme*. Universitas Catholica Lovaniensis. Dissertationes ad gradum magistri in facultate theologica, series 2, vol. 30. Gembloux: J. Duculot, 1937. Another very solid Roman Catholic contribution in this Louvain series. The documentation is superb.

Turrettini, François. *Notice biographique sur Bénédict Turrettini, théologien genevois du XVIIᵉ siècle*. Geneva, 1871.

Viénot, John. *Histoire de la réforme française de l'édit de Nantes à sa révocation*. Paris: Librairie Fischbacher, 1934.

——. *Histoire de la réforme française des origines à l'édit de Nantes*. Paris: Librairie Fischbacher, 1926. These two volumes by Viénot are both solid, though I cannot accept many of his conclusions regarding the nature of French Protestantism.

Viguié, Ariste. *Histoire de l'apologétique dans l'église réformée français*. Geneva, 1858.

Vinet, Alexandre. *Histoire de la prédication parmi les réformées de France au dix-septième siècle*. Paris, 1860.

Voeltzel, Rene. *Vraie et fausse église selon les théologiens protestants français du XVIIᵉ siècle*. Paris: Presses Universitaires de France, 1956.

Vuilleumier, Henri. *Histoire de l'église réformée du Pays de Vaud sous le régime bernois*. 4 vols. Lausanne, 1927–33. These volumes contain a wealth of information on the relationship of the Vaud Reformed Churches and those of France. They deserve a much broader use than they have received in the past.

Walzer, Michael. *The Revolution of the Saints*. Cambridge, Mass.: Harvard University Press, 1966. See the comments in chapter 1, note 61.

Warfield, Benjamin B. *Calvin and Calvinism*. New York: Oxford University Press, 1931. A very learned book, but one which presents the Calvin of orthodox reconstruction and so should be read critically with the original Calvin in mind.

Weber, Hans Emil. *Reformation, Orthodoxie und Rationalismus*. Beiträge zur Förderung Christlicher Theologie, vols. 37 and 51. Gütersloh, 1937 and 1951. Brilliant, perceptive studies which richly deserve translation into English.

Wendel, François. *Calvin: The Origins and Development of His Religious Thought*. Translated by Philip Mairet. New York: Harper

& Row, 1963. By far the best one-volume presentation of Calvin's life and thought. Wendel is thoroughly versed in Calvin and abreast of recent scholarship.

——. *L'Eglise de Strasbourg: Sa Constitution et son organisation 1532–1535*. Paris: Presses Universitaires de France, 1942.

Willis, E. David. *Calvin's Catholic Christology: The Function of the So-called Extra Calvinisticum in Calvin's Theology*. Leiden: Brill, 1966. A judicious presentation of a difficult topic, carefully documented and related to Calvin's thought *in extenso*.

SIGNIFICANT ARTICLES ON CALVIN, CALVINISM, AND SEVENTEENTH-CENTURY FRANCE

Archinard, A. "La Famille des Spanheim." *Bulletin de la société de l'histoire du protestantisme français* 12 (1863), 96–110.

——. "Les Théologiens du Nom de Tronchin." *Bulletin de la société de l'histoire du protestantisme français* 13 (1864), 175–83.

Armstrong, Brian G. Review of Laplanche, *Orthodoxie et prédication*. *Bulletin d'humanisme et renaissance* 28 (1966), 761–64.

Bonet-Maury, Gaston. "Le Protestantisme français et la république aux XVIe et XVIIe siècles." *Bulletin de la société de l'histoire du protestantisme français* 53 (1904), 364–84.

D'Angers, Julien-Eymard. "Problèmes et difficultés de l'humanisme chrétien, 1600–1642." *XVIIe Siècle*, nos. 62–63 (1964), pp. 4–29. Defines and describes humanism within the Roman Catholic communion in the early seventeenth century, a tradition which ran counter to the dominant scepticism within this Church.

De Richemond, A. "André Rivet et Guillaume Rivet de Champvernon." *Bulletin de la société de l'histoire du protestantisme français* 54 (1905), 315–25.

Dibon, Paul. "Le Refuge wallon précurseur du refuge huguenot." *XVIIe Siècle*, nos. 76–77 (1967), pp. 53–74.

Diestel, Ludwig. "Studien zur Föderaltheologie." *Jahrbücher für Deutsche Theologie* 10 (1865), 209–76.

Gray, Hanna. "Renaissance Humanism: The Pursuit of Eloquence." *Journal of the History of Ideas* 24 (1963), 498–514.

Joubert, L. "Les Années décisives de la réforme française, 1559–1562." *Etudes Théologiques et religieuses* 24 (1959), 213–38.

Kingdon, Robert M. "Calvinism and Democracy: Some Political Implications of Debates on French Reformed Church Government, 1562–1572." *American Historical Review* 69 (1964), 393–401. This interesting article shows that "democratic" ideas were prominent in the sixteenth-century Reformed Church.

———. "The First Expression of Theodore Beza's Political Ideas."
Archiv für Reformationsgeschichte 46 (1955), 88–100.

Labrousse, Elisabeth. "Le Refuge hollandais: Bayle et Jurieu." *XVIIᵉ Siècle*, nos. 76–77 (1967), pp. 75–93.

Mercier, Charles. "Les theories politiques des calvinistes en France au cours des guerres de religion." *Bulletin de la société de l'histoire du protestantisme français* 83 (1934), 225–60, 381–415.

Pine, Martin. "Pomponazzi and the Problem of 'Double Truth.'" *Journal of the History of Ideas* 29 (1968), 163–76.

Popkin, Richard H. "Skepticism and the Counter Reformation in France." *Archiv für Reformationsgeschichte* 51 (1960), 58–86.

Poujol, Jacques. "L'Ambassadeur d'Angleterre et la confession de foi du synode de 1559." *Bulletin de la société de l'histoire du protestantisme français* 105 (1959), 49–53.

Puaux, Frank. "L'Evolution des théories politiques du protestantisme français pendant la règne de Louis XIV." *Bulletin de la société de l'histoire du protestantisme français* 62 (1913), 386–413, 481–96.

Rex, Walter. "Pierre Bayle, Louis Tronchin et la querelle des Donatistes." *Bulletin de la société de l'histoire du protestantisme français* 105 (1959), 97–121.

———. "Pierre Bayle: The Theology and Politics of the Article on David." *Bibliothèque d'humanisme et renaissance* 24 (1962), 168–89.

Rist, Gilbert. "Modernité de la Méthode Théologique de Calvin." *Revue de théologie et philosophie*, no. 1 (1968), pp. 19–33. An exceptionally fine article, perhaps the best statement to be found on the nature of Calvin's theology.

Stauffer, Richard H. "Une Ouverture 'oecuménique' contestée: *La Reunion du christianisme*." *XVIIᵉ Siècle*, nos. 76–77 (1967), pp. 23–37.

Zuber, Roger. "Calvinisme et Classicisme." *XVIIᵉ Siècle*, nos. 76–77 (1967), pp. 5–22. The only article on this list about which I have serious doubts. It may be that liberal Huguenot thought was much more influential than Zuber recognizes.

INDEX

Abel, 156
Abraham, 155; and justification by faith, 227
Absolute predestination. *See* Predestination, doctrine of; God, doctrine of, absolute will
Absolute will of God. *See* God, doctrine of, absolute will
Accommodation. *See* God, doctrine of, knowledge of
Adam, 104, 146, 154, 155, 234
Alais, national synod of (1620), 83–84; Pierre du Moulin and, 134–35
Alcalá, University of, 128
Alençon, national synod of (1637), 60, 101, 103, 222; Amyraut's heresy trial at, 88–96; orthodox Calvinism and, 88–91
Alexander the Great, 253
Alien righteousness, in justification by faith, 229, 230, 238
Alsted, John Henry, 128
Ames, William, 141
Amsterdam, 16
Amyraut, Abel, 75n
Amyraut, Elizabeth, 77
Amyraut, Moïse: character, 71–74; cosmopolitanism, 5–6, 72, 127; irenicism, 72–73, 78, 88; early life, 74–88; education, 75; marriage, 76–77; installation at Saumur, 77, 79–80; heresy trial at Alençon, 88–96; later life and work, 96–119

RELATION OF THOUGHT TO
—Beza, 100, 158, 159–60
—Cameron, 42–43, 61, 76; on faith, 241, 242, 243
—Calvin, xviii, 99–101, 265–69 *passim;* on conditional grace, 201–2; on covenant of grace, 198–99; du Moulin on, 86–87; on faith, 259–62; on decrees of God, 163–65; on two-fold will of God, 186–87; on justification, 225, 226, 227, 228, 231, 233, 237, 239–40; on law-gospel distinction, 233; on predestination, 158–59, 160–65, 187–91
—de la Milletière, 96–99; on justification by faith, 228–31
—du Moulin, 61, 74, 84–87, 89, 90n, 91, 94, 97, 110–11, 115, 158, 179, 185–86, 188, 192, 193, 251, 263, 264
—Luther, on two-fold will of God, 200–201
—Lutheranism, 78
—orthodox Calvinism, xviii, 87–96, 98–99, 101, 102–4, 105–14, 165–66, 221
—Rivet, André, 105–6, 108, 112
—Rivet, Guillaume, 112
—Roman Catholicism, 7, 112; on justification by faith, 228–31
—Spanheim, Frederick, the elder, 102–13 *passim*

TEACHINGS
—antispeculative nature, 162–65, 184–87, 266–67
—on the atonement, 91, 92–93, 100, 104, 152–53, 174, 210–14
—on Christ and his work, 80, 175–77, 210–14, 225–26, 228–31, 238, 248
—on church government, 116

319